# The Fragile Fabric of Union

Studies in Early American Economy and Society
from the Library Company of Philadelphia
Cathy Matson, *Series Editor*

# The Fragile Fabric of Union

*Cotton, Federal Politics, and the Global Origins of the Civil War*

Brian Schoen

The Johns Hopkins University Press
*Baltimore*

© 2009 The Johns Hopkins University Press
All rights reserved. Published 2009
Printed in the United States of America on acid-free paper
9  8  7  6  5  4  3  2  1

The Johns Hopkins University Press
2715 North Charles Street
Baltimore, Maryland 21218-4363
www.press.jhu.edu

Library of Congress Cataloging-in-Publication Data

Schoen, Brian.
   The fragile fabric of Union : cotton, federal politics, and the global
origins of the Civil War / Brian Schoen.
       p. cm.—(Studies in early American economy and society from the
Library Company of Philadelphia)
   Includes bibliographical references and index.
   ISBN-13: 978-0-8018-9303-2 (hardcover : alk. paper)
   ISBN-10: 0-8018-9303-8 (hardcover : alk. paper)
   1. Southern States—Economic conditions—19th century.   2.
Southern States—Foreign economic relations—Europe—19th century.
3. Cotton trade—Southern States—History—19th century.   4. Cotton
trade—United States—History—19th century.   5. Cotton trade—
Political aspects—United States—History—19th century.   6. Secession—
United States—History.   7. United States—History—Civil War,
1861–1865—Causes.   I. Title.
   F213.S37 2009
973.7′1—dc22        2008050560

A catalog record for this book is available from the British Library.

*Special discounts are available for bulk purchases of this book. For more
information, please contact Special Sales at 410-516-6936 or specialsales@
press.jhu.edu.*

The Johns Hopkins University Press uses environmentally friendly book
materials, including recycled text paper that is composed of at least 30
percent post-consumer waste, whenever possible. All of our book papers
are acid-free, and our jackets and covers are printed on paper with
recycled content.

*To Kelli and Julia*

# Contents

# Series Editor's Foreword

This is the fifth title in Studies in Early American Economy and Society, a collaborative effort between the Johns Hopkins University Press and the Library Company of Philadelphia's Program in Early American Economy and Society (PEAES). In *The Fragile Fabric of Union: Cotton, Federal Politics, and the Global Origins of the Civil War,* Brian Schoen traces the bitter legacy of the American Revolution from Georgia and South Carolina, the two southernmost states of the new Union and the region whose identity featured both the most idiosyncratic and the most typically American characteristics of three postrevolutionary generations, to the opening areas of the expanding Cotton South in Mississippi and Alabama.

Through years of rebuilding an economy based on burgeoning world demand for their cotton and rice, expanding their ownership of slaves in the context of unprecedented slave liberation movements and British abolition, and establishing the contours of racial authority on Native American frontiers and slave plantations, the elites of these critical southern states consistently demonstrated how their power depended on solidifying international commercial relations. The domestic economy and society of Georgia and South Carolina, then additional new states, depended on their successful commercial position in the Atlantic world. However, as Schoen argues compellingly, southern partnership in the world of trade was rarely secure during the antebellum years to come; international inflation, shortages of exports, overdrawn international accounts, and the ravages of war and diplomacy were as much a threat to southern stability as were slave and frontier unrest from within. Meanwhile, state leaders struggled continually to create a satisfactory balance of political power between their states and the federal Union; the shifting contours of the southern political economy both reflected and conditioned the compromises they sought from the national government and their international trading partners. In forging these compromises, myriad Americans increasingly saw how the cotton economy and its reliance on slave labor had simultaneously tied together the political economies of southerners and northerners and set them on increasingly divergent economic paths until the Union itself could no longer bear the weight of unworkable tensions.

Schoen's argument about the fragility of southern states' position in the new nation and in the world of commerce is grounded on a sophisticated blending of sources that reveal not only the regional and global economic cultures but also the ideas set down in the print culture of southern political economists who were keenly aware of the destinies being shaped within the South and more widely in commercial networks throughout the Atlantic world. Schoen brilliantly weaves together the shifting conditions of international economy, regional policymaking, contested frontier and planter interests, and the free trade ideology that bubbled to the surface of southern discourses time and again. The expansive canvas on which Schoen works thus offers readers a unique opportunity to understand the place of these distinctive, yet quintessentially American, southern states in relation to the larger federal Union and to global conditions between the Revolution and Civil War.

PEAES is honored to include *The Fragile Fabric of Union* in this collaborative series. In the Economy Program's ongoing efforts to reach across scholarly disciplines and methodologies and in its aims to promote discussion of the early American economy in the broadest terms possible, Schoen's intellectually stimulating and deeply researched study is a most fitting addition.

Cathy Matson
Professor of History, University of Delaware
Director, Program in Early American Economy and Society

# Acknowledgments

This book is about the vast and often complicated web of relationships created by the material-minded growth and sale of a commodity. Researching and writing it has forced me to confront some of the basest of human motives, rationalizations, and actions. More often than not, however, the process has affirmed my faith in humanity, not least because of the generous people who have helped me through it.

The University of Virginia proved an ideal place to begin this project. It is, in part, my response to one of the many pearls of wisdom Edward Ayers offered during his seminar on the nineteenth-century South. While his call to "deprovincialize" the South was leading him toward a groundbreaking comparative study of two border counties, he showed great enthusiasm for my big-picture approach. With his usual kindness, he made time to read and discuss my work, despite increasing administrative responsibility. It and I are all the better for it.

Richard Drayton's British Empire seminar provided the chance to write a research paper exploring connections between the Cotton South and Great Britain, a paper I was fine filing away. Richard would not let me and for that I remain grateful. His consistent support for me and this project (even after he left for

Cambridge) has been more important than he may realize. As my research pushed me deeper into the political terrain of the antebellum United States, Michael Holt became an increasingly valuable resource.

More than anyone else Peter Onuf helped me realize this subject's potential. He generously shared his time and brilliant insights, guiding me through the intellectual history and political economy of the early Republic. Our many conversations and his willingness to read multiple drafts, regardless of their condition, made this book possible. As importantly, he modeled to me what it meant to be a responsible scholar and a good citizen of the academy. I hope he sees this book as a small token of my appreciation.

Having the likes of Peter Onuf and Edward Ayers as mentors comes with the added benefit of getting to know the other young scholars they attract. I had an especially talented, intellectually diverse, and remarkably encouraging cohort. Leonard Sadosky, Charles Irons, and Johann Neem offered regular encouragement and continue to enrich my personal and professional life. Sharon Murphy, Rob Parkinson, Watson Jennison, Dayo Mitchell, Susanna Lee, Aaron Sheehan-Dean, Sarah Hand Meacham, John Riedl, Carl Bon Tempo, Katherine Pierce, Benjamin Carp, Richard Samuelson, and Albrecht Koshnick, along with other members of the Early American Republic Seminar, endured early drafts and more conversations about cotton than they probably cared to. I remain indebted.

Other faculty at the University of Arkansas, Cambridge University, and the University of Virginia pointed me toward the field and helped me better understand the discipline. I am particularly thankful for my contact with David Sloan, David Edwards, Henry Tsai, Lynda Coon, Randall Woods, Suzanne McCray, Betty Wood, Mark Goldie, the late Stephen Innes, Charles McCurdy, Olivier Zunz, Nelson Lichtenstein, Maurie McInnes, Paul Halliday, Ed Russell, and Joseph Kett.

To my great fortune I entered the profession at California State University, Sacramento, where I had splendid colleagues and made cherished friends, among them Patrick Ettinger, Mona Siegel, Al Holland, Barbara Keys, Afshin Marashi, and Christopher Castaneda. In addition to being one of those, Charles Postel graciously read the entire manuscript, offering sage advice about content and process. This manuscript became a book at Ohio University, where my luck with co-workers has continued. Paul Milazzo, Mariana Dantas, Robert Ingram, Kevin Mattson, and Bruce Steiner all shared their input on specific portions of the book or the ideas informing them. Our chair, Norman Goda, has offered considerable wisdom and unwavering support as I brought this project to a close.

As this book evolved, a number of senior scholars in U.S. and Atlantic history graciously offered their insights, commented on conference presentations, or responded to published materials emerging from my research. I would like to thank P. J. Marshall, Joe Miller, Eliga Gould, John Larson, John Majewski, Michael O'Brien, Susanna Delfino, Marc Egnal, Larry Hudson, Herb Sloan, Andrew O'Shaughnessy, Douglas A. Irwin, L. Diane Barnes, and Jim Horn. Several others read all or significant portions of this book as it progressed toward completion: Adam Rothman, John James, James Read, Peter Coclanis, Frank Towers, Robin Einhorn, Andrew Shankman, and the anonymous reviewer for the Johns Hopkins University Press. Sven Beckert shared his extensive knowledge of the global cotton trade and read the entire manuscript. Exchanges with Walter Johnson and Scott Marler helped sharpen my understanding of developments in the Lower Mississippi Valley. Portions of chapter 2 were published in the *Journal of the Early Republic*, "Calculating the Price of Union: Republican Economic Nationalism and the Origins of Southern Sectionalism, 1790–1828" (Summer 2003). I would like to thank the anonymous readers and editors for that opportunity.

Studying the large and intricate tapestry that cotton wove through people's lives required considerable resources. A Batten Fellowship and a predoctoral fellowship from the Robert H. Smith International Center of Jefferson Studies provided funding at two critical moments. Fellowship and travel grants from the Corcoran Department of History and the College of Arts and Sciences at Virginia allowed me to make research trips to England, Georgia, and South Carolina. Research and Creativity Awards from California State University, Sacramento, permitted additional travel to the Carolinas, Georgia, Mississippi, Arkansas, and New Orleans. The generous support of the Program in Early American Economy and Society, particularly through a postdoctoral residential fellowship at the Library Company of Philadelphia, provided me the time necessary to complete the initial manuscript. Travel grants from Ohio University's history department and the College of Arts and Sciences made some final additions possible.

This money provided me the opportunity to burden more librarians and archivists than can be mentioned here by name. I would, however, like to thank the staffs at the British Public Record Office (now National Archives), British Library, John Rylands Library, Manchester Central Library, University of North Carolina at Chapel Hill, Duke University, South Carolina Historical Society, South Caroliniana Library, South Carolina State Archives, Mississippi State Archives, the Historic New Orleans Collection, Georgia Historical Society, Georgia State Archives, Tulane University, and the University of Arkansas. Special thanks are warranted for the staffs of the University of Virginia, Thomas Jefferson Library, and the Library Company of Philadelphia, whose consummate professionalism and generous assistance made this research not only possible but enjoyable. I kept interlibrary loan offices at UVA, Sacramento State, and Ohio University hopping and appreciate their help in shuttling microfilm, books, and obscure pamphlets to and fro, often on short notice.

I could not have asked for a more supportive series editor. Cathy Matson's backing paved the way for this book to go forward; her expertise in the early Republic helped me focus some of the themes discussed there. Seldom does an author have a press editor who is also an expert in his or her field. Robert J. Brugger generously offered both his skills as an editor and his quite considerable knowledge of the antebellum South. His assistant Josh Tong, my managing editor Linda Forlifer, and Michael Baker, who copyedited the manuscript, helped usher me through the final stages.

Finally, I want to thank my family for their unceasing love and support. My parents, Dale and Carol, were the first in their families to go to college. They taught me to appreciate education so much that I decided to make a career of it. Their examples of perseverance helped me make it here. Though I passed on their title suggestion, "Cotton, the Fabric of their Lives," I hope they and my sister, Lisa, know what a comfort they have been in my own life. I want to also thank my in-laws, Bob and the much-missed Kathy Coughlin. On several occasions their hospitality helped me through long stretches of writing and revisions.

No one has sacrificed more for this project than my wife, Kelli. She remains the greatest gift that graduate school gave me. Blessed with a first-rate mind, a sharp editor's eye, and saintly patience, she contributed to this project from start to finish. In the process she gave birth to our daughter, Julia, who has subsequently provided a welcome distraction and a great incentive to finish this book. I dedicate it to them, knowing that what they have given me is so much greater.

# Introduction

Americans past and present have had a difficult time fathoming why slavery in the U.S. South grew stronger rather than weaker as the nineteenth century progressed. That had not been its trajectory elsewhere during the modern age. All European powers but Spain ended the practice in their American colonies by the 1850s. Most of the new Latin American republics abolished it within two or three decades of achieving their independence. Why had the liberty-loving citizens of the United States allowed slavery "a vitality that was never anticipated by its friends or foes"? Cincinnati publisher and proponent of African colonization David Christy believed he knew why. In 1855 he urged his readers to look beyond local circumstances and national debates. "Slavery," he explained,

> is not an isolated system, but is so mingled with the business of the world, that it derives facilities from the most innocent transactions. Capital and labor, in Europe and America, are largely employed in the manufacture of cotton. These goods, to a great extent, may be seen freighting every vessel, from Christian nations, that traverses the seas of the globe; and filling the warehouses and shelves of the merchants, over two-thirds of the world. By the industry, skill,

and enterprise employed in the manufacture of cotton, mankind are better clothed; their comfort better promoted; general industry more highly stimulated; commerce more widely extended; and civilization more rapidly advanced, than in any preceding age.

As a "profound statesman," cotton "knows what measures will best sustain his throne," and its unwavering policy had been, Christy concluded, "to defeat all schemes of emancipation." "Cotton," in short, "was King." That left slavery, one South Carolinian later added, as its "queen-dowager."[1]

Lower South planters and politicians took great pride in such depictions of cotton and slavery's royal status, especially when they circulated in prominent Atlantic publications and through political discourse on the eve of the Civil War. Like sugar before it and oil after it, cotton's growth, manufacture, and sale defined an era in world economic history. The "white gold" served as the major commodity trade of the early nineteenth century and observers credited it with sparking (or at least greatly accelerating) industrial revolutions in Western Europe and the United States. Raw and finished cotton created networks of trade that circled the globe many times over and expanded European empires while destroying, reshaping, and at times empowering individuals' economic livelihoods. "King Cotton" affirmed slaveholders' central place in the larger global economy. So, too, did simple statistics. In the mid-1780s cotton goods composed only 6 percent of the value of British exports and the United States produced less than 0.2 percent of the raw cotton imported into Britain. By 1820 those percentages had risen to roughly 59 and 60 percent, respectively. In the years prior to the Civil War, at least two-thirds of the world's entire raw cotton supply (by now manufactured in large quantities on the European continent) was cultivated by enslaved African Americans working fields in the U.S. Lower South. This fact offered considerable psychological comfort to Lower South planters, politicians, and apologists, who were quick to remind abolitionist critics of slavery's centrality for the most vibrant commercial trade that the world had yet seen. For these reasons alone, any attempt to understand southern and U.S. history must place cotton alongside the much better-understood subject of slavery.[2]

Responsibly doing so requires rethinking a deterministic narrative in which the heavy emphasis on economic and social developments subsumes the personal choices and political contingencies that made cotton king. Anthropomorphizing their precious commodity enabled slaveholders, when it suited them, to abdicate individual moral responsibility and portray themselves as at the mercy of a power far greater than that of any person or group. Subsequent apologists for the South have found such a view useful in their efforts to redeem the South from history's harsh judgment. With markedly different intentions, a significant number of economists and historians, diversely inspired by Progressivism, classical Marxism, and dependency theory, have reached surprisingly similar conclusions. In many, perhaps most, interpretations of the last century, the people of the South, whether the bastard children of "merchant capitalism" or "retainers" to King Cotton, appear weak in the face of economic forces they could not hope to control. Accounts differ over how willingly, quickly, and completely the planters and farmers of the Lower South surrendered to their fate, but surrender they did, passively accepting, we are told, their subservient place in a capitalist world system fast passing by their outmoded slave society. Only when their traditional—some even say premodern—way of life came under attack from real or imagined threats did slaveholders rouse to defend themselves. Fear, anxiety, trepidation, reluctance, insanity, anger, honor: some combination of these emotions or other pathologies are thus made to carry the heavy burden of explaining why otherwise genteel and conservative white men partook in the seemingly desperate act of secession and civil war. The lamentations of Lower South propagandists, particularly during bleak economic or political times, provided just enough historical evidence to make such accounts believable, especially to scholars ready to accept slavery and agriculture as inherently antimodern or inclined to see history primarily through the lens of deeply rooted economic structures or cultural codes.[3]

These fatalistic assessments, however, have obscured more than they have illuminated the economic reality and geopolitical outlook of Lower South planters and politicians, which are the focus of this book. Though their economic lives were often circumscribed, contemporaries faced and made difficult choices, frequently with more positive perceptions of the outcomes than historians acknowledge. Individuals who chose to experiment with cotton did so not as hopeless agrarians but as entrepreneurs with opportunity and profits foremost in their minds. When hard economic times or political concerns about overdependence suggested the utility of reform, leaders did not throw up their hands in defeat or retrench within their atavistic slave society. Instead, they searched for reasonable alternatives and adjusted their behavior. That they often looked in different places than we would does not make their efforts illogical or unworthy of closer study. That they did not generally achieve the same degree of economic development as the world's two leading industrial powers (the northern United States and Great Britain) mattered. It did not, however, make them somehow less modern or, as some of their own and subsequent accounts have suggested, less motivated by material concerns. Planters, farmers, and the politicians who represented them jealously guarded and constantly sought to improve their position within the world economy in ways that would advance their own wealth and that of their communities.

When international and domestic circumstances such as foreign wars, high tariffs, and abolition endangered their investment in cotton or the slaves necessary to grow it, the region's politicians protected them with extreme vigilance. Most of their efforts took the form of peaceful, though often passionate, dialogue in the arenas of politics or print culture. On multiple occasions, however, they felt compelled to use coercion. When cotton growers believed that European belligerents had mistreated them and their countrymen, they responded with commercial and physical warfare. When the need to defend slavery and the opportunity to corner the raw cotton market suggested the wisdom of aggressive expansion, Lower South voters and politicians rallied to the cause and achieved surprising results. Though never acting in isolation, white farmers, planters, and merchants in the Lower South created a "Cotton South," preserved its profitability, and by the 1850s ensured its dominance of international raw cotton markets. This book explains how they accomplished this and at what cost to their region and the United States. The story is a tragedy, one in which greed and an integrated world's insatiable desire for cotton provided the incentive and the means for entrepreneurial planters to continue enslaving millions of souls and eventually to help inaugurate the bloodiest war in U.S. history.[4]

Placing cotton at the core of Lower South thought and action requires widening the lens used to examine decision-makers who are too often seen as provincial and studied exclusively within local, state, or national settings. Recent literature on modern slavery has been greatly enriched by the advances of Atlantic and global history, but these approaches have only rarely and recently informed our understanding of the white South. Yet individuals reliant on the cotton trade acted within a complex and ever-changing international landscape shaped most prominently by: wars in Europe; the erosion of European empires in the West; the rise of modern nation-states to replace them; the industrial takeoff of Europe and North America; the transportation revolution; the emergence of free trade as an economic ideal and a policy choice; a global depression in the late 1830s; the rise of nationalist movements in continental Europe in the late 1840s; and the continuation of European imperialism and coerced labor in Africa and Asia. Each of these events critically impacted commercial agrarians and merchants in the Cotton

States, who responded to them as private citizens seeking business partnerships, as intellectuals sharing an increasingly globalized public sphere, as officials of the U.S. government, and as strategists disgruntled by their current geopolitical situation. They thus have central interpretive significance for this book. Reintegrating Lower South elites into world events should raise some interesting questions for world historians, though this book's primary focus remains on explaining events framed within the histories of the American South and United States.[5]

To a considerable degree, the timing of cotton's rise to economic glory justifies keeping the nation-state central to the story. The vibrant cotton trade emerged within the context of nationalist movements, none perhaps more significant or successful than the creation of the United States. Historical actors in the Cotton States, though deeply integrated in transnational processes, acted within a particular national political framework: the federal system they helped create in 1787. Average Americans living in the nineteenth century had considerably less daily contact with the federal government than their descendants did. That did not, however, make their national government any less significant for their self-understanding or their pursuit of self-interest. Indeed Americans put significant psychological energy and political capital into their understanding of nationhood. They celebrated its birthday and contested its meaning. They penned eloquent prose with unabashedly patriotic messages. They also relied on the national government to respond to most of the external challenges they faced, and many of the domestic ones. It is probable that wealthy individuals engaged their national government more directly than those with fewer resources and less direct access to power. Elites, to be sure, disproportionately controlled and contested national and state-level politics. Consequently, they feature prominently in this discussion. Yet democratic ideas and processes deeply affected the Lower South— if not as thoroughly as elsewhere in the United States, almost certainly more tangibly than most anyplace else in the world at that time. Yeoman farmers joined wealthy planters in voting their political leaders into office or in selecting the proxies who did. Together they and other interest groups wrote their congressmen and petitioned governments in an effort to shape public policy. When they suspected that the national government no longer served their interests, they passionately debated the matter, and majorities, at least in the Cotton States, decided to end one experiment with federalism and begin another.

If a republican system of federalism provided the legal framework for questions of great significance, the policies produced by this system often determined how Americans felt about each other and their government. Recent examinations of nationalism have appropriately highlighted the cultural forms and processes by which Americans created and contested their "imagined communities." We know, too, that words and "rhetorical modes" shaped historical understanding in important ways. Exploring the imagined community and rhetoric that cotton created at home and abroad requires that we look much more closely at how perceived interest shaped policies and identities. Perhaps the best way to accomplish this is through the study of *political economy*. The term carried significant weight for contemporaries, who invoked it to explain everything from the economic relationships individuals formed, to the government policies statesmen passed, to the supposedly natural laws governing the economy or relations between various polities. The term's flexibility has recently made it attractive to those historians of the early Republic interested in salvaging some of the lessons of economic history without accepting its often overly schematic methods and unambiguous conclusions. It is particularly well suited for this study, which presents neither a traditional economic nor an intellectual history but a discussion of how economic realities and ideological beliefs interacted to shape political perspectives and decisions. When properly balanced between its political and econometric components, *political economy* has the potential to prevent either economic determinism or intellectual vagaries from carrying too much explanatory power for the actions of thoughtful people with real but seldom clearly understood material interests. As an interpretive device it might also help bridge the growing divide between older political histories that give primacy to ideas and newer ones stressing institutions.[6]

Since the inception of the federal Union, debates over national political economy remained the most common and divisive challenges facing Americans. They forced politicians who represented diverse interests (commercial, industrial, various agrarian groups, slaveowners, and nonslaveholders, etc.) into an extended dialogue over what constitutional responsibilities they had to one another and what policies best served their own and their nation's interests. It should not, therefore, be surprising that arguments were raucous. On numerous occasions, the sites of national identity formation—the halls of Congress, boardinghouses, presidential campaigns, national newspapers and journals—were transformed into arenas for competing local and sectional interests to air their grievances or turn policy and public opinion toward their own ends. A sometimes remarkable faith that the nation's diverse parts shared a common destiny generally saw policymakers through these arguments with their patriotism intact. Federalism could, as James Madison famously suggested in *Federalist* 10, turn America's economic diversity into a political asset. Alexander Hamilton's much less heralded sequel assured Americans that the nation's interests were naturally complementary and that a stronger Union would bring collective economic growth. Yet even a deep faith in the Founders and their principles could not prevent politicians from pondering whether such harmony really existed.[7]

In fact, national and foreign policy generated a particularly blunt understanding of the Union for residents of a Cotton South so deeply invested in overseas trade and slavery. Often vexing struggles to define the Lower South's collective interests played out in local newspapers, state governments, regional associations, and two-party politics. Intraregional consensus often remained elusive, if not impossible. In this sense the Cotton South comports to the emphasis on heterogeneity that has recently defined southern scholarship. Fine state, local, and biographical accounts have mined, and hopefully will continue to mine, the "many Souths" known to have existed. Yet a number of these recent studies have also demonstrated the degree to which commercial cotton production and a slave-centered economy created political and economic bonds that united individuals otherwise separated by distance, class, gender, religious belief, or party affiliation. Instead of dropping another probe in hopes of finding yet another South, this project presumes that there is much to be gained by stepping back. It proposes that a broader perspective gives us a clearer picture of the terrain and allows us to see new paths of exploration and to revisit old ones with fresh insights. Cotton's pervasiveness throughout the region and its national and international significance make it "a South" worthy of closer study even if at a slightly lower resolution.[8]

Still, analyzing the Cotton South in a coherent fashion has required some difficult compromises. Perhaps the greatest involves terminology. Though commercial cotton cultivation took place in every slave state, this study is largely restricted to the four in which it was clearly dominant: South Carolina, Georgia, Mississippi, and Alabama. They were, undeniably, "Cotton States" and will be referred to as such. On occasion, and especially on the eve of the Civil War, contemporaries described Louisiana, Texas, and Florida as Cotton States because of the fact that many of the settled regions within their borders were also dedicated to raw cotton production. I have tried to avoid such an appellation in recognition of the more diversified agricultural base of those states. When I have ventured into discussions that include those states or refer to the precotton era, I have tried to limit myself to the broader descriptors: the Lower or Deep South, which are used here interchangeably. When referencing subjects that might apply specifically to cotton-growing regions in these and other states, most notably western Tennessee, pockets of North Carolina, and southern Arkansas, the term *cotton belt* or *Cotton South* is generally applied. The term *South* is even less precise and evolved over time. Here it is applied to those states, south of the Mason and Dixon Line, that were particularly committed to slavery. Such labels, as the debates discussed below demonstrate, do not imply that these regions were "static," nor do they suggest that a uniformity of thought or interest existed within them. The frequency with which these terms, especially the *South* and *Cotton States,* occur in the historical record does suggest that they offered significant interpretive value to contemporaries who shared an interest in cotton, slavery, or both.

This exploration of the Cotton South proceeds in a generally chronological fashion framed by particular political, economic, or diplomatic challenges (and in some cases, opportunities) that faced policymakers. Prior to cotton's emergence as an exportable crop, wide majorities of South Carolina and Georgia elites determined that only a stronger alliance with northern neighbors could provide real geopolitical security and protect the Lower South's interests in slaves, land, and wider overseas markets. The calculated decisions and compromises at Philadelphia, later ratified by state conventions, provided the national framework for government action as well as the primary reference points for regional understandings of American nationhood. The far-from-inevitable emergence of an Anglo-American cotton trade in the late 1790s, however, both reinforced and subtly challenged the commitment of residents of the Lower South to the federal Union and older understandings of political economy. Assisted by British and northern merchants and shipowners, the wealth accrued during cotton's first boom returned languishing economies in South Carolina and Georgia to prosperity. It did so, however, only by expanding the region's dependence on international trade with sworn adversaries and by deepening the region's commitment to African slavery. At a moment when mercantilist calculations continued to dictate policy, despite the introduction of revolutionary principles and free trade ideas into some circles, cotton began weaving together a powerful, interdependent trade between patriotic Americans and British enemies.

Events leading up to the War of 1812 forced politicians from cotton-growing regions to balance gingerly their need for British markets with their commitment to a Jeffersonian Republicanism essentially Anglophobic in character. The legacy of the sacrifices they supposed they made for "free trade and sailors' rights" during the Jeffersonian era indelibly shaped cotton southerners' perceptions of national political economy in the post-1815 period, when the oft-neglected tariff debates took center stage. The debates over revenue and commercial policies, which often intersected with other prominent issues, such as the Missouri Compromise, land distribution, African colonization, Negro Seaman's Acts, and internal improvements, consumed the politics of the 1820s and early 1830s. They reveal cotton communities' heightened concern about western and northern majorities' growing support for protectionist policies and antislavery gestures. The means and ends of the "American System," many believed, promised to destroy the free trade cause and the economic and social fabric of an ever-expanding Cotton South. The problem came to a head in South Carolina's efforts at nullification, but a general recognition of cotton's precarious political place in the Union prevailed in the other Cotton States as well.

The battle to protect slavery and free trade led citizens in these states to reevaluate their strategies in the postnullification period. Internally, they struggled, with limited success, to provide a united political front, to reform the regional economy, and to articulate a coherent proslavery response to abolition. Externally, they sought empowering commercial ties with the western United States and Europe as well as stronger political alliances within the Union. The emerging second party system provided alternate visions for a region reeling from a second panic in 1839 and a prolonged depression that wrecked many of their grander plans. The Whig Party temporarily benefited from the hard economic times, but internationally informed commitments to cotton and slavery eventually hitched the region to a Democratic Party wed to free trade and the annexation of Texas. Success on both of these issues marked a shift in Lower South geopolitical perceptions, helping to inaugurate a gradual rethinking of the region's relationship with its northern allies and European trading partners.

This book culminates by explaining this process and specifically by showing how domestic and foreign circumstances combined to shape the sectional crisis and make secession appear a desirable and viable option for the residents of the Cotton South. Domestic-centered interpretations of the origins of the Civil War have tended to see the Deep South as purely reactive, thus ignoring or seriously underestimating the proactive aspects of secession. Far from sinking into an agrarian-minded fatalism or honor-driven defense of tradition Lower South reformers and politicians continued to calculate action based on interest. They also saw reason for hope as well as concern. High cotton prices and peaking global demand offered planters a potentially bright future even as reformers aggressively sought to translate profits into a more diversified regional economy. With notable exceptions individuals with diverse interests believed that cotton provided leverage for slavery's future expansion, a policy option seen as providing significant economic and political benefits to the region's many groups.[9]

The Cotton South's forceful pursuit of both freer international trade and the expansion and protection of slavery resulted in a complicated political situation at home and abroad, one that severely weakened and eventually destroyed the fabric of union. The obstinacy of Cotton South politicians on policies ranging from navigation acts, to homesteading, to internal improvements, to the international slave trade, to the entrance of new states generated considerable mistrust within the Democratic Party and amongst a northern public increasingly tired of southern obstructionism. At the same time, an ambiguous but seemingly propitious international scene allowed cotton planters and politicians to envision that European policymakers would, unlike their northern Republican counterparts, oblige them by acting on cotton-centered interests rather than antislave sentiments. Broad regional faith in cotton's global power both informed secessionists' actions and provided them an indispensable tool for mobilizing otherwise reluctant confederates. In this sense, the march toward secession may not so much suggest a rejection of economic realism, as historians have commonly asserted, but an overabundance of faith in it. Deep South disunionists assumed that potential European allies and northern adversaries shared their conviction that cotton ruled global trade. That they had severely miscalculated would surprise not only individuals in the Cotton South, but many outside of it. King Cotton's ultimate failure also would have important ramifications for postwar interpretations of the conflict and southern history.

Indeed, the construction of historical memory provides a final analytical framework for this project. In addition to tracing all the policy issues in a time-specific manner and situating them within their broader geopolitical contexts, this work also depicts the larger and often contested legacy left by those policies. Previous decisions and compromises powerfully informed policymakers and observers. As circumstances changed, so did the meanings of past debates and policy choices. Politicians and publicists within the Lower South proved particularly adept at revising and internalizing their history, a practice which by the 1850s allowed them to reduce their own and the United States' complex past into merely a prelude to war. This development was by no means inevitable. Had any number of alternative constructions stressing federalism's continued benefits prevailed, unionism in the Lower South might have endured the crisis of 1860. It did not, however, and the region's relationship to cotton and commerce helps us understand why.

# Prologue, 1787

The American Revolution left a deep but ambiguous imprint on the two south-ernmost states of the new confederacy. Independence from Britain offered white Georgians and South Carolinians republican self-government and the opportu-nity to determine their own political, economic, and social fate. A humiliating British occupation, however, intensified provincial anxiety over the region's weakness within the nation and the world. Until British troops evacuated the Lower South in 1782, Georgia's delegates to the Continental Congress feared that northern states would sign a peace treaty, leaving Georgia and South Carolina permanently under British control.[1] A brutal civil war had also seriously destabi-lized a slave society, allowing approximately one-fourth of South Carolina's slaves and one-third of Georgia's to slip away, believing that freedom and better lives could be found within the British Empire. Within white society, the fighting left a legacy of bitterness among British occupiers, Loyalists, and patriot militias. The region, according to one historian, had been "ravaged by the war as no other sec-tion of the country. Its governmental processes had collapsed, and its society had disintegrated to the point that it approached John Locke's savage state of nature."[2] Revolutionaries, who in 1776 had famously declared that "the Laws of Nature and of Nature's God" entitled them to break and form new political bonds, wondered how benevolent nature really was and worried about what new political bands would be formed. Independence had been successfully achieved, but the consequences of that independence, or even its endurance, remained seriously in doubt.

Though welcomed, even peace and the return of civil governance did not ease fears. The Treaty of Paris granted a generous land settlement, including most British lands east of the Mississippi, but the "frontier" situation remained ominous. The return of East and West Florida to the long-despised Spanish further elevated concerns about some of the continent's largest and most tightly organized Indian tribes—the Creeks, Cherokees, and Seminoles. Fears of "savage" Indians and Spanish adversaries on porous borders heightened anxiety about the estimated 100,000 potentially dangerous Africans still living within them. Whereas many slaveholders farther north, including Virginians, considered emancipation a possibility, practically no whites in South Carolina or Georgia believed that the rights they had fought for would ever extend fully to black people. Many blacks, however, thought otherwise. A broken postwar economy and more frequent antislavery gestures by fellow Americans complicated the planters' task of subjugating, and in some cases resubjugating, slaves who had inherited their own revolutionary legacy.[3]

While whites united to deny blacks freedom, they remained deeply divided over how the postrevolutionary world should look. Frustrated with the conceit of coastal merchant and planter elites, previously marginalized groups sought to make state governments serve their interests, too. During the mid-1780s, political debates over land, debt, constitutions, and the international slave trade demonstrated to elites that these groups would not be easily silenced. Some historians have seen continuity and consensus in postwar politics, but from the perspective of contemporaries themselves—whether wealthy aristocrats, yeoman farm families, or slaves—the Revolution opened up a flood of new forces, new hopes, and new fears.[4]

Domestic stability and international security remained tied to another critical task: restoring the region to economic productivity. During the war, practical necessity and patriotic fervor had led Lower South residences toward subsistence production of corn, wheat, and low-grade cotton. Black and white women spun their own fabric to clothe themselves and their children. In peacetime, however, neither these crops nor the possible economic transition to manufacturing proved profitable. Moreover, the region's primary staple crops of rice, indigo, and tobacco had limited domestic appeal. Keeping elites wealthy, slaves' hands busy, nonelite whites content, and even foreign enemies at bay required reconnecting with the Atlantic economy.[5]

Exceedingly lucrative commerce during the colonial period, gleaned primarily from rice cultivation and a provisioning trade with the British West Indies, created high expectations for the postrevolutionary future. Planters and merchants anticipated great rewards from open and direct commerce with wartime allies. They soon discovered the harsh realities of their new world order. Inflation, shortages, and restricted access to European credit limited the states' ability to find new sources of trade. Consequently, planters, merchants, and farmers remained reliant on the only sources of money and goods that existed: British merchants who had stayed after the fighting had stopped. These men willingly provided new slaves and finished goods at high prices and often premised on high-interest loans. At the same time, British officials sought to reward loyal Canadians and punish Americans for their traitorous act. In addition to refusing to return slaves who were removed by the British navy, Westminster passed Orders in Council that reduced, and in some instances banned, the previously profitable British West Indian trade. A worsening balance of trade highlighted the incongruity between economic hopes and reality, forcing Lower South residents to confront their region's continued dependence on sworn enemies. These developments generated a constellation of challenges informing almost every state policy, from treatment of Loyalists to debtor legislation, naturalization laws, and commercial policies. Politicians of diverse backgrounds walked a fine line to preserve the meaning of the Revolution while also ensuring that procommercial policies maintained critical access to needed British trade and capital.[6]

Concerns about geopolitical security, renewed social harmony, and an abysmal economy pervaded the political culture of Georgia and South Carolina during the Confederation period. They occupied the minds of the region's delegates to Philadelphia's federal convention in 1787 and local representatives who overwhelmingly ratified the Constitution a year later. General Charles Cotesworth Pinckney, a respected state militia leader during the war and a drafter of the Constitution, candidly warned his state's ratification convention of the urgency of joining the new government: "We are so weak that by ourselves we could not form a union strong enough for the purpose of effectually protecting each other. Without union with the other states, South Carolina must soon fall. Is there any one among us so much a Quixote as to suppose that this state could long maintain her independence if she stood alone, or was only connected with the Southern States? I scarcely believe there is."[7] Georgians, who were fewer in number and further isolated geographically, remained in an even more precarious position. Anxiety about groups and forces both outside and within the Lower South propelled political representatives to welcome a stronger national government.[8]

At the Philadelphia Convention, however, Pinckney and his fellow delegates from the Lower South demonstrated much less humility, aggressively pursuing protections for their region's interest in commercial agriculture and slavery. While Upper South and Mid-Atlantic moderates like James Madison and James Wilson carefully sought consensus on principles and policies, intentionally evading unsavory topics such as slavery, Deep South delegates staked out more extreme positions in an effort to force real compromises. Though taking strong nationalist positions and siding with larger states on most major controversies, they repeatedly threatened to walk unless they received specific concessions on representation, slavery, and trade policy. Over the question of apportionment in the House of Representatives, the Georgia and South Carolina delegations insisted that protection of property and "justice" demanded slaves be fully counted in determining representation because "they are as productive of pecuniary resources, as those of the Northern States" and because "the security the Southn. States want is that their negroes may not be taken from them."[9]

Georgians and South Carolinians reluctantly had to accept that under the new government only 60 percent of their slaves would factor into lower house representation and subsequently the Electoral College. South Carolina's delegation did not vote for the three-fifths compromise; Georgia's did. Both states' efforts, however, had been instrumental in earning slaveholders a partial victory while making only a limited and potentially avoidable concession. Northerners at Philadelphia insisted that so long as slaveholders benefited from counting three-fifths of their slaves for congressional apportionment, they must also pay for three-fifths of their value if and when the federal government levied a "direct tax" on the states. But Americans generally favored drawing revenue from more easily hidden tariffs on imports, and politicians remained reluctant to pass "direct taxes." In those rare moments when they did, between 1789 and 1817, slaveholders fared rather well.[10]

Skilled politicians with litigious minds—six of eight had legal training—Georgia's and South Carolina's delegates parlayed a two-fifths "defeat" on the question of representation into partial victories elsewhere. As the five-man Committee of Detail began ironing out final points in late July, General Charles Cotesworth Pinckney "reminded the Convention that if the Committee should fail to insert some security to the Southern States against an emancipation of slaves, and taxes on exports, he should be bound by duty to his state to vote against their Report."[11] Almost as if to answer Pinckney's concern, the committee, which included Carolinian John Rutledge, cemented the three-fifths clause and prohibited Congress from banning the slave trade or passing export duties that could tax slave-grown staple commodities. In another measure favorable to the South, a two-thirds "super-majority" would be necessary to pass navigation acts that might be used to restrict foreign vessels' access to American markets for the benefit of northern merchants. In fact, only a clause that required a simple majority to pass other commercial legislation and the failure of the committee to refer expressly to "slavery" could be read as adverse to Lower South interests.

Northern representatives led by Rufus King and Gouverneur Morris stridently objected that too high a bar had been set for northern-friendly legislation while no bar existed at all for the continued importation of an acknowledged evil. The substance of the report sparked an uncharacteristically prolonged but illuminating debate over the morality of slavery, culminating in Virginian George Mason's fiery speech against "the pernicious effect" of slavery and a proposal by Marylander Luther Martin to prohibit or heavily tax the importation of new slaves.[12] In a revealing retort, Rutledge quickly urged that "religion & humanity had nothing to do with this question." Instead, he submitted, "interest alone is the governing principle with Nations—The true question at present is whether the Southn. States shall or shall not be parties to the Union." Indeed, according to Rutledge, northern interests should dictate continuing the trade as "the increase of Slaves . . . will increase the commodities of which they will become the carriers."[13] He would support the commerce clause but only "on condition that the subsequent part relating to negroes should also be agreed to."[14] In one of his few recorded comments, Georgia representative Abraham Baldwin concurred, informing the convention that Georgia—the only state at the time still legally importing slaves— would never submit to an abridgment of one of her "favorite prerogatives."[15] After an extended airing of the issues, the questions of the slave trade, navigation act, and export taxes returned to committee, where Morris hoped "these things may form a bargain among the Northern & Southern States."[16]

Another draft and more private and public negotiation yielded an accord more acceptable to northern representatives but in the final analysis still fairly favorable to the Lower South. With support from New Hampshire, Massachusetts, Connecticut, North Carolina, and Maryland, Georgia and South Carolina narrowly overcame the opposition of Virginians and other, Mid-Atlantic states to ensure that Congress could not prohibit the international slave trade until at least

1808, though they could pass a $10-per-head tax on each importation. In addition to another half victory for slavery, slaveholders enjoyed a complete success on the question of export duties. What would eventually become Article I, Section 9, ensured that the federal government could not pass export duties. Nor, according to a convoluted subsequent section, could individual states pass duties, except "what may be absolutely necessary for executing its inspection laws" and "subject to the revision and control of the Congress."[17]

Having used threats to secure significant protections for slavery and commercial agriculture, Pinckney then curried favor with northern allies by accentuating his region's vulnerability and exaggerating the sacrifices that he and his constituents would make on behalf of northern merchants. Dubiously asserting that "it was the true interest of the S. States to have no regulation of commerce," General Pinckney explained the reasons for their accommodation, considering the "liberal conduct towards the views of South Carolina [regarding the slave trade] and the interest the weak Southn. States had in being united with the strong Eastern States, he thought it proper that no fetters should be imposed on the power of making commercial regulations."[18] Pierce Butler similarly trumpeted the "concessions on the part of the S. States" and being "desirous of conciliating the affections of the East" dropped his opposition to a simple majority on navigation acts.[19] Both Madison and Martin confirmed that a bargain (which they both opposed) had been struck, the latter noting that he found "the *eastern* States, notwithstanding their *aversion to slavery*, were willing to indulge the southern States, at least with a temporary liberty to prosecute the *slave-trade*, provided the southern States would, in their turn, gratify them, by laying *no restriction on navigation acts*."[20] With all but one South Carolinian dropping their support for a higher threshold, that state joined northern ones to guarantee that all commercial legislation, including navigation acts, needed only a simple majority for approval.

Such maneuvering reflected shrewd and calculating politicians' early willingness to make concessions and reach compromises that would protect slavery. Making the most of every opportunity, South Carolina's delegation peddled their potential generosity on commercial matters into final assurances for slavery, securing the unopposed passage of a fugitive slave clause intended to prevent "any person bound to service or labor" from finding freedom if he or she escaped to increasingly freer states in the North.[21] The degree to which the Constitution was a proslavery document remains contested. The man at the center of much of the negotiations, General Pinckney, summarized his sense to South Carolina's state convention, "Considering all circumstances, we have made the best terms for the security of this species of property it was in our power to make. We would have made better if we could; but on the whole, I do not think them bad."[22] In short, political battles had been won, if not completely. Such was the cost of a union that the Lower South desperately felt it needed.

Afterward Charlestonian David Ramsay, a well-connected emigrant from Philadelphia, informed Massachusetts Federalist Benjamin Lincoln that compromises in Philadelphia had made local elites "much more Federal than formerly" and significantly elevated their esteem for New Englanders:

> This honest sentiment was avowed by the first characters: "New England has lost, and we have gained, by the war; and her suffering citizens ought to be our carriers, though a dearer freight should be the consequence." Your delegates never did a more politic thing, than in standing by those of South Carolina about negroes. Virginia deserted them, and was for an immediate stoppage of further importation. The [Old] dominion has lost much popularity by the conduct of her delegates on this head. The language now is "the Eastern states can soonest help us in case of invasion, and it is more our interest to encourage them and their shipping, than to join with or look up to Virginia." In short, sir, a revolution highly favorable to union has taken place; Federalism and liberality of sentiment have gained great ground.[23]

The flirtations with New England never blossomed into a marriage, but Ramsay's commentary suggests the shortsightedness of assuming simple North-South dichotomies.

Though their delegates' effort in Philadelphia highlighted the region's preoccupation with geopolitical security and slavery, Georgians and South Carolinians returned home ready to acknowledge the more immediate and positive reasons for ratifying the Constitution. As the Philadelphia Convention closed, John Rutledge admitted that even the big "concession" to the North, a simple majority on all commercial policies, might end up benefiting the region. "At the worst a navigation act could bear hard a little while only on the S. States. As we are laying the foundation for a great empire, we ought to take a permanent view of the subject," which included, he reminded his Lower South colleagues, "the necessity of securing the West India trade to this country."[24] Indeed, Ramsay's comments and subsequent state-level discussions demonstrate that, fears of northern economic domination aside, coastal elites with disproportionate state power believed the stronger national government *would* serve regional commercial interests.

By protecting private contracts and preventing states from passing deflationary currency policies, supporters at the ratification convention argued that the Constitution would restore international faith in a regional economy beset by inconsistent debtor relief laws and tariff schedules. South Carolinian Charles Pinckney drove the larger point home, arguing that the Constitution provided just the right tonic to cure the region's ills: "the one first and most sensibly felt" being "the destruction of our commerce" and its consequences, "the loss of credit, the inability in our citizens to pay taxes, and [the] languor of government."[25] A few Charleston delegates, purporting to represent the city's artisan community, even hoped that the national government might pass protective tariffs, something the state legislature had been reluctant to do. Acceptance of the Union would stabilize the Lower South's place within a stronger, more cooperative national economy and a less certain international one. The region might need nationally coordinated trade policy after all.[26]

Supporters claimed the Constitution also furthered this goal by providing the national government with paramount war-making capabilities and by elevating foreign treaties above state and even federal law, thus enhancing local responsibility and providing better diplomatic leverage. In fact, Charles Pinckney responded to skeptics within the state by declaring Article I, Section 10, which restricted states from interfering with diplomacy, currency regulation, contracts, or trade duties, the "soul of the Constitution" and essential "to cultivate those principles of public honor and private honesty which are the sure road to national character and happiness."[27] The Constitution's stronger diplomatic charge for the federal government had particular resonance in Georgia, a state simultaneously seeking to preserve an eastern mercantile economy and secure an inland empire protected from Spanish settlers and Indians. The document arrived just as a special legislative session was discussing recurring frontier problems and legislators quickly appointed a ratification convention in hopes that the new "general government" could "obtain a firm peace with Indians."[28] Merchant Joseph Clay believed this could be accomplished, but only if "the restraining power of the Union" limited white settlement, an action sure to anger many Georgians.[29] The treaty and war powers provisions provided tools, but as future diplomatic controversies later demonstrated, their perceived usefulness for serving regional interests depended very much on the circumstances.

Though many trade-conscious and slaveholding Georgians and Carolinians argued that the Union would provide a foundation for economic prosperity and geopolitical stability, some in the region remained skeptical of brokered compromises and the new government's powers. Anti-Federalists, as they became negatively labeled, feared that a tyrannical central government might use its new powers to thwart local autonomy. Such sentiments were strongest among backcountry yeomen, who were less involved in commercial agriculture and preoccupied with winning proportional representation within their respective states.[30] "A Georgian," writing in the *Gazette of the State of Georgia,* projected such a view onto the national political scene, arguing that unless the South received more representatives it would be exploited by a more populous North. The state's most prominent critic of the Constitution, Lachlan McIntosh, privately echoed those fears, recommending that Georgia "have a fair trial of its effects" for twenty years (not coincidentally the same year the slave trade could be banned), after which it could choose to readopt, amend, or void its ratification of the document.[31] During South Carolina's ratification debates, Rawlins Lowndes, a Charleston lawyer, protested that by making the constitution and treaties "the supreme law of the land" the new government would interfere with local and state governance. This, along with the numerical supremacy of commercial-minded "Easterners" who might be squeamish about the slave trade, would ensure over time that "the sun, of the Southern States would set, never to rise again."[32] Because they believed it unlikely that a South Carolinian or Georgian would ever hold the presidency, anti-Federalists were particularly sensitive about the judicial appointments and treaty-making powers that Article II vested in the executive branch. To them, *Union* ultimately connoted subservience to a numerically superior North. While their organizational skills proved ineffective against pro-Constitution advocates, their rhetoric and warnings remained guideposts to which later states' rights disciples and secessionists would return.[33]

Federalists responded that the sum would be more effective than the parts. *Union* implied strength and mutually beneficial cooperation on economic and political matters. The Constitution, they suggested, simply formalized the natural alliance that existed between the thirteen republics. In early 1788 these arguments won handily. Georgia state delegates unanimously ratified the Constitution in January, making their state the second to sanction the new government. In May, South Carolina followed when delegates approved the new system by a 2-to-1 margin. Morris & Brailsford, a Charleston-based firm with commercial dealings in both states, wrote Thomas Jefferson in France to convey the region's optimism in the wake of ratification. Should the "Federal System" be adopted by sister states, they believed "our Commerce will then experience the fruits of Order and Energy, and those Nations, who now view us with Contempt, who ridicule our Folly and Disunion, and who are enriching themselves on our Spoils, will gladly court our rising Consequence and be happy in granting us liberal Sums for the benefits we allow them from the participation in our Trade."[34] Lower South planters and merchants celebrated the news that, by the slightest of margins, New Hampshire, Virginia, and New York had ratified the Constitution. A union providing adequate, if not in their mind excessive, protection for slavery and the promise of commercial betterment would be inaugurated in 1789.[35]

Philadelphia entrepreneur Tench Coxe, who also eagerly embraced the Constitution, remained somewhat less certain about the new government's ability to serve his own and his state's particular interest in fostering American manufacturing, specifically in textiles. As delegates began assembling in Philadelphia in May 1787, Coxe addressed a crowd of like-minded individuals at the house of Benjamin Franklin, the convention's senior-most statesman. Later printed for and addressed "to the Honorable Members of the Convention, assembled at Philadelphia for fœderal purposes," Coxe's speech conveyed his hope that the planned constitutional reforms would protect American artisans and manufacturers by breaking down trade barriers between the states and erecting "general restrictions and prohibitions affecting foreign nations."[36] By August, private conversations with delegates must have had Coxe concerned. He revisited the subject of active support for American industry, this time before the Philadelphia Friends of American Manufacturing. A national government that supported American industry would, he urged, "improve our agriculture and teach us to explore the fossil and vegetable kingdoms" and "accelerate the improvement of our internal navigation and bring into action the dormant powers of nature and the elements—it will lead us once more into the paths of virtue by restoring frugality and industry, those potent antidotes to the vices of mankind and will give us real independence by rescuing us from the tyranny of foreign fashions, and the destructive torrent of luxury." But accomplishing all of this necessitated that the manufacturing interests be given the same care that commercial and agrarian interests had been given by "THE AUGUST BODY now sitting in our capital." He hoped the convention would encourage American industry by explicitly empowering Congress to pass protective tariffs on foreign goods and to offer direct bounties to manufacturers. The industry these policies would foster, Coxe concluded, would bring "more profit to the individual and riches to the nation" and achieve the country's "*Political Salvation*."[37]

It is not clear if the "august" delegates from South Carolina and Georgia attended either of Coxe's presentations or read his treatises, but Coxe seemed determined to persuade them that domestic industry would serve even planters' interests. In his circulated tract, he hoped that "southern planters would adopt the cultivation of" cotton, "an article from which the best informed manufacturers calculate the greatest profits, and on which some established factories depend."[38] Though cotton was still limited in growth, Coxe believed it capable of reengineering the national economy and uniting the nation's diverse interests in common cause. Cultivation by southern planters and processing by northern manufacturers would wean all regions from the lapsed economic dependence on their former imperial overlords.

Delegates may have heard Coxe's opinions, but his views do not appear to have factored heavily in the convention's deliberations. Broad consensus already existed that trade within the United States would be kept free, which was certainly key for Coxe's vision. But on the few occasions when individuals suggested more active protection for American manufacturing, most delegates refused to move beyond discussing tariff policy as a means of generating revenue or encouraging American shipping. Congress's enumerated powers included the authority "to regulate Commerce with foreign Nations, and among the several States," but proposals to give Congress the express power to aid manufacturers failed. Even more damning, however, the Constitution's prohibition on states levying their own import duties forced states like Pennsylvania to revoke protective measures in place since the Revolution. Subsequently, manufacturing proponents like Coxe would have to convince national politicians to adopt a liberal interpretation of the commerce and "general welfare" clauses to win meaningful support for specific domestic industries. The relative lack of support for manufacturing within the convention mirrored that of the nation as a whole. The commercial and agrarian majority had little desire to grant powers, seen by many as special privileges, that would raise prices for the many in order to support a few.[39]

Nor did the allure of cotton prove capable of winning southern delegates over to the cause. Indeed the crop seemed to have factored little in that hot summer's deliberations. While references to tobacco, rice, indigo, wheat, lumber, and even hemp appear throughout the convention records, cotton is scarcely mentioned. Delegates from Georgia and South Carolina were certainly intimately aware of the crop's usefulness. Under duress, many likely grew it in small amounts to clothe themselves and their slaves. But it had not yet been shown to have much commercial value, and individuals at home were only beginning to experiment with new varieties that would eventually prove profitable. After a decade and half of indebtedness and depressed markets for staple crops with few domestic consumers, delegates from South Carolina and Georgia (like those from many parts of the nation) came to the convention hoping to enhance their position within global trade, not to find new ways to restrict it. Had U.S. cotton cultivation and textile manufacturing emerged in the cooperative way Coxe envisioned, perhaps a very different national history would have been woven. Coxe and other supporters of manufacturing would instead have to pursue their goals without Lower South support.

In the final analysis, citizens from diverse places and backgrounds believed membership in a stronger union built around federalism and Madisonian pluralism would enable them to achieve the stability, security, and prosperity that political independence had failed to provide. A broad segment of South Carolina and Georgia shared these hopes, which helps explain the comparatively easy battles for ratification in those states. Yet the federal position also revealed tensions that would not be sorted out until after the Civil War. In order to win acceptance of a stronger federal government, supporters of the Constitution told constituents that a national harmony of interests existed and that passing more authority to a national government should not be feared. At the same time, however, the difficult compromises at the convention also suggested that the diversity of interests and peoples within this vast confederacy might be more disparate parts than an organic whole. Was the United States a natural nation or not? Patriots and policymakers continued to hope, claim, and even believe this was the case even as arguments over political economy, foreign policy, and slavery continually disrupted such optimistic visions. Verdicts on the effectiveness of the Union remained primarily based on the federal government's usefulness for its component members. Politicians in the First Congress soon discovered this as they struggled to find national solutions to local and international problems.

# CHAPTER ONE

# The Threads of a Global Loom

Cotton, Slavery, and Union in an Interdependent Atlantic,
1789–1820

A week before the Philadelphia Convention, readers of the *State Gazette of South Carolina* learned that an improved Atherton spinning machine had enabled the small town of Holywell, England, to spin enough cotton thread "in one day . . . as will surround the globe at the equator."[1] Neither the *Gazette*'s readers nor the "ingenious correspondent" who shared this information knew how symbolic this imagery would be. While cotton cloth's durability, washability, and breathability had made it increasingly attractive to consumers, the profits to be gained from it were only beginning to become apparent. In the mid-1780s, cotton goods composed only 6 percent of all British exports, a figure dwarfed by the centuries-old woolen industry's 29 percent. British manufacturers might be able to spin miles of thread efficiently, but a reliable source for raw cotton did not exist. Nor did their former North American colonists seem likely providers, as evidenced by the United States' earliest documented foray into British markets. In 1784 Liverpool custom agents confiscated eight bags of cotton from a U.S. ship. Believing it impossible that the new Republic could produce even this meager amount, they assumed it to be of West Indian origin and thus imported in violation of the navigation acts. After the affluent British merchant William Rathbone authenticated its

U.S. origin, the low-grade cotton was released, only to sit in a Liverpool warehouse for several months before being sold to a Derby cotton spinner.[2] Despite these inauspicious beginnings, within two decades the Lower South provided almost half of Great Britain's raw cotton supply. Finished cotton products composed over 40 percent of Britain's flourishing export trade. Together, the workers, mill owners, and merchants of the British midlands and the planters and slaves of the Lower South had inaugurated an international cotton empire that would soon encircle the globe.

The Anglo-American cotton trade that emerged in the last decade of the eighteenth century did so at a particularly critical moment in the development of international political economy and modern nation-state building. During the seventeenth and early eighteenth century, Europeans' efforts to secure empire and wealth led them across the Atlantic in search of land, labor, and supplies, creating vast systems of trade that generated considerable profits, much of it on the backs of African slaves and their descendants. Along with wealth, however, came repeated war as Europe's chief powers, especially Britain and France, competed more often than they collaborated. Alarmed by such developments, some mid-eighteenth-century theorists, most famously the French Physiocrats and Adam Smith, scorned the bitter fruits of what David Hume called the "jealousy of trade." They argued instead that great benefits could be gained from less government intervention, fewer national barriers, and the pursuit of freer trade. By so doing they laid much of the conceptual groundwork for what we now call classical economic liberalism.[3] In their day, however, most people saw these ideas as mere abstractions. Politicians, situated within empires, continued to make policy based on pragmatic concerns and premised largely on mercantilist ideologies. In short, powers sought to command as many economic resources as possible, to create a favorable balance of trade, and to control specie.

To a very significant degree, this pursuit of economic hegemony set the stage for a second series of events, equally important in their effects and collectively referred to as the "Age of Revolutions." The geopolitical landscape of the Western Hemisphere forever changed when thirteen of Britain's North American colonies declared themselves independent and created a new nation built upon the principles of republican government. The language and theories Americans used to justify their Revolution were not new, but the scale of their success was. Though imperfectly practiced, the ideals of liberty they proclaimed reached a wide audience in North America and abroad. Within the United States, poor whites, slaves, and others who had been disaffected during the colonial period seized on the language of freedom and equality to pursue their own interests and desires. The values of the American Revolution, transatlantic in origin, resonated abroad as well, and over the next half century people in Europe and the Western Hemisphere sought to create independent nations out of empires, to transform old monarchies into new republics, and even on occasion to challenge the labor system of slavery around which the Atlantic economy had emerged.[4]

It remained to be seen, however, if and how the era of revolution and nation-making would transform the empire-centered, mercantilist calculations of European leaders. Would the existence of these politically independent, material-rich nations like the United States compel European empires to abandon restrictions on trade policies and pursue freer trade? Or would these new nations perpetuate restrictive commercial measures of their own, using tools reminiscent of the empires that they had left—navigation acts, tariffs, duties, and so forth—to encourage their own nation-centered economies? In the 1780s and 1790s most American revolutionaries certainly hoped that the former would be the case. The Revolution had been predicated, in part at least, on breaking free from an empire that, according to one South Carolina planter-merchant, had "determined to bring the colonists into a State of Vassalage" by restricting American commerce and westward expansion.[5] Independence, enterprising Americans thought, would allow for better access to frontier lands and foreign markets. U.S. planters, farmers, and merchants rich in commodities could navigate their own commercial routes with fully extended sails. After Americans won their independence, however, neither their French or Dutch allies, nor their British adversaries, proved as accommodating as hoped. Mercantilism, calculated to help diversely composed and widely dispersed empires, remained the guiding principle of international trade. Disappointed and struggling through a severe postwar depression, Americans under the relatively weak framework of the Articles of Confederation found a united response all but impossible.

The new Constitution made available more easily deployed and powerful commercial weapons. Many in the first federal Congress hoped to use countervailing duties on foreign tonnage and tariffs on imported goods to respond to European policies and pry open foreign markets. Despite disagreements over specifics, proponents of these measures saw them as means toward the greater end of freer trade, and thus historians have often labeled them "neomercantilists." A few Americans saw them in a different light. Members of the artisan classes, especially, believed restricting American commerce presented the first step toward a different, domestic-centered vision of the American economy built around a vibrant industrial base capable of limiting dependence on foreign trade. A third group, which included powerful voices within the Washington administration, believed that unfettered trade with Britain remained the most reliable source of attracting much-needed capital and credit.[6]

In the broadest terms, these political and economic calculations competed to shape policy as planters in Georgia and South Carolina embarked on the cultivation of raw cotton for commercial profit. The crop's ascension would eventually prove critical for the creation of an Anglo-American free trade movement capable of altering economic worldviews and shifting national policies. In its infancy, however, cotton's revolutionary potential remained latent. Shortly after former Loyalists ushered in commercial cotton into the Sea Islands in the late 1780s, "patriotic" planters began cultivating it farther westward. Still relatively small in number and influence, cotton planters and the politicians representing them emerged as part of a loose Jeffersonian Republican coalition committed to neo-mercantilist policies that sought to reduce American economic dependence on Britain. In spite of Republican planter-politicians' own policies and widespread Anglophobia throughout the Lower South, a decade of peace and relatively open trade with Britain ushered in by Jay's Treaty allowed for a cotton revolution that transformed and revitalized the Lower South's economy. Entrepreneurial planters and industrious slaves converted available land into cotton fields, and Georgia, South Carolina, and the Lower Mississippi Valley rapidly emerged as major providers of raw cotton. This economic transformation, however, had quite counterrevolutionary effects, not least of these being continued dependence on trade with Britain and lethal blows to the hope for a gradual end to North American slavery. Cotton, to a very great degree, ensured that both international trade and America's national experiment would remain premised on slavery and its expansion.

## Cotton, Empire, and Nation

Historically, cotton's growth extended back to antiquity. People throughout the Mediterranean, Southeast Asia, and in Native American societies clothed themselves by producing and spinning it in small quantities. Cotton's rise to global prominence, however, had its origins in the cultural transformations of early modern Europe and the might of Britain's commercial empire. By the eighteenth century, increasingly delicate European sensibilities created what Norbert Elias called a rising "threshold of embarrassment."[7] Ever more consumer-conscious middle and working classes embraced elevated standards of cleanliness and fashion, placing high demand on easily washable and increasingly colorful cloth. Centuries-old woolen manufacturers continued to dominate British and other European markets through the eighteenth century, but cotton prints, first introduced into Britain by the East India Company in the 1690s, offered a practical alternative. Despite a legal ban on cotton imports enacted in 1721, Indian calicoes that could be more easily dyed and washed became increasingly popular.

Cotton's versatility meant it could be mixed with linen, even made into velvet, and used for window curtains, cheap britches, and handkerchiefs. Cotton cloth was less expensive than silk and could more easily be imprinted than wool or linen. Consequently, women of the mid- and late eighteenth century were presented with an astonishing array of patterned dresses printed predominantly on cotton cloth. As the eighteenth century progressed, status-conscious Britons of all backgrounds, including those in the North American colonies, took part in the social masquerade of refinement. They increasingly turned to printed cotton dresses and waistcoats and white cotton stockings, simultaneously raising the fashion standard and making it more attainable to the general public.[8]

Though other European countries pursued cotton manufacturing, existing structures and technological know-how gave Britain a considerable edge. After the largely ineffective ban on British cotton production expired in 1774, cotton manufacturers in Manchester and surrounding areas quickly entered into the same mercantilist and protectionist systems that had long aided wool producers. In the 1770s, inventions such as Hargreaves's spinning jenny, Arkwright's water frame, and Crompton's mule afforded Lancashire manufacturers the ability to manufacture textiles at a greatly accelerated rate. In just a few decades new technologies and government support transformed the British Midlands into the most powerful manufacturing metropolis the world had seen. Producing an array of goods—from fine corduroys and velvets for wealthy Britons, to cloth for petticoats popular amongst the rising middle class, to plainer, ready-made fustians worn by British workers—the industrialists of the Midlands found the making of cotton cloth a very profitable industry, despite a very limited supply of the raw material necessary to produce it. By the mid-1790s, British cotton products had risen to over 15 percent of that nation's exports.[9]

If domestic consumption gave cotton its start, Britain's vast commercial empire offered unique opportunities for its growth. Like their British counterparts, continental Europeans found the flexibility and affordability of cotton textiles attractive, even though they had only limited capacity to produce them. Consequently,

Table 1  Exports of British Produce, 1784–1856, by Commodity Group

| Commodity Group | 1784–86 | 1794–96 | 1804–6 | 1814–16 | 1824–26 | 1834–36 | 1844–46 | 1854–56 |
|---|---|---|---|---|---|---|---|---|
| Cotton goods | 766 (6.0) | 3,392 (15.6) | 15,871 (42.3) | 18,742 (42.1) | 16,879 (47.8) | 22,398 (48.5) | 25,835 (44.2) | 34,908 (34.1) |
| Woolen goods | 3,700 (29.2) | 5,194 (23.9) | 6,172 (16.4) | 7,866 (17.7) | 5,737 (16.3) | 7,037 (15.2) | 8,328 (14.2) | 10,802 (10.5) |
| Other textiles | 1,334 (10.6) | 2,313 (10.6) | 2,788 (7.4) | 3,628 (8.2) | 3,226 (9.1) | 4,523 (9.8) | 6,349 (10.9) | 13,018 (10.5) |
| Other manufacturers | 4,858 (38.3) | 8,144 (37.4) | 8,944 (23.8) | 7,783 (17.5) | 6,777 (19.2) | 8,125 (17.6) | 10,922 (18.7) | 24,363 (23.8) |
| Foodstuffs and raw materials | 2,032 (15.9) | 2,727 (12.5) | 3,760 (10.0) | 6,455 (14.5) | 2,679 (7.6) | 4,110 (8.9) | 6,986 (12.0) | 19,410 (18.9) |
| Total | 12,690 | 21,770 | 37,535 | 44,474 | 35,298 | 46,193 | 58,420 | 102,501 |

Source: Ralph Davis, *The Industrial Revolution and British Overseas Trade* (Atlantic Highlands, N.J.: Humanities Press, 1979), 15.
Note: Export values are given in thousands of British pounds. Numbers in parentheses are percentages.

Table 2    Destination of British Finished Cotton Exports
by Region, 1784–1856 (as percentage of exports)

|  | Europe | Asia and Africa | America and Australia |
|---|---|---|---|
| 1784–86 | 40.5 | 21.4 | 38.1 |
| 1794–96 | 22.6 | 5.8 | 71.6 |
| 1804–6 | 45.5 | 4.3 | 50.2 |
| 1814–16 | 60.1 | 1.9 | 38.0 |
| 1824–26 | 51.4 | 10.1 | 38.5 |
| 1834–36 | 47.4 | 18.1 | 34.5 |
| 1844–46 | 39.2 | 36.3 | 24.5 |
| 1854–56 | 29.4 | 39.6 | 31.0 |

*Source:* Ralph Davis, *The Industrial Revolution and British Overseas Trade* (Atlantic Highlands, N.J.: Humanities Press, 1979), 15.

especially during the Hanoverian period, Britain's cotton exports flourished in German and other continental markets, which in the mid-1780s consumed about 40 percent of British yarn and finished cotton goods. Britain's success also relied heavily on a "blue water" strategy that fostered trade with its ever-expanding imperial provinces throughout the world. Under this vision the profitability and standard of living for white Britons at home and abroad remained tied to imperial regulation and commercial expansion. British colonials, especially in warmer climates, further boosted demand for Lancashire cotton manufactures. Provincial settlers anxious to retain their British identities and forced to do so by navigation acts embraced metropolitan fashions, making them important consumers of the mother country's textiles. With little or no local cloth production, Canada and the West Indies purchased British textiles in large quantities. The settlement of Australia in the 1790s turned convicts into consumers. As the nineteenth century proceeded, cotton found a central place in what C. A. Bayly has called Britain's "new imperial age." The mechanisms of imperial governance sought to ensure that Britain's trading empire would be clothed in the so-called vegetable wool.[10]

Despite growing numbers of consumers, the expansion of Britain's cotton businesses required that manufacturers find steady supplies of raw cotton. Not surprisingly, Westminster followed traditional assumptions and sought to turn the imperial periphery into a producer of fine- and medium-quality raw cotton suitable for European and American tastes. In 1787 the Board of Trade sent Polish botanist Anton Pantaleon Hove to Bombay, India, on a two-year investigation of the successful cultivation methods employed there. Hove shipped over twenty varieties of seeds to London, where the board distributed them to interested

West Indian planters.[11] Combined with encouragement from island governments, these efforts met with some success. By 1790 West Indian cotton production had increased 50 percent. The next decade, however, saw supplies contract as unfavorable weather, plagues, and sugar's continuing profitability limited the crop's success in the Caribbean.[12] Manufacturers and officials also attempted to establish cotton plantations nearer the source of more bountiful labor in Africa and East India. In the 1780s and early 1790s investors created companies along the West African coast using both free black and slave labor to grow Persian and Indian seeds. Nature again interfered, as poor soil, insects, and the resulting bad crop yields convinced financiers that efforts there would be largely fruitless.[13]

The best chance for an imperial source of cotton remained the Indian subcontinent, but intra-imperial tensions and economic rivalries prevented that region from providing a sufficient supply. Midland manufacturers' need for raw materials clashed with the powerful East India Company's desire to import more lucrative textiles to the homeland. Manchester manufacturer Patrick Colquhoun bitterly attacked the continued flow of finished cotton products from India, advocating that East India should be kept only a harvester rather than a spinner of fine cotton. His wish would come true, and India would be deindustrialized, but not until much later in the nineteenth century. Instead, trying to balance the mother country's need for more raw cotton with the interests of the periphery, the Board of Trade approved policies to import a relatively small portion of the finest East Indian raw cotton available. The East India Company proved reluctant or unable to cooperate, and for the time East India remained only a secondary supplier.[14] Despite some diversification within Britain's Asian, African, and Caribbean possessions, officially sponsored efforts proved insufficient for the fast-growing needs of cotton manufactures. Nature, science, intra-imperial rivalries, and economics failed to cooperate with mercantilist calculations, thus paving the way for extra-imperial commercial relationships.

In 1790 the United States remained an improbable supplier, generating less than 0.2 percent of British raw cotton imports. Poor-quality strands homespun by patriotic women during the war had been critical for the war effort but afterward were deemed more suitable for clothing slaves than "refined" whites. In addition, slaveholders seeking reentrance into global commodity markets initially turned their slaves' efforts toward traditional crops, choosing to purchase cheap plain calicoes, known as Negro Cloth, from Britain rather than have slaves spin their own. When Anglo-French warfare in the early 1790s restricted British access to the continent, the United States assumed new importance for British manufacturers. Its citizens became, if only temporarily, the single largest market for the kingdom's cotton cloth. This meant that Americans, who retained their penchant for British styles, participated in cotton's early global business primarily as consumers of British cloth, helping to fuel that nation's cotton empire.[15]

This continued dependence on British fashion and textiles alarmed Americans from diverse backgrounds, many of whom united in an effort to wean themselves from the unpatriotic trade. Such attempts contributed to the raucous debates of the First Congress as diverse interests sought to use Congress's constitutional obligation to "lay and collect Taxes, Duties, Imposts and Excises to pay the Debts and provide for the common Defence and general Welfare" to benefit particular interests or agendas.[16] With alert constituents watching, congressmen had to ensure that the "grammar of political combat" they struggled to master achieved tangible results for voters at home. The task remained exceedingly difficult, given ambiguous understandings of the greater national good and the myriad interests demanding support. With a great deal at stake, debates over tonnage and revenue or impost bills quickly transformed into broader discussions about if and how the nation's competing interests could be harmonized into a coherent national political economy.[17]

Artisans and manufacturers believed the answer lay in higher levels of protection for American-made goods. Building on Tench Coxe's earlier treatises and emphasizing the trade deficit created by Americans' insatiable demand for British finished cloth, textile manufacturers, including proprietors of the Beverly Cotton Manufactory in Massachusetts and Thomas Ruston of Philadelphia, argued that true independence required that America manufacture its own cloth. They insisted that "Good Policy" and "Public Justice" dictated raising impost tariffs on finished goods and removing duties on raw materials needed to manufacture cloth—especially cotton, sheep's wool, and hemp.[18] The agrarian and mercantile interests dominating national politics may have sympathized with the goals of these arguments, but they rejected the idea of a majority of Americans paying higher taxes in order to protect a small minority of citizens. While Pennsylvania delegates pushed for a duty on imported textile goods of 12.5 percent, Georgia representative William Few successfully led a retreat back to a compromise level of 7.5 percent.[19] The final bill included that rate for most cotton goods.

Instead of promoting the domestic-centered vision of national political economy offered by northern artisans and manufacturers, the majority of legislators in the First Congress, including one of its leaders, James Madison, remained tied to the assumption that America's comparative advantage in agriculture meant it would continue to freight raw materials to European markets in exchange for more-complicated manufactured goods. Accepting this Atlantic-centered understanding of the economy did not, however, mean that agrarians in the First Congress wanted to keep the nation dependent on British merchants. Indeed discussions of commercial legislation raised the subject of how best to empower American merchants and diversify American markets. Madison, along with Secretary of State Jefferson, who had served in France, knew that the European continent and West Indian islands consumed much, if not most, of the South's colonial staple crops—especially wheat, rice, lumber, and tobacco. Colonial navigation acts had dictated the flow of goods to maximize revenue and benefit British merchants, but the Revolution had voided them. Ideally, Americans—now armed with the new Constitution's coercive tools—could end their overdependence on British creditors and merchants, empower U.S. commerce, and acquire direct access to French, Dutch, and Italian markets.

Seeking to capitalize on these new potentialities, the First Congress passed a system of tonnage duties to aid American merchants and shipbuilders. Foreign ships would be assessed a duty of 50 cents per ton while American-owned and -built ships would pay only 6 cents per ton upon arrival at U.S. ports. To further encourage trade with continental Europe, Madison and other Virginians led the push for additional discrimination against British ships. Resistance in the Senate and from the president, however, blocked this measure. In an attempt to pry open access to the British West Indian trade, a special navigation act did, however, target British vessels carrying goods from those islands to the United States. Congress also sent a strong message about its desire to circumscribe foreign participation in the coastal trade, allowing American vessels to pay a nominal annual registration fee while forcing foreign vessels to pay 50 cents per ton on every entrance into a U.S. port. Congress had sent a pretty clear message that it wished to support the use of American merchants and ships. Subsequent legislation furthered these efforts by adding a 10 percent duty on all goods imported on foreign vessels.[20]

Historians have generally assumed that the spokesmen for the Lower South remained united with their Virginia brethren on these policies, and by 1793 they would be. A closer look at the debates of the First Congress, however, demonstrates that Georgia and South Carolina's delegates were much more reluctant to pass highly discriminatory legislation against foreign powers generally and Britain particularly. Unique postwar circumstances help explain the Lower South's rejection of discriminatory duties. Like Virginia tobacco planters, South Carolina and Georgia planters had suffered mightily during the Revolution and from a deep depression afterward. But unlike Virginia and most northern states, Georgia and South Carolina officials' decision to allow British merchants to stay after military withdrawal led to the immediate resumption of direct trade with the British Empire. This fact created considerable tensions within Lower South society, including a fair amount of anti-British sentiment, especially in Charleston and the backcountry. In the halls of Congress, however, pragmatic interest prevailed.

In response to Madison's proposals, Georgia and South Carolina representatives demanded a more conciliatory trade policy. Lowcountry rice planter William Loughton Smith, who had spent most of the Revolution in Europe, admitted to his friend and South Carolina state legislator Edward Rutledge that "encouragemt. shod. be given to American shipping," but he feared that, if allowed "to indulge their inclinations," the New England states "wod. lay a tonnage equal to [pro]hibition on British Shipping, & then we shod be greatly embarrassed [about] how to export our crops."[21] Even two of the region's most vocal Anglophobes expressed great reluctance to target British traders. Aedanus Burke, who had earlier authored a scathing attack on the presence of British merchants in Charleston, admitted that "though in favor of South Carolina we vote in favor of Great Britain. Unfortunately it goes hand in hand" when commercial interests are involved.[22] Georgian James Jackson agreed, noting that "the southern states are obliged to make use of British vessels."[23] As Madison and Upper South representatives expressed general satisfaction with the First Congress's early tonnage bills and tariff schedules, Jackson reflected widespread dissatisfaction in the Lower South, complaining that the commercial legislation did not "bear equally" on his region. Southern staple growers, he lamented, had been "saddled to aggrandize the eastern" merchants and manufacturers, who "will never be content till [they] get the whole trade in their own hands."[24] Pierce Butler, a drafter of the Constitution, went even further, arguing that "locality and partiality had reigned" and expressing dismay that the "concessions" at the 1787 convention had been "so soon abused and taken advantage of."[25]

Such sentiments provided the setting for the first legislative concessions made specifically for U.S. cotton producers. As requested by manufacturers, the tariff measure emerging from the House had provided for the duty-free importation of raw cotton. But in the Senate, Georgians and South Carolinians refused to support the bill until a duty of 3 cents per pound on raw cotton was added. James Madison conveyed to a frustrated Tench Coxe that the duty had been a "concession to S.C. and Georgia who complained of sacrifices on almost every other article."[26] Coxe received an even more detailed analysis of the dynamics from his friend, Pennsylvania representative George Clymer, who candidly expressed the challenge of simultaneously fostering America's two infant cotton industries, whose short-term interests conflicted. Southern planters would not support higher protection for manufacturers in an "infant state" based solely on promised "future benefits." At the same time, because the South "could make no promise of supplying all the American demand in any short time," the tariffs necessary to encourage raw cotton growth harmed manufacturers, who needed inexpensive access to those goods. When prospective cotton planters "insisted upon this small tribute," they demonstrated the short-term impracticality of Coxe's initial vision, a harmony of interests between raw cotton producers and nascent textile manufacturers.[27]

In preparing his well-known 1789 Report on Manufacturing, Treasury Secretary Alexander Hamilton appreciated the difficulty, innovatively suggesting a middle course. Raw cotton would enter duty-free but cotton manufacturers would receive a bounty of 1 cent per pound for using domestic cotton. The idea might have helped harmonize cotton producers and manufacturers, but Congress—especially agrarian groups—remained skeptical of providing bounties to minority manufacturing interests. When it revisited the impost question in the spring of 1792, it rejected textile mill owners' requests and kept duties on finished goods and raw cotton at existing levels, thus continuing to benefit cotton planters but not manufacturers, who still required foreign fibers to meet demand. Legislation in subsequent congresses brought slightly better protection for American textile manufacturers, including 15 percent duties on imported textiles in 1797, but the 3-cent duty on raw cotton remained in effect until 1846.[28]

While Lower South opposition to protecting American manufacturers remained steady, developments in the Atlantic forced planters to rethink earlier assumptions about trade with Britain. The outbreak of France's revolutionary wars in the late spring of 1792 and Britain's entrance into the anti-French coalition the following year placed Americans in a precarious position between their revolutionary allies and their chief trading partner. Seeking to ensure that American neutrality did not harm British war efforts, Westminster issued Orders in Council that targeted American ships. In 1793 and 1794 as many as 350 American ships destined for France or her colonies were confiscated. Many Lower South planters, farmers, and merchants, angry at British belligerence, continued debt, and the failure to return escaped slaves grew more receptive to Virginia-led plans for retaliation.

Though claiming to adhere to free trade principles, Madison seized on Secretary of State Thomas Jefferson's 1793 Report on Commerce, which had stressed the advantages of increased trade with France, and proposed neomercantilist policies targeting trade with Britain. Discriminatory duties and tighter navigation acts would, both men hoped, end discriminatory practices or, at the least, secure American economic independence by properly rechanneling trade away from Britain. American merchants and shipowners needed to "obtain an equitable share in carrying our own produce," thus enabling Americans to "enjoy the actual benefit of advantages which nature and the spirit of our people entitle us to."[29] Even if European nations failed to embrace more conciliatory policies, Jeffersonians offered hope to manufacturers like Tench Coxe (who subsequently joined their ranks), suggesting that higher tariffs would indirectly protect domestic production by promoting the settlement of European mechanics and encouraging state governments to "open the resources of encouragement which are under their control."[30] Not surprisingly, Jefferson's reports and Madison's associated resolutions seized on revolutionary rhetoric promising all interests a second chance at the new markets that political independence and the Union had yet to furnish.[31]

The Republican opposition's arguments resonated with Lower South politicians, who only a few years earlier had rejected milder forms of economic coercion. Pierce Butler—a critic of Madison's discriminatory plans during the First Congress—supported the heavier measures, praising Madison for the "Manly manner in which You came forward" to move beyond "Half way restrictions" to a "Strong Measure" that would truly strike at the heart of "British influence" and commercial temptation. "All that are Patriotick, must be with you," he concluded.[32] Fellow Carolinian, Representative Thomas Carnes, lamented the "infamous, cruel, illegal, and unwarrantable conduct of Britain" aimed at "destroying our commerc [sic]" and spoke favorably of congressional action to retaliate economically and, if necessary, militarily.[33] Georgia's representative James Jackson and South Carolina's Edward Rutledge and Aedanus Burke agreed, challenging the administration to take a more actively pro-French position that supported the global cause of republicanism.[34] These individuals' efforts were instrumental in organizing state-level "republican" opposition to more conciliatory administration policies.

Anti-British positions seemed to have garnered even broader support amongst the public in South Carolina and Georgia, where a combination of economic, political, and social forces pushed Anglophobia to new heights despite the fact that Britain remained a potential market for the region's handful of cotton growers.

From a commercial and cultural perspective the French Revolution had created renewed excitement. Republican forces there allowed greater access to the West Indian carrying trade, providing rice planters and merchants involved in the provisioning trade a brighter economic forecast. Yet continued cycles of debt and dependence on British merchant communities in Charleston and Savannah continued to trouble the region. Legislation in each state had buffered American debtors somewhat from their coastal creditors, but with local economies still languishing and rice, indigo, and tobacco prices low, farmers and planters remained in dire straits. These conditions help explain South Carolinians' warm embrace of French ambassador Citizen Edmond-Charles Genet, who arrived in Charleston in April 1793 after his ship had been blown off course. Genet's visit drew great interest, spawning Democratic-Republican societies that advocated open support for the French Republic. Lower South merchants involved in trade with France, along with backcountry farmers and artisans, rallied to the liberty pole and demanded the United States recognize its ally's plight by severing all trade with Great Britain. Within this context, being a good American Republican necessitated not being sympathetic to Britain.

Not all politicians from the Lower South agreed that anti-British measures served regional or national interests. William Loughton Smith, who represented local Goose Creek rice planters enjoying close ties to Charleston's British merchants, emerged as a chief critic of Jefferson and Madison's plan. In Smith's view, commercial retaliation meant endangering the road to economic recovery by stripping American agriculture of its necessary markets and "violently" interrupting the importation of inexpensive and necessary British manufactures. Smith countered Jefferson's Report on Commerce and Madison's speeches by arguing that trade with Britain was far more important than that with France and "may, in most cases, be considered as a means of extending, instead of abridging our commerce."[35] Opposing his colleagues and the general public's apparent wishes, Smith became Alexander Hamilton's mouthpiece in Congress, urging a diplomatic solution that would prevent commercial or actual warfare. Fearing the potential for armed conflict, Washington preempted any congressional action by sending Supreme Court Justice John Jay to negotiate in London.

Jay's Treaty reflected the administration's desire to secure peace and retain direct trade with Britain even if it meant sacrificing some American interests. Though it did little to open the British West Indian trade or protect American sailors from impressments, it offered a framework to settle disputes over the U.S.-Canadian border, assured the removal of British forts from the Northwest, and guaranteed compensation for seized vessels. Perhaps most controversially, the treaty required reciprocal trading rights between the two nations, thus guaranteeing Britain most-favored-nation status for the next ten years. In this sense Jay's Treaty was, as Jacob Crowley has described it, a "liberal" document that came closer to free trade than any previous American policy.[36] Congressional opponents, however, believed the treaty a blatant attempt to preempt economic coercion and an unconstitutional infringement on Congress's control of commercial legislation. Once ratified, the supremacy of treaties under the Constitution would ensure that no special discrimination could be made against British shipping. What Madison had been attempting, with the support of South Carolina and Georgia Republicans, would be impossible. Opposition in the halls of Congress escalated, making it identifiable as perhaps the key moment in the formation of a Jeffersonian Republican political "party."

Reactions proliferated even more angrily through Lower South towns and farms. When the terms of the ratified treaty reached the region in July 1795, the Georgia and South Carolina public reacted strongly against what newspapers described as the "horrific" and "intimate political relation" that had been formed "with the old corrupt" government of Great Britain.[37] Within a month of publication, grand juries and town meetings in Charleston, Augusta, and throughout the countryside protested an agreement described by one Savannah assembly as "an infraction of the sovereignty, and independence of the United States, and derogatory to the honor, interest, and happiness" of American citizens.[38] Democratic-Republican societies rioted in the streets. Effigies of South Carolina's William Read and Georgia's James Gunn, the only senators south of Kentucky who voted for ratification, were hung alongside those of Jay, the alleged saboteur of American rights and honor.[39] Even political moderates like Lachlan McIntosh, John Rutledge, and Charles Pinckney publicly denounced the terms and spirit of the treaty in speeches and newspaper editorials.[40] A Federalist propaganda war waged by Smith and fellow representative Robert Goodloe Harper in late 1795 tempered Lower South opposition somewhat by demonstrating that the treaty had averted a potentially devastating conflict.[41] These moderating efforts, however, could not prevent the South Carolina legislature from demanding a constitutional amendment requiring House approval of treaties and declaring (by an astonishing margin of 70 to 9) that Jay's Treaty was "Highly Injurious to the General Interests" of the United States.[42]

In the Lower South, disappointment with Jay's Treaty reflected genuine concerns with both the treaty's symbolism and its specific terms. Complaints highlighted

Jay's unwillingness, as a representative of the federal government, to protect the interests of slaveholders. The treaty, one Augusta paper lamented, "is entirely silent on that important subject, the restoration of Negroes, and other property carried from this continent by the British troops," which had represented a substantial financial loss.[43] This omission was particularly alarming because it followed on the heels of northern representatives' willingness to discuss antislavery Quaker petitions and consider special taxes on slave importations. The treaty's failure to support the legal claims of slaveowners spawned charges by some Republicans that Federalists might not be trustworthy on sensitive matters involving slavery.

More broadly, however, opposition to Jay's Treaty reflected the region's frustrating indebtedness to British merchants, growing commitment to Virginia-led neomercantilism and widespread disgust over a document deemed incapable of freeing planters, farmers, and merchants from Britain's economic grip. The treaty allowed for the return of expelled Loyalists with full citizenship and forced the federal government to pay off individual debts to British citizens that had remained unsettled since 1783. Additionally, the terms concerning commerce in the West Indies had not, southern Republicans believed, been settled on terms sufficiently favorable to American commercial interests. Only the smallest of American vessels would be allowed to enter West Indian ports and even then only with restrictions. Furthermore, the treaty had not expressly distinguished between the origin of cotton imports, creating some ambiguity that the nascent Anglo-American cotton trade would be recognized. Perhaps most critical to the growing number of Madison and Jefferson supporters in the Lower South, the special privileges the agreement awarded Anglo-American trade restricted the nation's ability to use economic coercion to fight British commercial dominance.[44] For all of these reasons, Jay's Treaty led many South Carolinians and Georgians to question whether the federal government they had helped form would actually serve their perceived interests.[45]

An ever-complicated backcountry situation further alienated Georgians from the Washington administration. Centralization of foreign policy into an independent executive branch allowed Native Americans to protest directly to the president against state encroachment upon their lands. While Georgians had hoped that the Union would help them secure their vast backcountry lands against powerful Native American tribes, Washington and Secretary of War Henry Knox proved to be, at least relative to southern backcountry inhabitants, impartial brokers. Their approval of a 1790 treaty with Creek leader Alexander

McGillivray secured solemn "guarantees to the Creek Nations all lands within the limits of the United States to the westward and southward of the boundary described."[46] Much to the chagrin of Georgia's proexpansionist government—which had not been consulted—McGillivray had turned the federal government's treaty-making power against Georgia's self-declared rights of territorial sovereignty. Senate ratification of the treaty failed to solve the issue, as Georgian ruffians continued to settle on Creek lands. Only the calling out of federal and state troops in 1794 and the forced withdrawal of illegal settlements prevented bloodshed. Georgians' faith in the Washington administration remained severely damaged, making westward-looking Georgians more likely to support a growing opposition.

Though the decade of relative peace with southeastern tribes and relatively open trade with Britain provided an economic windfall for American cotton planters, many early growers, notably Pierce Butler, did not foresee this development and retained a heavily Anglophobic and antiadministration outlook. This was largely because U.S. textile mills, prior to 1794, absorbed almost all of the meager quantity of American cotton. The possibility of an Anglo-American cotton trade did not seem to have significantly factored into Jay's negotiations. The article restricting American participation in the West Indian carrying trade (Article 12) had not distinguished between the crop's places of origin, leading some planters to fear that U.S. fibers might be confiscated under the British navigation acts. In the treaty's final passage, however, at the insistence of southern delegates and with the approval of Treasury Secretary Hamilton, the Senate struck this article before ratifying it, and Britain tacitly accepted the change, at least as it regarded cotton. Nevertheless, cotton planters' embrace of Jeffersonian Republicanism, including its Anglophobic outlook and willingness to use economic coercion, had deep and lasting effects on the region's political culture. Pregnant with irony, even as local Republicans spilled much ink angrily denouncing Jay's Treaty, the peace it preserved provided the necessary backdrop for a vibrant Anglo-American cotton trade that returned the region to economic profitability.

## The Formation of a Transatlantic Cotton Interest

Despite their Anglophobia, few benefited more from the détente Jay's Treaty created than the cotton planters of the Lower South. Open direct trade enabled entrepreneurial Americans and Britons to rapidly create a highly profitable transatlantic partnership centered on cotton. This cash crop transformed the Lower

South so quickly that later commentators, informed by naturalism and evangelical Christianity, claimed that God or nature had foreordained the region for cotton production. Historians of the trade and the South have better appreciated secular forces and human agency. Yet even they often use the hindsight of King Cotton to paint the emergence of the Cotton South as either inherited or foreordained. In reality, slaves and entrepreneurial planters, many with deep personal connections to the British Empire, laid the groundwork for cotton's rise to prominence. By the mid-1790s they had acquired the technical expertise necessary to transform the region's forced labor and readily available land into major suppliers for cotton-hungry British manufacturers.

Despite production for household use in the 1770s, Lower South planters do not appear to have aggressively pursued cotton as a cash commodity immediately after the war. Indications of raw cotton sales or notices of cotton merchants infrequently appear in postwar newspaper advertisements, suggesting that planters initially returned their slaves to the cultivation of rice, indigo, and tobacco. Stagnant markets and bad harvests in the 1780s, however, led some to begin investing in commercial cotton. According to Whitemarsh Seabrook, an early chronicler of American cotton and one of its more successful growers, these efforts dated to 1786, when "cotton from various parts of the world was introduced into the Southern States and Louisiana" by risk-taking planters hoping to find a strand suitable for commercial manufacturing.[47]

Marginalized British Loyalists with continued access to the empire proved central to cotton's introduction into the Lower South. A Bahamian friend of future Georgia governor Josiah Tatnall forwarded him seeds that may have been part of the British Board of Trade's effort to encourage Caribbean cotton growth.[48] Tatnall distributed the seed for experimentation among his lowcountry friends, including, it seems, former Loyalist refugee Nichol Turnbull, who by 1789 had successfully planted the crop on his Sea Island lands. Another Loyalist, James Spaulding, established connections while in exile and eventually imported both seeds and a cotton gin invented by Bahama planter Joseph Eves.[49] So profitable did his family's cotton business become, that he managed to erase an estimated Revolutionary War debt of $100,000 and leave his son, Thomas, as one of the wealthiest planters in the region.[50] Frank Levett provides yet another example of the role that Loyalist refugees, black and white, played in early cotton cultivation. Forced to abandon his Georgia Sea Island lands at the end of the war, Levett, his family, and some one hundred slaves found haven in Jamaica and then the Bahamas. Finally allowed to reclaim his land in the mid-1780s, he and his slaves returned with valuable cultivation skills. Seeking to redeem his name and fortune, Levett claimed in 1789 to have successfully cultivated a commercially viable crop from the Pernambuco cotton seed.[51] Levett's slaves do not appear to have been alone in bringing Caribbean expertise in cotton production to U.S. shores. A December 1788 advertisement in the *Georgia Gazette* marketed a male slave from St. Croix known to be "well acquainted with the Culture of Cotton" and able to "construct a gin" and operate it, suggesting the important role that experienced Caribbean slaves played in achieving the goals of aspiring cotton planters.[52]

Impatient with official British efforts to create a supply of raw cotton within the empire, some Midland manufacturers took a more direct role in encouraging cotton growth. John Milne, an entrepreneur willing to transcend imperial boundaries who owned factories in Stockport, England, and in France, sent his son to Georgia, where he spent two years "stimulating and instructing the planters to the production of cotton." The younger Milne visited George Washington at Mount Vernon in 1789, leaving a favorable impression and prompting a letter from the president-elect to Thomas Jefferson predicting that cotton production in South Carolina and Georgia "must be of almost infinite consequence to America."[53] Despite these rosy forecasts, however, cotton remained an immature business through the early 1790s. In 1791 only about 2 million pounds of the crop were produced within the United States, a number that represented only 0.4 percent of total production worldwide.[54] While some planters willingly devoted land and labor to experiment with different seeds, they did so with considerable risk of failure. The fragile fibers of each species of cotton required particular planting techniques and growing conditions to flourish. Though profits could be high, so could the risk. Imported seeds were rarely ideal for the Lower South's particular soil and climate.

Consequently, southern planters and their slaves continued their own experimentation with seed hybridization and altered planting methods, staking their own place within the modern pursuit of progress. Planters were always, one Charleston factor noted in 1809, "changing the seed" to create an "improved-on Staple."[55] One of the earliest successes came along coastal Georgia and South Carolina in the Sea Islands, where Richard Leake successfully tested dozens of seeds of Asian, South American, and West Indian varieties before eventually settling on a hybridized black seed, believed to be of South American and West Indian origin. In 1793 Leake's experiments—along with the profits they brought him—led fellow planters, including Thomas Spaulding and Alexander McIver, to seek out his "Famous Cotton Seed."[56] In addition to being highly valued and well suited for the humid coastal climate, this long-staple variety proved advantageous because its seeds could be more easily removed, lessening the need for ginning. Experimentation also paid off in the more Anglophobic counties inland, where planters and farmers sought a variety of the cotton plant suitable for more arid upcountry regions. Though less valuable than the long-threaded Sea Island cotton, a green seed thought by some to have originated in Mexico proved capable of flourishing in the upland regions of Georgia, South Carolina, and later Alabama, Mississippi, and significant portions of Louisiana and Tennessee. Along with seed experimentation, growers tested different techniques, including adapting grain-cultivating methods of "drilling" the seeds into the ground and planting them in rows along ridges, all of which contributed to increasingly higher crop yields. By the 1820s the Lower South had become globally renowned for its advanced planting capabilities.[57]

Finding suitable seeds and growing techniques constituted only half the battle, especially for hopeful upland cotton growers struggling to remove the vexing seed from sticky fibers. Slaves skilled in the operating of cotton gins continued, with their masters' encouragement, to experiment. Northern ingenuity, along with continued southern tinkering, helped clear the final hurdle for extensive cotton production in the Lower South. Eli Whitney, a recent Yale graduate and aspiring schoolteacher, visited the Georgia plantation of Nathanael Greene's widow, Catherine, where he "invented" an improved gin using wire teeth well suited for removing the green seeds. By enabling slaves to gin large amounts of cotton more quickly, Whitney's prototype, further improved by local mechanics, provided the technological advancement American cotton growers, merchants, and manufacturers so desperately needed. The Rhode Island native likely perceived his invention as benefiting American manufacturers much more than British ones. Less than 10 percent of U.S. cotton appears to have been exported in 1793, and the continued tariffs on foreign raw cotton made finding a sufficient domestic supply imperative for struggling American textile producers.[58]

With proven techniques and seed types and prices that regularly exceeded 30 cents per pound, a growing number of planters began converting slaves and both coastal and inland plantations into the production of Sea Island or short-staple cotton. Familiar with its growth due to revolutionary experiments, American patriots joined Loyalist neighbors and embraced cotton as a path toward economic recovery. Peter Gaillard and Ralph Izard hoped to return to profitability and converted indebted indigo and rice plantations into cotton fields.[59] Whitney's success led Catherine Greene to expand cotton operations on her plantation,

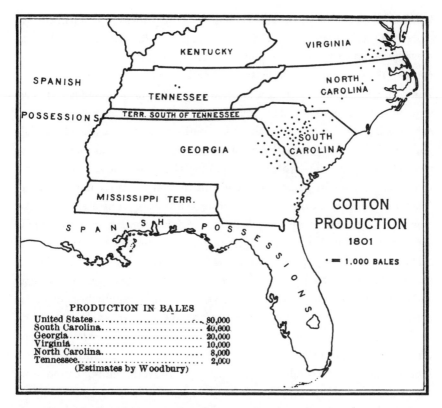

KENTUCKY

VIRGINIA

SPANISH

NORTH CAROLINA

TENNESSEE

POSSESSIONS

TERR. SOUTH OF TENNESSEE

GEORGIA

SOUTH CAROLINA

MISSISSIPPI TERR.

COTTON
PRODUCTION
1801

S P A N I S H

P O S S E S S I O N S

· ═ 1,000 BALES

PRODUCTION IN BALES
United States......................... 80,000
South Carolina........................ 40,000
Georgia.............................. 20,000
Virginia............................. 10,000
North Carolina....................... 8,000
Tennessee............................ 2,000
(Estimates by Woodbury)

U.S. cotton production in 1801, in the midst of its first great boom. From U.S. Department of Agriculture, *Atlas of Agriculture*, pt. 5: *The Crops of the United States*, Advance Sheets (December 15, 1915).

including leasing ginning capabilities to other planters, who ramped up their own growth. In 1793 Joseph Clay, a struggling Georgia merchant and rice planter, borrowed $32,000 to purchase an upland estate, cotton gin, and slaves. By 1800 Clay had repaid his loan and expanded his operation.[60] By 1799 a citizen of Chatham County, Georgia, praised cotton's profits within the Atlantic economy and encouraged fellow planters to shed their devotion to colonial crops like rice and indigo and embrace the "culture of cotton."[61]

Pierce Butler, signer of the Constitution and one of South Carolina's earliest Jeffersonians, emerged as an especially prominent beneficiary of cotton's glorious revolution. A closer look at his cotton business provides a brief window into the crop's economic potential and identifies the true foundation of cotton-created wealth. In 1774 Butler had purchased two tracts of land totaling 1,100 acres on the

Georgia Sea Island of St. Simons. Hampton, as the plantation was named, witnessed little activity during and immediately after the Revolution, a conflict that severely disrupted Butler's economic life. Occupying British soldiers evacuated many of the slaves kept at Butler's main South Carolina plantation.[62] After the war, poor financial circumstances forced him to sell some of his lands and to use remaining slaves as collateral to rebuild his lowcountry rice plantations. Despite experiencing some successes in the 1780s, Butler remained frustrated with lagging prices and in the 1790s began shifting more of his resources into cotton production. In 1794 he "ordered to Hampton about 115 [additional] workers," where he had them divided up into "3 or 4 distinct gangs" and required that they "plant *full 800* acres of Cotton."[63] The transition into heavy cultivation for market reaped Butler tremendous profits. With each field slave working an average of five acres of land and each acre yielding 150 pounds of cotton per year (selling for 36 cents per pound at 1795 prices), Butler's Hampton assets could have provided as much as $43,000 dollars per year. Given the fact that Butler soon owned three additional cotton plantations, it is little wonder that he rapidly became one of America's wealthiest men.[64] Butler's access to large numbers of slaves made his profits exceptional, but even planters with fewer hands could see handsome returns. Planters of Sea Island cotton on Edisto Island made an estimated $170 to $260 annually for each full-time field hand put to work tending cotton. Such profits provided incentive for Lower South planters to keep up or even expand their purchases of slaves, even as the price for prime field hands in Charleston's slave markets rose from $200 in 1790 to $400 by 1800.[65]

Increased ginning capabilities also enabled less well-off backcountry planters and farmers to realize tremendous profits from the production and sale of cotton. As early as 1796 the inland town of Camden petitioned the South Carolina legislature for a state inspection law that would enhance the quality and value of cotton and encourage its cultivation there. By 1805, travelers noted the degree to which "the culture of cotton has superseded that of tobacco," some even suggesting that it had "leveling effects" by providing poorer farmers better access to wealth.[66] Native farmers and small planters had to compete with a number of newcomers from northern states and abroad, lured by word of mouth or boosters, like Augusta, Georgia's, George Sibbald, who promised them backcountry lands "particularly adapted" to "the culture of cotton." Virginians and North Carolinians suffering from depressed tobacco prices found better economic prospects by moving to inland Georgia and eventually Alabama and Mississippi. Turn-of-the-century cotton boosters and speculators in upcountry lands could legitimately advertise the promise of profit to American and European audiences willing to embark on cotton production. Whether locals or immigrants, agrarian-minded men and women enthusiastically ushered upland cotton into inland regions, in most cases welcoming rather than resisting the market opportunities it offered them. Taken in the aggregate, these entrepreneurial efforts in different sections of Georgia and South Carolina upped total U.S. cotton production from 8 million pounds in 1795 to 48 million pounds by 1801. In five years the new crop had risen from relative obscurity to surpass rice, tobacco, and indigo as the chief agricultural commodity of the Lower South.[67]

U.S. planters were not the only ones to seize on cotton's rising fortunes. The Portuguese colony of Brazil provided some of the finest-quality thread, but ultimately poor infrastructure and social instability kept supply low. French settlers within Spanish-controlled Louisiana more successfully capitalized on high prices. By 1799 planter-merchant Julien Poydras noted that "the price of indigo does not interest me this year, I hardly made any and will get little from others." He and his neighbors were instead "all over head and ears in cotton" and by the end of that year Poydras had expanded his operations enough to need a "superb double mill to gin the cotton" to "profit by the present high prices." By August 1800, Poydras and a business partner could promise export of 122,000 bales of cotton from New Orleans, most of it destined for infant French textile operations.[68] These early efforts demonstrated the suitability of the Lower Mississippi Valley for cotton production, a fact that helped justify America's buying of Louisiana from the French in 1803. That Napoleon so quickly abandoned his vision for a renewed North American empire might also indicate that France's cotton manufacturers remained—in contrast to Britain's—peripheral in making imperial calculations. The Louisiana Purchase, coupled with cotton's march westward from the Atlantic, meant that by 1806 the United States had surpassed the West Indies by producing 80 million pounds of raw cotton.[69]

The ever-increasing volume of Lower South raw cotton rapidly exceeded American manufacturers' demand, further lessening Atlantic-centered planters' political support for domestic manufacturing. While prior to 1793, planters appear to have exported less than 10 percent of their crops, between 1796 and 1805 between 43 percent and 68 percent of each annual yield found its way to foreign markets. Though protected American markets and continental European consumers remained important, Britain fast emerged as the primary destination for southern-grown raw cotton. Nor could expanded production in the United States have been better timed for cotton-starved British manufacturers, whose search for imperial supplies had yielded disappointing results. After African experiments failed and East and West Indian output proved inadequate, British manufacturers turned to extra-imperial sources. To support their efforts and despite the risk of alienating still-powerful wool producers and West Indian planters, in 1792 British politicians took the unprecedented step of allowing foreign sources of raw cotton to enter the mother country duty-free on British ships and with only a 1-cent duty on foreign vessels.[70] This political measure underscored the growing importance of the kingdom's cotton industry and the necessity of looking beyond mercantilist systems for foreign raw supplies.

The Anglo-American cotton trade, then, resulted from a combination of local agency and external forces that encouraged cotton's expansion throughout the Lower South. U.S. duties against foreign raw cotton imports helped secure American producers' advantage within domestic markets. At the same time, Britain's decision to allow foreign cotton to enter duty-free critically aided Americans' ability to compete against traditional sources, the British West and East Indies. Had Jay's negotiations of 1794 failed and some form of warfare (actual or commercial) broken out between the United States and Great Britain, an entirely different history of the cotton trade might well have unfolded. In that event, Britain's pursuit of intra-imperial sources may have redoubled and more would have been done to foster cotton production in Brazil, Central America, Asia, Africa, or elsewhere. Nevertheless, at the critical moment when British cotton mills most needed new supplies, peace prevailed. Bags and bales of slave-cultivated cotton from the Lower South flowed through British ports to cotton mills, which transformed them into finished textiles traded around the globe. In the last five years of the eighteenth century, South Carolina and Georgia rose from obscurity to capture nearly 25 percent of the British market in raw cottons. Between 1806 and 1810, over half of Britain's raw cotton supply came from the United States, as planters accelerated the transformation of cultivatable land between the Atlantic coast and the Mississippi River Valley into a cotton empire.[71] As Britons expanded their dominance of the seas, landed U.S. slaveowners proved willing accomplices, providing a necessary commodity despite continued animosity toward their former imperial ruler.

Cotton's rapid ascendance relied upon and offered benefits to far more than simply Lower South planters and British manufacturers. In an era of inadequate commercial banking, this "economic miracle" could not have occurred without the help of native and British merchants who provided planters with capital, negotiated crop sales, and provided the vessels freighting cotton to British markets

Table 3    Sources of Raw Cotton Imported into Britain (as percentage of imports)

| | United States | Brazil | British West Indies | Mediter- ranean | East Indies, &c | Sundries |
|---|---|---|---|---|---|---|
| 1786–90 | 0.16 | 7.87 | 70.75 | 20.44 | 0.78 | 0.0 |
| 1796–1800 | 24.08 | 11.43 | 35.28 | 18.47 | 8.90 | 1.89 |
| 1806–10 | 53.14 | 16.07 | 16.23 | 1.28 | 12.78 | 0.49 |
| 1816–20 | 47.31 | 15.86 | 6.77 | 0.29 | 26.65 | 3.12 |
| 1826–30 | 74.50 | 10.45 | 2.23 | 2.76 | 9.57 | 0.49 |
| 1836–40 | 79.91 | 4.54 | 0.31 | 1.68 | 12.67 | 0.89 |
| 1846–50 | 81.13 | 3.76 | 0.12 | 2.04 | 12.76 | 0.19 |
| 1856–60 | 77.02 | 1.95 | 0.07 | 3.19 | 17.01 | 0.78 |

Source: Thomas Ellison, The Cotton Trade of Great Britain (1886; London: Frank Cass & Co., 1968), 86.

in Liverpool, Bristol, London, and Glasgow. Many of those merchants were locals. Daniel DeSaussure, Josiah Smith Jr., and Joseph Habersham emerged as important facilitators of the early cotton trade.[72] Especially as cultivation and commerce extended, Charleston, Savannah, and later Mobile and New Orleans commission merchants and factors formed important inland, interstate, and international partnerships. They often connected prospective buyers with sellers and handled the numerous incidental expenses of the trade such as warehouse storage, freight, and insurance. But British merchants remaining in Charleston and Savannah after the war offered more readily available credit, making them central to the trade's origins. Native merchants and shippers, meanwhile, suffered further losses when British navigation laws severely restricted their access to once-lucrative British West Indian markets. Unable to provide access to needed European goods or low-interest loans, South Carolina and Georgia merchants lost significant market shares to their British counterparts. A native merchant class remained critically important, but much of the region's export-import business went to British and increasingly to northern merchants, with locals increasingly serving as factors to outside firms. Others like Joseph Clay simply sold their mercantile interests and joined the profit-seekers investing in cotton and cheap western lands rather than turbulent Atlantic waters.[73]

A lack of detailed records and inventories makes it difficult to know the precise details of the Anglo-American cotton trade prior to 1820, but sources suggest that the earliest direct cotton shipments were consigned by planters to British merchants, who then shipped the crop directly to Glasgow or Liverpool. After successfully shedding their Loyalist leanings, the Tunno family—with connections in London and Charleston—emerged as important brokers for South Carolina and Georgia cotton. So, too, did James Gregorie, a British merchant who had been allowed to stay after the 1782 British occupation. As the trade continued to grow, new British profiteers also found their way to southeastern port cities throughout the early national and antebellum periods. Several members of the Molyneaux family of merchants settled in Savannah and built up a lucrative commercial business. Anthony and Edmund Molyneaux were retained as British consuls from 1826 through the 1860s, thus serving as political and economic cogs in a vast commercial empire.[74]

Though their importance would be overshadowed by the increasing number of northern-based commercial houses in the nineteenth century, both posted and itinerant Britons retained a vital role in the Lower South's economy, one largely ignored by historians.[75] In 1824, Godfrey Barnsley, the son of a cotton manufacturer and merchant, left Liverpool for Savannah, Georgia, where he brokered cotton for numerous European firms, including that of John Milne. Barnsley soon married into the wealthy Scarborough family and quickly used his dowry of land and slaves to supplement his mercantile interests with cotton plantations of his own.[76] Over the course of the early national and antebellum periods, such linkages provided cotton planters at least some access to Lancashire and London capitalists willing to invest significant amounts of money in the region. As late as 1820, foreign vessels still serviced between 25 and 30 percent of Savannah and Charleston's export trade, a significantly higher proportion than in other states.[77]

The burgeoning Anglo-American cotton trade did not, however, simply reconstitute older colonial trading patterns. The architecture of the federal Constitution and northerners' demands for cotton inaugurated some important changes in the national economy. Already by 1791 thirty-five of the forty-one shipowners who signed a "Petition of Masters of American Vessels in Charleston" were northerners, most of them from Massachusetts.[78] Heavy discrimination against foreign vessels participating in the internal coastal trade gave northern merchants a significant edge when it came to pricing. New England shipowners, and increasingly their Philadelphia and New York counterparts, transported bags or bales of cotton northward to American manufacturers duty-free. They then exported their surplus crops to British markets. In other instances, especially as the trade became more routine and financial networks more sophisticated, northern vessels carried a variety of domestic and foreign products from their home to southern ports. After loading with raw cotton, they would ride the trade winds back to Liverpool before returning to Philadelphia, Boston, or New York laden with

European goods. This emerging triangular trade benefited from the most favorable winds but also made economic sense, given South Carolina's and Georgia's limited capacities as consumers. These patterns stood in stark contrast to the direct trade between Charleston and English ports that dominated southern commerce during the colonial period.[79]

The takeoff of the Anglo-American cotton trade thus proved very profitable for northern merchants and factors, who flocked to southeastern ports in hopes of carving out profits from the newest cash crop. In 1804, for example, Boston merchant Nathan Appleton traveled south to Savannah and Charleston, working out partnerships with local factors and commission houses. Though initially cautious in his cotton purchases, Appleton soon saw the potential profits cotton offered and allowed his local agents more latitude in purchasing and transporting raw cotton to the North and Britain.[80] Other groups also benefited, including New England slavers who, at least until the slave trade's abolition in 1807, received high returns for continuing to supply coveted field hands. The creation of the Insurance Company of North America in Pennsylvania in 1794 and subsequent insurance companies in New York, Boston, New Haven, and Hartford allowed American exporters and importers to better protect their profits while providing handsome profits for shareholders. All of these developments enabled nineteenth-century northern interests to play a pivotal role in the transatlantic cotton trade.[81]

While some local merchants lamented the region's declining commercial sector, other residents accepted the economic rationale and trumpeted its patriotic implications. Though it might seem strange, one Georgian noted as early as 1801, "for a state . . . to permit other states, to import goods for her," such a reality was desirable because the wide assortment but limited quantity of goods needed in "inland stores" could not be provided by "any one port in Europe." More importantly, he added, facilitating commerce between the North and the South served patriotic ends, increasing the odds that southern merchants would purchase northern goods from northern merchants.[82] By tightening commercial relationships between the states of the new federal Union, the cotton trade embodied the cross-sectional coalition of interests envisioned by the founders, even as it deepened reliance on trade with Britain.[83]

By the beginning of the nineteenth century, a vast and intricate web of commerce already had created a regional, national, and global interest grounded in the raw cotton of the Lower South. Once partnerships were formed, choices for sale varied greatly in scale and scope. After a planter consigned part or all of an annual crop to a factor, usually in exchange for credit on supplies or notes, the factor was then responsible for finding a buyer. This could be done either through a northern or European broker, generally located in New York or Liverpool, or less commonly by dealing directly with any of a number of manufacturers who hired their own buyers to find the finest material at the source. The cotton's purchase would then be financed on extended credit, tying the trade into extensive financial networks involving major Anglo-American mercantile firms, especially those emerging in New York.[84] While the earliest financing of the trade appears to have relied on British financiers and commission houses, U.S. firms took over when war-related concerns created unease amongst European investors. By the 1820s, interlaced trade systems provided cotton growers and traders access to virtually any market in the world.[85]

Relinquishing more control to British and northern merchants did not necessarily mean that planters had auctioned off their economic freedom. High prices generated higher expectations and fierce competition for planters' crops. Agents for Manchester manufacturers McConnel & Kennedy repeatedly complained about their inability to purchase enough cotton, citing the "unwillingness of the owners to accept the present price" or the planters' "opinion that prices must be very high in Spring on account of the deficient supply."[86] Though planters could not defy the laws of supply or demand (delaying sale too long risked a glut the following year), initially those laws worked in their favor, as global demand generally exceeded supply.[87] Indeed, rising supply and demand led Lower South political economists to embrace the assumption, most prominently articulated by French savant Jean-Baptiste Say in 1803, that long-term gluts were impossible since increased output ultimately produced an enlarged market. Faith in this principle and continually escalating demand allayed fears about overproduction, despite increased growth in the Old Southwest.[88]

Factors in the cotton trade, regardless of geographic origins, thus remained highly dependent on good relationships with growers whose crops they marketed. Notwithstanding expected tensions during financial crises or isolated poor sales, the prospect of mutual gain made for good relations and even, at times, friendships. In the case of Wade Hampton and his Charleston factor, Christopher Fitzsimons, a business partnership became a familial one when Hampton's son married Fitzsimons's daughter.[89] Price listings and monthly or bimonthly cotton circulars enabled planters to make informed decisions: factors failing to serve their planters' best interests were quickly replaced by more responsive and effective competitors.[90] Though the producer-factor relationship ultimately depended on trust, planters commonly gave specific instructions to factors based on their own estimation of market forces. Small factors often provided the individual attention planters desired, but large merchant houses like Alexander Brown & Sons (with main branches in New York, Baltimore, and Liverpool) typically offered more diversified selling avenues and better financing options.[91] Mutual esteem or, if necessary, mutual interest ensured that, in the long run, factors did what they could to protect planters' interests within Atlantic markets.

## Cotton's "Revolution" and Its Limits

The cotton trade captured the economic imagination of Americans, though few understood what its long-term implications would be. Later nineteenth-century critics and twentieth-century historians have argued that cotton production simply perpetuated colonial economic patterns and the region's path toward dependence and economic backwardness.[92] One would be hard-pressed, however, to find such an analysis in the historical record of the 1790s. On the contrary, cotton cultivation seemed to offer unbounded promise to whites with a recent memory of wartime devastation and postwar depression. It allowed a return to prosperity for older but anxious elites and a new pathway for less well-off planters and farmers. Though directly or indirectly trade increasingly flowed to Britain after 1795, it did so on significantly better terms than the Lower South had recently experienced. The value of exports once again exceeded imports, returning Georgia and South Carolina to the favorable trade balances that they had enjoyed during the colonial period. High prices, Britain's and northern manufacturers' seemingly insatiable demand, and the eagerness with which foreign and domestic merchants marketed and financed the crop strongly countered the supposition that planters had succumbed to an unpatriotic dependence.

Increased reliance on northern merchants, vessels, and financiers, though viewed as a loss by Charleston merchants, seemed for others to be "a fortunate circumstance" because it harmonized sectional interests and promoted national pride.[93] Cotton's charm even seduced outside commentators. An 1802 contributor to Boston's *Columbian Centinel,* writing under the pseudonym "An American," spent an entire column "reviewing the immense benefits to be derived to our nation from the culture of cotton, in the great southern and southwestern division of the United States." In addition to generating profits and promoting manufacturing, the author noted, cotton's cultivation raised the value of the 60 million acres that Georgia had recently ceded to the federal government, the sale of which would help extinguish the national debt "with rapidity."[94] The increase in the number of cotton growers, a Philadelphia contributor noted, aided producers of grain and livestock, lumber and fish—in the aggregate, a much larger group—by lowering their own numbers and thus raising prices for their diminished output.[95] In short, America's great natural resources, especially cotton, should give all her citizens reason for great confidence: "It is clearly evident that no other nation in the world has so rich a prospect as ours."[96] For all of these reasons, few Americans would have disagreed with South Carolina governor John Drayton's 1800 declaration that cotton's positive effects represented a "matter of National Joy."[97] As such, the cotton revolution perpetuated a positive association with the American experiment even as it increasingly depended on trade with a political rival.

Other observers hoped that the cotton trade would overturn centuries-old mercantilist assumptions and usher in a new era of peace and freer global trade. As one American observer noted as early as 1802, the trade served "to promote mutual interest and harmony" between foreign governments.[98] "No state of things, between intelligent and well disposed nations is so happy," another argued, "as that which enables them to modify their business, so as to encrease [*sic*] to each other the fair benefits of their mutual intercourse." This, he concluded, was the "posture of affairs between this cotton raising country and the European manufacturing nations."[99] Trade, even trade between rivals, was mutually beneficial and should be celebrated.

These commentators harkened back to arguments favoring the Jay Treaty but also anticipated future cosmopolitan utopians who envisioned a day when global commerce would break down political animosity. Cotton, they argued, had provided some fleeting early victories. For much of the 1790s, British officials had allowed raw cotton, regardless of its origins, to enter duty-free, thus demonstrating some willingness to look beyond empire. So, too, had American cotton growers and carriers, who repeatedly rebuffed northern manufacturers' calls for higher protective duties on European textiles. Though born in an age of mercantilism, the Anglo-American cotton trade fostered a mutual dependence that provided early indications of the free trade movement that would eventually emerge in the 1820s.

The emergence of war in the Atlantic in 1803, however, quickly soured prospects for freer trade, causing great concern among those engaged in the transatlantic cotton trade. British officials quickly restored the tariff of 3 pence per pound on foreign cotton in an effort to mobilize their vast empire and finance yet another war with France. Such a measure encouraged the use of intra-imperial supplies while also raising much-needed revenue, but it provoked great frustration among British manufacturers, who, dependent as they were on American-grown cotton, feared the new duty's effects on their bottom lines. Their arguments, reprinted in numerous American newspapers, demonstrated cotton's growing centrality in the British economy and further affirmed American cotton planters' increasingly prominent place in the world economy. An 1803 *London Morning Chronicle* article reprinted in Charleston's *Carolina Gazette* declared that in 1782 the gross return of Britain's cotton manufacturers had not exceeded £2 million, but "from that period it had been in a regular progressive state of increase" and by 1802 "the return was twenty millions sterling, paying in wages thirteen millions, and furnishing employment to nearly a tenth part of the population of the island."[100]

British contemporaries expressed particular concern that the reintroduced duties on U.S. cotton might allow French manufacturers to buy the raw material cheaper and thus expand their rival industry. A Glasgow petition—featured prominently in American reports—noted that "54,000,000 pounds of cotton wool were imported into Great Britain in 1802; 30,000 tons of shipping, and 2,000 seamen were constantly employed in importing the wool, and exporting the manufactures into which it is here wrought; 80,000 persons are constantly employed in Great Britain in the cotton manufactures; their wages amount to 13,000,000 lbs. a year." With raw cotton so important to Britain's economy, attempting to draw revenue from it was "putting to hazard the source of national prosperity, and in truth exemplifying the old story of *killing the hen that lays golden eggs.*"[101] While highly protective tariffs on raw materials aided British wool and wheat producers and West Indian planters, they made little sense to Liverpool merchants and Manchester manufacturers.

Despite threats to American neutrality, cautiously optimistic observers hoped that southern raw cotton had become so important for Europe that it might insulate the United States from conflict. According to one, the greatness of America's natural resources, cotton foremost amongst them, meant that "under the guidance of a wise government and the smiles of a benign Providence, the people will have nothing to fear from the peace or the wars of Europe."[102] War might even lead Napoleon to foster France's own textile industry and provide America with a second major foreign market for its raw cotton. Though not fully realized until the mid-nineteenth century, this hope for an expanded continental market for American raw cotton periodically resurfaced among Republican-minded planters, most notably with Napoleon's proposal for a "Continental System" in 1806. But instead of a vibrant Franco-American cotton trade, the resumption of Anglo-French hostilities threatened to undermine American trade with both powers. Hopes of developing free trade in the Atlantic world had to be put on hold until more peaceful circumstances guided international discourse. As one South Carolinian had noted in 1797, the growing dissemination of the "theory of Adam Smith" might excite supporters but only "after the age of revolutions is over" (or at least the wars accompanying them) can one expect to see its "full force" exemplified through "the necessary laws of commerce between rival, though enlightened nations."[103] The violence, high duties, and commercial attacks that accompanied wars cast an ominous shadow over the future of free trade and of cotton.

The cotton trade's effect on international political economy remained in doubt, but not its reliance on enslaved black labor. The new staple crop restabilized slave-based lowcountry economies and intensified the entire Lower South's commitment to preserving an institution it believed necessary and even natural. It did so with little fanfare and to no one's surprise. Even before cotton had become significant, Lower South whites demonstrated a deep commitment to slavery. While northern states passed gradual emancipation laws and even Upper South slaveholders considered them or expressed personal doubts about slavery, South Carolinians and Georgians had far fewer qualms. While Virginians talked of the need to ban the international slave trade at the Philadelphia Convention, South Carolinians and Georgians would hear nothing of it. When Quakers forwarded modest antislavery petitions to the First Congress, Lower South politicians insisted that they be stricken from the record and that further discussion be suppressed. For early slave apologists like Governor John Drayton, cultivation of the rice fields and pine barrens necessitated slavery. Without it, "it is probable, in the scale of commerce and importance, she [South Carolina] would have been numbered among the least respectable states of the union."[104] Cotton, then, stepped into a region already wed to slavery and fast becoming versed in defending that institution from attacks rooted in revolutionary ideology and evangelical Christianity.

It emerged as a strong ally in the long-term development of proslavery defenses. In addition to preserving slavery in established areas, cotton's profitability ensured slavery would expand across the North American continent. Though some boosters advertised the crop as perfect for yeoman farmers, its westward march generally facilitated the spread of slavery. Without cotton, slavery would likely have still spread to the interior but certainly not as easily or quickly and never with as much impact. Rice and sugar—crops heavily reliant on slave labor—had yet to show profitability inland. The decline of tobacco prices increasingly weakened the institution of slavery in places where the "noxious weed" traditionally grew, leading many Virginia and North Carolina growers to sell off, or in rare instances free, surplus slaves. Cotton provided the incentive and the means for retaining its viability in the United States and expanding slaveholding within the Lower South.

New generations of whites enthusiastically joined slaveholding ranks. Far from being the victimized recipients of market forces and slavery, as some historians have portrayed, most backcountry farmers and planters eagerly embraced the crop and the labor system deemed necessary to grow cotton in large quantities.[105] Compared to rice or indigo, it required little initial capital, leading David Ramsay to conclude that the crop allowed "the poor" to become "of value" and "be elevated to this middle grade of society."[106] Certainly not all, or even most, backcountry families parlayed cotton into slaveownership or higher status, but enough did to keep the dream alive. Between 1790 and 1800, the slave population of the middle-country counties of Orangeburg, Cheraws, and Lower Camden increased 19 percent, 51 percent, and 139 percent, respectively. The slave population of upcountry counties farther west grew 65 percent over that same period and would increase by another 83 percent the following decade. The aggregate number of slaveholding families in the backcountry grew from 4,739 in 1790 to 10,237 in 1810, a majority of which owned between one and four slaves. By 1810 the total number of slaves in the South Carolina backcountry grew from 29,094 to 85,654, an increase of 194 percent.[107] Cotton's high prices provided enough capital for many yeoman farmers to invest in at least a couple of slaves to help tend the fields and realize greater wealth.

Much of this growth came from an increasingly vibrant domestic slave trade, but the continuing international trade also proved key in meeting cotton growers' demand. In 1803, backcountry representatives in the state assembly finally overcame the opposition of lowcountry planters and resumed slave imports, which petitioners claimed had been "a direct Bar to the Increase of the Wealth and population of the Upper and Middle Districts."[108] Atlantic slave traders, many of them northern-based, provided a critical supply, even after the federal government legally abolished the international trade beginning in 1808. The story of Lydia, a female slave brought into Carolina directly from Africa, demonstrates that cotton proved doubly important for keeping the international slave trade going. In 1805, she remembered, "a keg of liquor, and some yards of blue and red cotton cloth, were the principal" items with which she and twenty others from her tribe had been purchased.[109] With cotton cloth being preferred in tropical regions of Africa, it became a major currency for the late eighteenth-century and nineteenth-century slave trade. All told, before prohibition, the international slave trade imported an estimated 25,000 new slaves into South Carolina.[110]

The expansion of cotton and slavery in Georgia paralleled her sister state with more striking consequences. In 1790, Georgia produced 1,000 bales of cotton and the settled eastern half of the state had 29,264 slaves. By 1800, 20,000 bales were being produced by a slave population that had more than doubled to 59,232. In the next decade the slave population in the Sea Islands and coastal regions would grow to 91,154, while that in newly settled cotton lands in the West grew from 174 in 1800 to 14,064.[111] As in South Carolina, many of these slaves—an estimated 28,500—were foreign-born, since Georgia had kept its international slave trade open until fears spawned by Haitian violence led to its permanent closure in 1798.[112] After that, many of Georgia's new slaves came across the Savannah River from South Carolina or southward from the tobacco plantations of the Upper South. Charles Ball, a Maryland-born slave sold to the southern backcountry in 1805, described the primary engine driving more and more slaves, especially prime young hands, west:

> Cotton had not been higher for many years, and as a great many persons, especially young men, were moving off to the new purchase in Georgia, prime hands were in high demand, for the purpose of clearing the land in the new country—that the boys and girls, under twenty, would bring almost any price at present, in Columbia, for the purpose of picking the growing crop of cotton, which promised to be very heavy; and as most persons had planted more than their hands would be able to pick, young niggers, who would soon learn to pick cotton, were prime articles in the market.[113]

Indeed later historical scholarship demonstrates a rather close correlation between cotton prices and prices for slaves between the ages of eighteen and thirty until the 1850s.[114]

Many more slaves found that their forced migration toward cotton's fibrous fields did not end in the South Atlantic states. As early as the 1790s, but especially after the purchase of Louisiana in 1803 and the annexation of West Florida in 1810, cotton descended upon the fertile soil along the Mississippi River Valley, and slavery soon followed. While slavery, especially of Native Americans, had a long history along the Gulf of Mexico, the cotton boom that began in the 1790s brought planters and slaves eastward from Louisiana and westward from the Atlantic coastal states. The desire for profits, primarily derived from cotton, led local forces—allied with proslavery advocates elsewhere—to push for early territorial organization in 1798 so that a federal ban on slave importations could be lifted. Mississippi received approximately 9,000 foreign slaves, which along with Louisiana's 7,000 *legal* introductions ensured that the early cotton frontier remained a slave frontier as well. Even after prohibition began in 1808, historians have estimated, an additional 7,000 new slaves per decade entered the United States, most finding their ways to the cotton-producing areas of the Lower South. White cotton fields in the West would be tended by new generations of enslaved blacks.[115]

By keeping slavery exceedingly profitable and encouraging its expansion westward, cotton thwarted the two most practical measures for ending slavery: diffusion or recolonization. The most passive—and thus most popular—national vision for the extermination of slavery focused on faith in modern progress and realizable "laws of nature" that would see slavery (much like feudalism) die a natural death, as slavery would fail to make economic sense. Historians continue to debate whether this might have eventually been realized in the United States, as it was elsewhere. At the least, however, cotton's massive expansion across the Lower South postponed any such eventuality. Slaveholders with surplus slaves found it more profitable to sell them to traders "down river" than to allow them to purchase their own freedom or begin paying them wages. By driving slave prices up, cotton made colonization plans premised on compensation seem impractical.

The centralization of labor and capital on southwestern cotton plantations demonstrated slavery's continued viability, even economic vibrancy, in the face of revolutionary aspirations. Hence South Carolina governor John Drayton, in an early defense of the institution, could simultaneously assert that if slavery "be an evil, it will sooner, or later, effect its own cure" to only then conclude that in certain lands and climates it would never end because "nature, governed by unerring laws, which command the oak to be stronger than the willow, and the cypress to be taller than the shrub, has at the same time imposed on mankind certain restrictions, which can never be overcome."[116] Even Jefferson, a sometime proponent of diffusion and colonization, relinquished the possibility of slavery's early disappearance in the face of its growing strength. He confided to William Burwell in an 1805 letter that he had "long since given up the expectation of any early provision for the extinguishment of slavery among us."[117] Such was cotton's counterrevolution.

The cotton trade, however, did not just further regional defenses of slavery and defy national antislavery hopes. It also kept the fastest-growing segment of global trade dependent on enslaved Africans. Other than a few pockets of religiously motivated, antislavery groups and some revolutionary Frenchmen and Americans, few found this surprising or offensive. Since the Columbian encounter, slavery had been critical to Atlantic trade and empire building. As a transatlantic antislavery movement emerged and eventually had success, cotton planters repeatedly and accurately stressed their own enslaved laborers' continued centrality for global profits. By the 1830s proslavery apologists argued that not just the Lower South but the entire world required their slaves.[118] There were few more powerful proslavery arguments than that.

The cotton trade's rapid ascendance within the world economy furthered the miseries of hundreds of thousands, and eventually millions, of enslaved blacks forced to toil on Deep South fields. But for whites in that region and elsewhere, cotton had a very positive and immediate impact, returning elites to the prosperity they had experienced during the colonial period and allowing others to experience their first taste of commercial profits. The Lower South's ability to produce

WEEKS PICKING

"Hauling the Whole Week's Picking," *Nitta Yuma Pasties: Panels 1 and 2* (1840s). These watercolors depict the daily routines experienced by millions of slaves involved in the picking and transport of cotton. They were made by noted silhouette artist William Henry Brown and given to the William Henry Vick family, who owned a cotton plantation north of Vicksburg, Mississippi. Courtesy of the Historic New Orleans Collection, accession nos. 1975.93.1 and 1975.93.2.

copious amounts of raw cotton proved critical to the success of the British cotton industry and trade. The failure of imperial supplies made the Anglo-American trade an economic necessity for British manufacturers. Jay's Treaty made it a political possibility. Northern merchants, shipowners, and financiers who flocked to southern ports offering services and capital turned handsome profits preserving faith that the crop served national, as well as regional, interests. Individual choices combined with global developments to alter the world economy.

The growing economic power of the trade in raw and finished cotton ensured its entrance into the minds of policymakers on both sides of the Atlantic but toward what ends few could predict. The pragmatic commitments that the cotton trade fostered—including continued commitment to Atlantic trade and mutual dependence between political enemies—complicated national and empire-centered political economies. Some American planters, merchants, and politicians believed cotton provided not only wealth but also inducements to break down traditional animosities and usher in the revolutionary hope of wider commerce and free trade principles. Yet in Europe and America, these aspirations foundered on continued calculations of international trade as a zero-sum game. The resumption of war in 1803 even more seriously imperiled the cotton trade as the Atlantic became crowded with British and French fleets looking to undermine one another's business and attack each other's trade. Nationalism would be tested as policymakers struggled to define a federal policy capable of preserving patriotism and economic interest. Cotton growers would face difficult decisions over how to respond to belligerent acts by their essential trading partner, Great Britain.

# CHAPTER TWO

# Calculating the Cost of Union

Nationalism and Sectionalism in a Republican Era, 1796–1818

Even as the ligaments of an Anglo-American cotton trade were forming, geopolitical developments on both sides of the Atlantic threatened to rip them apart. The resumption of warfare between Britain and France in 1803 exposed the United States by placing it in a precarious position between its chief trading partner and its old ally. Again their neutral status initially enabled Mid-Atlantic and New England merchants to prosper by carrying West Indian produce back to Europe after a brief stopover in American ports. Just as in the 1790s, however, such profits coupled with wartime concerns eventually led European belligerents to turn on the United States. Impressments of American sailors and attacks on American cargo multiplied. Britain's naval supremacy, especially after the Royal Navy's destruction of the French fleet at the Battle of Trafalgar in 1805, enabled that nation to target American carriers and ensure that supplies were funneled to British rather than continental ports. Napoleon responded in kind, seizing any American ships he could to ensure that they did not aid his enemy's war effort. How would America respond to these overt challenges to its sovereignty and perceived rights? How would those Americans from cotton-growing regions react?

The challenges were familiar, but the party facing them had changed. In 1800, a diverse political coalition of the Federalist administration's opponents helped usher Thomas Jefferson into the presidency. Calling for a more decentralized government that would empower the states, provide equal protection for the nation's different interests, and thwart the supposed conspiracy of "Anglomen," Virginia-led Republicans took control of the executive and legislative branches. This loosely knit alliance, which included leading members of the emerging Cotton South, would be responsible for redressing Americans' grievances abroad. Like their Federalist predecessors, they sought neutrality, but a deep Anglophobia prevented them from signing a treaty which might have eased tensions. Instead they chose commercial and eventually military warfare, choices that dramatically but divergently affected the nation's various interests. By so doing they transformed discussions about retaliation into debates over the nature of the nation's political economy. Merchants, artisans, farmers, and planters, all claiming to stand with Jefferson, discussed their particular place within the nation and became hyper-aware of how real and hypothetical commercial policies affected their own interests. The arduous and ultimately unsuccessful attempt to find a peaceful solution that could both protect America's diverse interests and redress violations of American rights tested Republicans' vision of a decentralized economic union of equals.

Cotton growers found themselves in a particularly precarious position during this extended national debate, the results of which promised to affect dramatically their region's access to European markets. Like most Americans, they viewed French and especially British abuses against American sailors and ships as affronts to American sovereignty. Concern for the nation's international reputation and support for their merchant allies necessitated a response of one sort or another. Their own relatively peripheral geographic and political place within the Union and the Republican Party did not allow them to dictate policy, so most were inclined to defer to the Virginia-led party and the neomercantilist measures it had long embraced. The cotton trade's rising national and international importance, however, ensured that it would feature prominently in Republican efforts at commercial warfare. Yet, any response targeting Britain would seriously threaten, perhaps even paralyze, the still-young Anglo-American cotton trade deemed so central to the Lower South's economic growth. Navigating these various economic and political commitments forced groups in the Cotton South to perceive economic coercion and ultimately warfare against Great Britain as an affirmation of their patriotism and a sacrifice for the nation and Republicanism.

That many northern merchants neither desired nor appreciated southern-led measures allegedly undertaken for northerners' protection only increased inter-sectional frustrations. Eventually, the triumphal nationalism spawned by the war effort subsumed these deep tensions within the Jeffersonian Republican Party. Nevertheless, the process by which Americans had been led into a "Second War of Independence" revealed much about cotton's place within the nation and the world and would cast a long shadow on subsequent debates.

## The Cotton South and a Republican Coalition of "Equals"

By the late 1790s frustration over Federalist policies had led disparate and desper-ate groups to join forces to change the direction and policies of the federal gov-ernment. Critics of the administration believed the banking and commercial policies supported by Washington, Hamilton, and Adams encouraged corrupt-ing "artificial" interests, destructive consolidationist tendencies, and unnatural, even unpatriotic, subservience to Britain. According to these critics, the National Bank, with its unique mixture of wealthy private investors and public funds, tainted the party with elitism and favoritism on behalf of an eastern "paper aris-tocracy." Opponents of Jay's Treaty and friends of France, especially artisans and merchants not trading with Britain, lamented the continued commercial depen-dence on their former colonial master. Planters and farmers eyeing western lands were frustrated by Federalists, who slowed movement westward by restricting public land sales and recognizing at least some Native American land claims. Persons of all backgrounds lamented the low points of Federalist totalitarianism: the Alien and Sedition Acts, which targeted opposition and attempted to stymie debate. In place of all these abhorrent policies, Republicans promised a better, if only vaguely defined, policy of commercial empowerment and impartiality.

Geographically, the strongest and most consistent opposition came from southern states, where outrage against Jay's Treaty and Indian policy had been loudest. To be sure, pockets of Federalism remained, especially in banking and merchant committees of eastern Virginia and North Carolina. The rice grandees of South Carolina's lowcountry remained the Federalists' last stronghold in the region, three times offering Charles C. Pinckney as a presidential nominee. By 1800, however, the Lower South had turned heavily Jeffersonian. Tensions be-tween Georgia and the Washington administration over Indian treaties and the Yazoo land disputes had almost single-handedly driven that state into the opposi-tion. In South Carolina, Pierce Butler provided critical Republican leadership in the 1790s. Arguing that Hamilton's banking policies were of "no benefit to the landed interest" and that Federalist plans showed preferential treatment to merchants—especially British merchants—over agrarians, Butler helped attract a broad statewide coalition. Aiding him were backcountry planters, including transplanted-Virginian-turned-cotton-magnate Wade Hampton, who was frustrated with lowcountry Federalist control of state politics. Smaller planters and backcountry farmers, however, comprised the Republican rank and file and flocked to Jefferson, agreeing with one "Back-Countryman" that Jefferson was "the uniform, undeviating friend of the rights and liberties of his fellow citizen." By 1800 the state's electors would solidly vote for Jefferson, despite Pinckney's presence on the ticket.[1]

Notwithstanding their growing dependence on Britain, cotton producers formed a geographically and numerically expanding part of this Republican coalition. Though not all cotton planters were Republicans, most were, and the crop's rapid westward expansion continued to swell Jeffersonian ranks. Seeking their share of cotton's wealth, upcountry farmers in South Carolina and Georgia sought unhindered access to western lands at cheap prices. The proexpansionist policies of the Jeffersonian Republican Party could help them achieve their goals. Particularly in Georgia, desire for the opening of new lands to cotton cultivation fueled a mad dash westward that neither Federalist titleholders nor American Indian settlements could impede. Conflict over the Yazoo lands and the Washington and Adams administrations' attempts to provide some measure of legal protection for the Creeks and Cherokees mortally wounded Federalist politicians' popularity in that state. Even in South Carolina, despite the endurance of lowcountry Federalists, the desire for easier access to cheap western lands and policies favorable to borrowers made Republicans seem a natural ally. The emergence of a short-staple crop necessitated opening new lands and thus channeled most new producers, particularly in the backcountry and newly opened Southwest, into the emerging Republican Party.[2]

Republicans also seemed to offer the platform best suited to protect the Lower South's commitment to slavery. While slavery or opposition to it never played a central role in either party's political calculations, national politicians who raised their voices against slavery, such as Thomas Pickering and John Jay, generally held Federalist loyalties. The Jay Treaty had made Federalists' support of slaveholders' rights suspect, despite the efforts of William Loughton Smith and others. More generally, northern Federalists tended to favor policies that, though not abolitionist, were less accepting of slavery within the United States than the general

Republican Party line. Behind-the-scenes maneuvering by southern leaders like Madison in the early 1790s temporarily frustrated efforts to bring antislavery petitions before Congress and ensured that slavery would be legal in the Southwest Territories.[3]

Already by the late 1790s, the legacy and policies of Jeffersonians were finding favor in other parts of the country, too. Western farmers, taking note of Washington and Hamilton's crackdown on backcountry distillers in the Whiskey Rebellion, found political legitimization by joining Republican ranks. Jeffersonians seemed to be more sympathetic to debtors and, though their leaders were as wealthy as Federalists, less aristocratic in tone. But not just agrarians were frustrated with Federalist policies or attracted to Republican ones. Jefferson and Madison's calls for commercial retaliation in the 1790s attracted northeastern and Mid-Atlantic merchants looking for non-British markets overseas as well as artisans and mechanics in urban areas. Federalists had proven to be only passive supporters of manufacturing. By the mid-1790s, many manufacturers outside the shipping industry, such as Tench Coxe, found the neomercantilist restrictions proposed by Jefferson and Madison more attractive than a Hamiltonian plan premised on encouraging the importation of British goods. These would-be manufacturers first conceived of an alternative to the Atlantic-centered vision based on protection for domestic craft production in symbiosis with southern cotton cultivation. A number of urban craftsmen, especially in New York and Philadelphia, rallied to support an alternative to Federalist policies they perceived to be Anglophile in spirit and harmful in effect.[4]

Jeffersonians' affinity for commercial retaliation also made it a political home for a growing number of mercantile groups. Hamilton's policies had been boldly commerce-friendly, but his foreign policy remained strongly pro-British. Unlike his opponents in the cabinet and Congress, he and his followers had little patience for commercial discrimination meant to encourage shipping to the French and Spanish West Indies or continental Europe. As a result, a large number of wealthy merchants in port cities—such as the Crowninshields of Salem, James Nicholson of New York, Stephen Girard and John Swanwick of Philadelphia, and the Smiths of Baltimore—found the commercial and foreign policy agenda of the Republican opposition more attractive. The continued drawbacks and discriminatory tonnage duties on foreign—especially British—ships that Madison and Jefferson advocated would aid American shipping interests, especially those looking to capitalize on the reexport carrying trade between the West Indies and continental Europe.[5]

People from diverse regional and occupational backgrounds—northern artisans, merchants, tobacco and cotton planters, and western wheat farmers—coalesced into a politically powerful and generally united political opposition. They did so believing that Jefferson and his supporters could better protect their interests within Atlantic economies and preserve their understanding of the revolutionary legacy and the Constitution. Federalists had governed from on high by centralizing power into the hands of a few; Republicans, supporters claimed, would govern impartially and with consent. The Jeffersonian promise to free the nation from Federalist machinations and British dependence through an expansive commercial program drew different economic interests into a shared political agenda. Briefly stated, American agricultural goods from the Mid-Atlantic and South, including cotton, would be carried by commercial and shipping interests of the Northeast to foreign markets, strengthening all regions' positions in the Atlantic economy. Northern shippers would be able to gain access to colonial carrying trades. Small-scale domestic manufacturing would provide essential goods, but comparative advantage would ensure the importation of European finished goods and complete the cycle of international trade. The Jeffersonian plan would unite the nation's different parts behind a supposedly more patriotic, natural, and balanced political economy that offered mutually beneficial and less pro-British relationships within Atlantic economies.[6]

The vision was ambiguous, but in ambiguity lay political strength. The Jeffersonian concept of economic federation had broad appeal and seemed to provide something for everyone. The coalition of merchants, artisans, and planter-farmers, all desiring liberation from the perceived inequality of Hamiltonian policies, carried Jeffersonianism into the northern states in 1796 and into the presidency in 1800. Jefferson's first administration stressed Republican support for the nation's "four pillars of prosperity": agriculture, manufacturing, commerce, and navigation.[7] The new president recruited a regionally and occupationally diverse administration, headed by Secretary of State James Madison and Secretary of the Treasury Albert Gallatin, both staunch allies of commercial interests.[8] Fiscal policy prevented the development of a strong navy and in a fit of frustration Jefferson flirted with the idea of tying American commerce to Britain's fleet, but Madison, Gallatin, and other cabinet members of various backgrounds kept the administration focused on protecting the cross-regional and cross-sectoral coalition around which their government had grown.[9] Republicans in Congress further assisted American shipping by charging foreign vessels entering American ports with a "lighthouse" duty of 50 cents per ton.[10] Continued support for commerce as agriculture's "handmaiden" ensured that American shipping attained supremacy in interstate trade and the exportation of American produce. The Republican vision of economic federation was thus affirmed, inspiring hope that the tools of political economy could promote interregional harmony, preserve decentralized national government, and free America from dependence on Britain.[11]

This harmony would be tested by the reemergence of slavery into national politics in the wake of Louisiana's entrance into the Union and northern congressmen's effort to pass a $10 tax on imported slaves. Voting on the issues was not purely sectional or partisan, but such considerations factored heavily in the debates. Connecticut Federalist James Hillhouse pushed for banning entirely the importation of slaves into Louisiana from foreign or domestic sources. Local sugar and cotton planters insisted that any prohibition would mean that "cultivation must cease, the improvements of a century be destroyed." Despite the efforts of southern Republicans, led by Georgians and South Carolinians, both houses prohibited the foreign or interstate slave trade into the Orleans Territory, but appeals to Jeffersonian ideas of fairness preserved migrating slaveowners' right to take their slaves into the territory. Jeffersonians further muted the question by rapidly elevating the region to the second stage of territorial governance, allowing locals to reopen the interstate trade.[12]

A similar commitment to Jeffersonian "equality" helped Cotton South politicians undermine efforts to slow the international slave trade after South Carolina reopened the trade in 1803. South Carolina's action met with widespread disapproval, leading many state legislatures, including those of North Carolina, Tennessee, and Maryland, to request a constitutional amendment to shut down the importation immediately. Always the conciliators, Virginia Republican leaders worked feverishly to prevent a potentially explosive debate that would alienate their Lower South allies. Instead, national opponents of the slave trade countered South Carolina's bold action indirectly through a House proposal to levy a $10 tax on every slave imported. Supporters of the tax understood precisely the connection between cotton, slave prices, and continued imports, one noting that because each "slave on a cotton plantation would . . . clear for his master a net sum of two hundred dollars a year . . . No important article . . . would bear an impost so well." But Pennsylvania Republican Andrew Gregg, an opponent of the bill, astutely noted that the very high prices of cotton and slaves (his sources suggested $400 per slave) meant that planters "will think little of ten dollars" and thus "the tax cannot effect the object contemplated" of reducing the international traffic in slaves.[13]

In the end, South Carolinian and Georgian delegates of both parties success-fully prevented the broadly popular bill from passing, by arguing that the tax unfairly targeted a particular agricultural interest. According to Representative Thomas Lowndes, the tax "will fall exclusively upon the agriculture" of South Carolina and thus would reflect the "height of injustice." Regardless of whether the bill intended to restrict the trade or garner additional revenue, his colleague Benjamin Huger argued, "the fair principle of taxation is that every part of the Union should contribute equally."[14] Renewed efforts by antislavery forces in De-cember 1805 suggest that a majority approved of the $10 tax, but continued post-ponement of the tax bill reflected the general softness of that commitment and the "triumph" of Jeffersonian commitment to "equality" for whites. Though cit-ing their personal moral opposition to the slave trade, Cotton South representa-tives appealed to its necessity. Complaints about special discrimination's unequal effects helped cobble together enough support to permanently table the bill. The Republican coalition of equals muted the thorny issue of the growth and expan-sion of slavery, thus allowing newly arrived slaves to continue flowing onto ever-expanding cotton plantations.[15]

As Jefferson's first term came to a close, most supporters had reason to cele-brate. Gallatin had begun an aggressive and largely successful debt reduction program, even as a Republican-led Congress repealed excise taxes much hated by American farmers. To aid this fiscal effort, Jefferson slashed government expen-ditures, including those funding the army and navy. The resumption of war be-tween Britain and France in 1803 threatened to undermine commerce, but war-time conditions also created an unparalleled economic boom aiding both American producers and merchants. American exports jumped from $56 million in 1802 to $95 million in 1805 and broke the $100 million mark for the first time a year later. Cotton prices dropped somewhat, but the greatly increased quantity generated unprecedented wealth and prosperity. Tobacco did not fare as well, continuing its steady decline, but planters continued to shift into the production of wheat and corn, crops in high demand in war-torn Europe.[16] In addition, these crops increasingly reached new, non-British markets on the continent and in the West Indies. Shipping activities, benefiting from neutrality during international war, remained at high levels. Total tonnage in foreign trade broke 1 million in 1805 and even more remarkably, over 90 percent of that tonnage traveled on U.S. or mostly U.S.-owned ships, up from 59 percent in 1790.[17] Wartime conditions again enabled American merchants and shipowners to prosper, carrying West Indian products back to Europe with high rates of return. Wages for day farm laborers also rose from 57 cents per day to 80 cents per day between 1801 and 1804.[18] The acquisition of Louisiana in 1803, constitutional qualms aside, was widely popular and introduced a major new port into the regional and national economy.

In reality these positive economic developments stemmed as much from fortuitous circumstances in the Atlantic as from the wisdom of Republican policy. Politicians and voters, however, did not make that distinction. Republicans traded on the relative good times to secure electoral victories, decisively winning the presidential and congressional elections in 1804. Furthermore, Jefferson cemented Republican advances northward by winning every state but the Federalist bulwarks of Connecticut and Delaware. In his second inaugural address, he proclaimed his administration's successes at raising revenues, reducing the debt, and expanding trade and prosperity. He also congratulated the nation on "the union of sentiment now manifested so generally as auguring harmony and happiness to our future course."[19]

Within a year, however, "harmony and happiness" had given way to anxiety and frustration; Jefferson's second term would challenge the "union of sentiment" in ways few could have imagined. Unlike later approaches to national economy, the early Republican approach had remained premised on the integration of different interests for reciprocal benefit within the Atlantic trading system. It therefore remained dependent on favorable conditions within a trading system in which the young nation continued to have little diplomatic clout. Highlighting that fact, Britain withdrew its tacit acceptance of the reexport trade and in a May 16, 1805, Order in Council announced a strict blockade of continental Europe. Subsequent British naval action against American vessels, including the renewed impressments of American sailors, suggested that potentially ruinous retaliation lay ahead. With European goodwill rescinded and American prosperity threatened, the coalition of interests and Republicanism's experiment with economic federalism would be challenged. These developments were compounded by France's Milan and Berlin Decrees, which declared open hostility against American direct trade to Britain.

As these events unfolded, Republicans, and especially cotton planters, realized that despite sharing common goals and rhetoric, different groups within their partnership did not have converging interests. These differences rose to the surface as national politicians debated how best to respond to British and French belligerence. Merchants and planters both desired open access to overseas markets, but planters could use non-American merchants if American vessels were shut out. U.S. merchants demanded protection from foreign belligerence, but some forms of retaliation acceptable to agrarians, like nonimportation or embargo, threatened the very livelihood of commercial classes. Artisans and domestic producers generally benefited from restrictions on imports that farmers and planters could get more cheaply from abroad. Nor were the interests of agricultural groups always aligned. Different markets and competitors could shape different foreign policy objectives. Those producing food products like wheat, flour, and corn, for example, had a large domestic market and potential consumers throughout Europe, the Caribbean, and even parts of South America. This likely contributed to increased flexibility on foreign policy issues for Mid-Atlantic farmers and some Upper South growers. Producers of other southern staples, including tobacco and cotton, remained heavily dependent on British mills and markets and thus faced more circumscribed options.[20] Along with global geopolitical realities, each of these economic commitments framed the discussions and debates facing the nation from 1806 to 1815. Preserving the Republican vision of equal opportunity and the party itself would require compromise and sacrifice.

How far would Republicans go to protect the nation's carrying trade and especially those carriers involved in the indirect reexport trade of West Indian raw materials to European ports? For many mercantile Republicans, especially in Philadelphia and New York, the reexport trade had become an essential part of a newly diversified and more independent national economy. Neutrality had allowed for a thriving indirect commerce, as voyages between the Caribbean and Europe "broken" by stopovers in U.S. ports were partly legitimated by British courts in the 1800 *Polly* decision. Contrary to Jefferson's grim predictions and despite a severe slump when England and France returned to war in 1803, the carrying trade approached previous highs by the following year.[21] Southern agrarians feared that these profits resulted from an "unnatural" state of global war and noted that unlike the direct trade in American goods, this trade benefited only mercantile interests located almost exclusively in the port cities of Boston, Baltimore, New York, and Philadelphia. Consequently, the indirect trade's position within the Republican formula for economic balance remained uncertain at best.

Despite sharing the reservations of agrarians, a deeply ambivalent Jefferson—encouraged by Gallatin—continued to support the reexport trade during his first administration, justifying its importance for revenue-building, for de-Federalizing the Northeast, and as a symbol of national economic strength.[22] Accepting their mercantile political allies' belief that the reexport carrying trade warranted government support, southern administration and congressional Republicans acquiesced and even encouraged America's reexport carrying trade by continuing the drawback system. Through this process, begun in 1794, duties on raw materials imported into the United States were paid back upon export.[23] The policy presented a cheap and seemingly painless way of encouraging commercial development without harming other interests. It generated considerable profits for American merchants and shippers, including a number of Republican-minded ones. Broken vessels, however, had been expressly rejected in the 1804 *Essex* decision, and consequently the carrying trade's success now brought American navigation into direct conflict with the mighty British Empire to which cotton planters remained commercially tied. The newfound wealth from the cotton trade would be leveraged to support American mercantile interests.

## "The Honor of Bearing It Best": Cotton, Commercial Warfare, and War

When challenged by Great Britain in early 1806, the Jefferson Administration chose to respond with commercial restrictions rather than military force. As a result, foreign policy debates quickly transformed into tests of the limits of Jeffersonian economic federation, political unity, and national sentiment. The insidious threat posed by Britain helped preserve party unity by fostering compromise, but open discussion about which coercive tools best suited the United States' political economy heightened sectional and sectoral tensions. As each attempt at economic coercion failed and the nation's economic outlook appeared bleaker, southern Republican cotton producers updated their calculations of the cost of commercial warfare versus that of submission. Eventually they decided that the price of both exceeded that of war. Persistent opposition from Virginia Old Republicans, led by John Randolph, and Federalists, who urged free trade, served as a constant reminder of the sacrifices cotton producers made. By defending the ultimate form of equal suffering—embargo—against such opposition, Republicans in Congress forged a better understanding of the Cotton South's position within the nation and the Atlantic.

Lower South Republicans joined the rest of the nation in criticizing British belligerence. But debates over the appropriate response reveal that they calculated the precise economic effects that supporting the carrying trade would have. In March 1806 advocates of the reexport trade drew heavily on American revolutionary zeal to portray American reexporters as true "patriots" and the reexport trade as an integral part of the national political economy—"a necessary link in the chain of our society."[24] Citing Republican precedents, northern merchants argued that British attempts to "make a sweep of our whole trade" and suppress "the rapid and lofty soaring of the American eagle" must be met with a policy of complete nonimportation.[25] But mercantilist definitions of national interest ignored "certain distinctions which exist in the country," argued Georgia's Peter Early: "First of classes, agricultural and commercial, and secondly, distinctions arising from geographical position."[26] Unlike the direct trade, which carried agricultural goods to foreign markets, the "mushrooming" indirect trade, though lucrative, benefited only a narrow and geographically isolated interest. Why would agriculturists, Early asked, "consent to surrender the certainty of good markets and high prices for our produce, and brave the danger of a total stagnation, for the purpose of embarking in a hazardous contest with Great Britain for the carrying trade?" To do so would be to "jeopardize the whole agricultural interest of the nation for the sake of that which in our opinion produces no benefit to that interest."[27]

Agriculture in general would lose. Southern planters—particularly those growing cotton and tobacco—believed that they would bear the brunt of a policy advocated by (and for) their northern Republican colleagues. A lack of carriers or possible retaliatory measures against American shipping would reduce access to British markets, a frightening prospect for cotton suppliers. Early and others quite literally calculated the price of commercial warfare, citing recently released Treasury reports showing that a majority of domestic exports to Britain and her colonies were grown in the South.[28] Indeed, cotton alone made up over 50 percent of the value of all U.S. exports sent directly to the British Isles. In addition to the threat posed to that trade, the region's access to needed British manufactures—including cheap clothing for slaves—would be stymied. The southern economy would experience disproportionately negative effects from nonimportation by having to pay higher prices for a smaller supply of manufactured goods. Additionally, others charged, nonimportation would severely hinder the Republican goal of debt reduction due to the loss in direct trade.[29] To close markets with Britain would be "to surrender the principles of self-preservation" and "strip ourselves of the leading stimulus to human action."[30] Opponents of complete nonimportation insisted that neither the nation's "spirit" nor its account books made extremely restrictive measures desirable.[31]

The standoff over nonimportation marked the most severe test of Republican political economy to date. Open and often heated debate drew attention to distinctive sectional and sectoral interests. In the end both Republican merchants and producers compromised, rallying behind the weakened administration's proposal to ban only nonessential British imports, including much clothing.[32] As a result, the agreement intended to use America's role as a consumer, particularly of British textiles, as a weapon to win redress. With the exception of a few recalcitrant Randolphites, who likened the carrying trade to a "fungus of war,"[33] southerners joined the 87-35 House vote to approve partial nonimportation. This policy provided at least token resistance to British aggression. Just as importantly, it preserved party unity, leading Jefferson to tell Monroe that he had "never seen a H[ouse] of Representatives more solidly united in doing what they believe to be the best for the public interest."[34] Despite some reservations, Republicans had invoked nationalism on behalf of the reexport carrying trade, defining it as a sector worth affording protection. Southern and northern Republicans overwhelmingly supported the compromise, thus confirming their loyalty to the nation and party. In the end, at Jefferson's request, Congress postponed enactment of the bill in hopes that diplomatic negotiations would bring an amicable solution to the numerous disputes between the two nations.

It was in this context of compromise and fast-changing developments in Europe that Congress, with relatively little fanfare, abolished the foreign slave trade at the earliest moment the Constitution allowed. Whereas earlier efforts, including the $10 tax, had failed, Jefferson's December 1806 annual message pressured Congress to revisit the issue. Overwhelming consensus emerged over the termination of slave importations, with Georgia's Peter Early heading the House committee to draft the bill. Despite agreement on the major point, serious debate ensued in both houses over the breadth of the prohibition, the fate of both violators and individuals imported illegally, and the Senate bill's provision to outlaw the domestic coastal trade on ships under forty tons. This last policy drew the ire of most southerners, including Early and Randolph, who hinted at the future prospects of "disunion" and argued that the measure infringed on southerners' "right to private property," set a dangerous precedent, and undermined the development of the southwestern states. "After a long debate," most of it unrecorded, political brinksmanship and northern Republican disunity ultimately ensured that the domestic trade remained open by a House vote of 63 to 49 and Senate concurrence. In a further concession to the South, representatives from the Lower South ensured that "contraband" slaves, instead of being emancipated or returned to Africa, would be given to state governments, who could then sell them.[35] On March 2, 1807, Jefferson signed the bill into law, guaranteeing that no new slaves would be *legally* imported into the country after January 1, 1808. Even as it heightened sectionalist anxiety, concern over the broader international situation likely contributed to both sides' willingness to compromise and may have helped protect southern slaveholders' interests. In the end, the bill received little notice in the newspapers, as editors kept their eyes and columns firmly focused on events in Europe and breaking news of Aaron Burr's western "conspiracy."[36]

Shortly after signing the bill ending the nation's official participation in the international slave trade, Jefferson received the fruits of extended diplomatic negotiations between Britain and the United States. Throughout the fall of 1806, James Monroe and Jefferson's special envoy, Maryland Federalist William Pinkney, struggled to hash out an agreement with London officials that would end attacks on American ships and sailors while preserving America's access to British and non-British ports. The resulting treaty provided Americans a narrower definition of contraband and assured that merchants would be fairly compensated for any seizures, but it failed to stop impressments and, like the Jay Treaty, precluded Americans from employing any form of commercial coercion. Upon receipt of the treaty terms, Jefferson, his cabinet, and a group of merchant advisors found the treaty unacceptable. Wishing to avoid public debate over the matter, the president refused to send the treaty to the Senate for discussion or even to have its terms publicly disclosed.[37] British attacks on shipping increasingly targeted the direct trade of American goods to France, and tensions escalated after a British frigate fired upon the USS *Chesapeake* in June 1807. In November new Orders in Council, responding to Napoleon's Continental System, required American vessels to stop in British docks before traveling to French-held ports. Most egregiously to cotton planters, it required a specific license for transit in cotton and added a prohibitively high reexport tax of 9 pence per pound on foreign raw cotton, in essence giving Britain a de facto monopoly on that critical crop. With an increasingly bleak forecast for American commerce and no prospects of diplomatic redress, southern and northern Republicans rallied behind the administration's decision to pursue radical legislation. With quick and overwhelming support, in December 1807 Republicans implemented a complete embargo on the exportation of all American goods.[38]

Though initially conceived as a measure of protection and possible preparation for war, Jefferson's embargo quickly became a tool of economic coercion.[39] By removing American raw materials and foodstuffs from warring European consumers, the American government would force warring nations back to the bargaining table. The producer mentality that it reflected was rooted in specific calculations of market forces. Higher prices resulting from shortages in Europe and the West Indies would force the repeal of anti-American policies. In this regard, the coercive understanding of the embargo reflected a way of thinking typical of Republican political economy, which naïvely assumed that the nation's importance as an agricultural supplier could forcibly open European markets for American commerce. Because it was safe to assume that it would be unprofitable to carry goods to the United States and return empty-handed, supporters of the embargo also hoped to punish Britain by depriving it of a chief consumer market.[40] This, too, was consistent with a revolutionary tradition of commercial retaliation and Republicans' inflated estimation of European dependence on American buyers.

Cotton played a doubly central role in this risky game of commercial chess. British manufacturers, Jeffersonians supposed, could not survive the exorbitant prices resulting from the withdrawal of American raw cotton. Republican papers around the country reported the likely ill effects that the embargo would have on Britain's economy. Noting the number of people involved in the textile industry (a half million by many estimates) and British reliance on southern cotton for over half her supply, Republican politicians and editors believed it would be as effective as war and force an "honorable accommodation with that nation."[41] Furthermore, British industry was already impaired in selling finished textiles to continental Europeans, and the loss of American consumers, at the time their single largest overseas market, would break it. Mills would close; workers would lose their jobs; merchants would go broke. "England suffered" greatly, one Jeffersonian noted: "More than one-half of the sixty-one million pounds of cotton consumed in her [Britain's] mills were of American production, and the annual balance of our trade in her favor amounted to eight millions sterling. Our markets were important to her manufacturers."[42]

Such claims, however, did not go unchallenged, and opponents of the embargo noted the negative short- and long-term effects that it would have on American raw cotton producers. An address, the "Cotton Trade: To Southern Planters," argued that withholding cotton from Great Britain would only lead her to "supply herself from her East and West India Colonies," "destroy the French manufacturers," and leave Britain "to enjoy all the advantages of a monopoly" of the cotton business. "Jefferson's ignorance" and the embargo, another critic argued, would "thus render England independent of us forever, for that staple." In such an event, "Our *Cotton-planting* Nabobs" will bid "farewell to the *Golden Dreams of the South!*"[43] Such realism highlighted the dangerous gamble presented to American cotton planters through commercial warfare with their chief consumer.

The debates over the policies of commercial restrictions forced individuals from the Cotton South and elsewhere to conceive of their interests in specific regional ways and to seriously consider the cost that commercial restrictions would have on them. Such fears help explain the fact that several Georgia representatives initially voted against the measure. In the end, however, even they looked past the obvious tribulations and joined South Carolina's voting members in support of Jefferson's "experiment" and subsequent enforcement laws. They rallied behind the party line, believing it necessary to fight British attempts "to confine the European trade of America to Great Britain" and accepting the argument that *"whether it be a tax on stamps or on cotton . . . America will [not] submit to a direct attack on her sovereign and independent rights."*[44] Defense of the embargo also necessitated making a conscious link between southern agricultural production and American consumption—a premise at the heart of later tariff debates.

Georgia's William H. Crawford recognized the possibility of Britain finding new sources of raw materials, acknowledging the development of raw cotton in India and Brazil. But, he insisted, America's consumer market remained the decisive factor giving American suppliers an edge: "Great Britain must always purchase raw materials, but it is because we take her manufactures in exchange. So long as this state of things continues, so long they will continue to resort to our market."[45] A contributor to the Charleston *City Gazette* similarly minimized the threat of a rival Brazilian market, noting that Americans' superior purchasing power and political stability would make her a chief source.[46] These economic arguments, emphasizing the relationship between America's national purchasing power and its export prospects, defended the belief that the embargo, strictly enforced, could be effective, hitting Britain on two fronts: its production and export sectors.[47] As a result, reports about the cotton trade provided one measure of the success or failure of the embargo.

For the theory behind the embargo to work, Americans had to endure extreme self-deprivation. With American goods locked down in port warehouses, the American economy nearly ground to a halt.[48] Northeastern and Mid-Atlantic port cities felt the effects most deeply. Merchants and sailors lost their jobs. The transition of more capital into new manufacturing establishments had a minimal effect on the situation. Cut off from supplies, shopkeepers struggled, charging consumers inflated prices for those goods they had in stock. Protests against the embargo began almost immediately in the North. In the countryside conditions were slightly better. Wheat farmers and flour sellers still had large, if glutted, domestic markets but no longer had access to lucrative Atlantic ones. Those farther South were even worse off, however. Crops with only limited domestic markets—including cotton, tobacco, and rice—were blocked from their only major markets.

Despite the celebrated founding of new U.S. textile mills, the still-rudimentary state of American manufacturing left cotton planters especially concerned about an extended restriction of international trade.

The dramatic economic slowdown produced a major shift in Jeffersonian ideology. The rallying cry for equal opportunity for all became inverted into a patriotic request for equal suffering on behalf of party and nation.[49] Attempts by New England Federalists and a few commercial-minded Republicans to win relief for select fishing and shipping interests escalated the rhetoric of sacrifice and were derided by the party mainstream as "unpatriotic" attempts at "exclusive privilege."[50] Southern and northern Federalists, determining that national interest dictated a policy of free trade, were condemned by Republican leaders as "Anglomen" acting out of greed, party spirit, and cowardice.[51] D. R. Williams, who had missed the initial vote, admitted that he would have voted against the embargo, "conceiving it was a premature measure, but . . . now the nation had lifted its hand, he thought it proper to support . . . till death, or till it should be ascertained whether or not it would answer the intended purpose." Williams later argued that he remained a "friend to the embargo" because "its operation is impartial" and "blockaded" all groups equally.[52] Georgian George Troup favored heavy restrictions on the coastal trade to keep his own Savannah from becoming a smuggling point, because he felt the "embargo was best for the situation" and if effectively defended would produce "an honorable peace."[53] As late as a few weeks before its repeal, recognized violations of the principles of the embargo were met with stronger enforcement laws to ensure that particular groups were not given special relief.[54] The alliance of American commerce and agriculture, aimed initially at advancing America's cause within the Atlantic world, would now share the burden of protecting American commercial rights through uniform sacrifice.[55]

Because Republicans defined patriotism in terms of a citizen's willingness to sacrifice for the common good, debates quickly degenerated into contests over whose region or interest had suffered most for the nation. Republicans affirmed their party loyalty by supporting the policy of self-abnegation, while Federalists complained bitterly about its damaging effects on commercial regions, some even charging southern Republicans with "enslaving the country."[56] Southerners had little patience for northern grievances, instead arguing that the embargo "operated to the injury of the Southern States more than to the injury of the commercial States" because "it was impossible for us to find a market for our produce but by foreign commerce."[57] Producers of cotton and tobacco crops, which had little or no domestic market and rapidly falling prices, felt particularly "justified in asserting that there is no section of the Union whose interests are more immediately affected by the measure than the Southern States."[58] As a result, the South "lose[s] the capital of the trade," Nathaniel Macon argued, "whilst they [the Northeast] lose but the profits to be made upon the export and import."[59] Additionally, some southerners believed that "the States who call themselves commercial States . . . may emphatically be called manufacturing States" and could more easily adjust to the cessation of trade, particularly given their surplus banking capital.[60]

At home, Georgians and South Carolinians boasted that "the Embargo bears heavy on us, but there are no people, generally speaking, who bear it more cheerfully."[61] In Congress, these states' representatives quickly squashed northern representatives' attempts to allow specific exemptions to the policy. Local papers provided images of the superior sacrifice of southern Republicans. News of the frequent protests against the embargo in northern port cities like Boston and Providence met with harsh criticism in the Georgian and South Carolinian press.[62] When a reprinted letter of a Charleston merchant noted that the embargo would have to end before the next cotton crop came in the fall, national and local Republicans dismissed it as "federalist" propaganda or likely a "fabricated" attempt by the British ministry to "keep up the public spirit."[63] At militia gatherings and Fourth of July celebrations, participants toasted the embargo as "a wise, just, provident and the *only measure*," asking for "Union and energy to enforce it until we can traverse the ocean like a free nation." Others chastised smugglers as "the worst enemies of America, and only worthy to be the mercenary slaves of tyrants." One lowcountry reveler shared his feelings about the embargo by using the word itself to spell out "Every Moderate Brave American that Respects Good Order."[64] William Ellison's Independence Day oration urged Camden, South Carolina, residents to "bear with patience the inconveniences of the Embargo, and convince the nations of Europe we can live without their merchandize."[65] But this type of creativity was not necessary to create awareness of self-deprivation. The simple and necessary act of consuming fewer and worse-quality goods at higher prices reminded the everyday consumer, male and female, of the "patriotism" they were displaying for their nation. It also, of course, reminded them of their nation's continued impotence within the larger Atlantic state system.

Citizens of the Cotton South furthered their self-righteousness by arguing that they suffered for an extraregional interest. One western legislator nicely summarized the sentiment felt by all agrarian Republicans, noting in particular that agriculture had other options: "The people I represent are an agricultural

"Non Intercourse or Dignified Retirement" (1809), Peter Pencill (pseudonym). Critics of Jefferson's embargo focused on its adverse effects on American fashion and its pro-French attributes. This satirical cartoon plays on words and references Jefferson's embargo policy and his break with Old Republicans like John Taylor: "What a fine thing it is, to feel independent of all Taylors! I have stript myself rather than submit to London or Parisian Fashion! Dear me! How unwise it would be ever more to recur to the London Cut! It never suited me, they are always wrong in their Measures." Napoleon cheers him on: "Bravissimo! Mon Uncle Thomas! I give you maparele d'honneur, séconde qualité, dat I am very much content of you—you ave only to take off de Chémise car c'est de la Toile d'Irelande and you will ave donné one grand example of one sacrifice généreux." American Prints, no. 233, by permission of the Houghton Library, Harvard University.

people, and I ask the gentlemen of what importance it is to them whether their produce is carried in foreign or American vessels? For what are the agricultural people now suffering, but to maintain our maritime rights: Sir, we are willing to discard all calculations of profit or loss, and make a common cause with our brethren of other States in defense of our national rights and independence."[66] Even loyal Republican southerners recognized that foreign shipping alternatives were as viable, and under the circumstances more accessible, than American shipping. Federalists and a small cadre of Old Republicans led by John Randolph continued to remind them of it. Decrying the embargo as unwise and possibly even unconstitutional, Randolph argued that a perverted "notion of honor or dignity" had misled Americans to entrust her "precious interests" into a "leaky vessel." American agrarians needed free trade to markets, even if it meant accepting British commercial dominance.[67] Randolph's claims were immediately condemned as unpatriotic, heresies within a Republican Party whose rhetoric and policy had been largely based on anti-British thought. Nevertheless, they also reminded more loyal southern Republicans of what must have seemed a tempting alternative and of the depth of their own sacrifice.

Throughout most of 1808, indications from Britain suggested that cotton growers had reason to be concerned. As conditions worsened in the South and prices for goods rose, cotton prices remained low in Britain. Large crops the preceding two years, reinforced by merchants' rush to get crops out to sea before the embargo went into effect in January, left Britain with surpluses into the summer. Despite protests against the Orders in Council from Liverpool merchants and opposition MPs, a ban on sending even British raw cotton to the continent stretched manufacturers' supply, and the government's policies remained broadly supported.[68] By midyear, however, British factors began to report "a very rapid advance" on the price of raw cotton in Liverpool and by mid-September the "increasing scarcity of cotton" meant American upland cotton had "already reached a price unprecedented."[69] December and January prices for both Sea Island and upland cotton in London were over double their comparable 1807 levels.[70] High prices incentivized smuggling, and Liverpool consul James Maury reported the illegal importation of just under 6,000 bales of cotton in December and January. Though the rhetoric of sacrifice did not conform to reality for such smugglers, most planters continued to suffer intolerably low local prices. They did so believing that British repeal of the Orders in Council was near. A letter from Manchester, reprinted in the early fall, painted a picture of "*poor, emaciated, half-famished, distressed*" subjects crying, "Give us food or we perish," and organizing to overturn "Despots and Aristocrats."[71] Based only on this evidence—echoed in British journals throughout the fall of 1808—and ignoring the severe dislocation in northeastern merchant towns and no indications of change from British officials, some in the South continued to hold out hope that the embargo might yet work. Self-congratulatory planters, believing they sacrificed for sectors concentrated outside of their jurisdiction, were primed for a sense of betrayal when northern Republicans led the charge to end the embargo.

In the winter of 1808–1809, northern political allies led by John Quincy Adams engineered a retreat from the embargo and toward a less punishing form of economic coercion.[72] In late 1808, reports from France suggesting that the belligerents happily accepted American self-abnegation eroded Republican support for the measure. Worsening conditions in northeastern cities gave more credence to Federalist claims that Jefferson aimed to ruin northern commerce. Northern merchants and seamen simply couldn't afford the type of "protection" southern administrations were offering. As the North became unified behind repeal, northern representatives successfully appealed to several southern and western Republicans. Republicans increasingly backed away from the embargo, citing economic concerns and the fear that Federalist gains in the 1808 elections represented the people's unwillingness to support the policy.[73] For these individuals, the party's future became dependent on sacrificing what had been the most important symbol of party unity. This interregional coalition began moving the legislature toward a softer policy of economic coercion through partial repeal and nonintercourse with Britain and France.

Histories of the embargo have generally ended here with its abandonment, ignoring or explaining away continued southern support as blind loyalty to Jefferson. Indeed Jefferson's embargo rightfully remains one of the most questionable policy choices of the early United States. The merchants it was reported to protect despised it. Its failure had disastrous long- and short-term effects for all economic sectors, manufacturers excepted. Its ineffectiveness as a foreign policy tool made these consequences seem unnecessary, making support for the embargo seem only idealistic stubbornness about a severely miscalculated "cause."[74] Such harsh judgments, however, need not preclude deeper and more revealing explorations into why many in the Lower South continued to support the embargo and the meaning that this support would come to have. Southern legislators feverishly attempted to preserve it—at least temporarily—even after proposals setting a repeal date had passed.[75] When Georgian George Troup joined Nathaniel Macon to mount a last-ditch effort to preserve the embargo through the summer, all but three Georgia and South Carolina representatives supported them.[76] Even after Jefferson and Madison had publicly abandoned the policy, Southerners favoring it continued to pride themselves on having been "Embargo men," loyal to their principles and country.[77]

The fact that the Cotton South experienced some of the worst short-term consequences of the measure makes explaining the region's long-term support difficult.[78] That support reflected, in part, sincere anger at the targeted measures taken by Britain against American cotton and concerns about a British monopoly. Some earnestly hoped that Napoleon's Continental System could foster more cotton manufacturing in France and thus provide an alternate direct market that needed protecting. Abandoning the policy without securing an end to British Orders would be like abandoning the field just as many believed the enemy was weakened. Though not yet reaching the power over international markets that it would in the 1820s, cotton's rapid rise gave Georgians and South Carolinians supreme confidence that withholding it could exact change in British policy and protect national honor. Under this belief, cotton retained its credentials as a patriotic crop helping the entire nation. Another likely reason for planters' willingness to endure self-deprivation was that, self-praise aside, they were better suited to handle the economic dislocations stemming from the policy. Slaves were diverted from cotton production to corn and encouraged to spin their own rudimentary cloth. According to one student of regional responses to the embargo, South Carolina "turned more energetically to household manufacturers" than any other state had.[79]

But enduring southern support for the embargo also reflected clear-minded and self-interested calculations concerning the policy of nonintercourse that would replace it. Massachusetts Republican Ezekiel Bacon, who served as an intermediary between southern and northern Republicans, characterized the southern mindset best in January 1809: "Our Southern friends . . . now tell us . . . that they are willing to support our commercial rights by the present System [embargo] or by War as we shall think best, but that they will never consent to take non-intercourse & non-importation as a substitute for the Embargo, that they will in Preference to this give up the whole ground of resistance to belligerent aggressions."[80] This sentiment against nonimportation or partial repeal through nonintercourse evolved from the ways market forces affected different regions and crops. While wheat and flour exports had potential friendly markets in the Mediterranean and South America, particularly after the removal of Portugal's Crown to Brazil in 1808, cotton sold almost exclusively in British or French-controlled markets specifically excluded by the act. This in part explains why Mid-Atlantic agrarians were far more willing to support partial repeal than were southern producers.[81] Nonintercourse, however, would provide considerably less market incentive for cotton, as backlogged supplies would not be able to reach their primary markets legally.

In reality, of course, cotton would and eventually did go to neutral ports and was then reexported to British and French destinations. Planters foresaw this possibility but believed that the effects of such an unpatriotic indirect trade would have little benefit for them, as their crops would flood a limited number of outlets, driving prices down to unbearably low levels. Nonimportation or nonintercourse freed up American commerce and aided American manufacturing and wheat producers but did so, embargo supporters argued, at continued expense to southern agriculturists. High demand to ship products overseas would elevate the prices that shippers and merchants could require, a problem that would be compounded by high insurance rates resulting from the perilous conditions of the British-controlled ocean. Allowing this, William H. Crawford of Georgia declared, would be "like paying tributes."[82] The meager profits promised for agriculture "would not pay the risk and freight, much less the duty." In the end, "the planter would receive no reward for his labor."[83] Additionally, northern manufacturers could demand high prices under monopolistic conditions at the expense of American consumers. With all goods likely to end up in British hands, Britain would triumphantly benefit from a situation that offered only false hope to American cotton exporters.[84] "When the embargo is repealed," he concluded, "war, or submission is plain ground, but all between, is mere whipping the devil round the stump."[85] The nation would have eliminated its last bit of leverage without having accomplished a thing.

Cotton South activists argued that ending the embargo without declaring war would transform the policy of equal suffering into one of inherently and grossly unequal distress. An important "ground of objection . . . noticed by the gentleman from South Carolina (Mr. D. R. Williams)," a sympathetic congressman noted, was that: "Putting the non-intercourse in place of the embargo, relieves one part of the Union, and imposes the pressure upon the other part. The embargo operates equally in a great degree on the different parts of the Union. The non-intercourse would press most severely on the Southern and Western States, who depend chiefly on the immediate exchange of their produce for foreign goods." Williams and others perceived a more subtle threat to planter interests because the new policy did not allow British and French access to American ports and "would throw almost the whole commerce of the nation into the hands of the Eastern States, without competition, and also add a premium on their manufacturers at the expense of the agricultural interests to the South and West. Foreign goods being excluded, the manufacturing States would furnish the rest of the Union with their manufactured goods at their own prices."[86] In language eerily similar to that of later tariff debates, South Carolina's John Taylor agreed, emphasizing that nonintercourse "operated unequally on different parts of the Union" and had, in effect, been a "tax on the people generally of the Southern States . . . under the pretense of resistance."[87]

For many Old Republicans too much had been sacrificed already and the best course was to drop all resistance, even if it meant economic submission to England. John Randolph and his followers joined Federalists, arguing that Republicans had no one to blame but themselves and harkening back to the rejected Monroe-Pinkney Treaty as a missed opportunity.[88] The majority of other Cotton South leaders, however, remained faithful to their definition of party and union, beginning an early cry for war. When that was found impracticable and the embargo's fate was permanently sealed, politicians choked back their anger. Senator Crawford privately but vehemently attacked northern abandonment: "If we can get out of this scrape, I for one will suffer the [British] to impress every Yankee in the nation if found upon the high seas, & to interpolate new principles into the law of nations as often as they please. The Yankees have brought the nation into the scrape, & have in Congress en masse deserted it in the hour of trial."[89] Fellow Georgian George Troup more publicly condemned the northern merchants he believed had proved themselves selfishly "ready to sacrifice the Honor and independence of the nation for a little trade in codfish & potash."[90] Unlike the uncompromising John Randolph, these Southerners had stood behind the embargo to protect commercial interests. Now those interests had, they believed, turned their back on southern efforts and the policy of equal suffering. Even southerners without strong ties to the Republican Party, like David Ramsay, lamented this development. In his *History of South Carolina,* first published in 1809, Ramsay described the "chain of suffering" encircling South Carolina, noting that "while others contended that they suffered most from the embargo, the Carolinians with justice preferred their claim to the honor of bearing it best." If only it had been "as patiently borne in every part of the Union as it was in Carolina," he concluded, "the issue would probably have been very different, and certainly more to the honor of the United States."[91] To the embargo's most militant supporters in the South, northern Republicans had betrayed the nation and party, thus allowing southerners to reaffirm their own alleged superior sacrifice.

With the embargo's end on March 4, 1809, the equal suffering it entailed promised to become radically unequal. The policy of economic federation seemed in shambles and foreign policy rudderless. "We have gone too far to recede," Crawford wrote, but "are so frightened with dissention [*sic*] at home that we dare not advance."[92] For the first time in these critical debates, southern unity was completely fractured. Some dissenters like Randolph joined Federalists and argued for submission; other party loyalists argued for a new embargo and war. Still others joined northern representatives in pursuing a different form of economic coercion. Nationalism continued to endure as even those southerners feeling betrayed recognized that the problem stemmed primarily from Britain's abuse of its naval supremacy and her laws that steered raw cotton to her own manufacturers. Furthermore, the spring agreement between Madison and British minister David Erskine raised expectations that diplomacy would preserve peace and gain recognition of American commercial rights. This détente, coupled with Madison's suspension of the nonintercourse agreement, muted and temporarily delayed the crisis within the Republicans' economic federation. Westminster's rejection of the agreement, however, meant enactment of the much-despised policy of nonintercourse on August 10, 1809.

Its implementation confirmed the fears of critics within the Cotton States. Charleston agents notified British buyers that indirect avenues for trade were available. British vessels could meet unprincipled American merchants at Amelia Island, Lisbon, or Cadiz. American cotton flooded into these channels, and prices for both Sea Island and upcountry cotton dropped well below preembargo levels. At the same time the price of freight through these indirect channels rose from an average of about $1.50 per pound in 1807 to over $3 per pound in late 1809, even reaching $4 in December 1809.[93] As the winter 1809–1810 session approached, the administration and a coalition including most southern Republicans were determined to mitigate the discriminatory consequences of nonintercourse and recement the theory of economic federation. The tool they selected was an American navigation act, commonly known as Macon's Bill No. 1, which intended to open direct trade with Europe, but only on American shipping. The proposal, similar to one presented by Madison in the 1790s, was carefully constructed to exclude British and French shipping from American ports while restricting American access to neutral ports, where illicit trade with Britain had developed. This, proponents believed, would legislate the most essential form of economic union by binding commerce to diverse agricultural interests through direct trade with Europe. It was also hoped that the burden would be shifted to the belligerents, perhaps giving them incentive to drop bellicose measures in order to regain access to the American trade. Given the bill's emphasis on the direct trade to Europe, solid southern support should not be too surprising.

As a matter of theory, however, endorsement of Macon No. 1 marked a significant reversal in southern policy. Dating back to 1787, anti-Federalists, and even Federalists, in the South had feared a northern commercial monopoly of the region.[94] Now southern delegates proposed legislating such a monopoly, if only for a temporary period. Troup, a steady cynic of northern merchant intentions, expressed his frustration to Georgia's governor, arguing that the "rights" of the southern states were being "shamefully sacrificed" to the "undue weight" of the East. "Individuals" were daily "detached from the Southern and Western interests, and made to unite in measures which have for their object the prosperity merely of New England navigation and fisheries." For Troup, it seemed the only way to put an end to these dangerous precedents was to declare war.[95]

As other southerners rallied behind Macon No. 1 they again applauded themselves on their patriotic sacrifices. Macon himself was baffled to find that the primary opposition came not from the South, where he expected it, but rather from the North.[96] Eventually the administration won enough New England and Mid-Atlantic representatives to win a close but firm victory (73 to 52). In fact, it was the stubbornness of more hawkish Mid-Atlantic mercantile interests in the Senate, not the failure of northern or southern support, that ultimately killed the navigation bill. Less compromising Republicans—several of them involved in the indirect trade—joined Federalist opposition and tipped the balance away from Macon's Bill and toward a policy of open but armed trade.[97] In the end stalemate between the two houses went unbroken. Rushing to beat the session's end, in May legislators adopted an impotent proposal offered by South Carolina's John Taylor. Macon's No. 2, as Taylor's proposal became known, dropped nonintercourse but promised to reimpose it on the enemy of whomever ended its belligerence. It was openly acknowledged to be one step away from submission.[98]

As its opponents predicted, Macon's No. 2 opened the door for a geopolitical debacle and drove the United States further away from Britain. Just as importantly, it all but closed the door to further attempts at economic coercion. As Kentucky senator George Bibb put it, "I do not expect any substantial benefit from negotiation—and look to a war or a most base and disgraceful submission as the only alternatives."[99] The British consul at Norfolk agreed: "After the Hurricane of Passion in which the Congress opened their Session, it is truly laughable to witness the miserable, feeble, Puff, in which they evaporated. It is indeed a very comfortable reflection that with every disposition to injure Great Britain, they have found themselves totally unable to do so."[100] Recognizing that embargo was impossible and that submission was potentially ruinous because of the British monopoly that would result, sentiments within the Lower South increasingly turned toward the only option left: war against Britain.

In addition to laughter, Macon's Bill No. 2 triggered a resurgence of international trade and a diplomatic debacle. Cotton again flowed directly to Liverpool, but prices fell to all-time lows, from 15.5 pence for a pound of upland in May to 11.5 by November to 11.25 by the following February. Sea Island prices dropped almost as dramatically, from 25 to 22.5 to 21.5 over those same periods.[101] In the meantime, Napoleon, seeing an opportunity to pit the United States against Britain, offered conditional promises to relax his decrees against American shipping. The gestures, conveyed in a letter from the Duke of Cadore, triggered a debate in the United States over whether America needed to impose sanctions against Britain. Months of waiting demonstrated that the Orders in Council would not be repealed, leading Madison to conclude that some action was necessary. At the president's request, Congress convened for its winter session and began debating a new nonintercourse bill directed at Britain. In February, after a rigorous debate, a nonimportation agreement was settled on as the appropriate recourse to give Britain one final chance to repeal its Orders in Council and end its belligerence. Instead, Britain rejected the claim that France's policy had changed, and continued to target American shipping.

These events brought little relief to the Lower South. Cotton prices continued to drop after implementation of nonimportation—down to 10.5 pence throughout much of the summer of 1811. A new spate of impressments and open clashes on the high seas between British and American vessels increased tensions in the summer of 1811. The situation in Charleston became so bad that Margaret Izard Manigault, the daughter of wealthy planter Ralph Izard and wife of South Carolina grandee Gabriel Manigault, lamented everything from cotton prices as low as 8 cents, to a serious money shortage, to an end to Charleston parties.[102] The social scene, however, was the least of South Carolina's concerns. Fall elections in South Carolina sent three hawkish young congressmen—John C. Calhoun, William Lowndes, and Langdon Cheves—to the House. Each had already expressed serious reservations about the restrictive system and a determination to end foreign injustice.

This triumvirate made an immediate impression. The freshly arrived British minister, Augustus J. Foster, found South Carolina's congressmen particularly "resolute" and observed that they "seemed to have great influence and were very cool and decided on the propriety of going to war in order to protect the Commerce of the Country."[103] The events of the previous years had done little to suggest to them and others that anything else would work. Nonimportation, embargo, nonintercourse, another round of nonimportation, vacillating cotton prices, and restricted purchases of British goods throughout the period had placed great stress on the American economy. Yet through it all Westminster had remained unwilling to repeal the Orders in Council. Even when their delegate, Mr. Erskine, had achieved a reasonable compromise, British officials at home rejected it outright. Negotiation had been "resorted to time after time, till it is become hopeless," Calhoun told the House, urging it to reject "the restrictive system persisted in to avoid war, and in the vain expectation of returning justice."[104] In the meantime, Americans from every state had endured self-deprivation, humiliation, and some of the most serious infighting seen in the young Republic.

A seasoned veteran of the debates, D. R. Williams angrily appealed for action and cited the poor conditions of his own state: "Inquire into the state of the cotton market; where is the crop of 1810? A curse to him who meddled with it. Where is that of 1811? Rotting at home in the hands of the grower, waiting the repeal of the Orders in Council."[105] It remained debatable who was primarily to blame. Randolph insisted that the Republicans' insane efforts at commercial warfare had created the low prices, and decried war as unwise. There was much truth in this claim, and nearly universal disgust with the Republican tools of economic coercion meant they could only be defended as "efforts to maintain peace and independence," not on grounds of their expediency for winning redress. Yet the vast majority of southern representatives from the Cotton South, led by John C. Calhoun, insisted that "the people of that section . . . did not attribute" the low cotton prices "to the efforts of their government" but rather the "hand of foreign injustice." Rather, "they know well, without the market to the continent, the deep and steady current of supply will glut that of Great Britain."[106] This assertion, though made with conviction, had questionable merit.

Given the relatively small amount of American raw cotton that actually went to the continent, it would be hard to assert that this—more than American efforts to cut off supplies—led to gluts when trade was opened and contributed to lower prices for cotton producers. Albert Gallatin's influential 1806 report on commerce with Great Britain suggested that from 1802 through 1804, 82 percent of exported raw cotton went to British ports.[107] Nevertheless, choosing the gendered language of patriotic militancy rather than submission, Calhoun insisted that the Cotton South was "not prepared for the colonial state to which again that power is endeavoring to reduce us. The manly spirit of that section of our country will not submit to be regulated by any foreign power." "War is the only means of redress," he told his chief adversary, Virginian John Randolph, whom he implied was encouraging a "resigned submission as the best remedy."[108] In the end, the House and Senate agreed with Calhoun and the Committee on Foreign Relations report that he helped draft, which demanded that Britain's "desolating war upon our unprotected commerce" must be answered. "The just complaints of our merchants," "the unhappy case of our impressed seamen," even the "cries of their wives & children" demanded the nation's protection. "We must resist," the committee concluded; "the patriotic fire of the Revolution" must be summoned and the nation put on a war footing.[109] Facing complete submission to Britain and public humiliation at the expense of a growing number of militants within Congress, Madison began rallying the party behind war preparations, sparking a prolonged debate that ultimately culminated in a declaration of war against Britain on June 17, 1812.

If, as has been claimed, the decision for war was a reluctant attempt to preserve party and national unity, then a significant part of that calculation was the need to preserve cohesion behind Republican economic federation. Southerners had taken a long and tumultuous journey, applying every form of economic coercion within the Jeffersonian repertoire. The nation had shown itself too undisciplined to achieve success with the most extreme form of commercial warfare: complete embargo. Nonintercourse and nonimportation were unacceptable because of their inequitable results for various sectors and regions. Submission had been unacceptable, particularly because it kept American interests at the mercy of British naval dominance. Those most actively pushing for taking up arms had come to fear something worse than war: a continuation of what Kentucky congressman Joseph Desha called "imbecile measures."[110] South Carolinian Langdon Cheves agreed, stating that "the restrictive system, as a mode of resistance . . . has never been a favorite with me."[111] Experience proved to the young firebrand John C. Calhoun that commercial restrictions were "improper to us" and "caused distrust at home and contempt abroad," thus making war "unavoidable."[112] Submission promised to ruin the country economically, giving Britain a monopoly, but further measures of economic coercion threatened to undermine Republican control or even dissolve the Union. The early and consistent strength of the war movement in the South also represented an explosion of frustration at the plummeting cotton and tobacco prices resulting from British policy. War, in effect, was the only option that could potentially win relief from the British noose *and* end the possibility of discriminatory commercial measures within the nation.[113]

Critically, the decision for war reinforced southern patriotism, prevented a political crisis within Republicanism, and preserved ideas of economic union.

Republicans would militarily defend national sovereignty and protect the agricultural and commercial interests of the nation. For a few southern Federalists and Quids who believed the war to be contrary to the nation's interest, the decision represented a "metaphysical" war tearing the very channels of trade through which America's lifeblood flowed.[114] The means did not justify the ends. Many looked back at the Monroe-Pinkney Treaty, blaming Jefferson and Madison for a lost opportunity at reconciliation.[115] Though small in number, the existence of these voices cannot be dismissed, because the themes they articulated—cordial diplomatic relationships with Britain and decentralized national government— would become attractive to later groups in the Cotton South. Their arguments gained further credence as British efforts to increase raw cotton supplies from East India cast doubt on the assumption that the United States' rise within international markets would continue.

The failures of the decade forced Republicans in the Cotton South to shelve, until the Civil War, the idea of using economic coercion as a means of gaining diplomatic redress. The growth of British dependence on southern raw cotton had empowered them and the Republican Party to believe commercial warfare had a chance. The embargo, nonimportation, and nonintercourse had been premised on the belief that restricting British access to southern raw cotton and American cloth consumers would protect American merchants. Every policy had failed miserably. Calhoun believed that this realization and the move toward war had commenced a "new era in our politicks." Prior to 1812 "conductors of affairs, have attempted to avoid and remove difficulties by a sort of political management. They thought, that national honor and interest could be both maintained and respected, not by war, or a preparation for it; but by commercial arrangements and negotiations." Such an approach "might suit an inconsiderable nation," but "experience has proved it improper for us. Its effects have been distrust at home and contempt abroad." In Calhoun's dawning of a new age: "We will defend ourselves by force" not by meek attempts at economic coercion.[116] The gamble that had leveraged America's natural resources (especially cotton) and consumer power against British naval supremacy and diplomacy had failed. "Free trade and sailors rights" must be protected through actual war.

Mobilization for that conflict reopened the likelihood of embargo or nonimportation of British goods. Even under wartime conditions, however, some Cotton South representatives remained reluctant toward continued restrictions. Calhoun's pragmatism and desire to cast off old measures led him to take the minority position and recommend ending the "restrictive system" completely, even allowing trade with the nation's archenemy. Instead, he suggested allowing imports, but at high tariffs, so as to obtain needed goods and raise the government revenues necessary to prosecute the war. "The conclusion is strong," Calhoun argued as early as June 1812, "that you cannot extend your commercial pressure on the enemy beyond, or at least much beyond, the operation of high duties." Calhoun and his colleagues lost the argument in the short run, and the administration's proposal for nonintercourse prevailed.[117] Along with wartime conditions, this policy ensured that southern cotton planters' suffering would continue as they and the rest of the nation mobilized for war. Average cotton prices overseas rose considerably, but the trade sank to all-time lows. In 1813, only 18,640 bags of U.S. cotton entered Liverpool, compared to 97,624 in 1811 and 143,756 in 1807, the preembargo year.[118] Glutted national markets dipped domestic prices to historic lows of 10.5 cents per pound for upland cotton.[119] Calhoun and his colleagues from the Cotton South continued to press for an end to nonimportation. Finally in 1814, for diplomatic reasons and in view of its apparent ineffectiveness, Madison agreed to end nonintercourse, thus ending the commercial restrictive system that had more or less guided policy for the past decade.[120]

The Republican affair with the restrictive system died a pitiful death, in the midst of a war that had at least partly resulted from its failure. During these political economic debates, the nationalism of southerners had been greatly heightened as they believed themselves to have discounted their own interest and sacrificed for northern commercial interests and the greater national good of economic federation. Simultaneously, the emphasis of economic coercion and its potential for sectional inequality within the Union pointed many Southerners toward the wisdom of pursuing freer trade. These debates proved to be a watershed in southern economic thought. Gone were the Republican arguments that foreign policy disputes could or should be fought with commercial warfare through nonimportation, nonintercourse, or embargoes. Calhoun's proposition for higher tariffs retained some traction, but politicians throughout the South, and especially the Cotton South, increasingly turned to protecting and extending free trade, regardless of whether that trade perpetuated dependency on Great Britain. In the process of fighting commercial and military war, however, developments in the North had caused the balance of economic interests within the Union to change, leading to a new postwar crisis over the proper form of national political economy.

The War of 1812 had other important consequences for the Cotton South. Tennessee cotton planter Andrew Jackson's persistent attacks against noncooperative Native American tribes provided devastating blows on several of the Lower Creek tribes, while intimidating many others and opening up vast new tracts of cheap but fertile land. Budding entrepreneurs increasingly looked westward to Alabama and Mississippi to find their fortunes in cotton. In addition, Jackson's defeat of British forces outside of New Orleans (his troops hiding behind stacked cotton bales) made him a national hero and allowed the region and the nation to claim symbolic victory, despite the fact that the battle took place after a peace treaty had already been signed. The War of 1812 thus provided most in the Cotton South with the perception at least that they had fought and won a war that had expanded their landed cotton empire and heightened the nation's respect abroad.[121]

## Peace Abroad, Dissension at Home: Republicans Active and Passive

After peace mercifully arrived in 1815, the battle over economic federation resumed with increased fervor, though this time under new political and economic circumstances. American "victory" heightened nationalism while laying the groundwork for a more energetic federal agenda. Different postwar calculations about a protective tariff forced competing visions within the Republican coalition into the open. A sizable portion of northern and western Republicans recalculated the original balance of economic federation, embracing the burgeoning manufacturing sector as a means toward a stronger and more self-sufficient economy. Though more aware of the limits of self-sufficiency than their northern colleagues, a group of active nationalists in the Cotton South led by Calhoun accepted protection as a means to bind the Union together and enhance national and regional standing within the Atlantic economy. These arguments angered a second group of passive nationalists, who believed that such efforts denied their earlier sacrifices on behalf of freer trade.[122] Increasingly, the commercial arguments of Randolph gained legitimacy as free trade Southerners began to question the wisdom of continued compromise believed to adversely affect cotton interests. The difficult and imprecise nature of the calculations allowed for a significant range of responses within these two conceptual approaches. Unlike earlier debates, however, peacetime conditions and the Federalist Party's collapse were gradually removing powerful centripetal forces that had united Republicans.

Far from being neo-Federalist in sentiment, National Republican calls for protection after 1815 drew from neomercantilist precedent and traditional Republican concerns over economic dependence on Britain. What's more, protectionism remained consistent with the party desire to cement a cross-sectional and cross-sectoral alliance by uniting manufacturing, commerce, and agriculture behind a common, albeit recalibrated, understanding of economic union. In 1810, Tench Coxe repeated his calls for a stronger domestic economy uniting textile manufacturing and cotton planters.[123] Simultaneously Philadelphia Republican representative Adam Seybert argued that government protection of a vibrant manufacturing sector, as commerce had been defended, would preserve the "peace, honor, and independence" of the nation."[124] At the time, with few exceptions, southern agrarians and northern merchants dismissed Seybert's ideas as outside the properly balanced, Atlantic-centered Jeffersonian political economy. After the war, however, more developed domestic manufacturing led individuals like Henry Clay and Calhoun to revisit the issue and begin to appreciate the benefits of increased economic independence through a more integrated domestic economy. The decade of commercial and actual war had already helped lay the foundation by creating more home industry. Full implementation, however, required internal improvements and protection of America's infant manufactures from the European goods expected to flood into American markets. A protective tariff promised to support both by raising the necessary revenue to pay off a massive war debt, support public works, and protect American goods from less expensive European ones.

Southern support for this agenda was critical, but outside of Kentucky hemp producers and Louisiana sugar growers few policymakers believed protection would greatly help southern agrarians.[125] Fewer still imagined that manufacturing would emerge as profitable within the rural South. Southern fiscal conservatives supported the 1816 tariff bill primarily for its role in providing needed revenue, but supporters and opponents alike recognized that it was primarily intended to foster a more united domestic economy and a secure nation.[126] Ensuring increased American political and economic strength necessitated a stronger center and, not surprisingly, National Republicans turned to political economy. Calhoun argued that Americans must "bind together more closely our widely-spread Republic." The tariff "was to greatly increase our mutual dependence and intercourse; and will, as a necessary consequence, excite an increased attention to internal improvement—a subject every way so intimately connected with the ultimate attainment of national strength, and the perfection of our political institutions."[127] The previous decade had convinced many Republicans of the underlying weakness of America's political union. The "extension and organization" of the federal Union had protected it from the old threats of centralization and submission but had "exposed us to a new and terrible danger—disunion."[128] Sectionalism, evidenced most dramatically by the Hartford Convention, had threatened the idea of union itself.

Critically, Calhoun's perception of the recent past had suggested to him that the nation could never "be indifferent to dangers from abroad." In fact, he "considered as the plain dictate of wisdom, in peace to prepare for war." Not to do so would be to "indulge in the phantom of eternal peace."[129] National prosperity, indeed the American nation, had been at the mercy of European powers, which, despite the settlement at Vienna, promised to be at war again in the near future. It was improbable and undesirable that America should try to challenge British naval supremacy, but an aggressive campaign for internal improvements and a stronger domestic economy would better isolate America from the hazards of inevitable future conflicts while providing stronger military preparedness should America be dragged into war again.

As horrific as the previous decade had been, according to protectionists, a unique opportunity had been created and needed to be seized. By creating a vibrant domestic manufacturing base for national security, an unfortunate past of "restrictive measures and war" could be transformed into a promising future, "more valuable than the repeal of the Edict of Nantz [sic]," which had brought thousands of skilled Protestants to England.[130] Linking agricultural production to internal manufacturing would provide options independent from the tumultuous Atlantic world while also ensuring that America would have the tools necessary for better military preparedness. Success for this plan, however, required an adequate national demand, and American manufacturers could not compete with cheaper European imports without tariff protection.

Where Calhoun saw opportunity, critics from the Cotton South saw perverse economic calculation, faithlessness, potential disaster, and dangerous precedents. Calhoun's chief southern opponent, Representative Thomas Telfair of Georgia, emphasized that America's future lay with the current "natural" balance of the Jeffersonian economy: "The extent of territory, the exuberance of our soil, the genius of our people, the principles of our political institutions, have in their combination decreed, as by a law of nature, that for years to come, the citizens of America shall obtain their subsistence by agriculture and commerce."[131] Encouraging manufacturing through artificial measures "would fain issue a counter order, to withdraw industry from its natural and accustomed channels, and, by our laws, force into a state of prematurety [sic] the manufacturing enterprise of this country."[132] Outside of Congress, Virginian John Taylor of Caroline County made the same arguments, comparing protectionist measures to the "artificial" British system that Americans had fought to remove themselves from in 1776 and again in 1812.[133] Though they did not necessarily embrace Taylor's pastoralism, early advocates of free trade from the Cotton South did find more pragmatic elements of his discussion a useful premise from which to argue.

To this group of free traders, protectionism seemed to undermine the very reason the war had been fought. The use of commercial restrictions made sense if the goal was protecting national rights and interests from violations by European powers. It was ill suited, however, for a period of peace, particularly one in which Britain appeared willing to relax some of its more onerous protectionist policies, as evidenced by the Convention of 1815, which jointly ended discriminating duties on British and American shipping.[134] In the context of European belligerence against America, the free trade arguments embraced by Old Republicans and Federalists had been perceived as unpatriotic submission. In the context of global peace, however, they could enthusiastically be embraced as the key to reviving American agriculture and trade.

Free traders felt that making self-sufficiency a national priority required abandoning the majority view, which had sacrificed so much to win free and open trade for northern merchants. They deemed higher tariffs unfair in theory and practice, forcing southern consumers to pay duties beyond revenue purposes and consequently reroute natural economic channels. Charity from commerce and agriculture, which had suffered for the last decade, was being demanded for American mechanics and manufacturers, the only interests that had prospered during the period. Telfair emphasized that the tariff would be, like the earlier policies of nonimportation, grossly discriminatory to agrarians and unequal to "the planter of this country . . . who consumes the article manufactured, [and] shall be made to pay the difference between the wages of labor in the factory and field, together with the difference of profit which superior skill in the foreign manufacturer gives over the manufacturer of this country. In one word, all articles are made dear to the consumer, whether of foreign or domestic fabrication, merely that the manufacturer may derive a profit upon his capital." Furthermore, he submitted, the producers within the country were not in a "condition sufficiently thriving to make this sacrifice." Agriculturalists added to such claims by highlighting the poor conditions of American agriculture in the wake of terrible conditions within the Atlantic.[135]

These Republicans emphasized the personal sacrifice that the nation's agricultural interest—led by the southern cotton farmers—had made for commerce. Increased free direct trade with Europe offered the hope of peacetime prosperity.

For Telfair, support for the tariff was shortsighted and failed to recognize the precedent that it would set for aiding a "favorate [*sic*] class of the community by a tax upon the rest" and creating the conditions for a new monopoly.[136] Free traders like Telfair and Taylor rejected claims that protection would bind the Union together. Instead, they submitted, as Randolph had earlier (regarding protection of commerce), that the means proposed by Calhoun and Clay undid the ends. Providing special protection for a minority interest threatened to reintroduce Federalist consolidationist economic policies. Ultimately, redistributive policies would alienate particular groups, exacerbating rather than dampening sectionalist feelings. Protection, opponents contended, threatened to destroy the Union from within.

Free trade Southerners, who eventually turned to states' rights to protect their interests, were not initially the successors of "faithless" men that history has portrayed. Instead they believed themselves to be carrying the true torch of American constitutionalism and the original formula of Republican economic federation. Randolph and some Old Republicans may have had critical reservations about the wisdom of union, but most opponents to the protectionist agenda conceived of themselves as having willingly and repeatedly sacrificed for the principles of the Union. As they saw it, they had stood as the guardians of the principles for which the nation had fought: free trade, decentralized political government, and nondiscriminatory practices: "The liberties of this people and the independence of this Government, rest on a basis too firmly laid in their very genius and nature to require such protection." To passive nationalists, Calhoun and his colleagues had lost their faith, turning to artificial measures that men like Telfair refused to adopt because they "denoted the absence of all ideas of self-government."[137]

Though Calhoun's belief in the necessity of military preparedness justified his national vision, the economic arguments presented by free traders did not ring completely hollow with the Carolinian, who himself had opposed the restrictionist measures of the Madison administration. In fact, southern opposition to the tariff forced him to define his support around the belief that protection for manufacturers ultimately served the long-term economic interests of the agrarian South. Stronger domestic textile manufacturing would provide a richer domestic outlet for raw cotton and create an alternative to a risky Atlantic trade. Consequently, European powers would be unable to take American supplies for granted. Ultimately, Calhoun argued, protection would provide the cheapest way to support American commerce and agriculture within the Atlantic economy. By increasing American leverage in the pursuit of commercial agriculture, a stronger manufacturing base would replace the need for a costly navy—something most southerners had long opposed.[138] Such calculations were premised on realpolitik and supported by the recent experience of war. Lower South support for the tariff of 1816, then, was premised on the likelihood of future conflict, American vulnerability in the Atlantic world, and the assumption that the development of stable domestic manufactures in the North would provide long-term benefits to southern planters.

Several other factors muted the tension that might have erupted during these early tariff debates. The high tide of Republican nationalism in the wake of the War of 1812 took some time to subside. As importantly, the debate over the 1816 tariff did not break down along clear sectional lines. Just as the South remained split, substantial numbers of northern commercial groups and agrarians, especially those looking to profit from the resumption of the direct cotton trade with Europe, opposed the call for protection by northern manufacturers. Finally Monroe's election in 1816 perpetuated the belief that the South remained at the helm, providing hope that protectionists within the region would soon come to their senses. Other Republicans in the region could also soften the effects of protection, and even partly support it, by accentuating its fiscally responsible nature and believing it to be just a temporary measure.

Warlike conditions and immediate postwar policy had a major effect on the cotton trade. During the war, prices rose, but in largely inaccessible Liverpool markets. Large quantities of cotton flooded available American markets, especially in New York, where prices hovered between 10 and 15 cents per pound.[139] The severe restriction of overseas trade allowed northern financiers and shippers to consolidate their control over the coastal cotton trade. Prior to 1805 British or southern merchants provided much of the credit that fueled the cotton trade. When peace returned in April 1815, one Savannah agent notified his Manchester buyers of an important change: "Should you direct us to make purchases of cotton on your account, we would recommend you to nominate some substantial houses at the northward to endorse our Bills on you and dispose of them there, and on whom we could pass drafts for purchases made, with greater facility than disposing of our Bills on you here. This practice has been pursued here and has been found to answer every purpose."[140] Largely cut off from British credit and markets and lacking adequate sources within the region, planters and their factors relied on northern houses and merchants to provide needed advances.

Restricted overseas markets and increased domestic consumption of cotton also heightened the importance of the coastal trade in cotton and northern merchants' role in facilitating it. In 1817, Congress passed a Navigation Act which excluded foreign vessels from the intercoastal trade. Northern shippers, whose share in the foreign export trade had dipped from 90 percent to 77 percent, were given a monopoly of interstate commerce and its most lucrative component, the carrying of cotton from southern to northern ports. The bill, proposed by Georgia's John Forsyth and amended by South Carolinian William Lowndes, demonstrated the Cotton South's continued desire to cement the economic alliance between northern commerce and southern cotton. In the course of the largely unrecorded debates, Lowndes, Calhoun, and Georgians Forsyth and Richard Wilde discussed whether foreign participation in the coastal trade should be completely prohibited or just discriminated against; few, however, opposed providing American merchants an advantageous position within the trade. Not surprisingly, John Randolph remained the chief opponent, arguing that once again the nation was providing a northern monopoly and interfering with trade. Unfortunately, no roll call vote for this bill seems to exist, but it seems quite likely that leadership from the Lower South was critical for its passage.[141] Far from lamenting southern dependency on northern merchants, as they later would, representatives from the Cotton South were legislating it as part of a desire to bind the nation's commercial and agrarian interests together toward mutual benefit.

The Republican era and the second "war of independence" left a complicated legacy for the Lower South. A sizable bloc of southern politicians led by John C. Calhoun had agitated for war against Britain in order to protect America's shipping and commercial interests. "The sailors have claimed our protection," Calhoun told Congress, and "such generous sympathy for those who stand connected to us only by the ties of citizenship does honor to our country . . . Our history abounds with many instances of this sympathy of the whole with any part. When it ceases to be natural, we will cease to be one nation. It constitutes our real union. The rest is form."[142] Calhoun's exhortations on behalf of northeastern sailors and traders earned him and his southern colleagues the historical label of patriotic "nationalists."[143] And yet even the war's supporters such as George Troup and William Crawford could join its critics and question whether the last decade had demonstrated that such sympathy was always honorable, natural, or necessary. For them, the decade had witnessed considerable frustration as southern agrarians repeatedly sacrificed their rights and their interests to what Troup called the "undue weight of" the East and the "prosperity of New England navigation and fisheries."[144] The egregious abuses of British naval supremacy and French policy led most to blame foreign belligerence for the problems and to reject John Randolph's calls for submission. Yet regardless of the level of enthusiasm for the fighting, all in the Cotton South realized that sacrifice for country came at a sectional cost. Most Republicans in the Lower South rallied to protect the alliance between northern commerce and southern agriculture, even when the protective measures closed off access to British markets on which the cotton trade depended. In this light, contemporaries saw their sacrifice as anything but qualified.[145]

Indeed, these memories from the Republican era of embargo and war continued to inform debates on the horizon, namely, the tariff debates of the 1820s and those over the expansion of slavery. In 1844, in the midst of the crisis over Texas annexation, Calhoun and other southerners would proudly recall their region's role in defending the Union in 1812, complaining that "the zeal, which the South has ever evinced to defend the North . . . [would] never be reciprocated." With historic license, Calhoun argued that though the Revolution and the War of 1812 had "originated in causes much more Northern than Southern; and still more strikingly was that the case in the last war [1812] . . . the generous South, ever devoted to the liberty and honor of the country, and true to its engagements, poured out freely her means, in blood and money, for the common cause, without asking whether she was to be the gainer or loser."[146] Ironies abound. Many, perhaps most, merchants had never asked for the harmful form this "generosity" took. Indeed for many northern Federalists and a growing number of northern Republicans, the conduct of slaveholding Jeffersonians in the War of 1812 period had exacerbated antisouthern feeling and may have heightened their attacks against slavery, though politically the issue had remained secondary to commercial and foreign policy issues.[147] In sum, the perceived compromises made by southern nationalists in the earlier period helped heighten southern sectionalism after economic and geopolitical circumstances, most importantly the growth of abolition and protariff movements in the North, forced the South to conceive of itself as a minority. National victory in the early Republican era proved a Trojan horse for more section-minded southerners of a later age. Compromising southern nationalists ushered in a capacious understanding of national economic interest in order to win and maintain Republican prominence nationally. The South's battle against national protection for manufacturers proved especially contentious precisely because southerners had already fought—and some believed won—an international battle to protect the nation's commercial rights and free trade.

# CHAPTER THREE

# Protecting Slavery and Free Trade

## The Political Economy of Cotton, 1818–1833

In the midst of attacks against slavery in 1856, South Carolina historian and commentator Louisa McCord exclaimed that though "men and prejudices have gone against us . . . the noble science, not perhaps too justly named Political Economy will and must be our judge." McCord's confidence that political economy would justify the Slave South has seemed unfathomable to subsequent scholars who see slavery as both unjustifiable and economically backward. Such a verdict remained far less clear in the mid-nineteenth century, especially in a region rapidly becoming the chief supplier for the world's most profitable business. Many, perhaps most, commentators in the Deep South shared McCord's faith in the "science whose object is the weal[th] of nations."[1] Though Cotton State planters and politicians were certainly not the first or only to embrace political economy, and particularly laissez-faire axioms, few in the western world repeated them as often as they did. Their rhetoric emerged in 1819–1820 out of a direct and pragmatic response to "restrictionist" policies against the movement of labor, capital, and trade. The conviction that followed drew inspiration from changing international circumstances and growing trends in Atlantic intellectual circles, as war-weary

Europeans and many Americans turned away from bloody battlefields and toward the creation of a more peaceful and profitable global system.

The "modern discipline *par excellence*" provided children of the Enlightenment something that the subjective vagaries of moral philosophy, romanticism, and theology could not: supposedly objective laws that explained individual and collective action.[2] Few politicians understood the intricate arguments of Adam Smith, Jean-Baptiste Say, or David Ricardo, but as casual readers they freely quoted simplified versions to garner support for their positions. Most believers shared a commitment to Adam Smith's understanding of political economy, defined by him as "a branch of the science of a statesman or legislator" intended "to enrich both the people and the sovereign."[3] Groups within the United States could not agree, however, on what precisely that meant. Adjusting to peace in Europe and the new opportunities presented by successful revolutions in Latin America proved exceedingly divisive for U.S. citizens, who disagreed over the past's meaning and the future's direction. The fierce debates over the subject elevated the apparent divergence of economic interests and even raised the specter of disunion.

Political histories of this era have tended to relegate the tariff debate to mere background for the purportedly more important stories, seen by some as the crisis over slavery sparked by the Missouri controversy, and by others as the looming bank war and capitalism's final triumph over democratic agrarians.[4] This deemphasis, especially when coupled with a lack of awareness of international political economy, has led many histories to see cries against active protection—particularly from South Carolinians—as insincere or part of a shadow war against forces threatening slavery. Slavery and laissez-faire ideals were, of course, enmeshed but in more subtle, complicated, and less all-consuming ways than have been previously suggested. Cotton South opponents of protection predicated their position on the assumption that (barring a cataclysmic event) slavery and the commercial agrarianism it supported would and should remain a permanent fixture in their locales. They also saw freer trade as necessary for slavery's continued profitability, and thus some perceived protection as an indirect effort to undermine slavery. Protecting slavery and foreign commerce led most cotton planters, merchants, and politicians to seek a passive national economic policy, even as they continued to expand local estate regulations deemed necessary to safeguard slavery.[5]

Nor were many troubled by the theoretical contradiction between free trade arguments for the unrestricted flow of labor and capital and the system of slavery they sought to perpetuate. When forced to pragmatically confront the potential challenge that freer trade presented to slavery—in the form of free black sailors involved in trade—local and state officials compromised but did not discard their intellectual commitment to free trade. Instead, they racialized it, contending that classical economic theory applied only to whites and not to allegedly lazy slaves or incendiary black Jacobins. Sporadically enforced "Negro Seaman's Acts" sought to preserve slavery by curtailing the number of free blacks entering into port while still allowing "safe" commerce to enter. Though further flattening white understandings of African Americans, these racist arguments and laws enabled politicians to continue to embrace modern macroeconomic principles. Few northern politicians recognized the contradiction; fewer still wanted to point them out. For the vast majority of political combatants, then, the tariff debates represented a high-stakes disagreement over divergent understandings of national political economy.

The protracted struggle between free traders and protectionists dominated national politics from 1820 to 1833. The battles took place in local assemblies, on the floors and in the halls of Congress, in Washington parlors, and on the pages of an ever-proliferating number of local, regional, and national newspapers. Neither a defunct national Federalist Party nor a splintered Jeffersonian Republican one could temper zeal or compel easy compromises. Unharnessed from cross-regional partisanship, localist and at times sectionalized political perspectives burst forth, providing a highly charged discourse that informed regional collective identity and challenged individuals' faith in Madisonian pluralism. Understanding these ferocious tariff debates requires appreciating not only local and state-level dynamics but also national and international developments that informed thought and action. Uncovering the precise rationale for antiprotectionist arguments reveals much about the evolution of regional self-perception in the Cotton South and helps explain political events that very nearly fractured the Union.

## Panic and Protection

The return of peace in Europe and the North Atlantic renewed a vibrant cotton trade but under altered global conditions. The failure of Napoleon's Continental System again allowed British manufacturers relatively unimpeded access to the European continent. British merchants extended their commercial trade in Southeast Asia, where they began exporting cheap machine-spun cotton in 1817, and in China, where they compensated for an unfavorable balance of trade by unloading cheap cotton cloth. European conflict also had helped foster Latin American freedom, with potential benefits for other nations. Black Haitians had finally secured their independence from France in 1804 and insurgents from the Rio de la Plata region in the south to New Spain similarly sought to liberate themselves from the weakened Spanish Empire. Despite an official alliance with Spain, British merchants long familiar with the region provided arms to many. Peace at the Congress of Vienna freed Britain from specific commitments to the Spanish crown, further increasing trade to the region. By the mid-1820s trade to South America amounted to £5 million, or 13 percent of all British exports. Over half of that amount came in the form of cotton textiles.[6]

As the engines of Britain's industrial machines roared back to full capacity, Lower South planters capitalized on soaring prices. In Charleston average Sea Island prices rose from wartime lows under 20 cents per pound in 1812–1813 to century highs of well over 40 cents after 1815. More numerous growers of upland cotton also profited greatly from open trade. Liverpool shortages drove short-staple prices to around 20 pence between 1815 and 1818. In the bustling new place of interchange, New York, upland cotton prices peaked at nearly 30 cents in 1816 before dropping to the still highly lucrative price of 24 cents in 1818. Charleston's prices remained comparable, rising from around 17 cents in April 1815 to between 26 and 35 from the following winter through 1818.[7]

This profitability occurred despite increased competition from a rapidly expanding cotton belt. Crippling blows to Indians during the war opened new lands in Alabama and Mississippi, which by 1820 accounted for one-half of the United States' total raw cotton supply. Cheap federal lands and high cotton prices brought new prospectors hoping to find their fortune in cotton. After buying federal lands in Huntsville, Alabama, "which ten years ago belonged to the Cherokee," young Virginian John Campbell declared his amazement that the region's "wealth exceeds anything I have ever heard of."[8] Along the Mississippi Delta, cotton planters benefited from New Orleans markets that fetched nearly 30 cents a pound in 1817.[9] Large federal land sales in the Southwest led real estate prices to rise, fueling increased speculation. Farmers and planters alike took out loans to purchase lands they believed could be transformed into windfalls for themselves and their progeny.[10]

The forcing of slaves back onto old and newly cleared cotton lands netted copious amounts of coveted fibers. Total raw cotton exports rose from 17.8 million pounds in 1814 to nearly 83 million in 1815 to a new high of almost 92.5 million pounds in 1818. Lowcountry Sea Island cotton growers especially benefited, as exports jumped from 2.5 million pounds in 1814 to 8.4 million in 1815 to a record high of 9.9 million the following year.[11] In short, the resumption of Anglo-American trade and control of the necessary labor enabled southeastern cotton planters to finally cash in on the long-anticipated rewards after a decade of suffering.

Benefits from renewed international trade, especially in cotton, extended to northern businesses, too, further accelerating that region's economic growth and broadening national financial and commercial networks. Northeastern merchants, bolstered by the de facto monopoly of the coastal trade they achieved during commercial and military warfare and the de jure one granted by the 1817 Navigation Act, captured an even larger portion of the cotton business. This, along with other acts designed to retaliate against continued British restrictions on the West Indian trade, reduced the tonnage of British ships entering the United States from 174,935 in 1817 to 36,333 in 1819.[12]

The demands of people moving inland and goods heading to ports wove together new domestic and international financial networks and launched a banking boom. New York City, in particular, consolidated its position as the chief northern financial city and port of exchange for European goods and American raw materials, especially southern cotton. Success led investors, who previously traded stocks on the curbs of Wall Street, to rent indoor space and create a formal association, the New York Stock Exchange, which opened its doors in March 1817. The following January, the city's booming Atlantic trade created enough demand to inaugurate the first regular packet lines between Liverpool and the United States.[13]

While the economies of the Lower South and northern commercial centers recovered and expanded, other sectors and localities struggled mightily. By 1818 western and Mid-Atlantic grain farmers faced a particularly uncertain future. Demilitarization at home and abroad, good crops in Europe, and British Corn Laws designed to protect English farmers diminished overseas demand for American wheat and flour. Their combined export value dropped from nearly $18 million in 1817 to just under $12 million the following year.[14] Depressed tobacco prices also hindered postwar recovery in the Upper South, leading thousands like Campbell to bring their families and slaves to the fertile cotton fields of the Southwest.[15] Participants in the West Indian reexport trade continued to suffer. Despite being a partial cause of the war and a major goal of Secretary of State John Quincy Adams's postwar diplomacy, the West Indian reexport trade declined in economic and political significance after 1817.[16] The development removed residential support for that business from the once-significant ports of Charleston and Savannah.

Northern manufacturers, especially newly established Mid-Atlantic mill owners, remained most vulnerable to the resumption of Atlantic trade. They had benefited tremendously from the war, even gaining enough political support to retain protective tariff levels in 1816. Afterward, however, British cloth, iron, and other supplies flooded American ports with generally higher-quality goods at significantly lower prices. Under these conditions, many American textile producers simply could not compete, especially with the moderately protective levels scheduled to vanish altogether by 1820.[17] Though imports dropped in 1817 and 1818, American manufacturers' economic prospects continued to worsen, making it arrestingly clear that without further protection many businesses would soon be bankrupt.

A nationwide panic in 1819 accelerated their and many others' demise as the postwar economic boom enjoyed by some gave way to a bust experienced by all. Contemporaries reached little consensus over what or who bore primary responsibility, but its effects were clear. Insolvency, foreclosures, and massive unemployment affected nearly every region of the country. Urban areas experienced concentrated misery, but rural residents also felt severe dislocation. The bottom dropped out of American commodities, bringing wheat markets to new lows. A contraction in Britain's textile industry led to a rapid decline in raw cotton prices, with New Orleans upland cotton dropping from 23.5 cents per pound in December 1818 to 14.5 cents in January 1819. Two months later Charleston prices experienced a similar decline. As one Mobile newspaperman noted, "The flattering hopes of the planter in obtaining the high prices for his cotton, to which he has been accustomed, will not soon again be realized."[18]

Politicians had few tools with which to respond and forged even less consensus over how to react. Many in the cotton belt shared the aforementioned Alabama editor's assessment that "the market is glutted" due to overproduction at home and the "nearly equal" combined supply from "a formidable rivalry" with South America, the East Indies, and the West Indies planters. This semifatalistic commentator could only advise his readers to "go on with zeal, in the full assurance that although they may not receive the highest prices for their crops, yet their labors will be handsomely rewarded."[19] New Englanders and other easterners less affected by bank failures also chose passivity, simply scolding the rest of the nation for irresponsible land speculation and fiscal mismanagement. Other orthodox Republicans, including many in the South and West, blamed the Second Bank, demanding greater oversight of joint private and public ventures.

Those who had struggled even before the panic, however, focused their wrath on systemic problems and demanded more proactive national measures. Mid-Atlantic manufacturers and western farmers in particular targeted the specie drain resulting from overdependence on international trade, and channeled their economic woes into a desperate cry for federal assistance. A diverse coalition of Republicans insisted that fostering a "home market" become *the* primary objective of national economic policy. Leading the call was Irish immigrant and nationally known publisher Matthew Carey, whose broadly disseminated 1819 address before the Society for the Promotion of National Industry stressed that Britain had consciously undermined American manufacturing by quickly resuming postwar trade. Carey cited a parliamentary speech by Henry Broughman suggesting that "it was well worth while [for Britain] to incur a loss upon the first exportation in order by the glut to stifle in the cradle those rising manufactures in the United States which the war had forced into existence contrary to the usual course of things."[20] In response, Carey claimed, America must fully develop its domestic market and thus protect manufacturers, merchants, and agrarians from a hostile Atlantic trading system.

Judging national wealth to be an ability to meet the collective needs of its citizenry rather than simply a sum of individual economic parts, protectionists like Carey and Baltimore's Daniel Raymond urged a more holistic approach to national political economy.[21] Redefining self-sufficiency as the true mark of economic interest, Carey declared that "the mighty question was whether we shall be really or nominally independent."[22] He worked with Pennsylvania state senator and lobbyist Condy Raguet and second-term western Pennsylvania congressman Henry Baldwin to transform words into congressional action. Using his position as chairman of the newly formed Committee on Manufactures, Baldwin maneuvered behind the scenes to garner support for a higher protective tariff. He found a staunch ally in planter and fellow National Republican Henry Clay, whose Kentucky constituency of wheat and hemp growers had also struggled before and after the panic. On March 22, 1820, Baldwin introduced a bill calling for a protective tariff that would elevate imposts to an average of 33.3 percent.[23] Carey's pen and Baldwin's lobbying transformed the mild protection that active Republican nationalists had quietly achieved in 1816 into a campaign for a full-scale "protectionist" system.

Baldwin's bill entered a sectionalized political landscape still reeling from Missouri's controversial application for admission to the Union as a slave state. The previous year Alabama had joined Mississippi in achieving statehood with little resistance. Representatives, even northern ones, widely assumed that these states' cotton economies, "pregnant with future greatness," would require not only their current enslaved inhabitants but also access to more through the domestic slave trade.[24] Congress remained less convinced about Missouri's need, and northern representatives sought to curtail slaveholding ambitions that had helped them control the executive branch and, to a great extent, national policy.[25] Arguing from a variety of political, economic, and moral grounds, antislavery restrictionists in the House pushed through acts freezing slave emigration into Missouri and requiring gradual emancipation. Senators more sympathetic to slavery's extension narrowly defeated the measure just before the end of the spring 1819 session. News of the controversy spread to the local level, drawing responses ranging from anger to indifference. Returning home during the 1819 recess, South Carolina representative Charles Pinckney remained shocked that in Charleston, "scarcely a word was said of the Missouri question; no man there ever supposed that one of such magnitude was before you." Though Lower South representatives fiercely opposed any antislavery measures, the possibility that restriction might channel a larger and cheaper supply of surplus slaves to the Southwest perhaps blunted the people's response.[26]

While the public remained largely focused on the deepening effects of the panic, when the Sixteenth Congress convened in December, Missouri retook its place atop the agenda, and fiery emotions burst forth. Southern extremists threatened disunion and northern counterparts retorted that "it would have been happier for us if the Mississippi [River] had been an eternal torrent of burning lava."[27] Henry Clay privately predicted the dissolution of the Union within five years, and Secretary of War John C. Calhoun purportedly told Secretary of State John Quincy Adams that an independent South would be forced "to form an alliance, offensive and defensive, with Great Britain."[28] The fiery emotions swirling around the Missouri debate horrified the shrinking number of living "Founders." Jefferson believed them a "firebell in the night." Madison yearned for a tariff fight that would "divide the nation in so checkered a manner as is usual."[29] In the end, however, a convergence of factors, including economic interest, provided the context for the critical compromise that paved the way for Missouri's entrance as a slave state but precluded the extension of slavery in the remainder territory north of the 36° 30′ parallel.

Fear of a Federalist political reemergence, Maine's looming deadline for admission to statehood, and more recently President Monroe's own influence and aspiration for reelection have adequately explained why calmer heads prevailed. But deepening economic concerns also helped push key moderates, especially from the pivotal state of Pennsylvania, to compromise on what one described as an "odious and distracting question."[30] Monroe leaned heavily on his recent appointment as bank director, Philadelphian Nicholas Biddle, to personally lobby numerous delegates toward compromise. The most public "northern men with southern principles," or "dough faces" as John Randolph negatively labeled them, remained Henry Baldwin, whose single-minded desire to see a higher tariff made him one of the South's most vocal supporters during open debate. In private Baldwin whipped up enough northern conversions, including textile factory owner Samuel Moore, to narrowly force the compromise through.[31] Shortly after Monroe signed the compromise into law, Baldwin renewed his stalled tariff measure. The subsequent debate provided some of the "checkered" political groupings that Madison hoped for but not, ultimately, the results that Baldwin had worked so hard to achieve.

Baldwin's bill, which passed the House 90 to 78 before failing by one vote in the Senate, revealed the attractiveness of a domestic-centered economy for a wide swath of Americans. The center for support remained those sectors and localities that had experienced the toughest transition to peace. Mid-Atlantic states that had embarked on manufacturing, New York, Pennsylvania, New Jersey, and Delaware, recognized the desirability of protecting their struggling infant mills. Wheat farmers there, and in the western states of Ohio, Illinois, and Indiana, frustrated over Corn Laws banning their entrance into British markets, also found the idea of a stronger home market appealing. Senators and representatives from these seven states favored the bill 74 to 3.[32]

Even some planters in the Slave South believed Baldwin's bill potentially beneficial. Kentucky slaveholder and hemp producer Henry Clay proved to be one of the most fervent protectionists, arguing that a larger domestic manufacturing base would stimulate and liberate U.S. agriculture: "For the sake of the surplus of the produce of our agricultural labor, all eyes are constantly turned upon the markets of Liverpool . . . in the interior of the country there exists a perfect paralysis. Encourage fabrication at home, and there would instantly arise animation and a healthful circulation throughout all parts of the Republic."[33] Significant, though not dominant, constituencies in Maryland, Kentucky, and Tennessee agreed, as did many Louisiana sugar planters, who desperately needed protection from resurrected Caribbean sugar plantations.

Pragmatic economic concerns likely dictated these groups' support for a protective tariff, but the bill's advocates also believed they offered a desirable recalibration of the nation's political economy that would further bind the Republic's primary interests together. The first Republican economic federation had joined agricultural and commercial sectors within Atlantic commerce. A new economic union, assisted by legislated protection, would turn inward to facilitate a more vibrant trade between American farmers and planters in the countryside and manufacturers and workers living in towns and cities. A more economically balanced, self-sufficient, and politically unified national polity would result. Protectionists persuasively demonstrated that patriotism, self-preservation, and humanity, in addition to self-interest, necessitated protective tariffs.

Their arguments consciously harkened back to earlier Jeffersonian Republican measures but opportunistically recast the meaning of Madison and Jefferson's tariff proposals and navigation acts. Commercial warfare during those men's administrations, tariff supporters argued, had been aimed not only at retaliation or opening new foreign markets but also at increasing American self-sufficiency. Jefferson himself had, they noted, argued for discriminatory duties and famously instructed Benjamin Austin in 1816 that "we must put the manufacturer by the side of the agriculturist."[34] The origins and ends of American protectionism were predominantly domestic, but Atlantic developments also informed them. In addition to eyeing the British Corn Laws with chagrin, others like Clay hoped that the apparent dissolution of the Spanish Empire might create a hemispheric "American System" that would make the United States the political big brother and economic provider for the infant republics of the lower hemisphere.[35]

Despite a broad and diverse coalition supporting it, Baldwin's bill also inspired strong animosity. Opinion in New England—tied to both international commerce and domestic manufacturing—remained split with Federalist-minded journals and newspapers, including the *North American Review*, actively resisting what many saw as a return to mercantilist policies. With rare exceptions, agrarians and merchants in the Republican-dominated tobacco regions vehemently opposed the measure. All representatives from the older Cotton States of South Carolina and Georgia and the newer ones of Alabama and Mississippi opposed it. Arguments ranged from accusations of manufacturers' mismanagement to Treasury Department concerns that a prohibitive duty would create a revenue shortfall and necessitate reinstating internal taxation, a much-despised wartime necessity that Republicans had abandoned in 1817. The most extensive critique, however, focused on micro- and macroeconomic concerns and was presented by

William Lowndes, ironically a chief author of the 1816 tariff.[36] His analysis, along with the many others that followed, demonstrates the range of concerns tariff opponents had. They pointedly contradicted the claim that antiprotectionists "feared the *revenues*" generated by tariffs more than their "*expense.*"[37]

Like most early antiprotection arguments, Lowndes's response originated in interest not in abstract theory or a special animus for manufacturing. "Leaving . . . his Virginia friends" to sort out the theoretical and constitutional implications of protection, he outlined the practical cost of higher protection for nonprotected industries: "You say that it is important to encourage the manufacture of cotton. Be it so. We know that, however it be disguised, this can only be done at the expense of other classes of society. Is it not proper to inquire what expense is necessary; what would be adequate?"[38] His answer was emphatic: especially during widespread economic troubles, protective tariffs would inefficiently distribute America's limited capital and labor and prove politically self-defeating. By "directing the largest amounts of these into branches which require most encouragement, we really divert them from those into which they would flow with most advantage. Thus every branch of industry which is entirely safe from foreign competition . . . must be injured by the encouragement of those which draw from them their resources of capital and labor."[39] "How perfectly illusory all duties upon importation must prove for the protection of our agricultural industry," he concluded, because the supply of wheat, cotton, and tobacco would always exceed domestic demand.[40] Furthermore, American farmers and planters, themselves struggling from the panic, could no longer afford to supplement northern industrialists and workers.[41] A disproportionately burdensome tariff, Lowndes concluded, would not create a beneficial home market or a stronger union but political strife and a fierce struggle between the various interests within the Union for a limited stock of human and financial capital.[42]

Rather then redistributing wealth to experimental or infant industries, Lowndes concluded, Americans should continue pursuing their natural comparative advantage in growing and selling agricultural products for Atlantic markets and producing manufacturing goods safe from foreign competition. The panic, they argued, had been part of a natural cycle, a temporary and necessary adjustment from the wartime bust and postwar boom. It would provide its own natural remedy for manufacturers' woes. Severe drops in the cost of labor and raw materials would enable healthy manufacturers to survive under current tariff levels without additional harm to the nation's agricultural majority.[43] Federalists, former Federalists, and Republicans from the South and northern commercial areas, especially in New York City and New England, voiced similar concerns and shared the same fearful picture of the means and effects of Clay and Mid-Atlantic protectionists' plans.

To these arguments, antiprotectionist Republicans added a unique partisan bent. Higher tariffs negated rather than fulfilled earlier sacrifices on behalf of "free trade and sailors rights" and violated the very ideals around which the Jeffersonian coalition had formed. Interest and history, they argued, demanded broadening, not restricting, international trade. Shed of the Anglophobic prewar mercantilism central to Jeffersonian Republican calculations, southern agrarians in the cotton belt gravitated toward an unabashed commitment to free trade, even with the nation's former adversary. Not numerous enough to prevail in the House, "free trade" Republicans nevertheless found just enough Senate votes to torpedo Baldwin's bill and temporarily forestall protectionist efforts. The spring 1820 debate reflected the incongruity of local interests within the Republican Party more than the spirit of compromise and collaboration that eventually prevailed during the Missouri controversies. Much to Baldwin and Clay's ire, procedural maneuvering by opponents and the Monroe administration's unwillingness to push the issue prevented even serious discussion for the next four years.

Tariffs never inspired the same emotion or horrific images that slave-related debates did. Yet unlike many of those debates, the tariff promised immediate and likely unequal effects on the nation's diverse interests. It involved government revenue and thus quickly became entangled with other major domestic policy questions, including public land sales and the funding of internal improvements. As with all commercial measures, the protracted tariff battles started in 1820 forced close analysis of international trade and thus foreign policy. Because the stakes—both short- and long-term—were so high, compromise proved elusive. While it took two years to settle the debate over Missouri, it took over twelve years and more fully developed threats of violence to reach a compromise over tariff policy. This was largely because the tariff debates became economically, politically, and even legally intertwined with the issue of slavery. Nevertheless, to let the Missouri Compromise and subsequent debates overshadow the semi-independent questions raised by the battle between protection and free trade misleads more than it illuminates. Only by probing the specific logic of the Cotton South's embrace of free trade theory and practice can regional thought and the politics of the Jacksonian period be properly understood.

## Cotton and a Harmonious Domestic and International Division of Labor

In early December 1820, fearing that a protective tariff would "again be presented to the consideration of Congress," a large Charleston gathering of free traders met to send a message.[44] In a petition drafted by Stephen Elliot, a noted botanist and the first president of the Charleston Literary and Philosophical Society, and Robert Hayne, the state's ambitious young attorney general and future U.S. senator, the Charleston group rooted arguments against protection in local interests masked as "natural principles."[45] When Henry Clay proposed raising tariff levels to an average of 33 percent in 1824, petitioners throughout the country again mobilized. Diverse rural and urban communities in the Lower South and congressmen from the lowcountry to the Mississippi River drew inspiration from Hayne and Elliot's petition. Together these counteroffensives integrated pragmatic concerns, appeals to natural law, and a Jeffersonian-derived sense of political justice into a well-developed free trade attack on the American System.[46]

Elliot and Hayne wove together common assumptions about climate, racial slavery, and demography, drawing the conclusion that the Cotton South, and indeed the entire nation, would long remain an agricultural power. The vast and rich fields of the South, combined with its hot climate, ensured that the deficiency in white labor necessary for manufacturing would not be "soon if ever supplied." Destined to "continue to raise provisions, articles of the first necessity for man in every climate," the 1820 memorialists contended that the South had a "peculiar interest" to see "that our interchange with the world should be free; that the markets for the consumption of our produce should be extended as widely as the habitation of man." Consequently, "to force . . . to the loom and workshop much of the labor and capital which are now employed in agriculture and commerce" would be "unpropitious" and premature. In a country as naturally well endowed and sparsely populated as the United States, they declared with no apparent sense of irony, it was "self-evident" that "labor and capital should be permitted to seek and find their own employment."[47]

The Charleston memorialists framed their argument, keenly aware of changing international developments and protection's "possible (we may say probable) effects . . . on the great staple of our country." Restricted access during the war and high demand afterward had forced Britain to drop all discriminatory duties on U.S. raw cotton importations, meaning "our cotton is now admitted into Great Britain on terms as liberal as the cotton of any foreign nation." "Let us not flatter ourselves," the petitioners warned, "that the statesmen of Europe will permit a system of restrictions to be partial in its operations." If "this trade in the future shall be beneficial only to ourselves, she may on her part, prohibit totally the introduction into her ports of our cotton, our rice, our tobacco and turn to . . . Brazil and the East Indies [which] can even now furnish her with these articles." In addition, "the new Governments, too, arising in South America, possess an immense extent of territory adapted to the production of cotton, and tobacco, and flour, and rice." "On all sides," southern planters "shall meet competitors in the consuming markets ready to avail themselves of our errors and profit by our mistakes; ready to occupy any position which we may abandon, or from which we may be driven." Britain would find such a trade even more desirable because unlike a protected, northern-dominated Anglo-American trade, "her general intercourse with these countries" would be free and open and "exclusively in her own vessels, and her ship owners and her seamen would equally profit by this direction of her commerce."[48]

The recent memory of restricted international trade and cotton's earlier failure as a coercive tool led inland cotton planters to also envision protection as a new and, in the long run, even more damaging form of commercial warfare. "We fear," a Darlington, South Carolina, assembly claimed in 1824, that the tariff "will moreover, produce a re-action on the part of Great Britain, if not all Europe, which will bear on our interest alone."[49] Petitioners from Beaufort to Putnam County, Georgia, "viewed in dismay a state of things which makes it the interest of foreign manufacturers to *encourage* the growth of that article elsewhere; and, *as soon as sufficient supplies can be had from other places, to exclude ours altogether.*"[50] Great Britain consented to relative free trade in cotton, the Charleston memorialists argued, because "to her the general commerce of the United States is highly important and because our consumption of her manufactures offers an equivalent for the advantages we now enjoy."[51] For American cotton planters to stay ahead of the competition, the United States, they believed, must complete the cycle of international trade by purchasing finished goods, especially textiles, from Britain.

In addition to these potential threats, protective tariffs promised to have an immediate and disproportionately negative impact on southern agriculturists, who saw it as extending northern groups' "monopolistic" tendencies already aided by the nation's new navigation laws. Drawing upon well-rehearsed Jeffersonian rhetoric, petitioners from the Cotton South lamented protection's allegedly "unequal" and thus "unjust" effects. The citizens of Madison, Georgia, saw in the "deceptive and false" tariff a "policy of trammeling the great interests of commerce and agriculture . . . for the purposes of virtually encouraging a monopoly, they consider as unsound and fraught with consequences the most destructive and dangerous to the union of this republic."[52] Darlington, South Carolina, residents agreed, believing the tariff reported out of committee in 1824 "will be most ruinous to their interests" and "its operation, on this part of the Union, and on the agriculturists in particular, will be, not only burthensome and oppressive but entirely ruinous."[53] A Darien, Georgia, petition concurred with traditional Republican rhetoric, proposing that the tariff's effects "would be partial, and grievous in this operation, by the sacrifice of the interest of the largest portion of the citizens of these states, to a smaller portion."[54]

Critics rejected the belief that a more vibrant home market would aid cotton planters, noting as Mississippi representative Christopher Rankin did, that domestic manufacturers could not possibly consume the approximately 420,000 bales of cotton sold to Great Britain. The fact that between 1816 and 1824 planters exported between two-thirds and three-fourths of their cotton crop led Ranklin— a Pennsylvanian-born representative from Natchez, Mississippi—to conclude that "the idea of a home market for either our produce or manufactures to any considerable extent, is most fallacious" had "no foundation in reason or truth, but is calculated to delude and deceive the people." In fact, the very expansive supply of cotton cultivation required that planters from the Southeast and Southwest unite against high tariffs. Especially following recent relief from British taxes, cotton growers found little appeal in a more independent home market, particularly one in which they would have to pay higher prices for finished goods, including cheap textiles necessary for clothing their slaves.[55]

Lower South planters and politicians also emphatically rejected the claim that a viable export trade to South America would soften the blow of possibly reduced trade to Europe. The idea may have benefited some sectors, but it seemed absurd to cotton growers. If northern textile manufactures needed protection of 30 to 50 percent to subsist in domestic markets, where they had the advantage of lower transportation costs and domestic supplies, how could they possibly compete in unprotected foreign markets? No new consumers of cotton would be found, as South Americans had extremely limited industrial capacity and many were already being clothed in American cotton spun in British mills. Protective tariffs, they concluded, would only stymie efforts to cement commercial ties with South America by creating unnecessary artificial barriers.

Though largely driven by local interests, opposition to protection, in the Cotton South at least, did *not* reflect a provincial worldview or a turn away from modern economic thought. On the contrary, commentators in the Cotton South knew that their livelihoods depended on the mechanical process of turning raw cotton into finished cloth. Professor Thomas Cooper, the Lower South's preeminent political economist of the 1820s, understood that process well. The London-born Cooper, a self-taught chemist, had developed a bleaching technique for calico fabric and worked for James Watt's textile mills before a temporary downturn in 1793 caused the firm to go bankrupt. Financial trouble and his own increasingly radical political views (expressed through his sympathy with French Jacobins) led him to immigrate to the United States. Continued French sympathies led to an arrest under the Alien and Sedition Acts, and his unorthodox religious beliefs deprived him of a position at Thomas Jefferson's university in Charlottesville.

Cooper found a more hospitable welcome at South Carolina College in Columbia, where he trained dozens of future politicians on the subject of political economy. His personal experience and firsthand knowledge of mill-town poverty led him to the older Jeffersonian conclusion that agricultural pursuits were morally superior, healthier, and fostered more independence than manufacturing ones. As a believer in utilitarianism (his father-in-law Joseph Priestley was its ostensible founder) and a "proponent of modernity," though, Cooper recognized that manufacturing advanced individual and national wealth, created jobs, and stimulated agriculture. Neither he, nor his occasional adversary Jacob Cardozo, granted agriculture or commerce any intrinsic economic superiority over manufacturing.[56] Instead, the problem, as Lowndes had framed it earlier, was one of means not ends. Manufacturing was a worthwhile pursuit, but employing protective tariffs, as the Darien petitioners noted, was "nothing more or less than making a partial good, an universal evil."[57] Similarly, the Georgia state legislature conceded that "no *arts* can be more *useful* than agriculture and manufactures," before concluding that protective tariffs violated equal protection, "the fundamental principle" of the Constitution.[58]

Conceptually these and ensuing laissez-faire arguments were rooted in libertarian and Enlightenment ideas about human action and natural law. David Hume's notion that unharnessed individual impulses could serve largely beneficial societal ends translated quite well into a Smithian justification for a commercialized society where individuals acted on their own interests and created the most efficient and balanced economy. A Virginia ally, Philip P. Barbour, summarized the essential argument: "An instinct [is] implanted in man, the master-spring of his actions, which through life, impels him to a perpetual endeavour to better his condition" and "increase his portion of wealth."[59] Consequently, as South Carolina's James Hamilton Jr. noted, "labor and capital, if left to their own direction, will always seek, and find, their most prosperous investment." It was therefore sufficient to confide in "the sagacity of individuals who, by a law of nature, invariably in its operation, will pursue that department of industry which promises to yield either immediately or ultimately the greatest profit."[60] Rejecting the protectionists' understanding of a national economy, they and most free traders contended that the "national [wealth] is but the aggregate of individual wealth."[61]

This particularly optimistic understanding of nature's direction derived from the belief that America's extensive and fertile lands—furthered by the acquisitions of Louisiana in 1803 and Florida in 1819—promised long-term "natural" protection from the Old World problems that European political economists identified. In the dire projections of Thomas Malthus and others, natural labor distributions ended in doomsday prophecies of overpopulation and a fierce battle for scarce supplies. Southern free traders, buoyed by slavery, accepted these conditions insofar as they applied to Europe (sometimes blaming protection for creating them), but in the view of political economists such as Cardozo, the "agency of Nature concurrently with the labour and ingenuity of Man" connoted positive blessings rather than devolution into economic and social chaos. Southerners thus laid claim to liberal economic principles against a "restrictive system," enabling them to argue—and even earnestly believe—that despite their commitment to slavery, or perhaps even because of it, they were the true disciples of "liberal" economic thought and free action. In short, they proposed that they were the protectors of the nineteenth-century (white) American dream.[62]

Slaves who heard or read such arguments while daily facing police regulations limiting their movement must have found them surreal and dizzyingly hypocritical. The Cotton South's "liberal" free trade vision, unlike that of most nineteenth-century classical economists, remained predicated on the perpetuation of slavery, a fact made pointedly clear when in one breath South Carolina governor Stephen Miller decried protection for "sapping the foundation of the honest labor and constitutional rights of other sections" and in the next launched into a defense of slavery as "not a national evil . . . but a national benefit."[63] From the 1820 Charleston petitioners to the northern-born Ranklin, slaveholders who supported free trade unblinkingly claimed that *their* "labor and industry" were being "sacrificed to promote those of the manufacturers."[64] Several factors helped mitigate the now apparent contradiction. The continued presence of slavery throughout European empires and the relative meagerness of political abolitionism in the United States did not, for the time at least, make slavery in the United States particularly exceptional. For those few seeking logical consistency, evolving Enlightenment understandings about race and climate provided new theories that eased the transition by racializing the economic world. Perhaps most importantly, though, protectionists were not inclined to alienate potential supporters by interjecting slavery into the debate.

While some, like Henry Clay and Louisiana sugar planters, believed slavery and protection compatible, slavery and the Lower South's devotion to laissez-faire policies generally reinforced one another. The Charleston 1820 free trade memorial assumed that a shortage of white workers and reliance on African slaves, attributable to a semitropical climate, would keep the region committed to commercial agrarianism and away from manufacturers, at least for the foreseeable future.[65] Slaveholders also feared, accurately if modern economists are to be believed, that declining raw cotton prices and greater expenses resulting from high tariffs on so-called Negro Cloth would directly hurt their profit margins.[66] Over the long haul, redistributive policies threatened to make slavery unprofitable, leading Governor Miller to conclude that the "unparalleled . . . history of legislation" was an effort to "either directly *or indirectly* deprive us of the use of them."[67] In the aftermath of Denmark Vesey's failed 1822 conspiracy, slaveholders feared that further economic trouble might destabilize already fragile slave-master relationships.

The very decisions that South Carolina's legislators made after Vesey's trial, however, revealed an inescapable challenge presented by free commerce in a slave society. Believing that Vesey's West Indian origins and long career at sea had inspired his alleged plot, the state legislature quickly enacted a law requiring the imprisonment of any free black sailors who arrived in port. When confronted with a pragmatic problem that pitted free trade against self-preservation, state officials initially chose to keep the law at their disposal but not enforce it. When a "Charleston Association" composed of ambitious lowcountrymen pressed the matter, semiprivate enforcement of this "Negro Seaman's Act" inaugurated legal challenges that brought southern slaveholders into direct conflict with ship captains who relied heavily on black sailors. American vessel owners claimed that imprisonment (and the required payment of fines) violated the federal Constitution's equal protection and commerce clauses. Representatives of British victims claimed it infringed upon the 1815 and 1818 Commercial Conventions, which guaranteed them free access to American ports.[68]

South Carolinians defended the act as a "mere police regulation" reserved to their state under the Constitution and Bill of Rights. The argument failed to convince Supreme Court justice William Johnson, who while on circuit in 1823 heard an appeal of a Jamaican-born sailor arrested under the act, Henry Elkison. The native Charlestonian ruled in *Elkison v. Deliesseline,* that the law infringed upon Congress's paramount right to negotiate treaties and regulate commerce, a position also affirmed by Attorney General William Wirt. The ruling forced state officials and the local press into a frenzied defense of the law, and the state legislature reaffirmed it with only moderate alterations to avoid conflict with free blacks on board armed naval vessels.[69] Eventually, however, the federal government's and, after several decades, the international, response proved more pliable than initial reactions indicated. Though Johnson brilliantly defended his ruling against the law's constitutionality, even he admitted that circumstance and the limitations of the Judiciary Act of 1789 prevented him from giving Elkison relief or stopping enforcement of the act. Chief Justice John Marshall privately viewed Johnson's initial verdict as rash and unnecessary. Six months later he delicately avoided the issue when handing down the landmark *Gibbons v. Ogden,* in which he asserted congressional supremacy over interstate and international commerce but, unlike Johnson, stopped short of denying state concurrent powers.[70]

Most importantly, by the height of the nullification crisis, Jackson's first two attorney generals, Georgian John Berrien and future chief justice Roger Taney, took the position that a slightly modified act was "a necessary measure of internal police, not in conflict with the Constitution or in violation of the convention with Great Britain."[71] By Jackson's second term, the legal and political climate remained comfortable enough for Georgia and North Carolina to pass their own acts. All of the Cotton and Gulf States except Mississippi eventually followed with acts "quarantining" free black sailors from slaves. No president before the Civil War directly threatened these measures, and the few times Congress discussed them little came of it. Especially for the acts' victims, domestic and foreign, Federalism provided a Gordian knot unable to protect black rights.

Responding to Johnson's rulings and subsequent challenges, nevertheless, did shape the Lower South's political outlook, especially in South Carolina. Most obviously, the controversy elevated concern over the federal government's sensitivity toward slaveholders' needs and furthered a regional drift toward states' rights constitutionalism. In particular, Johnson's ruling, coupled with *Gibbons v. Ogden,* increased skepticism of the federal court's ability to favorably resolve questions involving the constitutionality of protective tariffs. Consequently, it intensified political efforts against legislative protection. When those proved unsuccessful, it led citizens from the Carolina coast to the Mississippi Delta to consider new constitutional remedies. The legal and ideological challenges raised by the law may have also increased the urgency of offering a more articulate and racialized proslavery argument capable of deflecting future challenges. It may not be coincidence that William Harper, who took up that task with zeal in the mid-1830s, had been the recorder for the state supreme court during early battles over the law. Protecting slavery and free trade required convincing northern whites, especially shipowners, that free blacks needed strict supervision.

The Negro Seaman's controversy continued to vex relationships between South Carolina and Britain until the late 1850s and would not find resolution with northern states like Massachusetts until repealed after the Civil War. In the meantime, these coastal slave states had to balance their earnest desire for freer commerce in goods with their perceived need to control some of those who might be tasked with loading and unloading it. This seems to have been done with strategic rather than uniform enforcement. Nevertheless, whenever domestic or internal threats to slavery arose, its apologists had to suspend their faith in laissez-faire and fall back on what Edwin Holland called "the first and great law of nature—SELF-PRESERVATION" from the South's "Jacobins."[72] The sometimes dramatic decline in the percentage of African American crewmembers on ships heading into ports covered by the acts may indicate that the Lower South's campaign for lily-white free trade had some effect.[73]

These laws' existence certainly did not mean, however, that slaveholders insincerely forwarded free trade arguments or sought to otherwise limit their commercial contact. In actuality the recognizable inconvenience created by the Negro Seaman's Acts elevated the importance of keeping duties low to avoid scaring off trade any more than absolutely necessary. In a rejection of older Jeffersonian rhetoric and occasionally policy, Cooper concluded in 1824 that "it is impossible and undesirable to render us independent of foreign nations."[74] Representative Ranklin agreed, telling his congressional colleagues that "the dependence of nations and parts of a nation on each other are marked in the varieties of soil and of climate, and in the dispositions of Providence," which taught "men and nations that they are and must be dependent on each other."[75] By embracing free trade in goods and the mutual interdependence of nations, southerners attempted to seize the moral high ground and, remarkably, even recast themselves as forward-facing ambassadors of goodwill—a position they continued to stress throughout the antebellum period.[76] While many tobacco and rice exports accepted this contention, it held the most weight with those who where enmeshed with the cotton trade and believed that the ever-expanding British Empire provided the best means of extending markets for cotton textiles.[77]

Worldwide progress of the free trade cause significantly informed the growing number of free trade ideologues within the Cotton South. They repeatedly invoked what South Carolinian James Hamilton called the "English doctrine" and sage wisdom of the "worthy old philosopher," Adam Smith.[78] Even as slaveholders nervously eyed William Wilberforce's parliamentary advances and British consuls' efforts against the vexing and inconsistent enforcement of the Negro Seaman's Act, southerners hailed the stirrings of a British free trade movement, symbolically marked by Alexander Baring's 1820 London petition protesting the Corn Laws. More concretely, however, Tory governments had begun to lower, and in some cases eliminate, tariffs on raw materials. These developments in Britain were particularly significant for Cooper, who singled out "the recent applications of the principles of Political Economy, by the enlightened Ministry of Great Britain" under the Canning, Huskisson, and Lord Liverpool administrations. His assemblage of classroom lectures, published in the influential *Lectures on the Elements of Political Economy* optimistically claimed that "the *mercantile system,* its fallacies, and its imperfections are now well understood in Great Britain."[79] Such developments and ideas circulated in lecture and printed form and informed an entire generation of amateur free trade political economists.

These changes led antiprotectionists, especially Cooper, to shed Jeffersonianism of the pragmatically inspired neomercantilism of previous decades and imbue it with a deep faith that freer commerce was transforming the international system into a peaceful one. "We now," Cooper asserted, "gain a glimpse of the dawn of a new day; and of peace on earth, and good will toward men." The principle of "cutting the throats or devastating the property of those who would be . . . customers and consumers" is being abandoned.[80] In place of jealousies of trade that had led to repeated warfare, the world stood on the brink of a more hopeful new order in which politicians recognized that "a state of mutual wants, and mutual dependence, among nations, has been appointed by God Almighty in the common order of nature."[81] Freer intercourse, in Cooper's calculations, compelled practical peace because "mutual interest is associated with mutual peace and good will."[82] Protection undermined this potential world, threatening to return the Atlantic network back into a theater of commercial and actual warfare.

This faith, especially as it related to British policy and global peace, reflected a highly selective understanding of the realities of official European commitment to free trade. Protectionists themselves repeatedly highlighted this point, occasionally referring to free traders as deluded "utopians" who rejected a patriotic "American System" for what Henry Clay called "the British Colonial System."[83] Though need for some raw materials, like cotton, had led Britain to stress interdependence and liberalize commercial legislation, restrictive measures on others, like grain imports, served as a reminder that interest rather than ideology shaped policy and hindered freer trade on both sides of the Atlantic. Indeed the British minister to the United States believed that had the Corn Laws been repealed, the 1824 tariffs would not have been supported by western farmers.[84] Despite these realities, even the ever-cynical Anglophobe, John C. Calhoun, found developments abroad encouraging enough to drop his protectionist propensities and embrace freer trade. "The more I reflect on it," he wrote Virginia senator Waller Tazewell, "the more deeply am I impressed with the belief, that at London and Paris the death blow may be given to the odious system of monopoly, which is now praying [sic] on the vitals of the community."[85] He would not say the same about northerners within the Union, who, he increasingly believed, were feasting on the profits of southern cotton.

Challenging protectionism politically, of course, required moving beyond local interest, cosmopolitan utopianism, or name-calling. It necessitated offering reasons for why freer trade benefited the nation's other interests. This led southern free traders to place cotton at the center of the national economy and to stress that a harmonious political and economic union required preserving the traditional Atlantic-centered economy they alleged had "naturally" emerged since the Founding. John C. Calhoun summarized the entire debate to Secretary of the Treasury Samuel D. Ingham in 1830, as "a struggle for the home market": "Were you to leave us free," Calhoun explained, "we would send our staples abroad, bring home foreign articles in return, and after supplying ourselves, would exchange the ballance [sic] with you for all of the products of farming, as distinguished [from] planting, and those articles of manufacture, which you would have an advantage over the foreign."[86] Because cotton exports had become the single most valuable export commodity (accounting for around 30% of the value of U.S. exports), such a claim had some basis in reality, though never as deeply as free traders contended.[87]

They did, however, assert, fairly and often, that the cotton business had created a national division of labor that benefited other sectors. The Charleston petitioners highlighted what many knew to be true, that liberal commerce in cotton assisted northeastern businesses: "In fact, this trade is now chiefly carried on in the

*Table 4*    Value of Total U.S. Exports and Cotton Exports, Average Prices

| Year | Total Exports[a] (dollars) | Cotton Exports[a] | | Average Annual Prices (cents/pound) | |
|---|---|---|---|---|---|
| | | Dollars | % of Total | Sea Island[b] | Short-Staple[c] |
| 1815 | 52,557,753 | 17,529,000 | 33 | 37.9 | 27.3 |
| 1816 | 81,920,452 | 24,106,000 | 29 | 44.8 | 25.4 |
| 1817 | 87,671,569 | 22,627,614 | 26 | 43.5 | 29.8 |
| 1818 | 93,281,133 | 31,334,258 | 34 | 63.2 | 21.5 |
| 1819 | 70,142,521 | 21,081,760 | 30 | 42.1 | 14.3 |
| 1820 | 69,692,000 | 22,308,667 | 32 | 32.8 | 15.2 |
| 1821 | 54,596,000 | 20,157,484 | 37 | 26.7 | 17.4 |
| 1822 | 61,350,000 | 24,035,058 | 39 | 24.8 | 11.5 |
| 1823 | 68,326,000 | 20,445,520 | 30 | 24.5 | 14.5 |
| 1824 | 68,972,000 | 21,947,401 | 32 | 24.6 | 17.9 |
| 1825 | 90,738,000 | 36,846,649 | 41 | 54.3 | 11.9 |
| 1826 | 72,891,000 | 25,025,214 | 34 | 32.7 | 9.3 |
| 1827 | 74,310,000 | 29,359,545 | 40 | 21.1 | 9.7 |
| 1828 | 64,021,000 | 22,487,229 | 35 | 25.6 | 9.8 |
| 1829 | 67,435,000 | 26,575,311 | 39 | 22.9 | 8.9 |
| 1830 | 71,761,000 | 29,674,883 | 41 | 24.8 | 8.4 |
| 1831 | 72,296,000 | 25,289,492 | 35 | 20 | 9 |
| 1832 | 81,521,000 | 31,724,682 | 39 | 18.2 | 10 |
| 1833 | 87,529,000 | 36,191,105 | 41 | 20.2 | 11.2 |
| 1834 | 102,260,000 | 49,448,402 | 48 | 25.1 | 15.5 |
| 1835 | 115,216,000 | 64,961,302 | 56 | 34.8 | 15.2 |
| 1836 | 124,339,000 | 71,284,925 | 57 | 39.5 | 13.3 |
| 1837 | 111,443,000 | 63,240,102 | 57 | 46 | 9 |

vessels of the United States; and by this means some of our most important man-ufactures (those connected with ship building) are encouraged, and the security and reputation of our country are increased by the seamen it nurtures and pro-tects." The rapid rise of New York's commercial life suggested that the financing and carrying of raw cotton proved extremely lucrative to northeastern bankers, merchants, and insurers involved in exporting, all of whom would be hurt by a restriction of international trade. Indeed, by the mid-1820s American carriers, mostly based in the Northeast, monopolized the foreign trade, controlling 95 percent of imports and almost 90 percent of the total export trade.[88] Northern and western agrarians were also thought to have benefited from cotton's rise to international power. The crop's profitability had converted Lower South lands to cotton cultivation, and for basic subsistence, corn. Consequently, the Deep South

| Year | Total Exports[a] (dollars) | Cotton Exports[a] | | Average Annual Prices (cents/pound) | |
|---|---|---|---|---|---|
| | | Dollars | % of Total | Sea Island[b] | Short-Staple[c] |
| 1838 | 104,979,000 | 61,556,811 | 59 | 35.3 | 12.4 |
| 1839 | 112,252,000 | 61,238,982 | 55 | 38.7 | 7.9 |
| 1840 | 123,669,000 | 63,870,307 | 52 | 22.5 | 9.1 |
| 1841 | 111,817,000 | 54,330,341 | 49 | 26.8 | 7.8 |
| 1842 | 99,878,000 | 47,593,464 | 48 | 18.1 | 5.7 |
| 1843 | 82,826,000 | 49,119,806 | 59 | 16.6 | 7.5 |
| 1844 | 105,746,000 | 54,063,501 | 51 | 18.8 | 5.5 |
| 1845 | 106,040,000 | 51,739,643 | 49 | 26.6 | 6.8 |
| 1846 | 109,583,000 | 42,767,341 | 39 | 26.6 | 9.9 |
| 1847 | 156,742,000 | 53,415,848 | 34 | 31.4 | 7 |
| 1848 | 138,191,000 | 61,998,294 | 45 | 19 | 5.8 |
| 1849 | 140,351,000 | 66,396,967 | 47 | 23.2 | 10.8 |
| 1850 | 144,376,000 | 71,984,616 | 50 | 27.8 | 11.7 |
| 1851 | 188,915,000 | 112,315,317 | 59 | 29.3 | 7.4 |
| 1852 | 166,984,000 | 87,965,732 | 53 | 37.2 | 9.1 |
| 1853 | 203,489,000 | 109,456,404 | 54 | 41.2 | 8.8 |
| 1854 | 237,044,000 | 93,596,220 | 39 | 33.4 | 8.4 |
| 1855 | 218,910,000 | 88,143,844 | 40 | 31.6 | 9.1 |
| 1856 | 281,219,000 | 128,382,351 | 46 | 39.8 | 12.4 |
| 1857 | 293,824,000 | 131,575,859 | 45 | 38.1 | 11.2 |
| 1858 | 272,011,000 | 131,386,661 | 48 | 29.3 | 11.5 |
| 1859 | 292,902,000 | 161,434,923 | 55 | 35.2 | 10.8 |
| 1860 | 333,576,000 | 191,806,555 | 58 | 47 | 11.1 |

[a]Taken from Stuart Bruchey, *Cotton and the Growth of the American Economy, 1970–1860* (New York: Harcourt, Brace & World, 1967), table 3.K.

[b]Annual Averages of Monthly Prices from Charleston, taken from ibid., table 3.Q.

[c]Weighted Annual Averages at New Orleans, taken from ibid., table 3.P.

had, free traders claimed, become heavily reliant on more northward states for wheat, flour, and livestock. While later southern political economists fretted about a lack of agricultural diversification and dependence on northern products, politicians of the Jacksonian period praised such a development as perpetuating a *natural* harmony of economic interests that fostered interregional cooperation and preserved the Union.

Protection, free trade advocates claimed, would destroy what God, nature, and the Union had provided. According to St. Luke's Parish memorialists, restricting international commerce would make "all the cities on our Atlantic coast, at present the depots of commerce, and the outlets for our agricultural products . . .

decline and languish in comparative insignificance."[89] Backcountry South Carolina representative, George McDuffie, agreed and suggested that consumers would be forced to pay twice as much for needed goods, like clothing. Cotton planters would have to curtail their purchase of western foodstuffs and northern products. If protection continued for long, McDuffie argued, planters would begin providing all of their own food supplies and even manufacture their own finished goods. Indeed after the 1828 tariff passed, McDuffie backed up his threats with action and invested (along with other prominent South Carolinians, including Calhoun's brother-in-law) in several upcountry textile manufacturers. Southern plantations, nationalists like McDuffie suggested, would devolve into their own little self-sufficient "home markets," endangering the ties of brotherhood that nature and the Constitution had created. Measures taken to establish an unrealistic American System would have the adverse effect of destroying the modest one that already existed.[90]

For multiple reasons, then, Cotton South opposition to protection should not be seen as a turn away from "imaginative agrarian nationalism to an increasingly provincial regionalism."[91] For one, free traders believed that they—and more particularly the global cotton trade they were enmeshed in—were finally bringing actual international political economy in line with Adam Smith's theories of how national wealth and international peace should be achieved.[92] The means (tariffs) and ends (self-sufficiency) of protectionism, they decried, were antiquated, even counterproductive for a rapidly globalizing world. Economic independence remained undesirable and impossible, especially for the ever-growing number of cotton planters dependent on an expanding British Empire to find new consumers for their crops and the cloth made from them. Secondly, antitariff arguments pointedly suggested that protectionists sought to fleece the wealth of the agrarian majority and redistribute it to a regionally defined minority interest.[93] Put more accurately, then, southern free traders promoted a vision of America as a dynamic commercial agrarian nation capable of exploiting the conditions of global peace and seeking to lead the world toward the ultimate triumph of free trade. By so doing they believed themselves to be adherents to the newest "science," dutifully if selectively stressing a naturally harmonious and equitable division of labor both within the nation and internationally.

Free traders embarked on these intellectual and political efforts, increasingly compelled to believe that free trade and unfree black labor were both natural and mutually reinforcing. In growing numbers they concluded that the federal government had no business meddling in international trade or

"The Monkey System or 'Everyone for Himself at the Expense of His Neighbor'"
(Philadelphia, 1831), E. W. Clay. Southern free traders and their shrinking number of
northern allies viewed the American System as creating a competition for resources
that would undermine rather than enhance national unity. Here Henry Clay wel-
comes John C. Calhoun: "Walk in! Walk in! and see the new improved grand original
American System!" A dour Daniel Webster sits turning a music box and singing,
"Hail Columbia! Happy land!" as Calhoun exclaims, "What a humbug!" In the back,
monkeys in cages labeled "home consumption" and "internal improvements" fight for
one another's food. Courtesy of the Library Company of Philadelphia.

domestic slavery. To them the argument against protection seemed increasingly
self-evident as peace with and in Europe, Anglo-American cooperation in preserving Latin American independence, and an expanding British trading empire reinforced their faith in a new era of economic cooperation with former
enemies. By the mid-1820s southerners had picked up the free trade cause with
considerable zeal and declared that their opponents were attempting to rewrite
heavenly decree. Unlike in 1820, however, in 1824 southern free trade arguments could not win enough northern senators to prevent passage of a protective tariff that raised average duties—including those on woolens and cottons—
to 33.3 percent. To politicians and the people of the Cotton South, its passage

signified a shift in national policy and a radically altered regional political calculus.

## "Unequal" Protection under the Law and Cotton's Minority Status

Cotton planters began the debates over protection as part of a national Republican majority that was controlled largely by western and southern agrarians but also included growing numbers of northern mechanics, farmers, and merchants. Even as the Jeffersonian party unraveled in the 1820s, Lower South politicians, particularly those with national commitments from the preceding decade, seized every opportunity to appeal to Republican ideals they believed might protect an agricultural and commercial free trade majority. After 1824, however, as the rest of the nation legislated and eventually increased protection, leaders in the Cotton South became increasingly aware of the incongruity of their slave-derived, internationally based cotton business with the political protectionism winning the day. Southern hemp growers and sugar planters' support for these measures and Virginians' contemplation of gradual emancipation during that state's constitutional convention exacerbated concern. Hard-fought political battles suggested an alarming reality: both nationally and within the Slave South, cotton growers and their shrinking number of allies no longer had the political clout necessary to protect their economic interests.

Economic pressures made the political argument all the more pressing. While cataclysmic predictions that Britain would stop buying southern cotton proved inaccurate, exports of raw cotton did precipitously drop from 583,000 to 505,000 bales in 1824. A steady trade resumed, but prices plummeted to less than 10 cents a pound by 1826 and remained stagnant for the rest of the decade.[94] Commentators understood that much of the problem came from saturated markets resulting from production in the newly settled Southwest. That competition heightened concern about out-migration from South Carolina and Georgia, which subsequently drove real estate down and increased political opposition to the cheap sale of federal lands. Southeastern planters, accustomed to a fairly vibrant Atlantic trade and predisposed to see protection as a rejection of earlier sacrifices, took the decline in trade especially hard. Yet far from exacerbating anger with their neighbors to the west, these realities only increased the necessity of politically uniting eastern and western planters against a protective tariff they largely blamed for declining cotton prices and continued economic woes. Unlike the

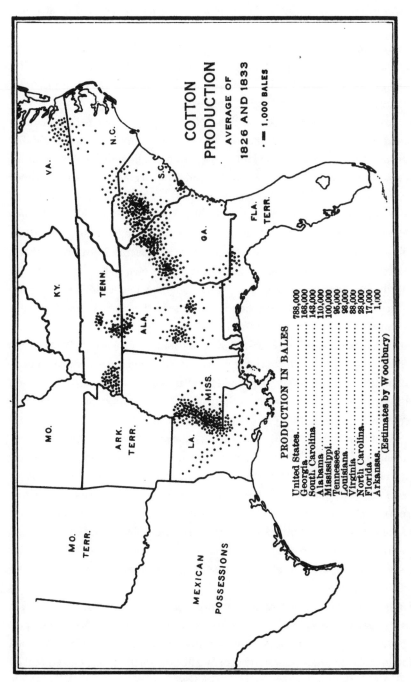

COTTON
PRODUCTION
AVERAGE OF
1826 AND 1833
= 1,000 BALES

PRODUCTION IN BALES
United States.......... 788,000
Georgia............... 168,000
South Carolina........ 143,000
Alabama.............. 110,000
Mississippi........... 100,000
Tennessee............. 95,000
Louisiana............. 98,000
Virginia.............. 88,000
North Carolina........ 28,000
Florida............... 17,000
Arkansas.............. 1,000
(Estimates by Woodbury)

Cotton production in the South between 1826 and 1833. From U.S. Department of Agriculture, *Atlas of Agriculture*, pt. 5: *The Crops of the United States*, Advance Sheets (December 15, 1915).

pre–War of 1812 period, they did so without the benefit of a united Jeffersonian party.

Instead, the passage of the 1824 tariff suggested that the original Jeffersonian party had fragmented beyond recognition. While Virginia tobacco farmers remained firmly committed to free trade and states' rights through the 1830s, other key Republican regions had warmly embraced protectionist policies. The Mid-Atlantic states of Pennsylvania, Maryland, New Jersey, and New York, previously the conduit for Jeffersonianism into the North, now led the nation toward higher tariffs that directly hurt cotton planters' pocketbooks. Equally troubling, the alliance with western states like Kentucky and Ohio seemed imperiled, as they extended their support for higher tariffs in hopes of enhancing domestic markets. John Quincy Adams's election, with very little support in the cotton belt, provided evidence of how fractured the Republican Party had become, while failing to provide much clarity to inter- or intraregional alignments. Most Cotton States supported the Jackson-Calhoun ticket; Georgia their own states' rights Republican William Crawford. Their lack of success led many to question other Republicans' commitment to the intersectional harmony they had patriotically supported during Jefferson's and Madison's presidencies.[95]

At the same time, the 1824 tariff debate left southern free trade Republicans also relying on odd bedfellows: the remnants of New England Federalism. Previous opponents of Jefferson's embargo and the War of 1812 now provided the Cotton South's strongest allies against protection, though they would respond to defeat in different ways. During the 1824 debate, southerners celebrated the "vigor" and "genius" of Daniel Webster's speeches against the protective system. James Hamilton submitted that the "unanswerable argument of that gentleman" had "scarcely left the honorable Speaker (Mr. Clay) an inch of ground to stand."[96] Applause for Webster extended outside of Congress. As late as the 1840s, at least one southern journal cited his 1820 speech at Faneuil Hall as free trade gospel.[97] As the primary advocate for northern commercial interests, Daniel Webster seemed a loyal ally in the free trade fight. So, too, was Alexander and Edward Everett's *North American Review,* which initially advocated free trade principles by publishing articles heavily critical of protection.[98]

Unlike northeastern Federalists, however, Lower South Republicans viewed defeat in 1824 as reason to move away from centralized control of economic policy, including federal funding for internal improvements. McDuffie abandoned his nationalist stance on that issue shortly after the tariff of 1824 passed and by 1825 had embraced a position he had criticized Georgians for advocating only four years earlier.[99] Mississippians and Alabamians more slowly abandoned the belief that an activist national political economy might serve their interests, continuing to seek federal support for roads. By 1827, however, even their legislatures questioned the constitutionality of such projects and expressed disdain for policies that might keep protective tariffs high.[100]

Anger aside, in 1824 free traders took comfort in the belief that the nation's agricultural and commercial majority would soon see the error of submitting its interest to a small manufacturing minority. Ranklin warned "ye tariff men" that "there is but a step between the throne and the scaffold": "When people shall have discovered that this home market is all a fallacy; that the cry for the protection of manufactures, and domestic industry . . . prostrates all the best interests of the country, and saps the foundation of its liberty, this triumph will soon end." The nation would ultimately reject the protective principle and the "beautiful fabric, erected with so much care and industry, will bury in its ruin its most zealous advocates."[101] Hopes for repeal were premised, however, on the pessimistic assumption that a high tariff would adversely affect northern commerce and agriculture. On the contrary, when corn, hemp, and wheat prices jumped in 1825 and again in 1826 farmers attributed it to the wisdom of the American System.[102] Far from retreat, protectionism continued to win new converts, even as northern manufacturers asked for higher levels to protect their still-slim profit margins.

These developments confirmed the fears of the 1820 Charleston petitioners, who had predicted that, once accepted, the principle would tie the nation to the policy: "When thousands, perhaps millions of dollars shall have been invested in manufactures, with the assurance of public support and protection, we know not how, with justice, this system could be abandoned, and the property vested under such assurance be devoted to irretrievable destruction." It was, they warned, "impossible to point out the limits at which this system will rest." With ever-greater portions of capital and labor seduced into manufacturing, the nation's wealthy and the needy alike would be dependent on its success. When the levels of support were found to be too low "the Government, even reluctantly, and with a consciousness of its errors" would be forced "into more disastrous measures—to the imposition of still higher duties."[103] This analysis seemed prophetic when, in 1827, northern wool manufacturers asked for higher protective levels for American cloth makers.

Believing the 1824 tariff insufficient and attributing their continued troubles to what Delaware mill owner Eleuterre DuPont described as "fluctuations in our home market, caused by the excessive and irregular importations," woolen manufacturers demanded that tariffs on woolen goods be raised and minimum valuation rules applied to limit the importation of cheaper-quality woolens.[104] A Woolens Bill promising levels of 50 percent passed the House in February by an eleven-vote margin but met narrow defeat in the Senate when Vice President John C. Calhoun's tie-breaking vote ensured that the measure would be tabled until Congress's next session. The pattern of the vote provided cause for concern throughout the Cotton South. Notably, arch–free trader Daniel Webster joined a majority of New England's congressional delegation in support of the measure, marking a shift in that region's views on protection. Editors and contributors of the Boston-based *North American Review* expressed support for higher tariffs, further evidence of New England's turn away from free trade. Exasperated by narrow defeat, Massachusetts representative Edward Everett told a Boston meeting that the reduction of British tariffs on raw wool gave that nation's industrialists heightened advantages within global cotton markets and made the 1824 tariff insufficient for New England woolen manufacturers. In a powerful precedent for sectionalized collective action, a hundred elected delegates from states north of North Carolina assembled in Harrisburg, Pennsylvania, in the late summer to express their grievances and insist on more congressional protection for northern manufacturers.

Free traders weighed their options and prepared for battle. In January 1827, the Alabama senate and house followed their South Carolina and Virginia counterparts in declaring that Congress had no right to distribute funds for internal improvements within states and denouncing protective tariffs as "an unconstitutional exercise of power and . . . highly oppressive and partial in its operation."[105] Senator William King decried that "every feature" of the American System was "marked with injustice and oppression."[106] In the early summer the Charleston Chamber of Commerce made it its "solemn duty" to "manfully" prepare "a series of defensive measures having in view, the clear decided and unanimous expression of the opinion of the South States" against the "united and active" efforts of New England and Mid-Atlantic manufacturers to use "the *power* of legislation exclusively for the benefit of particular portions of the country and a particular description of labor, against the *justice* of taxing the planter and the merchant for the benefit of the manufacturer."[107]

A few South Carolinians believed "justice" might demand action before unity. From Columbia, Thomas Cooper painted a bleak future for the South, famously insisting that planters "calculate the value of our union." Manufacturing is a "hydra," he submitted, "with the motto of *monopoly* and the desire to command *exclusively* every market." After considerable passiveness, "the planting interest, refusing to become the dupes have at length after a series of successful attacks upon them during the past ten years, become the victims of manufacturing monopoly." Should the trend that started in 1816 continue, Cooper argued, in a short time the "earnings of the south [would be] transferred to the north" and the "many sacrificed to the few." The American System turned out to be a most "unequal alliance" and the South would have to consider secession.[108] Not surprisingly, Cooper's perspective led him to focus on the political and economic concerns about consolidation; he said little about slavery.

The same could not be said about Florida-born and English-educated lowcountry planter Robert Turnbull, who painted an even bleaker political picture. In his view a "majority of the nation," composed of the "interests of the North and West, are diametrically opposed to the interests of the South." "Our true interest," Turnbull repeated, "is a free and uninterrupted commerce with the whole world, and particularly with England, where are the work shops of sufficient extent, to work up the raw material which we raise, and are in danger of raising in too great abundance." According to Turnbull, easterners' commitments to manufacturers and westerners' desire for federally sponsored internal improvements had created an alliance behind a loose construction of the Constitution's "general welfare" and "necessary and proper" clauses. The South, on the other hand, would neither benefit from these policies nor from the constitutional interpretations supporting them. Like the British Stamp Act of old, the tariff "ALREADY HAS RIVITED the CHAINS around the neck and the feet of Southern industry."[109]

In his lengthy diatribe, Turnbull, unlike Cooper, also highlighted concerns that the "firm *consolidated* national government" created by protectionism would take direct aim against slavery, a point made all the more real when the American Colonization Society petitioned the federal government for financial support in 1827. Support for the organization amongst Upper South officials, including that of former president James Madison and Secretary of State Henry Clay, alarmed Deep South observers even more. Clay's active involvement led some to assume that the federally funded antislavery organization would be funded by higher duties. In addition to paying higher taxes, cotton planters would be faced with higher labor costs, resulting from a restricted market as slaves were freed and sent back to Africa. Though political connections between the ACS and protection were indirect at best, some like Turnbull and Governor Miller saw them as an insensitive two-pronged attack on Deep South rights and pocketbooks. They turned toward laissez-faire arguments to urge the federal government to reject any legislation targeting or aiding a particular group. Labor, like capital, should be allowed to flow naturally wherever it was needed. Barring a change of sentiments in Washington, Turnbull concluded that extraconstitutional actions must be used to resist the powerful hand that the general government had begun to wield. Most found Turnbull and Cooper's talk treasonous, and calls for secession were widely denounced.

Nevertheless residents of other Cotton States found the constitutionality of protective tariffs questionable even if they condemned any discussion of violence or secession. Darien, Georgia's, 1824 petition had appealed to "that sacred charter, the constitution of the United States" and challenged the constitutionality of taxes "levied, not for the *common* defence, not for the *common* prosperity, but to foster, in *particular* sections, a forced and unnatural state of things."[110] Preparing for the 1828 tariff battle, Georgia's state legislature drafted its own lengthy and quite obstinate remonstrance against the "usurpations of the General Government" in its efforts to support protective tariffs and internal improvements that were "violative of the fundamental principles of its institutions." That memorial, forwarded to Congress in January, struck a slightly more conciliatory tone than South Carolina firebrands but still urged resistance against "the crying injustice of such an unconstitutional measure" that manufacturers were demanding.[111]

Attacking this, along with federally funded internal improvements, Georgia's elected officials warmly embraced the compact theory of government, arguing that the federal Constitution "did not convey sovereign power generally, but sovereign power limited to particular cases." Except for those areas specifically granted to the general government, "the people act alone by their state authorities; this right is not with the executive or judicial authorities of the State; the conclusion is irresistible that their representatives in General Assembly must have the right to protect the State from the usurpations of the General Government, and to remonstrate against any act that shall *encroach* upon the *powers* reserved by the people and *granted* to their *own Government*." It referenced the same revolutionary metaphor that Turnbull had, noting that "if necessary, we could produce more instances than is furnished by the American Revolution, that a long course of abuse, encroachment, and oppression followed up after repeated warnings and respectful expostulations have terminated in a convulsion fatal to the affections which generally bind together either men or nations." Though they would "not pretend, at present, to recommend the mode of OPPOSITION," they urged "that this State ought to *oppose,* in every possible shape, the exercise of the power on the part of the General Government to encourage domestic manufactures or to promote internal improvement."[112] The argument shared the same logic and much of the same language as those penned by would-be South Carolina nullifiers.

More humble in tone and unwilling to invoke compact theory, Alabama's general assembly nonetheless demonstrated its agreement with more-expressive southeastern planters. It followed up a memorial from the previous year, reiterating that state's conviction that to "impose a duty on any article of foreign commerce" designed "to exclude the foreign in favor of the domestic fabric . . . cannot be sustained as an incidental or implied power" and is "fraught with frightful danger." "This alarming principle" of protection, Alabamians concluded, "leads to the union of the worst of human passions" and thus "renders it odious and unfit to mingle in human affairs. Its natural offspring is monopoly, and its natural tendency is to divide the community into nabobs and paupers." The Alabama government even contested the Harrisburg Convention's "right to assemble and petition Congress."[113] Though undoubtedly some artisans, a few newspaper editors, and even a few politicians with national aspirations, like Andrew Jackson, took softer positions on protection or reserved judgment, majorities in the Cotton South—or at least majorities of their elected officials—angrily voiced their displeasure should Congress act on textile manufacturers' demands.

In early 1828, however, Congress did just that as a more united Northeast and Northwest, along with a handful of protectionists from the more northern slaveholding states, came forward with higher rates aimed at protecting northern manufacturers. Believing the bill likely to pass—and blaming it in part on Martin Van Buren's effort to put Jackson in the White House—South Carolinians campaigned to, in McDuffie's words, "fight the devil with fire" by raising duties on raw wool to levels so high that New England's representatives would be denied its benefits and thus reject the bill.[114] The experiment backfired, however, when Webster won even higher duties for manufactured goods, and a majority of New England senators swallowed the bitter poison. Even harsher levels of protection on textiles had once again been fastened on consumers. Cotton planters continued to suffer stagnant prices. Those South Carolinians at the forefront of the desperate effort wavered between befuddlement at their miscalculation and anger, taking passage of such an intentionally bad bill as evidence they might never achieve relief through traditional channels.

When protection confirmed its ascendancy in 1828, with the so-called Tariff of Abominations, arch–free traders decried their increasingly desperate situation as a minority in need of relief from an oppressive majority. Seeking to cohere a more systematic theory from which to oppose the tariff at the state level, South Carolinians turned to a theory of state interposition or nullification, which Vice President John C. Calhoun advanced anonymously and forcefully in a late fall 1828 "Exposition and Protest." This position intended to preserve the Union from the threat of secession and remove grievances by allowing special state conventions to veto legislation they believed unconstitutional. Practically, Calhoun's version of the theory, later embraced by most nullifiers, shifted the burden of proof for controversial national policies like the tariff (and slavery) to a supermajority equivalent to the two-thirds or three-fourths of a majority required for a constitutional amendment.

Unable to secure a free trade majority within Congress, Calhoun and other nullifiers acknowledged their minority status, or in language presumed to be more appropriate for the Cotton South's economic importance, their status as one of the nation's "concurrent majorities."[115] Calhoun's Exposition followed a tortured logic in justifying the principle but provided a specific mechanism for the practical measure of nullification. Supporters believed the theory had its roots in the "principles of 1798" and the Virginia and Kentucky Resolutions. They also had a long (and not completely inaccurate) list of specific instances where northern and southern states had interposed their political will to undermine or ignore specific federal laws. In these efforts, South Carolinians even found a seemingly unlikely ally in former protectionist Condy Raguet, whose Philadelphia and Washington papers embraced the logic of states' rights theory and provided a national platform for nullification. Though the rest of the region continued to decry the tariff, the Exposition's bluntness, remedy, and broader implications convinced few outside of South Carolina and Georgia. Tainted by the occasional secessionist rhetoric coming from the Palmetto State, nullification received the condemnation of a broad number of prominent politicians and state legislatures, even in the Deep South.

Instead of new constitutional mechanisms, most voters in the region placed their faith for redress of all grievances in the election of two of their own, Tennessean Andrew Jackson and John C. Calhoun. By late 1828 cries against the tariff gave way to electioneering to remove Adams and his supporters (who many

mistakenly blamed for the tariff) from national office. General regional agreement on tariff reform kept it from being a central issue, but Senate candidate
Thomas Buck Reed advanced his ultimately successful candidacy by recalling an
earlier circular in which he had declared the "restrictive system, at war with the
spirit of the present age" and unconstitutional. Protection, he continued, would
more appropriately "be called the 'Gothic System,' because it originated in times
of great ignorance, when the principles of commerce were not at all understood."
"There is," he urged, "no constitutional power in Congress to pass" protective
tariffs like the 1828 law. Protection over time, he argued, would "smite with a
heavy hand ... the terrified inhabitants of the whole cotton growing region."
"Lastly," he concluded, "I firmly and honestly believe, the effect of the system is to
transfer the wealth of the nation, from one portion of the country to another."[116]
Like many others of the Jacksonian faithful, however, Reed believed that Jackson's election would defuse the problem by leading to a tariff reduction. Aided by
their dominance in the Cotton States, Jackson and Calhoun provided Martin Van
Buren's coalescing party with a sweeping victory.

Jackson's election proved critical in slowing the Cotton States' drift toward
open resistance to federal power, especially in western Georgia, Alabama, and
Mississippi. At the request of Georgia's governor, Jackson withdrew federal troops
that his predecessor had stationed to protect Native Americans. In 1830 he exerted his considerable influence to get congressional approval for an Indian Removal Act that gave him authority to pressure southern tribes to vacate their
lands. This, along with his Maysville Road veto of the same year, assured many
supporters of states rights that Jackson's view of the federal government approxi-
mated their own. Jackson's attorney general, Georgian John Berrien, reversed
earlier executive opinions and declared Justice Department support for the constitutionality of the Negro Seaman's Acts. The president's efforts to reign in an
allegedly meddlesome federal government, however, stopped short of rejecting
protection. The general may or may not have seen the benefits of protection, but
he had remained elusive on the issue. He had voted for the 1824 tariff during his
brief congressional stint but done so citing "revenue" reasons. Regardless, Jackson's unwillingness to attack the bloated 1828 tariff may have served a more immediate political end. Protecting his power and the cross-regional party it rested
on prevented Jackson from further alienating northern supporters already frustrated with Jackson's concessions to southern states' righters.[117]

By 1830 the patience of arch–free traders in the Cotton South had worn thin.
Even from their minority position, however, they looked for opportunities to

reclaim a national free trade majority within Congress. Reeling from the loss of allies, representatives from the Lower Southeast, led by Robert Hayne, hoped to grant westerners a favorable land policy in exchange for support for a lower tariff. For southeasterners the endorsement of a favorable land policy drew upon the natural alliance they supposed western and southern agrarians shared. It was, nevertheless, presented as a sacrifice. Worsening cotton prices in the 1820s, blamed in part on competition from the Southwest, and concerns over the loss of community in the East had led southeasterners like George McDuffie to question further westward expansion and support higher land prices. The political debate over land policy had initially broken down along east-west rather than north-south lines.[118] Thus, Hayne hoped that his firm support for open access to western lands would be perceived as a generous gesture and solicit repayment from north-western politicians who had supported the 1828 tariff.

The opportunity arose when, in January 1830, Connecticut representative Samuel Foot proposed a bill intending to advance the American System by slowing westward expansion and keeping capital and labor in the East. In response, Missourian Thomas Hart Benton decried the plan as "a most complex scheme of injustice, which taxes the South to injure the West, to pauperize the poor of the North." He appealed to the "solid phalanx of the South" and true northeastern Republicans to reject Foot's proposal and instead open up the sale of more lands to both encourage western development and limit the necessity for higher tariffs.[119] Hayne seized on Benton's call, believing it the perfect opportunity to reveal to westerners the dire consequences of the American System and the maliciousness of the special interests advocating it. Repeatedly equating western oppression over land policy with southern oppression at the hands of the tariff, Hayne and his allies hoped to bring the westerners to their senses and win enough votes to overturn protection. Rising to defend New England from the slanderous attacks, Daniel Webster refuted the argument that New England had sought to exploit anyone, correctly pointing out that he and his region had been late to join the protectionist cause. After Hayne—who initially refrained from raising the question of constitutionality—hinted at nullification, Webster brilliantly shifted the debate away from the initial question and toward the sanctity of the Union. In what John Quincy Adams would call a "tapeworm debate" that lasted nearly three months, congressmen rehashed the history of almost every major contested issue since the Union had been created.[120] The so-called Webster-Hayne debate joined a long list of other key moments in the alleged march toward southern secession. Such hindsight has obscured the event's meaning and significance.[121]

History grants Webster a clear victory in the intellectual and rhetorical joust, but contemporaries remained less certain. Hayne himself did not retreat into a defensive posture and instead aggressively supported his state's stance, contending that the moral high ground had always been with the South and free trade. Hayne charged that the Northeast had demonstrated repeated hypocrisy and inconsistency. On January 25 Hayne regaled the Senate with a prolonged history of national economy, constitutional thought, and patriotism. Calling attention to the New England "peace party" and "Hartford Convention," Hayne proclaimed that it was the South (and South Carolina particularly) that had "done more for the honor and prosperity of the country" during that critical time. "With generous devotion to country," the South had protected northern and New England seamen in the name of "free trade and sailor's rights!" The South, Hayne reminded western senators, had supported the idea of cheap western lands from an early date and even sought to promote federal internal improvements that would benefit the West. Beginning in 1824, however, a new alliance had been formed between northern manufacturers and western agrarians that linked internal improvements to a more devious protectionist ploy that raised national taxes and exploited the South. With an aging Madison denouncing South Carolina's version of state interposition, Hayne suggested that the deceased Jefferson's understanding of the principles of '98 justified his state's potential nullification.[122]

After the tiresome debate, all sides carefully watched for partisan consequences. The defeat of Foot's amendment led supporters of Benton (supposed by many to be Jackson's proxy) and Hayne (a favorite of the Calhounites) to claim victory. Henry Clay heard repeated denunciations of nullification as evidence that Hayne and his state remained marginalized, and he celebrated the victory of his new ally, Webster. A close examination by historian Daniel Feller suggests that the debate over the Foot amendment briefly opened the door for a political alliance between some in the South and the Northwest, as Hayne had hoped. Indeed in 1830 southeastern Jacksonians conceded a minor victory to prodevelopment westerners, accepting the doctrine of preemption, which allowed squatters the right to purchase land. Though they rejected the idea of ceding lands to the states, fearing such a policy would create a revenue problem and necessitate higher tariffs, they overwhelmingly joined Benton's graduation policy, which would gradually lower prices for western lands in order to encourage purchase and settlement. In fact, only the overwhelming New England and Mid-Atlantic opposition and a reversal from Ohio, the only western state to have already sold most of its lands, prevented the graduation bill from passing.[123]

Remaining western states had the choice of fighting congressional action through their own resort to nullification, a position proposed by the Indiana and Mississippi legislatures, which declared the federal government's claim to land within their boundaries as "invalid, null, and void."[124] But such action would have greatly alienated the nation's least powerful and most vulnerable states from valuable commercial partners in the Northeast and from a federal government they depended on for everything from debtor relief to internal improvements to continued protection from Native Americans. As a result westerners remained good Madisonians, rejecting questionable constitutional claims and biding their time until better political circumstances allowed for a more favorable public land policy.[125]

In the final analysis then, the Southeast's attempted "trade" of cheaper land for freer trade highlighted continued western and northeastern tensions but not a commitment on the West's part to end protection and certainly not support for Carolina-style nullification. With the exception of Benton, Hayne's efforts failed to seduce congressmen away from protection. When Congress revisited the tariff, western representatives continued to support protection on most goods, resulting in only a largely symbolic reduction on tea, coffee, salt, and sugar, one of the few southern products receiving protection. Seen as a trifling bill with no effect, South Carolina nullifiers heightened their cries for state action and accelerated their efforts to, in the words of Senator William Smith, "destroy internal improvements" so as to "leave no motive for the tariff."[126] Their efforts, however, only further alienated them from northwesterners, who coveted resources to build roads and canals that would link them to profitable eastern commercial centers. Jackson's veto of the Maysville Road heading through Henry Clay's Kentucky provided some hope, but subsequent support for several other internal improvement bills made even that appear only a political jab at his longtime rival.

The president lost more political capital amongst antitariff constituents in the Lower South when, in December, he reiterated his support for a distribution policy that would allocate surplus federal funds to the individual states to pursue their own projects. At a Jefferson Day dinner, Alabama's Clement Clay directly attacked Jackson's handling of the matter and the people's money, toasting that "the best and fairest mode is to leave it in the pockets of the people who made it—the rightful owners." Clay's colleague, Representative D. H. Lewis—subsequently praised by Charleston nullifiers for his "eloquent cooperation" in the state's rights cause—asked for "the resurrection of the Constitution."[127] Calhoun decried the distribution plan as "the most dangerous, unconstitutional, and absurd project ever devised by any government." South Carolina nullifiers prepared for action. Yet, Jackson's plan went nowhere in Congress and hope returned that the fast-approaching retirement of the federal debt might serve as a final opportunity to reduce the tariff.[128]

Determined to make the most of the opportunity, Lower South politicians rallied to a national call sent forth through Condy Raguet's network of states' rights papers to attend a "Free Trade Convention" to be held in Philadelphia in October of 1831.[129] The convention, attended by South Carolina nullifiers as well as their critics, intended to provide a symbolic answer to the 1827 Harrisburg Convention and a way of mobilizing for a legislative attack against the tariff. Public meetings and local elections throughout the United States sent representatives from every state but Missouri. Those elected or in attendance included many esteemed figures, such as former treasury secretary Albert Gallatin, the son of Massachusetts arch-Federalist Theodore Sedgwick, and former Virginia congressman and recently appointed federal judge Philip Barbour. Even aging chief justice John Marshall put in an honorary appearance, joining several foreign dignitaries in the gallery of the Musical Fund Hall. Raguet was elected secretary and recorded the proceedings for posterity in his *Banner of the Constitution*.[130]

On the surface the minutes of the week-long convention suggest modest hope for Cotton South delegates—who attended the convention in significant numbers. After ensuring that convention votes would be based on the number of attendees rather than one per state, those believing protection to be not only unwise but unconstitutional exerted considerable influence on the convention's "Address to the People of the United States." Berrien, who had recently resigned the attorney generalship and expressed some sympathy toward nullifiers even as he rejected their remedy, chaired the drafting committee. The fruits of his and the rest of the committee's work was an eleven-page address that the convention passed by an overwhelming vote of 158 to 29 and circulated throughout the nation. Though nullifiers ultimately failed to win an unconditional denunciation of the tariff as unconstitutional, the address noted that "a numerous and respectable portion . . . utterly deny—the constitutional power of Congress to enact it."[131] Revealingly, former treasury secretary Albert Gallatin's attempt to further weaken the language failed by a vote of 149 to 32 (including near unanimity amongst delegates from southern states). The final report contained a tortured but sincere attempt to meet nullifiers partway by admitting that the tariff of 1828 could be viewed as an "abuse of the taxing power" and that its victims had been "deprived of the protection of the Justice Department," empowering them to "unite . . . in correcting the evil, by peaceable and constitutional means." The vast majority of southern delegates outside of South Carolina, and even many from the North, accepted the possibility that the 1828 tariff could be seen as unconstitutional even if they refused to challenge Congress's right to "lay and collect duties."[132] Raguet himself supported the idea that Congress had no power to support manufacturing and considered nullification a viable option.[133] The convention had been so noncommittal on the question of constitutionality that several outside observers, including two major Washington, D.C., papers, the *Daily National Intelligencer* and the *Daily National Journal,* mistakenly concluded that it had "declared the tariff laws unconstitutional."[134]

In the end, however, the Philadelphia Convention provided free traders from the South less of a boon than many anticipated. Seemingly anxious that the debate over Gallatin's amendment might splinter the symbolic unity needed to force congressional action, the convention abruptly adjourned. Gallatin, having lost his proposal to avoid the question of constitutionality altogether, convinced the body to empower a special committee, composed of one member from each state, to prepare the memorial to Congress. Having thus neutralized the South's numerical dominance of the convention, he then took the lead in drafting a memorial far more moderate than other committee members, including Berrien and South Carolina nullifier William Harper, wanted.

Harper and Virginia's representative on the drafting committee, William and Mary professor Thomas Dew (both men later acclaimed for their mutually reinforcing proslavery treatises), proceeded to draft a spirited condemnation of Gallatin's petition, claiming that it failed to capture the spirit of the convention's work. Observing the final product, John C. Calhoun lamented to longtime friend and future nullifier Francis Pickens that Gallatin, once a political chieftain of the Jeffersonian party, "has betrayed the South." Feeling a deep sense that northern free traders had proven unwilling or unable to address the issue head-on, Calhoun concluded that "we have nothing to hope from the action of the General Government" and "must rely on the exercise of our reserved rights for redress."[135] For a few South Carolinians, including perhaps Calhoun, the principle of state interposition had become an end unto itself—a precedent for anticipated future debates over slavery. It should not be forgotten, however, that the driving force behind nullification originated out of grievances over the tariff's perceived unequal effects, a sincere and broadly held belief that protection abused the spirit, and perhaps the letter, of the Constitution, and a heightened sense that, northern free traders, as Calhoun told his brother-in-law, had "been more anxious to conciliate the powers that be, than to do justice to the South."[136]

While South Carolina radicals laid the groundwork for a nullification convention, others in the Cotton South more patiently waited to see if redress could be had within Congress. Joining Gallatin's memorial before Congress was a new tariff schedule proposed by the treasury secretary, Louis McLane. Noting the expected retirement of the national debt in 1833, McLane urged Congress to allow more goods to be moved to the duty-free list and proposed a reduction or elimination of minimum valuation on cheap goods, including textiles, a clear concession to slaveholders frustrated with high taxes on Negro Cloth. Largely with the help of former president John Quincy Adams, who had returned to the House, a tariff bill emerged that met some but not all of the free traders' demands. In its final form the tariff of 1832 increased the number of goods added to the duty-free list and lowered minimum valuations on Negro Cloth from 45 to 5 percent. Yet seeing opportunity within the compromise, manufacturers allied with Henry Clay managed to retain protective levels for iron and most other textile goods and actually increased the levels of protection on higher-quality cloth from 45 to 50 percent.[137] The bill had the desired effect of muting opposition in much of the South, but not in Georgia and South Carolina, whose delegations opposed the measure 6 to 1 and 6 to 3, respectively. Alabama and Mississippi congressmen remained almost equally divided over the bill. Georgia, Mississippi, and Alabama's legislatures, however, continued to question the tariff's constitutionality, the last declaring that though "unequal, unjust, oppressive, and against the spirit, true intent, and meaning of the Constitution," the 1832 tariff would be accepted only as a "harbinger of better times, as a pledge that Congress will, at no distant period, abandon the principle of protection altogether."[138]

South Carolinian nullifiers, further alarmed by federal colonization plans and Virginia's frank discussion of gradual emancipation in early 1832, pressed even harder to remedy the problem and perhaps, they hoped, establish precedent for potential problems over slavery that lay ahead of them. In October two-thirds of South Carolina legislators called special elections for a convention to nullify the 1828 and 1832 tariffs and demanded that the federal government end protectionism. Despite efforts by unorganized unionists within the state to prevent it, nullifiers elected largely from counties that produced the most cotton and had the most slaves, won control of the convention and declared that after February 1, 1833, these tariffs would not be collected within the state. A federal attempt to enforce the law would be "inconsistent with the longer continuance of South Carolina in the Union."[139]

The remaining Cotton States contemplated how to respond. In Georgia a fierce battle over nullification gained the radicals a larger following than has generally been admitted. Alabamians and Mississippians were less receptive, and their legislatures condemned nullification. Yet, reflecting on the various state resolutions that had emerged in Virginia, North Carolina, and the other Cotton States since the 1832 tariff, one North Carolina paper aptly noted that "it will thus be seen that every one of these six *farming* States have pronounced the tariff laws, not only oppressive and unjust, but, also, unconstitutional."[140] Moderate majorities throughout the Cotton States suggested a meeting of southern states or a larger constitutional convention to contemplate solutions. Fear that nullifiers would seize control of such a body aborted the convention idea.

Most individuals in the Cotton South deemed peace within union more desirable than a potential civil war, further reduction in the tariff, or nullification, a policy that Alabama's state legislature decried as "unsound in theory and dangerous in practice, that as a remedy was unconstitutional and essentially revolutionary, leading in its consequences to anarchy and civil discord, and finally to the dissolution of the Union."[141] In Georgia, loyalty to Jackson, who had in effect voided a court order and forced Cherokee removal, helped prevent nullification from seizing that state. In the developing southwestern states of Alabama and Mississippi, Indian removal, along with lingering aspirations for internal improvement projects, continued to suggest the value of an active central government. These states also had no major commercial ports and little institutional memory of the past sacrifices so critical to the rhetoric of South Carolina and Georgia resistance. Consequently, when South Carolina nullifiers continued forward, the rest of the Lower South states joined Virginia in an effort to pressure all sides back to the bargaining table.

Jackson and his supporters in Congress offered an olive branch in the form of further tariff reductions and threatened the use of the sword by passing a "Force Bill," which threatened to use federal troops to ensure that tariffs were collected. Deep South states took the carrot and continued to condemn nullification, though they remained squeamish about Jackson's threat of force. Seeing the writing on the wall, South Carolina promised more time. Calhoun and Clay worked feverishly to find a solution that would end the standoff. The subsequent Compromise of 1833 provided a face-saving gesture, but substantively its gains for cotton planters were longer-, rather than shorter-term. Tariffs would be reduced gradually (about 10% a year) over the next nine years, until finally a revenue-derived rate of 20 percent would be enforced in 1842. Having failed in their bid to eliminate protection as a principle and establish new constitutional precedents, South Carolina nullifiers stepped back from the brink, though not before symbolically nullifying Jackson's Force Bill.[142] The entire experience had done nothing to win them political friends. Yet, to make the moral of the political drama that played out over the previous thirteen years a story chiefly of South Carolina's political isolation and failure is, to a great extent, to miss the deeper implications of the tariff debate, namely, the Cotton South's resounding rejection of a nation-centered economy.

In shifting the nature of the debate from not how but *if* a united national harmony of interests existed, the 1820s punctured the illusion of a natural national economic federation that had sustained the first Republican Party. The cries of supporters of the American System for home markets, self-sufficiency, and protective tariffs fell, to a very great extent, on deaf ears in the Cotton states. Certainly small minorities of artisans and manufacturers and a very small number of newspapers in the region challenged the free trade mantra, but the overwhelming majority of inhabitants—whether involved in the marketplace or not—rejected the protectionist vision as undesirable and perhaps even unconstitutional. Under these conditions cotton growers—hypersensitive about slavery, protecting their bottom lines, and preserving their need for international trade—had developed a litmus test that calculated a national policy's wisdom based, not on its perceived utility for the greater good, but on its sectional cost.

The perspective had not become retrenched until the late 1820s, but as early as 1820 the Charleston memorialists had rigidly argued that "every system of restriction, of monopoly, of particular privilege" was "particularly hostile to the general spirit of our constitution."[143] Simply by making the tariff debate a test, not of national good, but of constitutionality, South Carolinians (aided, it should be noted, by Virginians like John Taylor and Philip Barbour) had sharpened all cotton planters' awareness of potential abuse coming from within the Union, even from previously assumed "natural" allies like western farmers. Whether from more aristocratic or democratic state political cultures, planters and farmers within the cotton belt agreed with the Alabama legislature's assertion that protection threatened to "destroy the equipoise of the General Government."[144] Furthermore, though nullification seemed politically imprudent to most, the right to secede had gained important endorsements throughout the region.[145]

The widely shared free trade principles and, nullifiers claimed, the potential remedy had been Jeffersonian in inspiration. Yet, by 1832 the spirit and the tone prevalent throughout the Cotton South were anything but. Jeffersonian Republicans *had* sought to tear down allegedly consolidationist Federalist policies and put less burdensome and more equitable national ones in their place. Yet, in their desire to slay the larger British dragon, Jefferson, Madison, and earlier Jeffersonians had proved willing, indeed at times even eager to pass neomercantilist commercial policies that appealed to broad groups and retained as their larger goal the harmonization of the nation's diverse interests. Without a shared enemy, at home or abroad, and during a time of Atlantic peace, the centripetal forces that previously had restrained tensions within Jeffersonian political economy gave way. The Missouri Compromise previewed a *possible* two-sectional division, drawn between free and slave states, one almost too horrible for Jefferson and others to imagine. Though less terrifying in some ways, the tariff debates, as well as those involving land policies, and to a lesser extent the National Bank and internal improvements, demonstrated a deeply troubling lived reality.

Even more directly than the War of 1812, the debate over national political economy demonstrated that interests of the political nation were not just incongruous but might be openly hostile to one another. South Carolina pressed the issue, but Alabama, Mississippi, and Georgia also took the lesson. In the Cotton South, and in pockets of the Upper South, the nation had been temporarily deconstructed into its distinct economic parts, and a ridiculously high standard of "equality" under the Constitution had been elevated as a standard for wise policies. For cotton planters, who believed they had been most abused, the sentiment of shared sacrifice for a greater good that had dominated Jeffersonian thinking gave way to the belief, admittedly overdrawn, that further sacrifice came primarily at their expense.

The change in political economic thought—the perceived dissolution of a harmony of interests and escalated concerns about unequal policies—heightened Cotton South fears of economic monopoly and ultimately political consolidation. By shaking the Lower South's faith in national political economy, the debates of the 1820s provided the underpinnings for an alternate economic vision stressing the desirability of a regional economy more independent from the North. Paralleling these concerns was another large one. If cotton could not command the economic and political allies to overturn protection, if there existed no harmony of interests, what would be the future fate of the region's primary source of southern wealth, slavery? Meeting that growing threat, many in the Cotton

South felt, required consciously investing the rest of the nation, especially the West, in slavery and in a southern economy centered on cotton and free trade. This project—along with fear of slave insurrections—helps explain the urgency with which southern ideologues responded to the relatively small numbers of northern abolitionists.[146]

# CHAPTER FOUR

# Building Bridges to the West and the World

Empowerment and Anxiety in the Second Party System, 1834–1848

The end of the nullification crisis brought widespread relief but did not alleviate political or economic concerns in the Cotton South. Debates, primarily over the tariff, called into question the existence of naturally complementary interests within the Union and highlighted the possibility that northern majorities (aided by sympathetic southerners) would pass policies adversely affecting Lower South interest in cotton and slaves. The perceived abandonment by northwestern politicians, who supported protection and proposed federal funds for colonization, loomed particularly ominously. Disagreement over nullification and Jackson's Force Bill, as well as the bank war, created lasting internal tensions that left the region politically divided. Some feared that the lack of unity might embolden northern antislavery groups to mount further attacks against slavery. The proliferation of abolitionist mailings and congressional petitions which urged immediate rather than gradual emancipation confirmed these concerns and provided issues around which self-conscious "sectionalists" attempted to redefine southern politics.

Economically, the postnullification picture remained mixed, highlighting a distinction between southeastern and southwestern planters that shaped the policy choices of both. The population and economy of the Southwest continued to grow, by 1834 providing almost 60 percent of the total national production of cotton, the price of which jumped from 11.2 cents to 15.5 cents in New Orleans markets. In the case of Mississippi and Alabama, however, wealth frequently found its way to Savannah and New Orleans ports, frustrating those states' politicians and demonstrating the fierce intraregional rivalry for trade. The situation remained less optimistic in the East, and especially for lowcountry planters. Average monthly prices for Sea Island cotton continued to fall, reaching new lows of 19 cents per pound in 1833 before rebounding to 23.2 cents the following year. More generally, southeastern politicians had become frighteningly aware of the *relative* decline of commerce and land values compared to northern states and booming economies in the southwestern cotton belt. Soil depletion fueled concerns that out-migration would slowly sap Georgia and South Carolina's wealth and power.

Within this context, southeastern groups advocated aggressive economic reforms they believed would bring commercial empowerment while also rebuilding economic and political bridges to old allies elsewhere. In the mid-1830s individuals and communities hoped that cooperative state-sponsored internal improvements and direct trade would revitalize a southern and western coalition that could prevent further federal action against slavery and free trade. Optimistic beginnings, however, gave way to internal dissension and a prolonged depression that eroded regional confidence. These, along with a significant head start by northeastern port cities, thwarted efforts to rechannel trade to southern cities. Few, if any, questioned the region's continued reliance on cotton and slavery, but competing visions emerged over how best to transform cotton's wealth into greater strength. Continued economic woes and the political debates that resulted (often framed around banking policy) undermined Democratic Party dominance. A young Whig Party actively, and at times successfully, competed for political office, generally conforming regional politics to the much-studied second party system.

Disunity over major economic policies only heightened the need for a firm and united voice against British and northern abolitionists. Even that proved elusive, but the 1830s and 1840s witnessed a transition within the Cotton South toward a proslavery perspective that highlighted slavery's compatibility with modern economic systems as well as its alleged benevolence for slaves and masters. Defending slavery emerged as a central aspect of both Jacksonian and Whig appeals. Though often drawing religious and moral claims into a paternalism-centered justification of slavery, apologists relied heavily on political economic arguments and especially the continued international importance of slave-grown cotton. The doomsday scenarios of antitariff politicians had proven inaccurate and Britain, the North, and the world were more dependent on southern cotton in 1845 than they had been in 1830. Appeals to economic sensibilities—though often overdrawn—allowed proslavery writers to define their opponents as hypocrites and appeal to potential allies on grounds of material interest. Yet, the intensification of antislavery attacks against the South also increased the need to ensure continued southern dominance of the raw cotton market, ultimately necessitating action to expand production into trans-Mississippi lands.

As always, policymakers observed these political and economic debates within a vortex of local, regional, national, and international commitments. The global cotton trade continued to tie the South, quite willingly, to Britain, which in 1846 joined the United States in further tariff reductions. Yet, the Lower South's economic partners also remained a major threat as the heart of emancipationist sentiment and, after 1834, action. Fearing their chief consumers might foster antislavery action and an alternate supply in Texas, Democratic-minded politicians and a majority of voters demanded annexation as necessary for regional economic and geopolitical security. Lower South Whigs who remained lukewarm about territorial expansion found themselves marginalized as their opponents maneuvered themselves into the inner sanctum of national Democratic Party power. With one of their own ascending to executive power, cotton Democrats seemed king as they, along with northern and western allies, steered federal policy toward Texas annexation, the apparent triumph of free trade, and eventually an unintended war with Mexico. Nationalism reached newfound heights even as its fruits paved the way for sectional animosity. Cotton proved decisive in shaping the region's political and economic response to international developments and the second party system.

## Publishing the "Banns" of Marriage: The Search for Lower South Commercial Advancement

In the summer of 1836, economic and political concerns led representatives from nine southern and western states to attend a massive railroad convention. On July 4—a date symbolically chosen by the South Carolinian organizers—380 representatives converged on Knoxville, Tennessee, for the widely advertised event. The delegates were diverse. Farmers, planters, manufacturers, merchants, nullifiers, unionists, and Jacksonians as well as many members of the still-coalescing

Whig opposition—all convened with the belief that a railroad project designed to link the Ohio River Valley and the Atlantic at Charleston might assist their local and state interests. After some discussion over the route, an appointed committee unanimously affirmed the project. In his presidential toast, the meeting's chief architect, nullifier Robert Y. Hayne, applauded "the South and West—We have published the banns—if any one know ought why these two should not be joined together, let him speak now, or forever after hold his peace."[1] The Charleston and Cincinnati Railroad represented one example of the Cotton South's commitment to commercial advancement. Its ultimate fate, however, highlighted the challenges of creating an independent southern commercial sector and the difficulty of achieving intrasectional cooperation toward common ends.

The Knoxville Convention drew on a long southeastern tradition of embracing technology for commercial development. Historians of internal improvements have wrongly interpreted opposition to Clay's American System as aversion to internal improvements generally. Even as the tariff debates of the 1820s soured southeastern support for *federally* funded internal improvements, South Carolina and Georgia had actually accelerated transportation projects within their states.[2] The burgeoning cotton regions of Alabama and Mississippi also aggressively sought—though they were delayed in finding—an infrastructure that brought commerce and progress to their newly opened plantations and commercial towns. In effort, if not always in results, the Cotton South sought to quicken communications and advance trade through the use of steamships and railroads. Already, Georgia investors had financed the first partially steam-powered Atlantic crossing in 1819, a venture which, though symbolically important, ended in financial disaster.[3] Steam proved to be more successful on land and, despite the upheaval of nullification, moderate Charleston merchants successfully won incorporation for the South Carolina Canal & Railroad Company. Upon completion in 1833, their ambitious project, a steam railroad linking Charleston to the Savannah River at Hamburg, became (briefly) the longest railroad in the world. Georgians were not far behind. Perhaps inspired and alarmed by the steady progress of the Charleston-Hamburg Railroad, activists in Eatonton and Athens brought that state into the railroad era by creating a line connecting the cotton-rich lands of central Georgia to Augusta and its water access to the Atlantic, through Savannah.[4] These generally successful ventures fueled grander schemes to unite the Southeast and the West via rail.

These new projects, like the Charleston-Cincinnati Railroad, differed from earlier endeavors in one important way: they self-consciously faced outward and were designed to enhance the Lower South's share of interstate and international commerce. The "prosperity of the Southern and Western States, and the full development of their resources," a South Carolina committee composed of former unionists, moderates, and nullifiers declared, necessitated the completion of an Ohio-Southeastern line.[5] A steam-powered Trans-Appalachian Railroad, according to Hayne, would revitalize South Carolina's commercial sector by increasing trade with the burgeoning West. Currently, he noted, western produce and livestock traveled directly on difficult mountain wagon roads or indirectly by water via the Ohio River to New Orleans or by way of the Great Lakes, Erie Canal, and New York. These circuitous routes added unnecessary transportation costs, insurance, and time. A carefully located railway, promoters estimated, would reduce formerly tortuous journeys to five or six days, thereby increasing the market for western flour and corn and augmenting the value of land and labor along the road. From South Carolina's perspective, the accelerated travel from the coast to the West would increase the potential consumers of foreign imports, again making Charleston an attractive location for international trade. Southern, rather than northern, merchants would become the middlemen for foreign goods and western grains.[6]

Proponents calculated the line with specific political as well as economic ends, seeking to "multiply the cords of sympathy" between western producers and southern planters and "removing as far as possible the sources of mutual ignorance and jealousy" created by the recent "political combinations" of the northeastern and western states. The implication was clear: an alliance between the South and West remained possible, notwithstanding differences over tariff protection. Better commerce and trade would disentangle the protectionist political web and possibly prevent an antislavery coalition by reorienting the West and South in natural economic, and by extension political, harmony. Revitalized "ties of mutual interest and dependence" would resurrect the old Republican alliance of farmers and planters, making them "one body of citizens united by community interests."[7]

Framed within the context of abolitionist petitioning and mailing campaigns (including many from Ohio), Hayne and his close partner, former unionist Alexander Blanding, told prospective investors that the railroad project would protect the "peculiar institution of the South . . . so little understood in other portions of the Union that it has lately been assailed." "An establishment of such an intercourse with the Western States, as is now proposed," Hayne argued, would have a powerful tendency to avert the "dire calamity" of disunion over the issue of slavery.[8] When Kentucky interests sought to make the terminus Louisville, instead of Cincinnati, Blanding told Charlestonians that though Louisville might be more lucrative, "in a political point of view" he much preferred Cincinnati. A connection there "detaches from the East a powerful confederate in our political struggles, as far as commercial and social intercourse can produce that effect; and may have a tendency to keep Ohio our friend on the slave question."[9] In the end, planners agreed to run a branch line to Louisville, to ensure the maximum political *and* economic effect. Promoters hoped internal improvements like the Louisville, Cincinnati, and Charleston Railroad, as it subsequently became known, would work toward slaveholding ends.[10]

Set within the postnullification period, the project also had considerable symbolic value. South Carolinians, whether unionists or nullifiers, perceived it as a way of mending political fences with outsiders who had scolded them for their political brinksmanship. Promoters also anticipated that the project's success would demonstrate that major public works did not necessitate federal funding. The financial burden for these projects would fall primarily on the states and the private citizens within them. South Carolina adopted the companies' outward-looking agenda with surprising speed and financial support, appropriating $10,000 to cover initial surveying expenses, providing a $2 million loan and giving the company banking rights, a notable measure for an otherwise fiscally conservative state.[11] When subscriptions opened in the fall of 1836, South Carolina's loan of $2 million, along with $1.4 million of private South Carolina funds, enabled the company to proceed with the first branch, beginning the task of joining Charleston with Columbia. Optimism continued into 1838, despite the Panic of 1837. Promoters had always believed the expensive project would necessitate foreign investment. In London, James Hamilton Jr. succeeded in selling project bonds, thus acquiring $500,000 in British specie to support the newly chartered Southwestern Railroad Bank.[12] Initial enthusiasm transcended local boosterism. In addition to the celebratory Knoxville Convention, the editor of the *American Railroad Journal* thought the project "sure of ultimate accomplishment."[13]

The success of the venture, however, necessitated cooperation from other states, and South Carolina officers, including Blanding, Hayne, and future Confederate treasurer C. C. Memminger, shuttled to various state legislatures seeking assistance. North Carolina, Tennessee, and Kentucky—states through which the proposed route would travel—granted charters, but political support never translated into monetary backing, particularly when panic conditions gripped the nation in 1837 and again in 1839. Henry Clay accurately described the situation in

August 1838, telling a friend that a South Carolina delegation to the Kentucky legislature would receive "more soft words than hard money."[14] Even as South Carolina managers continued to advocate the beneficial results of a direct line to Ohio, the lack of financial support elsewhere undermined the project's viability.[15] Throughout the project's life South Carolinians possessed five-sixths of the company's shares. The request by North Carolina and Tennessee to withdraw from the project in 1840 and the death of Hayne and Blanding terminated efforts at the original route. Until a similar project was resurrected in the 1850s, a branch line that connected Charleston to Columbia remained the only tangible accomplishment of the company, which was rechartered and prospered as the South Carolina Railroad Company.[16]

While the Louisville, Cincinnati, and Charleston Railroad passed away, the vision of a western and southeastern rail connection did not. At the Knoxville Convention, a Georgia delegation had proposed that an alternate line through its state would best link the Atlantic to the West. After winning the rights to build their own road to Knoxville, where it would connect with the larger project, Georgia railroad interests called for a statewide railroad convention. In November 1836, 116 delegates met and proposed the state-funded construction of a road from central Georgia to the Tennessee River. Other private and municipal companies would be allowed access to the interstate trade by running lines to a terminus, at what would eventually become Atlanta. Participants intended to transform the Tennessee River into a southern version of the Ohio River, thus capturing for Savannah the trade that currently traveled down the Mississippi to New Orleans.[17] The legislature, with united support from the state's central and northern sections and Savannah, warmly embraced the plan chartering the Western and Atlantic Railroad and boldly agreed to pay the entire cost. After a survey, grading began for the roadbed in 1838 and continued to completion, though the prolonged economic depression of the early 1840s temporarily suspended efforts.[18] Compared with the South Carolina plan, Georgia's project offered a more modest route, benefiting from already-existing railroad projects and waterways. It had a more immediate impact on the state's commercial success and depended less on potentially uninterested state legislatures to the north.[19] The state's generous support for the project provided additional stability. Indeed from 1841 to 1850 railroad spending—much of it for the Western-Atlantic—composed one-third of the state's entire budget![20]

Georgians were not the only ones to recognize the advantages of their plan, which would eventually become the heart of the Cotton South's railroad network.

During a visit to Athens shortly after the Knoxville Convention, John C. Calhoun, though a director of the South Carolina railroad, praised his neighbors' efforts. In a published communiqué to Augustin Clayton, Calhoun suggested that Georgia's "position gives her great and commanding advantages in reference to rail roads; more so . . . than any other State in the Union." Through a "generous rivalry," South Carolina and Georgia could work together to "unite the South Atlantic . . . with the great bosom of the Mississippi and its vast tributaries."[21] Other directors shared Calhoun's appraisal of the benefits of a more westward route, one he personally scouted on two trips. In October 1837 the Charleston-Cincinnati project purchased the Charleston and Hamburg line, a rail it hoped would eventually link to the Georgia project.[22] Even as the trade of the Northwest remained a goal, southern sectionalists believed that tapping into other southern state projects would unite the South. Writing to Alabamian David Hubbard, Calhoun expressed his belief that the Georgia route would "do more to unite & conciliate the slave-holding States, than can be effected by any thing else, and will change not only the commerce, but the politicks of the Union."[23] Just as in 1816, internal improvements were to help tie different polities together. This time, however, Calhoun wanted commerce and trade to bind together a southern party against the forces of northern consolidation and abolition. His friend George McDuffie agreed, noting that it was "of the utmost importance to unite the planting states."[24]

Internal improvement promoters in Georgia, the Cotton State most committed to such projects, shared much in common with South Carolina's more sectionally minded agenda. But profits more than politics remained Georgia investors' main concern, and until the 1850s they refused to allow a bridge linking the two projects, fearing it would undermine Savannah's efforts at commercial advancement. Though not universally popular, this and other railroad projects received widespread acclaim from Georgia's diverse economic sectors. Central Georgia's nascent manufacturers heralded the access to raw materials and markets offered by the state's railroads. Inland town shopkeepers and merchants commended projects that allowed them to more cheaply receive their goods. Moreover, these and other internal improvements continued to serve the interests of cotton, providing backcountry planters and farmers easier access to markets in port cities and even creating a few important inland towns.[25] Though hit hard by the cotton depression of the 1840s, Georgia's private and public projects did come to fruition in the 1850s, eventually turning Atlanta from a backcountry town into one of the more vibrant regional commercial centers. By then, higher cotton prices had spawned unprecedented railroad planning throughout the region, even leading many to envision a transcontinental railroad that could capture the Pacific trade for the South. Despite considerable desire, Alabama and Mississippi's efforts remained more meager, leaving much of those states' commerce flowing out of state to Savannah, New Orleans, and in some instances, Memphis.

Early state and local railroad conventions laid the groundwork for four more comprehensive regional commercial conventions that shared the goals of economic liberation from the Northeast and increased direct commerce with Europe.[26] While the Panic of 1837 caused great distress for many investors, particularly in the Southwest, where scarce specie became scarcer and debt heightened, the more severe consequences for northern commercial centers actually provided hope for southeastern economic visionaries. The collapse of northern banks, they thought, presented an opportunity to reroute European commerce and capital in a direction more advantageous to southern planters and merchants. At the behest of the citizens of Athens, Georgia, delegates were invited to gather in Augusta in October 1837 to "attempt a new organization of our commercial relations with Europe" and remedy the "unequal state" of things between southern and northern commerce.[27] These conventions, like preceding railroad meetings, stressed commercial outreach, but they also emphasized regional financial empowerment. "The disruption of the existing channels of trade," a resolution passed at the 1838 Augusta Convention suggested, "afford an opportunity of breaking down the trammels which have so long fettered our commerce and of restoring the South to its natural advantages."[28] The convention reflected the region's continued faith in "natural" economies, free trade policies, and the structural soundness of its slave economy.

Though participants placed significant blame on the "unequal" operations of protection, they eschewed discriminatory measures against northern goods or merchants. Instead a committee report, apparently written by George McDuffie but unanimously approved, suggested that in addition to the "involuntary tribute" exacted by the tariff, cotton growers paid a "voluntary tribute" (estimated to be $10 million a year) in service fees and transportation costs for an unnecessary indirect trade through northern cities.[29] In essence, the Cotton South had offered up its commercial independence to the North at a considerable cost. Ending this tribute would provide the capital necessary to expand internal improvements and commercial ventures. As a result, southern merchants and planters would become the suppliers for an expanding West: "If Georgia and South Carolina . . . would bring their individual energies and resources to the completion of those lines of communication connecting their atlantic [*sic*] cities with the navigable waters of the West the day would not be distant when our most ardent hopes and sanguine anticipations would be realized."[30] To further inspire merchant and planter associations, the first convention, held in October 1837, petitioned state legislatures to pass limited liability laws for copartnerships, a policy subsequently enacted by Georgia, South Carolina, Alabama, and Tennessee.[31]

Finally, the conventions encouraged southern banks to form direct connections with European capitalists and even establish agencies in major financial centers. The widespread financial chaos in 1837 gave initial hope that European investors would willingly put money into the relatively conservative and less adversely affected banks of Georgia and South Carolina. The half million in specie that James Hamilton acquired in 1838 for the Charleston-Cincinnati Railroad Company furthered expectations. Even in the financially devastated regions of the Southwest, optimism for increased Anglo-southern partnerships briefly flourished. In late 1837, executors for the Planters and Merchants Bank of Mobile employed the British consul, James Baker, to attract London capital for their fledgling bank.[32] Baker's confidential correspondence with the British Foreign Office reflected both initial enthusiasm for Anglo-American financial connections and the limits of British official government support.[33]

Like southern free traders, Baker accepted "the political and commercial importance of countenancing the Southern section of the United States in their present efforts of opening a direct trade and intercourse with Great Britain." He actively sought to induce London banks "to cooperate with the Southern States in bringing about this beneficial arrangement." Citing the 1837 Augusta Convention and subsequent passage of favorable bankruptcy laws, Baker told Viscount Palmerston's assistant that he had great faith British merchants and bankers would find southern ports attractive places to do business. Already, he also noted, many London capitalists had "greatly aided" his efforts on behalf of the Mobile Bank. Accepting the anticonsolidation position of many southern Democrats, Baker decried what he saw as Nicholas Biddle's Philadelphia Bank of the United States' efforts to monopolize Anglo-American commerce by opening a London agency. He urged the British government to guard against such developments and to encourage direct trade and capital flows to the U.S. South.[34] An official response does not seem to exist, but according to Baker, "Lord Palmerston did not enter into my views with regard to American Affairs."[35]

If official government support was not forthcoming, a good cotton crop and decent prices in 1838 did heighten expectations for Anglo-southern trade, leading private British merchants to expand their contacts and investments in the region.[36] The London-based Baring Brothers, who had previously only provided credit for the trade, contacted Mobile, Augusta, Savannah, and Charleston firms in 1837, hoping to purchase cotton, "the great staple by which we hope to make up for all our losses."[37] Baring's primary competitor, the Baltimore and Liverpool house of Alexander Brown & Company, also expanded cotton operations in 1838.[38] Ever imaginative, George McDuffie traveled to Manchester in spring 1839, hoping to cut out all middlemen and form direct partnerships with British manufacturers. Associations of twenty-five to thirty planters would pool their cotton and sell directly to English manufacturers in exchange for finished products at, they hoped, well below the normal cost. He hoped to convince them that "after '42 when no duty will exceed 20 per cent, Negro plains and every plantation supply can be advantageously imported." Surplus funds would aid other efforts, though nothing permanent appears to have come from the experiment.[39]

Supporters of direct trade did not necessarily see their efforts as incompatible with the goals of increased regional self-sufficiency or the encouragement of southern manufacturing. Entrepreneurial inland planters frequently invested in manufacturing and internal improvement projects as a way to diversify their economic portfolios.[40] McDuffie himself had invested in and helped manage a small textile mill in the South Carolina upcountry even as he continued to pursue exchanges with Manchester. The South's bountiful raw supply of cotton and ready access to water power would enable southern manufacturers to catch up rapidly with their northern neighbors. Reformers assumed that fostering southern textile factories would subsequently trigger wider investment in other industries necessary for their support, such as metalworking. Over time, some argued, they might even become an exporter of simple cloth, eyeing Latin American markets, and especially the slave populations of Brazil, as potential wearers of southern-produced cloth. Reformers also saw the natural development of specialized manufactures as compatible with commercial agriculture, slavery, and the goal of attracting more direct trade with Europe. The conventions themselves emphasized the need for planters to economize and become more self-sufficient by providing their own foodstuffs, actions thought necessary to free up additional capital for commercial houses, internal improvements, and manufacturing establishments.[41]

These and other ventures problematize a common assumption—dating back to Marxist and Progressive histories—that the Cotton South had fallen into a complacent and static agrarianism. Even after the hindsight of developmental economics, these efforts at commercial empowerment and industrial development seem futile, at times even naïve. Historians and economists alike have pointed out, perhaps accurately, that slavery and other systemic problems like low population densities necessarily hindered efforts at economic development relative to the North and Britain.[42] Contemporaries, though aware of the problem of limited consumer markets and overinvestment in cotton and slaves, eschewed any fatalistic assessment. Cotton and slavery remained, in their minds, structural strengths, and the mid- to late 1830s reflected a period of optimism for developers in the Cotton South who sought to resurrect the once-proud ports of Savannah and Charleston or to create new ones in Natchez and Mobile. The anticipated end of the protective tariff and rising cotton prices encouraged planters and merchants to try harnessing cotton's wealth for the promotion of broader local and regional advancement. By empowering themselves and local merchants to replace northern factors, southern sectionalists hoped to achieve lasting economic prosperity and win the western political allies necessary to preserve free trade and protect slavery in the event of further challenges from northern abolitionists. They sought to alter, not preserve, an agrarian regional distinctiveness.[43]

Instead of focusing on the problems presented by a slave economy, reformers in the Lower South perceived challenges and opportunities within the context of the global economy. In that context the financial crisis of 1839 and subsequent international depression of the early 1840s, rather than deeper structural arguments, provided the lens through which Lower South residents eyed economic and political decisions. The experiences of Mississippi's John A. Quitman between the mid-1830s and early 1840s provides a revealing window into how the euphoria of one of the region's many entrepreneurs transformed to economic misery. Quitman, a native New Yorker, had moved to Natchez in 1821 after failing to find his fortune in Ohio. Trained as a lawyer, he initially remained politically loyal to his northeastern roots and actively supported John Quincy Adams and the National Republicans in 1824. By 1832 however, Quitman had fully adapted to Lower South life, purchasing two cotton plantations and the slaves to tend them. The acquisitions transformed his political outlook rather dramatically, leading him to embrace John C. Calhoun and nullification. Though he gave no specific reason for his shift to states' rights thinking, his embrace of cotton cultivation and slaveownership no doubt heightened his concern about protective tariffs, northern abolitionism, and a federal government strong enough to implement both.[44]

Quitman's conversion to Calhounism and his desire for profits furthered, rather than inhibited, his avid campaigning for internal improvements and banks. Like many, however, he increasingly turned to the state rather than the federal government to pursue them. Determined that he and Mississippi would benefit from the improving spirit, Quitman attended two railroad meetings in 1834 and proposed a railroad linking new cotton lands to Natchez. By 1836, threats of a New Orleans and Tennessee connection that might bypass Natchez and capture northern Mississippi markets led the Mississippi legislature to charter and fund the Mississippi Railroad Company, with Quitman as one of nine directors. His efforts earned him the praise of the *Mississippi Free Trader,* and several local assemblies celebrated "Our Railroad," proclaiming it "a great and noble enterprise" conceived to commence a "new era in our State History."[45] Despite the Panic of 1837, progress on the railroad between Natchez and Jackson continued, and fourteen miles had been completed by April 1838.

These local efforts gained new sectional importance after a meeting with Robert Hayne, then touring to attract support for South Carolina's project. Instantly taken with one another, the two businessmen publicly praised the other's efforts and affirmed the goal of sectional commercial advancement through improved internal improvements and direct trade. Quitman provided Hayne speaking opportunities in Jackson and Natchez, where audiences celebrated the Carolinian's plan to unite the Southeast and Southwest and dispel sectional animosity between the Northwest and South. Perhaps inspired by Hayne's vision, Quitman intensified his commitment to bring about direct trade between Natchez and Europe. Following his purchase of shares in the Natchez Steam Packet Company—which in 1839 shipped 40,000 cotton bales directly to Europe—Quitman became commissioner for the Mississippi Importing Company, a newly chartered company that also advocated direct trade with Europe. Acknowledging his efforts, in February 1839 colleagues appointed Quitman to travel to Charleston for the last of the 1830s commercial conventions to promote railroad development and direct trade.[46]

Despite these accolades, however, worsening economic conditions instead led Quitman to Europe in search of investors to prop up his flagging bank bonds and ensure the long-term viability of his main passion, the railroad. In May 1839, Quitman and fellow director Joseph Thacher left for London, where they learned firsthand that the Panics of 1837 and 1839 had been truly international in scale. English bankers and merchants short of capital proved unwilling to invest overseas, particularly in downtrodden American state markets. As one correspondent informed him, "The Bank of England, 'the leader of Europe,' seems to be against America." Later encounters with the Rothschilds' firm in Frankfort and banking houses in Belgium and France proved equally fruitless. By late August, Quitman was back in London lamenting that "the commercial revolution . . . has reached England and I fear an end is put to our borrowing money, securities, or stocks." The failed trip left his entrepreneurial project in "ruinous consequences."[47] It did indeed. The rest of the railroad's directors, fully expecting a fresh influx of capital, had extended operations that could no longer be paid for. By early 1840 it was clear that the bank was short on specie and that the company could not pay its debts. Natchez merchants refused to accept company bank notes, and within six months Democratic governor Alexander McNutt revoked the bank's charter. The emaciated company was doomed, and a debt-riddled Quitman had to temporarily abandon his political career. In Quitman's mind these failed efforts resulted neither from slavery nor from a bias against railroads or banks. The culprit, he believed, was a global depression that had caused a significant drop in the value of Mississippi's most valuable commodity, cotton, and thus a withdrawal of domestic and European capital.

The Panic of 1839 and the prolonged depression that followed undercut the boisterous efforts to raise local capital, while also simultaneously restricting European investment in the region. Baring, Brown, and other merchant houses withdrew from investing in either cotton or state bonds. Southerners could not agree on whether exogenous or internal forces were primarily to blame for the Panic of 1839. The debate itself fueled partisan politics, with many Democrats in the Southwest joining McNutt in displaying familiar Jacksonian antibank ideas. They suggested that the panic had been primarily the fault of irresponsible banks that overextended credit for land, labor, and internal improvements. Others looked elsewhere, blaming foreign specie flow, trade fluctuations, and a withdrawal of foreign investment for failed projects. If Quitman's case is any indication, then both international and domestic forces coalesced to undermine improvement projects in the Cotton South.[48]

Regardless of the cause, the immediate and long-term effects of the panic devastated the region. Lower cotton prices left investors unable to pay off their debts, much less invest in new projects. Mississippi's infamous defaulting on foreign-held bonds practically ended British interest in that state until after the Civil War. "Wild cat" banking ventures from the 1830s went bankrupt, creating havoc in Alabama and Mississippi. Financial institutions stable enough to avoid closing, including most Georgia and South Carolina banks, chose survival over potentially risky investments. State governments quickly responded by tightening government controls over corporations and granting considerably fewer new charters between 1840 and 1845 than they had in the preceding five-year period.[49]

This does not mean that without the Panic of 1839 and the following depression the Lower South would have succeeded in creating large commercial metropolises with surplus capital or attracted more direct trade with the West and Europe. Disproportionate investment in land and slaves, structural aspects that subsequent historians and economists have seen as slowing commercial and industrial development, remained in place. In addition, northern canals, especially the Erie, and railroads had already made deep inroads into the Midwest, all but ensuring that New York and other northern cities would continue to dominate trade there, with New Orleans capturing much of the rest. Yet Quitman and others' experiences do suggest why and how contemporaries overlooked so-called systemic problems (which they saw as strengths) to embrace a more contingent explanation for their initial failures at diversification. Just at the time when businesses, planters, legislatures, and even many farmers invested themselves both intellectually and financially in economic development and diversification, their endeavors were plagued by circumstances that many believed beyond their control.

The goal of reengineering a more favorable national economy through internal improvement and direct trade with Europe and the West stumbled during the early 1840s but resumed when prosperity and some European capital returned in the late 1840s. Even though the panic did raise some skepticism about free trade policies, reformers believed the goal of economic diversification could be achieved within a larger framework emphasizing global interdependence and the ideal of international free trade. Unlike in the early national period, however, reformers no longer conceded that a natural division of labor dictated that southern crops travel indirectly through northern hands. They remained divided, however, between those future Whigs, who foresaw the utility of some federal intervention in the economy, and Democrats, who preferred little or none. Despite the setbacks of the late 1830s, politicians in the Lower South continued to desire sectional economic matrimony with the West and sectional commercial development as a means toward prosperity and power.

## American Proslavery Thought in the Age
## of British Abolition

By the mid-1830s it was becoming increasingly clear that preserving political allies would necessitate blunting an increasingly virulent antislavery movement. In
the decade after the nullification era, concerns about protecting slavery spread
well beyond South Carolina, which led a regional campaign to silence antislavery
voices and convince a wider world of slavery's compatibility with modernity and,
to receptive audiences, its moral justness. The continued centrality of slave-grown
U.S. cotton for global markets—despite fears that protection would ruin them—
empowered Lower South slaveholders in their efforts. The widespread economic
dislocation created in the late 1830s demonstrated just how adaptable American
proslavery thought could be. In flush times, slavery proved its economic profitability, in poorer ones, its alleged humanity. Recent historical scholarship has
come to appreciate the multifaceted nature of American antislavery belief; scholars of proslavery thought must do the same, recognizing that slave apologists
offered a variety of justifications, the adaptability (we might say inconsistency) of
which served as an important asset in their political efforts.[50]

The impetus for this surge of proslavery thought and action resulted largely
from developments on the ground, including Denmark Vesey–like conspiracies
and Nat Turner–like actions. Yet fears over how to deal with slave insurgency had
long existed. What changed by the mid-1830s was the heightened tone and aggressiveness of antislavery voices outside the region and visible signs of success in the
British Empire. Humbly presented petitions by Quaker pacifists gave way to the
fiery rhetoric of William Lloyd Garrison, the son of a Massachusetts merchant,
whose first edition of the *Liberator* (1831) promised an uncompromising approach
to the question of slavery. Such voices drew further inspiration from Britain's
demonstration that slavery could be abolished on a grand scale. Shortly after
South Carolinians revoked their ordinance of nullification against the tariff and
nullified the Force Act in March 1833, the British Parliament resumed a debate
over slavery in its provinces. Watching developments from his position as chargé
d'affaires to Belgium, Charleston unionist Hugh Legaré wrote privately that matters would be made worse because "the House of Commons will probably have
passed a bill for universal emancipation . . . which, added to St. Domingo, will
present you, at the mouth of the Mississippi, a black population of some 2,000,000
free from all restraint and ready for any mischief."[51] The August Emancipation

Act confirmed Legaré's fears, by compensating slaveholders £20 million and demonstrating the possibility of abolition's success.

This long-anticipated, and in the South much-feared, event provided the lens through which Lower South slaveholders—long in contact with West Indian planters and already sensitized about free black sailors—tracked the debate within their own country. In August 1833, writers for the *Charleston Mercury* returned to comparisons Robert Turnbull had made in 1827, cautioning slaveholders to be proactive in preventing antislavery forces from seizing the U.S. national government as they had the British. The once-powerful West Indian planter lobby found its institutions beholden to a hostile centralized government that had been seized by a once-fringe antislavery movement. As they had during the tariff debates, southerners might face the same fate "if our masters of the majority think it proper to ape the caprices of British fanaticisms, or in any mode whatever to legislate for her oppression." Duff Green, an avid Calhoun supporter and prominent editor of the Washington-based *United States Telegraph*, reprinted Lower South concerns while expounding a few of his own. Northern abolitionists, he argued, were following the same playbook as their British counterparts: "They wanted to instruct them a little better in religion, and who could object to that? Then they wanted to instruct them to be better clothed—by law. Then the owner must do this thing and the slave must do that—until finally," Green contended, it was thought best that the slaves be freed and their owners compensated.[52]

British abolition placed the Lower South's proslavery thought further outside of mainstream western moral and religious thought, allowing one Mississippi Fourth of July orator to now refer to slavery as the United States' "peculiar domestic institution."[53] With the French and English colonies having abandoned chattel slavery and most of Spain's former possessions doing so after achieving independence, slavery remained legal only in the United States and Africa, as well as Spain and Portugal's few remaining colonial possessions, most significantly Cuba and Brazil. The transatlantic abolitionist movement promised to hone its efforts on the most powerful and democratic slave power: the planters of the U.S. South. "The great slave question has started in England," Charlestonian Charles Drayton II wrote, "if realized [it] will transfer a great bearing on the United States: of course the whole evil will fall on the Southern section." Consciously timed to build on the momentum, the American Anti-Slavery Society convened in December 1833. Confirmed in their fears, southern moralists began a more deliberate proslavery response. "Pliny," an anonymous contributor to the *Charleston Mercury*, turned to the classical world and nostalgically praised slavery as a system that perpetuated the "natural" benevolence that premodern systems of mutual allegiance had supposedly promoted. But different and drastic times also called for new methods. "Planters," Drayton concluded, "must entertain views of the future different from those of existing times, that they may be prepared to bear the brunt of the baneful change in the coming state of affairs."[54]

The frightening reality of this new world order became apparent in the summer of 1835, when thousands of abolitionist mailings arrived in the Lower South. They were, with the tacit approval of Andrew Jackson and his postmaster general, Amos Kendall, quickly suppressed. When abolitionist petitions to Congress spiked in December of 1835, newly elected representative James Henry Hammond and seasoned veteran senator John C. Calhoun performed procedural gymnastics designed to demoralize their opponents by having the petitions immediately returned without a hearing. Perceived by northerners and even some southerners as a violation of the right to petition the federal government, their efforts partly failed but did ultimately achieve a compromise gag rule ensuring that all petitions regarding slavery would be received but immediately tabled, a policy that Congress annually renewed until 1844.[55] Even as Lower South slaveholders continued to claim that their economic commitment to free trade reflected their "liberal" attitude, their assault on abolition made their politics anything but.

As national politicians hurriedly erected levies to block the supposed tide of abolition within the nation, Lower South writers furthered new arguments to foster regional unity and convince outsiders that slavery remained not only morally and theologically sound but necessary for the advancement of commerce and western civilization. Much historical study has focused on the religious underpinnings of proslavery thought, and rightly so. Yet, the most ardent proslavery theorists—Edward Brown, Thomas Dew, William Harper, James Henry Hammond, Josiah Nott, and others—preferred, in Harper's words, to contend that Christianity had "nothing to do with the matter, except, indeed, that the total silence of its Divine Author" suggests "He considered the institution as altogether a matter of political expediency."[56] While preachers battled over the morality of slavery in print and in synod meetings, national politicians and their publicists remained largely focused on more material modes of analysis and "the common moral sense of mankind." In this they relied on their familiarity with free trade theory, the adverse economic impact of British emancipation, and especially the world's growing dependence on slave-grown raw cotton. When cracks in proslavery economic thought appeared, a fresh influx of race theory helped smooth them over, allowing slavery's apologists to argue for the continued necessity of black enslavement for the region, the nation, and the world. For pragmatic minds, the battle over slavery's morality mattered less than convincing northern moderates that it remained in their interest to protect slavery and that, by consequence, abolition threatened national economic prosperity and political security.

South Carolinian William Harper led the charge, delivering a speech before the South Carolina Society for the Advancement of Learning that was subsequently edited and published in 1838 as the *Memoir on Slavery*. A manifesto for future apologists, Harper's text provides a particularly revealing look at proslavery ideologues' turn toward newer justifications. Though defensive, it reflects little of the psychological or moral angst that historians typically attribute to slave apologists. Instead, Harper wove together a proslavery argument firmly rooted in modernity and grounded in the circumstances of global commercial expansion and fluctuating economic conditions, including developments within the British Empire and the 1837 panic. Harper's treatise nicely accompanied southern efforts at economic development, free trade, and the expansionist political agenda that came to dominate the 1840s.[57]

Reflecting his global outlook, Harper framed his discussion around the work of Edward Gibbon Wakefield, the eminent British political economist, social critic, and author of *England and America: A Comparison of the Social and Political State of Both Nations* (1833). In Harper's hands and despite Wakefield's antislavery premises, *England and America*—republished in New York in 1834—became a catalogue of the historical, social, and economic reasons for why slavery provided the ideal path toward modern civilization. Wakefield, whose goal had been to encourage English colonization, contended that England's so-called white slaves lived in material economic conditions worse than those of American slaves. Citing longer life spans and better diets in the United States, he argued that "the peasant of the south of England suffers nearly all of the evils but enjoys none of the advantages of slavery."[58] Wakefield then affirmed southern claims that early colonization, slavery, and successful commercial agriculture historically reinforced one another, also proposing "*the situation of America* [namely labor shortages] *does afford some sort of apology for the foul stain upon her character.*"[59] Wakefield thus perversely provided Harper the "objective" commentary from which to construct a material and economic justification for slavery, one that subsequently resulted in a moral justification based largely on utilitarian grounds.

To Harper, Wakefield's England represented both the epitome and the nadir of modern civilization. In Harper's imagination, Britain—not least because of its commercial dominance of the world—remained the most civilized nation on the globe. Yet, its path toward civilization had come at a considerable cost and contained, according to Harper, the seeds of its own destruction. While the fierce competition for labor produced "excellence in art and knowledge," it also created gross inequality, working-class misery, and the middle-class anxiety so vividly evidenced in Wakefield's account. In societies such as England, Wakefield and Harper contended, when the supply of labor exceeded demand, wages dropped and employers became decreasingly concerned with the health and well-being of their employees. As material conditions worsened, desperation would lead workers to take to the streets and overturn society. In the long term, Harper anticipated, such class warfare would destroy British civilization from within. For Wakefield the vicious cycle that placed free whites in a situation worse than slavery could be broken by balancing labor supply and demand, through the prohibition of Irish immigration and the encouragement of South African and Australian colonization, Wakefield's primary hobbyhorse. Yet Harper believed that Wakefield's attempt to eliminate Malthusian population pressures hindered the very competition for labor necessary for progress and civilization in a free labor society.[60]

Slavery on the other hand, Harper concluded, concentrated both labor and capital in the hands of those best able to direct them, mitigating the economic competition between the two while still allowing it to be directed toward common economic ends. Especially in areas with vast lands, like newly colonized nations or more sparsely populated regions like the southern United States, concentrations of capital with labor had to be coerced in order to be successful. This "universal" proposition gained further credence, Harper believed, when applied to tropical climates, which (by Wakefield's own account) had only been commercially successful when built upon slave labor. For Harper, the reason was simple. Abundant land led to settler dispersion and thus removed the concentration of labor necessary for larger-scale market production. Hot weather disinclined many to work, especially with abundant vegetation so easily available. Coerced labor, particularly in the form of permanent slavery, prevented this from happening by placing human capital at the clear direction of individual masters with the knowledge and desire to pursue trade and civility.[61]

According to Harper's logic, slavery even remained a flexible enough institution to question the traditional axiom that it was only suitable for agrarian societies. Unlike the 1820 Charlestonian memorial, which had emphasized that the South's slave labor prevented it from becoming a manufacturing center, Harper

implied that slavery could be deployed in any number of economic pursuits because slaveholders could channel their labor wherever they wanted. The South
could industrialize without the need for dense urban areas. As Wakefield had
admitted, slave masters were in certain instances the ideal types of capitalists,
able to direct otherwise uncoordinated labor toward the most profitable ends.
Slaves were already being used to construct railroads, mines, and mills across the
South. Not all in the Lower South accepted the idea that slaves should be used in
southern factories, especially in combination with free labor. Nor did they necessarily believe that slavery could or should industrialize the region as quickly as
free laborers were transforming the Northeast. Yet, Harper and others increasingly believed that slavery could forward rather than retard economic progress and
diversification, albeit along a different route and pace than free labor societies.[62]

White "capitalists" could thus enact the competition necessary for advancement and civilization because of their near complete control of labor. Harper in
essence provided one of the first systematic examinations of what Jeffrey Young
has recently referred to as "corporate individualism."[63] Harper accepted the classical economists' argument that free labor was cheaper than slave labor, but argued that this presented the precise moral problem of free labor capitalism. Intense competition for inexpensive voluntary labor lowered its value, leading to
exploitation that pitted labor and capital against one another. By Harper's analysis slavery, precisely because it required a long-term investment in the welfare of
the laboring class, had the reverse effect. As later southern politicians repeatedly stated, slavery aligned labor and capital in a more harmonious relationship.
As a result it *"anticipates the benefits of civilization, and retards the evils of
civilization."*[64]

The contrasts between free and slave society seemed particularly acute given
the immediate context of the panics gripping Britain and the United States in
1837: "In periods of commercial revulsion and distress, like the present, the distress, in countries of free labor, falls principally on the laborers. In those of slave
labor, it falls almost exclusively on the employer. In the former, when a business
becomes unprofitable, the employer dismisses or lowers their wages. But with us,
it is the very period at which we are least able to dismiss our laborers."[65] Forced to
live on reduced rations or sold away from family members, the slaves of an indebted owner no doubt disagreed. But for self-pitying and self-congratulating
slaveowners like Harper, the first indications of a prolonged global recession and
high unemployment in the North prompted a quick elevation of the allegedly "pa-
ternalistic" results of proslavery economics. Paternalism did not mean rejecting

modern economic sensibilities. Rather, apologists came to the striking conclusion that the very wisdom of the slave system stemmed from its ability to merge good business practice and moral purpose to advance profit and humanity.[66]

Harper's carefully reasoned (if flawed) argument derived from modern understandings of modern processes, including a material-based worldview, expanding global commerce, and a commitment to societal progress. In so doing, however, it flattened humanity down to the most base and basic level, perpetuating a deeply racist perspective that ignored the individual hopes and desires of the slaves so central to the future "progress" slaveholders envisioned. Harper's inegalitarian premises rejected a basic tenant of Enlightenment natural rights theory, which he believed "ornamental" and "sentimental." In its place, Harper offered his own version of natural history, one with strong linkages forward to late nineteenth-century Social Darwinism, in which "the proclivity of natural man is to domineer or to be subservient." Attacking the primary intellectual justifications behind abolitionism—that slavery contradicted the will of God or Nature—Harper and subsequent theorists retained their fealty to supposedly natural economic and social principles.[67] Unlike earlier proslavery authors, however, who merely emphasized the blessings of a hierarchical or semifeudal agrarian society, Harper and his intellectual heirs presented a vibrant, malleable proslavery ideology capable of adjusting to a range of circumstances and deflecting a variety of charges. Not surprisingly, then, Harper's writings circulated throughout the Lower South, joining Thomas Dew's as staples of the proslavery lexicon.

Harper and subsequent proslavery apologists drew heavily on the increased global importance of southern cotton and the ongoing free trade movement, stressing the importance of slavery to interests outside the South. At the Founding, those in the Lower South had defended slavery as a necessity for regional economic development. For Harper the products of slavery, especially cotton, had become critical components of the national and global economy. Drawing on inflated arguments repeatedly made during the tariff debates, he insisted that "the products of slave labor furnish more than two-thirds of the materials of our foreign commerce, which the industry of those [northeastern] States is employed in transporting and exchanging." "Among the slaveholding States is to be found the great market for all the productions of their industry, of whatever kind," meaning that "the prosperity of those [northern and western] States, therefore, and the civilization of their cities, have been for the most part created by the existence of Slavery."[68] In addition, he invoked the redistributive effects of the tariff, arguing that slavery had, in part, given northern workers higher wages and a

partial reprieve from the harsh conditions seen in Britain, thus temporarily averting the vicious consequences of free labor competition. In essence Harper had
translated lessons from the tariff debates into a double-edged proslavery sword,
contending that slavery benefited not only those regions where it existed but also
those that traded and manufactured the products of slaves. Harper's bold theories
might have only been possible within the unique political and social climate of
South Carolina, but his deeply materialistic conclusions resonated much more
broadly in light of the global context within which they were proposed.

Cotton Southerners explained both the reasons for and effects of British emancipation in ways comparable to Harper's materialist analysis. Some concerned
slaveholders asserted that British emancipation had resulted from the triumph of
sheer religious fanaticism over reasoned economic interest. Other self-taught political economists, however, including Duff Green and John C. Calhoun, immediately searched for deeper structural reasons for abolitionists' apparent success.
British policymakers, they privately and publicly argued, had been seduced by
"manufacturers, as well as those connected with the East India interest" who, according to Green, desired to reroute British imperial trade toward the East Indies
in order to "open a larger market for the productions of England" and be furnished with "supplies of tropical productions [including cotton], at a cheaper
rate." This "powerful inducement to change the direction of trade" could only be
achieved by undermining West Indian commerce, and it was calculated that "the
emancipation of the slaves will diminish the quantity of West India productions,
without much diminishing the demand for British Productions."[69]

Another observer of the cotton industry took his cynicism a step further and
argued that abolition had been little more than an effort "to promote the aggrandizement of her Eastern Empire" in hopes of developing an alternative to British
dependence on Southern cotton. It was an economic decision first and "humanity . . . only an after thought."[70] Misled by the economic arguments of different
imperial interests, another writer concluded, the British government had taken a
"false" position and accepted the East India Company's belief that emancipation
in the West Indies would greatly elevate the value of free labor in the East.[71] Politicians' mistake, slaveholders hypothesized, would come at an enormous price to
Britons of all races. After emancipation turned West Indian slaves into "apprentices," southerners scrutinized the West Indies to evaluate the relative productivity of slave and postemancipated societies. Predisposed to accept negative reports
coming out of the region and having learned to view international trade statistics as the primary mark of civility, regional commentators did not take long to

conclude that emancipation had been a complete failure. While abolitionists praised the relative peace that persisted during the transition to freedom, southern planters and papers used the sharp drop-off in exports and imports to condemn the "ruinous" effects that emancipation had on the staple economies of the West Indies. What one historian has called "the painful transition to freedom" further fueled arguments about the material and economic benefits of slavery.[72]

Regional propagandists used the decline in West Indian commercial productivity to bolster another much more problematic aspect of their evolving proslavery argument: the claim that people of African descent lacked initiative and were lazy. One self-serving article reprinted from an Ohio newspaper in the *Southern Quarterly Review* alleged that the Jamaican chief of police, a former Virginia slave, publicly proclaimed that he had never seen a "coloured community in [a] slave State so debased so indulent [*sic*], so vicious and so impoverished, as are the free negroes in Jamaica." In a remark revealing the apocryphal nature of the story, the chief allegedly stated he "would prefer living with his master in Virginia, if he could be reinstated."[73] In reality, the individual initiative, not laziness, of free persons had been the source of the downturn in West Indian trade. Caribbean freedmen and -women, much as those in the United States attempted to do immediately after the Civil War, asserted freedom from their former masters by leaving the plantation and setting up independent, self-sufficient homesteads. Few whites, even in Britain, recognized this distinction, however. Driven by a commercial-centered view of progress, slaveholders turned a remarkable attempt at self-empowerment into further "evidence" for racist assumptions that by the 1830s were gaining support, even among pseudoscientists.

In the final analysis, then, British emancipation had a more complicated legacy than has typically been assumed. As Drayton and Legaré had feared, success empowered British and American abolitionists to focus on eradicating slavery in the U.S. South. Even as American blacks celebrated August "Emancipation days" with their Caribbean counterparts, slaveholders' myopic, commerce-centered worldview (tinctured with racist assumptions), provided a powerful device for spreading the proslavery economic gospel. Those in the region who remained squeamish about accepting slavery as a permanent and morally just institution, in light of developments in Haiti and the British West Indies, accepted it as a modern necessity. In fact proslavery thinkers accused abolitionists of rolling back material and cultural advancement. One need only look southward to the British West Indies, they argued, for concrete evidence that emancipation reversed the progress of western civilization. According to one southern commentator,

"Slave Emancipation; or, John Bull Gulled out of Twenty Millions" (England, 1833). In this antiabolitionist satire, the "philosopher" William Wilberforce leads a tour through the slave quarters, lobbying "Johnny Bull" for the funds necessary to finance emancipation. Bull, representing the British public, believes it an attempt at extortion and expresses deeper concern about the "poor innocent factory children." Behind him a gluttonous "slave-robber" and Whig politician conspire to pick Britain's pocket of £20 million for compensation to slaveowners. On the right, heavily racialized depictions of persons of color celebrate with rum and tobacco but without understanding what emancipation means, one thankful that "massa Boll pays for it" and the other decrying that "Jonny Bool" "be one dam fool." Cynical views of British abolition such as this fostered Lower South confidence in its own slave system. Courtesy of the Library Company of Philadelphia.

emancipation had, in total, resulted in the loss of $800 million, leading to widespread destitution and creating a "much worse state of slavery than the African race in the slaveholding states of our Union."[74]

Official efforts to import coolie labor from Asia and contracted Africans began in 1844 and further fueled proslavery responses, even leading the southwestern press to argue that the British government had been guilty of "criminal hypocrisy," criticizing southern slaveholders while under "the name of apprentice consigning" workers "to perpetual servitude."[75] All of this proved to one Natchez editor writing in 1845 that Britain, "led by the overwhelming influence of the East

India Company," had only "nominally abolished slavery" and, realizing the error of its ways, had essentially reopened the Atlantic slave trade under another name.[76] The economic recessions of the 1820s and early 1840s may have provided slaveholders some reason to think free labor more efficient than slave labor, but the results of British abolition suggested to them that emancipation guaranteed complete economic ruin.

These developments deepened the Lower South's commitment to proslavery thought, but observers remained somewhat more anxious over whether emancipation would bolster the East Indian economy and create a viable competitor in the raw cotton market. In 1839 Britain, as part of an effort to revitalize East India's economy, sent a covert operative, Thomas Bayles, to the South to recruit potential planters willing to move to India and teach southern growing practices.[77] Bayles apparently did not protect his cover as British officials had instructed him to. In 1842 the *Southern Quarterly Review* noted that two years earlier the "agent" had procured "eight or nine young men" "to go to India to teach their overseers the art of making cotton on the improved method of Louisiana and Mississippi," taking with them superior American seeds and knowledge of cotton gins.[78] In 1841 British entrepreneurs again sought to bring the crop to readily available labor in the Niger River Valley of West Africa, a move that, because slavery was still common in Africa, southerners perceived as an effort to turn African slavery against American slavery. These measures, however, largely failed. Contrary to the expectations of abolitionists and officials, India plunged into a recession from which it would not recover until the late 1850s. The declining production of overseas colonies adversely affected British workers, whose jobs were dependent on colonial materials and markets. This, in turn, arguably injured working segments of English society, which could no longer command high prices for their products.[79] In sum, slaveholders predictably used these developments to confirm their argument that tropical and semitropical plants like cotton were best grown with enslaved blacks controlled by educated whites. Efforts to toy with this supposedly naturally determined relationship would have harmful consequences for all.

Continued British dependence on U.S. cotton subsequently informed Lower South views of British foreign policy and her abolitionist stance toward the United States, provoking a level of Anglophobia not seen since the War of 1812. Observing the situation in 1842, one observer contended that British manufacturers and East Indians "wish to break up all competition elsewhere, particularly the competition arising from slave labor in the United States."[80] As early as 1842, some contended that British jealousy of American cotton and commerce had led her to consciously interject abolition into U.S. politics in hopes that a state of perpetual warfare between the North and South would leave Britain economically supreme.[81] A more charitable and accurate view of British policies would have perceived it as a peaceful effort to wean the British textile economy from its dependence on southern cotton and slave labor. Propagandists in the Cotton South instead supposed that British efforts reflected a desperate attempt to recapture the revenue lost from abolition and destroy slavery in the United States without any regard for the calamity it would create. Such arguments would prove critical in defining the region's response to Texas annexation.

Observers also molded evidence coming out of the British Isles to bolster Harper's conclusions and further a proslavery critique of free labor. The continuing poor economic conditions throughout Europe and America in the early 1840s provided slaveholders with ample verification of the humanitarian problems possible in free labor economies. This was particularly the case in James Hammond's renowned 1845 letters to British abolitionist Thomas Clarkson. In the late 1830s and early 1840s, reports of atrocious social conditions within British urban centers became the target of parliamentary investigations, ultimately culminating in extensive debate and legislative reforms. Printed in 1842, these documents emboldened Hammond to condemn British society for its destitution, vice, and exploitation of women and children. The result was a catalogue of the material and moral abuses witnessed within Britain's towns and countryside: "It is stated by your Commission that forty thousand persons in Liverpool, and fifteen thousand in Manchester, live in cellars; while twenty-two thousand in England pass the night in barns, tents, or the open air."[82] Challenging British abolitionists directly, Hammond declared: "When you look around you, how dare you talk to us before the world of Slavery? For the condition of your wretched laborers, you, and every Briton, who is not one of them, are responsible before God and man. If you are really humane, philanthropic, and charitable, here are objects for you. Relieve them. Emancipate them. Raise them from the condition of brutes, to the level of human beings—of American slaves, at least."[83] The conditions of slavery, if not its name, continued throughout the world, Hammond opportunistically concluded.

The increased prominence of labor problems in Britain and the North reframed slaveholders' anxieties over the constant threat of slave insurrections. Traditional commentary had emphasized the unique instability that slavery created. In 1787, Lower South leaders cited security from insurrection as a reason to join the larger federal Union. The recent experiences of Denmark Vesey and Nat

Turner had reminded anxious slaveholders of the damage that could be caused by uprisings of enslaved peoples. But in the late antebellum period, southern elites increasingly framed these fears within the context of the universal challenges of suppressing class and racial warfare. Observations of riots in northern and British cities and the emerging critique of free society provided confidence, however false, that slave society was no more, and possibly even less, insecure than non-slaveholding societies. In the 1840s the rise of workers' parties in the North and socialists in Europe (culminating in the 1848 revolutions) would be deployed to show that the dislocations of free society were leading to dangerous political instability for free societies as well. Southerners continued to take comfort in the fact that their localities and state governments would always take the steps necessary for their protection, as evidenced by continued enforcement of the Negro Seaman's Acts. Indeed these laws—though still challenged in northern federal courts—gained increased legal support after the unrelated case of *Milne v. New York* more clearly established states' policing power.[84] Nor did Lower South slaveholders assume that they were destined to be at the losing end of this prolonged struggle. Indeed their political maneuvering within the Union secured them several apparent victories in their campaign to prevent external forces from fomenting rebellion within their slave populations. The conquests of East and West Florida and the recent Indian removals allayed concerns by removing potential disruptive elements from inside and outside the borders of the Deep South. The successful annexation of Texas and preservation of slavery there would provide an even larger buffer zone for slaveholders in the Deep South by removing a potential haven for escaped slaves.

The logic of these arguments was directly challenged and often rejected by many contemporaries, most especially by free blacks and former slaves, whose narratives provided clear evidence of their capabilities. Neither the moral, economic, or racial contentions of southern slaveholders retained the coherence necessary to stand the test of time or science. Nevertheless, the arrogance and aggressiveness with which they rationalized them, particularly during a period of economic depression and the advancement of scientific racism, should prevent us from assuming that they believed their institution destined for obscurity. From their perspective, the intellectual dilemmas they faced were neither so terribly deep nor so paralyzing as to generate pessimism about the future.[85] This knowledge might help redefine the way we measure southern responses to antislavery movements. While southerners hoped that moral and religious arguments would mute political enemies and win allies, their defense depended primarily on convincing others of the continued economic viability of slavery for their region and the world. Thus a major challenge of the 1850s would be to convince others that cotton's utility to the world warranted further accommodation, even as southerners themselves sought to create a regionally diversified economy that rerouted capital and labor toward increased self-sufficiency.

While the gag order attempted to limit the reach of antislavery sentiments, slaveholders—especially in the Deep South—framed a more virulent proslavery ideology that by the early 1840s empowered southern intellectuals and politicians of a variety of political and economic outlooks. It seemed particularly well suited for a Democratic political agenda stressing westward expansion and unimpeded access to overseas markets. But economic reformers seeking to increase the region's commercial and manufacturing potential could apply Harper's examples of concentrated capital and labor to support slavery's shift toward manufacturing and envision a route toward industrialization without the potentially harmful effects of urbanization or intraracial class warfare. The proslavery argument failed to bring political unity to the region or convince everyone that slavery remained a perpetually desirable or moral institution. But the apparent negative effects of emancipation in the British West Indies and slave-grown cotton's continued dominance left few in the Deep South doubting that national and global progress depended on their special institution. Whether they could convince outsiders of this and halt the abolitionist advance remained much less clear. They would have to do so within a second party system that, because of its interregional composition, could neither fully accept nor reject their proslavery axioms. It remained to be seen whether the national Whig or Democratic Party would best serve cotton's interest.

## The Second Party System in the Cotton South

Low cotton prices, widespread economic depression, heightened antislavery attacks, internal dissension, and delayed internal improvement projects—by 1840 the tempered optimism of the mid-1830s had given way to a sense of economic despair. Depression and the desire to attract northern allies capable of protecting contested regional interests reshaped the political landscape within the Cotton South, leading state and local leaders (outside of South Carolina) to welcome the second party system. Increasingly vocal defenses of slavery as a positive good marginalized the region from a small number of conscience voters in the North and a few in the Upper South. Leaders in the Democratic or Whig national parties, however, granted slaveholders many of the political accommodations they demanded. Martin Van Buren had proved an important ally in arranging the House's gag rule in 1836. By 1840 antislavery Whigs had become so frustrated with their party's pandering to slaveholders that they formed their own political organ, the Liberty Party. The southern wings of both parties actively embraced what has been called the "Politics of Slavery," highlighting accommodationist northerners within their own ranks and accusing opponents of fraternizing with antislavery northerners. Yet both national parties' early willingness to protect, or appear to protect, slaveholders' interests generally left other issues to determine actual political loyalties. While ethnicity and religion (often pivoting around Catholic immigrants) played a significant role in determining party allegiance elsewhere, they played less of a role in the Lower South. Instead, ideas about how to redress worsening economic conditions provided the primary determinants of party strength, especially in the period from 1839 to 1844.[86]

The economic jolts brought on by the panic and blamed on Jacksonian Democrats' poor stewardship of the economy helped local Whig recruiting efforts. Especially in cotton-growing regions, wealthier planters and merchants favoring banks and desiring railroads found a home in the Whig Party, though not perhaps as uniformly as some historians have asserted.[87] At the national level, the presidential face-off between William Henry Harrison and Martin Van Buren has often been portrayed as a popularity contest won by a more balanced ticket, hard cider electioneering, and catchy campaign slogans. Even if Harrison was high on style and intentionally ambiguous on substance, the success of the "Tippecanoe and Tyler too" campaign within the Cotton South at least demonstrated the region's frustration with current economic conditions. Four years earlier the "Opposition" refused to accept Harrison as its presidential nominee, turning instead to Tennessee slaveholder Hugh White, who had a disappointing showing and won only Georgia by a very slim majority. The Jacksonian Democratic legacy, carried on by a New Yorker, Martin Van Buren, won solid victories in Alabama and Mississippi.[88]

By 1840, however, promises of a return to economic prosperity and sound fiscal and economic policy helped carry Harrison into the White House and Whigs into state legislatures. Despite the Whigs' poor showing only a year earlier in state elections, Harrison won comfortable majorities in Georgia and Mississippi. Even in Alabama, a Democratic stronghold, Harrison made significant inroads. The results of state-level elections also reflected the Whig ascendancy in the wake of the 1839 panic. In Alabama, Whig candidates gained seventeen house seats between 1839 and 1840, leaving Democrats with only a narrow majority of 51 to 49. Georgia and Mississippi Whigs also rebounded from big losses in 1839 to win majorities within those states' lower houses.[89] Both locally and nationally the Whig Party successfully painted itself as the party of prosperity and its opponents as the source of economic ruin.

The political wars over fiscal policy generally conformed loyalties in the Lower South to national developments.[90] Van Buren's Independent Treasury plan and hard-money propensity during a time of scarcity provided a particularly fruitful target for Whig candidates. Jacksonians' apparent inability to properly handle state-level banking or internal improvements also made state officials a target of the mounting opposition. The supposition that Whigs would help stabilize the local and national economy and facilitate more internal improvements especially contributed to Whiggery's advances in the commercial centers and black belt regions of the Cotton South. The Whig charges, however, did not go unanswered. Commitment to Van Buren's Treasury plan and the party's currency policy continued to resonate with many Democrats in the Lower South.

The removal of federal funds from the nation's banking system would, Cotton Democrats argued, stymie consolidationist policies they believed had harmed southern interests. According to Calhoun, who again briefly flirted with the Democratic establishment over the issue, "If the separation should be completely consummated, its [the federal government's] power will be reduced more than half. The whole banking interest will become the antagonist, instead of the ally, of high duties, extravagant expenditure & heavy surpluses."[91] Misplaced rumors that Bank of the United States president Nicholas Biddle's meddling in the cotton market prevented new financial arrangements with Europe and worsened the financial crisis compounded the hatred.[92] Democrats throughout the South saw the separation of banks and federal government as a key blow to northeastern monopolists.

The bank wars always retained a particularly localized tone, but one not dissimilar from debates in northern states. South Carolina and Georgia Democrats largely restricted their opposition to national and northern banks and proclaimed a desire to reform, not eliminate, state banks. In the Southeast, banking and paper money (based on sound money) remained "as legitimate and as lawful a business as planting cotton or making bricks," declared Georgia's *Macon Telegraph*.[93] In no small way, this was because Democrats and Whigs in the Atlantic states remained most committed to attracting the commercial capital they believed necessary to diversify their economy. The same was not necessarily true in the

Gulf States of Mississippi and Alabama, where Democrats unleashed venomous attacks on all banks, which they blamed for the panics, depreciation in state bonds, and widespread bankruptcy. Antibank governors, aided by radical Democrats, outmaneuvered bank supporters within their own party (including John Quitman) and catered to widespread popular dissatisfaction fanned by the banks' suspension of payments, accusations of corruption, and suspicion that funny money had created the crisis. Their campaign largely succeeded in limiting the number and power of states' banks, thus drawing state parties closer to radical agrarian and Loco Foco Democrats in the North and West.[94]

Throughout the cotton belt, Whigs argued that Democratic attacks on banks, state or national, and "soft currency" had gone too far, threatening to halt the wheels of commerce, undermine internal improvements, and prevent economic diversification. Though many southern Whigs happily attacked Democratic mismanagement of state-controlled banks, they insisted that private, and especially commercial, banks must be protected and believed some form of national oversight necessary. Economic stability, internal improvements, and future economic growth, they suggested, depended on banks. As antibank Democrats seized on a worsening fiscal situation to advance their agenda in 1841 and 1842, Alabama and Mississippi Whigs—particularly from commercial areas—responded that reform rather than repudiation offered the only solution.[95] After Harrison's untimely death, Whig congressmen from the Lower South, led by Georgia's John Berrien, fought hard to overturn John Tyler's unexpected veto of a third national bank.[96] In part disillusioned by Tyler's retreat from what they believed a major party plank, Georgia Whigs met in June 1842 and expressed their support for Henry Clay in the presidential election that was still two years away.[97]

Clay, once vilified as the founder of the exploitative American System, saw his political fortunes rise in a short period, thanks to woeful economic conditions. In addition to Clay's pro–National Bank policy, Whigs (in part seeking to keep the Central Railroad afloat and fund other improvement projects) also found his policy of public land distribution attractive. Realizing that direct federal support for internal improvements might be politically impossible, Clay envisioned indirect support by distributing revenues from the sale of federal lands to the states at a ratio determined by their relative population. Southern Democrats and most westerners hated the plan, favoring devaluation or John Calhoun's plan for cession to the states, which could then use the revenue to build public works. Whigs, on the other hand, especially in the land-strapped state of Georgia, preferred Clay's plan because it would provide them monies necessary for state improvement projects. Had it not been for the attractiveness of Clay's economic agenda, Georgia Whig leaders might otherwise have found Tyler, with an impeccable record on slavery and free trade, an ideal Whig. Instead they helped force him out of the party. These southern Whigs feared that a passive national economic policy would only worsen their situation, ultimately paralyzing economic recovery.[98] They proposed as remedies a new national bank or, when that seemed unlikely, depositing federal funds in existing banks. In so doing they drew closer to the national Whig Party orthodoxy. In this, at least, they sincerely waved the party banner.

Ultimately, however, constituents' continued commitment to a more sectionally defined economic agenda—centered on cotton commerce and international trade along with slavery's expansion westward—limited the region's embrace of central planks of national Whiggery. The degree to which cotton had itself become a form of currency may have limited the appeal of a more nationalized banking policy. Even more significantly, however, the reemergence of the tariff question in 1842 and 1844 strained party loyalty, suggesting that Lower South Whigs could still not fully embrace the American System. Since 1833, protective tariffs had received little political attention, with most groups accepting the compromise tariff of 1833, at least publicly. By 1841, however, projected federal deficits and poor economic conditions led northern Whigs to embrace a higher tariff for both revenue and protectionist reasons. A face-off between supporters of Tyler's generally lower-tariff approach and pro-protectionist members of his own party led to a prolonged debate—one ultimately culminating in the passage of a tariff justified partially on revenue grounds but also because it provided extra protection for manufactures. Opponents argued that the proposal violated the sanctity of the compromise that had saved the Union a decade earlier, but their efforts to overturn the tariff in 1844 failed.

The tariff debates of the early 1840s rekindled the sectional rhetoric of the 1820s, particularly in the minds of Deep South Democrats. Rhetorically, and in places substantively, the argument looked much like those of the 1820s. Statistical tables drawn from the recently published 1840 census simply replaced those offered up the previous decade, supporting similar analyses.[99] Not surprisingly, South Carolinians and Georgia Democrats responded most vociferously, threatening to disrupt interstate trade. According to Robert Barnwell Rhett, "If the protective policy is wise and just with foreign nations, it must be equally so between the States, for there is far more intercourse and affinity of interests between portions of the United States and foreign nations, than between different portions of the Union."[100] George McDuffie threatened to act on Rhett's suggestion, saying he might resign his Senate seat so that he could bring a measure before the South Carolina legislature that would tax all domestic manufactured goods not produced in the state. Georgia's Seaborn Jones agreed, suggesting that southern states might fight a protective tariff, not with nullification, but with "retaliatory legislation" passing countervailing "excise duties upon manufactured articles which have not paid revenue duty to the Government."[101]

Such avowed threats remained rare until the 1850s because they raised the specter of unconstitutionality (though the issue would be debated) and undermined the very beliefs being argued for: that nature and the Founding Fathers had a distinct affinity for free trade policies. Still, Alabama representative Arthur Bagby warned, the tariff would "tax ten planters for the benefit of one manufacturer" and "oppresses and plunders one section for the benefit of another."[102] Samuel Gwin of Mississippi concurred, suggesting that tariff advocates were "sowing the seed of bitter dissensions in our future legislation. You will either force the South to change her products altogether, and become your competitors in manufacturers; or we will force you to repeal your tariff laws."[103] The tariff debates of the 1840s again highlighted the difference between an American System focused on home markets and a region oriented toward overseas markets and fearing itself already overly dependent on northern merchants to reach them.

As with the debates of the 1820s, the grain-producing western states provided the major swing votes in 1842 and 1844. Accordingly, tariff supporters again highlighted that the restrictions on imports provided by the British Corn Laws should make grain producers leary of free trade. In response southern Democrats offered somewhat strained cotton-centered arguments, suggesting that "the constituents of gentlemen of the West [were] all indirectly cotton-growers themselves." "They," Gwin proposed, "sent their supplies to feed the South; sell them for the cotton planter's bill on New York or Liverpool, where he has shipped his cotton; and with these bills pay their debts, or make purchases in the Northern cities. Thus the money received by the cotton grower rests, at length, in the pockets of the grain-grower." Westerners' refusal to hold to the compromise tariff of 1833 and free trade would mean "that a crisis in the history of the West and Southwest is at hand. If we, the most natural allies on earth, go to war, it will be a breach never to be healed."[104] Groups in the cotton belt remained baffled that northern agrarians continued to rebuff their supposedly natural partners, a clear indication that they had not yet sufficiently invested the West in free trade. Just as in earlier debates, both Gwin and Bagby—though ostensibly westerners themselves—suspected

Table 5  M. A. Cooper's Summary Table of Congressmen Representing Party and Interest Affiliation

| Sectional Interests of Representative | Representing farmers or planters | | Representing farmers and manufacturers, or merchants | | Representing mercantile and manufacturing | | Exclusive manufacturing interests | Farming and manufacturing interests mixed |
|---|---|---|---|---|---|---|---|---|
| | Democrats | Whigs | Democrats | Whigs | Democrats | Whigs | | |
| From North and East | 27 | 24 | 12 | 37 | 7 | 16 | 23 | 49 |
| From South | 41 | 20 | 7 | 8 | 0 | 0 | 0 | 15 |
| From West | 9 | 33 | 0 | 0 | 0 | 0 | 0 | 0 |
| Total | 77 | 77 | 19 | 45 | 7 | 16 | 23 | 64 |

*Source: Congressional Globe*, 27th Cong., 2nd sess., appendix, 836.

that northwestern support for the 1842 tariff had been bought by northeastern support for internal improvements and a more favorable distribution of the revenue from land sales.[105]

While free traders' analysis had changed little since the 1820s, political circumstances had changed a great deal. The context of a functioning two-party system fundamentally altered the debates as both national parties pressured their members to support or oppose the measure regardless of their location. To demonstrate that point and put pressure on his Georgia Whig colleagues, Democratic representative Mark Anthony Cooper used census data and "private intelligence" to generate a detailed table identifying the party affiliation of every individual in Congress and the combination of interests (manufacturing, farming, planting, mercantile) in their respective districts. After showing the concentration of mercantile and manufacturing in the Northeast and planting and farming in the South and West, he suggested that the only explanation for the tariff that appeared likely to pass was "purely political" action by Whigs who "yield" the "best interests" of their constituents over to the influence of "party feeling." In actuality, the presence of more sizable manufacturing in Upper South states, like Virginia and North Carolina, helped their numerous Whig politicians support protection on grounds of interest and party.[106]

The same was far less true in the cotton-dominated states of Mississippi, Alabama, Georgia, and South Carolina. In these states, despite the growth of some nascent manufacturing, there remained very little political support for a protective tariff. As a result, the Cotton South could potentially become even more isolated from its Upper South neighbors, a fact highlighted when one Maryland representative charged that "the Cotton States" had, as demonstrated by the compromise tariff, sabotaged national economic policy. Mississippi Democrat Samuel Gwin correctly perceived the charge as a partisan attempt to represent the "cotton-growing section of the Union . . . as the antagonist to the other great interests of the country, especially to the grain-growing tobacco, and manufacturing interests."[107] Convincing themselves and their colleagues that this was not the case remained difficult, particularly in the midst of a national recession that begged for government action.

For the first time, southern Democrats hoped to attract some northern manufacturers to the free trade cause. The lack of significant South American industry and the more advanced capabilities of U.S. factories might, free traders suggested, allow northern manufactures to compete with British counterparts—an idea thought ludicrous in the 1820s. Northern manufacturers still thought the idea a bad one. The political wedge between them and southern free traders remained significant, despite their mutual dependence. In his analysis of American politics, Edward Wakefield had proposed that southern slaveholders should embrace protection because "the force of the whole Union [was] required to preserve Slavery, to keep the slaves down." Harper reflected wider southern regional opinion "most indignantly repudiate[ing] his conclusion, that we are bound to submit to a tariff of protection, as an expedient for retaining our slaves."[108] Whether a stronger alliance with manufacturers would have better protected slavery politically is not clear. But continued Lower South resistance to tariff protection certainly did not encourage northern manufacturers to serve southern interests. This doesn't mean that southern slaveholders subverted the protection of slavery to their commitment to free trade. On the contrary, they continued to believe the two closely intertwined because abandoning free trade would limit the region's profitability, thus undermining slavery's viability.[109]

With little economic optimism at home, Lower South Democrats looked abroad, reaffirming their commitment to free trade principles. "The true American policy," Gwin suggested, "is to encourage the purchase of our cotton, rice, and tobacco, on the continent of Europe; our manufacturers in the South American States; our breadstuffs in the colonies of Spain, France, and Great Britain; and if possible, open the European market to the same." Doing so, he believed, was the best policy internationally and domestically because "commerce with the whole world will be promoted, extended markets secured for the products of our whole country, and a sufficient revenue supplied, at a low rate of duties, to meet the wants of Government." In making their case, cotton Democrats highlighted recent global developments they believed would benefit American commerce, agriculture, and manufacturing. The creation of a stronger manufacturing sector in continental Europe provided one source of hope: "He must be an inattentive observer of events in Europe who does not see that a great revolution is taking place on that continent as regards commerce and manufacturers. The continental system of Napoleon, which was a theory in his time, is now put into practical operation. Instead of nationals on the continent of Europe being dependent upon English manufacturers for consumption, they are becoming the great rivals of that great manufacturing people, both at home and abroad."[110] Already since 1833 balance of trade statistics with France had increasingly favored the United States. Particularly encouraging, in mid-1844 the Tyler administration presented the Senate with a commercial treaty with the German states of the Zollverein which offered the duty-free importation of cotton and reduced tariffs on other staple goods in exchange for lower import taxes on some manufactures.

The rise of new European manufacturing sectors would, free trade Democrats thought, have a ripple effect on British commerce and ultimately benefit American merchants and agrarians by providing indirect access to new markets in Asia and Africa. "England must have an outlet for her manufactured products," Gwin noted. The "loss of the market on the continent of Europe" had forced her to look to other continents, as evidenced by increased British trade with Africa and the Opium Wars, which Gwin contended had been fought to open Chinese markets. If the United States preserved its direct trade with Britain, Gwin continued, Americans would gain access to these new markets, which otherwise they had "neither . . . the military or the will to do" on their own. This would, of course, be particularly beneficial to cotton growers, who had historically been Britain's primary source of raw cotton. The Cotton South would once again benefit tremendously from that nation's expanding commercial empire. In short, southern Democrats argued, this period of economic depression warranted expanding markets, not restricting them with tariff barriers.[111]

The region's commitment to cotton culture continued to tie the region and its voters to a policy of free trade. As a result, the tariff debates of 1842 and 1844 placed Whigs from the Cotton States in an awkward position—forced to choose between party loyalty and prevailing local opinion. In 1841 and 1842 only Georgia's six Whig representatives and one senator faced the problem. In an effort to bring them along, Clay tied the tariff to a distribution scheme popular in Georgia. The attempt offered Georgia's Whigs some political cover, which Senator John Berrien furthered by successfully proposing an amendment that would suspend distribution when any tariff rates exceeded 20 percent. In the following session, however, Clay determined that those rates were too low for the necessary revenue and argued that they needed to be raised to 30 percent. Ultimately the distribution bill, which Lower South Whigs supported, and the tariff bill, which they opposed, had to be separated.[112]

Without the perks of funding for improvements and facing opportunistic Democrats determined to exploit the tariff issue at home, Georgia Whigs distanced themselves from the 1842 tariff. James Meriwether and Richard Habersham blasted the measure. In a daring counterattack Hiram Warren deflected criticism back to the Democrats, suggesting that their unwillingness to consider a revenue tariff had in fact violated the compromise tariff and created severe deficits. The Democrats, not the Whigs, were responsible for the budgetary problem and thus had only themselves to blame. Revealingly, however, even Warren ended up voting against the bill, on grounds that it was "too protectionist." After Tyler signed the tariff into law, emphasizing that it was a revenue measure, Lower South Whig parties astutely reversed themselves, insisting that any protective effects were purely incidental.[113]

The tariff question remained a political thorn in the side of Cotton South Whiggery. When George McDuffie launched an 1844 Senate campaign to repeal the 1842 tariff, Lower South Whigs led by John Berrien first tried to quash the action by claiming that revenue legislation must come from the House and then by noting that the doomsday scenarios Democrats had offered had not materialized: "I know that the price of southern produce has not fallen since these duties were imposed. I know too, that the prices of articles of southern consumption have not risen, but have been sensibly diminished." If anything, the national economy had witnessed a general recovery, even if cotton regions had not. "The friends of free trade," fellow Georgian Robert Toombs argued, "assume that all commodities will, necessarily and invariably, and in all markets, sell for their natural price." Calling into question the fundamental premise of free trade thought, he contended that "this proposition, so far from being generally true, is almost universally untrue. The market price is seldom, in any market, the same as the natural price; and even this natural price, from the very nature of its constituent elements, is subject to an infinite variety of disturbing causes, and like, the market price, is as variable as the winds."[114]

In South Carolina, William Gregg, founder of the Graniteville Company and heralded as the most successful textile manufacturer in the South, chastised Democrats for investing energy in opposing the tariff rather than using it to advance southern industry.[115] Berrien agreed, contending that the "march of this manufacturing spirit is still onward and southward." Citing the creation of manufactories along riverways in South Carolina, Georgia, Alabama, and Arkansas, he noted in heavily sectionalized language that "our northern brethren will not, therefore . . . be permitted any longer to play this game altogether alone. They must divide the 'plunder,' and share with us of the South some of the 'enormous profits' which they have been hitherto exclusively enjoying." Berrien and Toombs did not defend the principle of protection overtly, but they did reject the Democrats' common refrain that Great Britain and other European powers were disposed toward freer trade.[116] Unlike in 1842, however, in 1844 Berrien and three of his four Lower South Whig colleagues, including Alabama's James Dellet, backed up their words with votes supporting the tariff. If a revenue tariff was necessary, it might as well discriminate in order to support American and, they hoped, southern industry.

Even as declining regional economic conditions led a few Whig leaders and the small but growing number of manufacturers to recognize protection's potential benefits, majorities continued to disavow its usefulness for cotton's commerce. Berrien acknowledged as much, noting "how little influence my judgment on this question will have, or can claim to have, with the great body of my countrymen."[117] Protectionist claims that higher tariffs aided cotton growers did not conform to planters' economic reality. Cotton prices had continued to drop after passage of the 1842 tariff, fetching only 5.6 cents a pound in 1845, by far the lowest price of the antebellum period.[118] Though it would have supported his arguments before Congress, Toombs did not join the chorus of northern voices contending that protection raised the domestic price of cotton. Instead, he noted that protection had beneficial results for corn and wheat growers and suggested that planters diversify their crops and investments.[119]

In addition, free trade Democrats made a logical argument that tariffs, especially on European iron, actually hindered the South's efforts to build manufacturing establishments and railroads. Adding to Lower South Whigs' troubles, the Whig-controlled Senate rejected the Zollverein Treaty in June, a move that clearly hurt regional efforts to attract direct trade and new raw cotton markets on the continent. Despite their support for banking and some individuals' growing skepticism of free trade, Whig politicians from the region could not fully embrace a major premise of the American System. Tyler's excommunication from the Whig Party after his Second Bank veto only worsened the plight of Lower South Whigs, who now had to negotiate minefields within their own party. Already limited in their ability to worship fully at what Joel Silbey has called the "shrine of party," Whigs in the cotton belt thus remained exceedingly vulnerable when the long-suppressed subject of Texas annexation took center stage in 1844.[120]

Some Americans had desired Texas almost as soon as that province declared its independence from Mexico in 1836. Fear of war and party division, however, kept even sympathetic Jacksonians from debating the policy, despite Texans' own express desire to join the United States. Those responsible for igniting the proannexationist movement in the early 1840s and their motives are well known. Concerns over slavery—and especially rumors of a British abolitionist plot in Texas—motivated Tyler and his political advisors Duff Green, Abel Upshur, and John C. Calhoun to act. For this paramount reason, Thomas Hietala has convincingly demonstrated that annexationists, especially with ties to the Lower South, actively sought to dominate the global raw cotton market, a motive Tyler admitted had been primary. Those at the center of this movement saw these two tasks as integrally related to a third: defeating Britain in a perceived commercial war and thus advancing the free trade cause at home and abroad. Context and a closer examination of Atlantic developments reveal how and why politicians converted initial anxiety into a momentous political and diplomatic triumph for a crop they could now call "King."[121]

Duff Green, the man perhaps most responsible for fueling annexationist concern and action, did so from London, where Tyler had sent him in 1841 as a confidential agent tasked with monitoring developments and convincing Britons to pursue freer trade. In the process of explaining his slow progress, Green, a well-connected newspaperman and John C. Calhoun's son-in-law, believed he had made a discovery, both ominous and reaffirming. The inability of Britain's postemancipation colonies to produce raw materials as cheaply as slave labor in the United States, Brazil, and Cuba, he told Calhoun, had made it "impossible" for her "to maintain her commercial and manufacturing superiority." She faced two options: accept freer trade with slaveholding powers or continue protecting her own raw materials and waging war against "slavery and the slave trade" in hopes of increasing the "cost of producing the raw material" in slave-growing regions. Early indications, according to Green, were that she had decided on the latter course. Despite a moderate reduction of the Corn Laws in 1842, British politicians—partly at the insistence of antislavery groups—had continued discriminatory duties against foreign-grown raw materials. Those included highly protective tariffs on foreign sugar and grains and a more modest 5 percent tariff on cotton, a policy meant to raise revenue and increase intraimperial supplies. Antislavery lobbyists also demanded special discrimination against slave-grown commodities, a principle that Peel's government accepted regarding sugar in early 1844. Collectively this, along with British efforts to restrict credit and specie from U.S. markets, suggested that Americans must recognize "that this is a commercial war."[122]

A U.S. victory "can be accomplished without war," Green continued, but "the only means of doing it, is to be prepared for war." He advised Calhoun to "unite all parties" behind such preparations and predicted that "if England be defeated in the present movement, she has no alternative but to fall back on free trade."[123] By the summer of 1843, rumors that British officials were negotiating with the Texans and promising them diplomatic assistance in exchange for emancipation and free trade convinced Green that Britain's incendiary fight had reached new levels. She now sought not just to harm the United States commercially but to make Texas a haven for escaped slaves and ruin the South.[124] Letters to Calhoun and Secretary of State Upshur—two men whose instincts told them the same thing—helped mobilize Tyler and his few allies in Congress for annexation. In early 1844 Upshur and Tyler negotiated a treaty with the Texas minister to the United States.

As usual Calhoun, who became secretary of state after Upshur's death in early 1844, saw not only need but political opportunity. Now was the perfect chance to test northerners' support for slaveholders' rights. If they passed, great; if not, Calhoun believed, fellow slaveholders would at last realize the depth of the political crisis they faced at home and unite. With that apparent strategy in mind, Calhoun sent the Senate (along with other treaty documents) his own belated and unnecessary response to a British official letter denying any specific designs on Texas but admitting a desire to "procure the general abolition of slavery." His now-famous April letter to British minister Richard Pakenham caused an immediate stir. Pulling no punches Calhoun directly accused the British government of all that he and Duff Green had long believed. Real politics, not kind hearts, dictated actual policy. Abolition's economic failure and India's inability to compete with slave-grown cotton and sugar had led Britain to push emancipation schemes elsewhere. Anyone who doubted it, Calhoun suggested, just needed to look at Britain's recent importation of contracted indentured labor from East India and Africa to the West Indies. A few more charges of hypocrisy and Calhoun concluded with a strident proslavery analysis highlighting slavery's relative economic profitability in tropical climates. For good measure Calhoun drew on the highly inaccurate census data of 1840 to suggest that Africans lived longer, less crime-ridden, and better lives in slavery than outside of it.[125]

Subsequent correspondence and public comments provided further insight into the South Carolinian's mind. In May, he rather revealingly offered Pennsylvania Democrat Francis Wharton a partly revisionist historical account of "three memorable occasions, the war of the Revolution, that of 1812, and the threatened war of the Maine boundary, when the interests of the north was mainly involved." In those occasions "the generous South, ever devoted to the liberty and honor of the country . . . poured out freely her means, in blood and money, for the common cause, without asking whether she was to be the gainer or loser." The North now had an opportunity to do the same, but he suspected that the South's "zeal" would "never be reciprocated."[126] Calhoun expanded upon his economic understanding of the crisis and his definition of the South's security in a widely circulated August letter to the recently appointed minister to France, Alabama's William R. King. British officials, he argued, had been duped by abolitionists "to combine philanthropy with profit and power" under the principle that "tropical products can be produced cheaper by free African labor and East Indian labor, than by slave labor." "The experiment had been a costly one," he contended, using a *Blackwood's Edinburgh Magazine* article to demonstrate that tropical products grown by slaveholding nations far surpassed those grown in British free labor possessions. Britain's unscrupulous attempt to level efficient slave economies in order to rejuvenate languishing free labor colonies must be stopped.[127] If Calhoun thought such efforts would unite the nation or the South behind annexation, he grossly miscalculated. For a variety of reasons (some economic), Whigs, even southern ones like Henry Clay and Alexander Stephens, wanted little to do with annexation. Nor, after Calhoun had sectionalized the subject, did many northern Democrats.

More tactful but no less expansionist-minded Lower South Democrats stood poised to make the most of the bad situation that Calhoun had created. A more savvy approach might even provide a silver lining. If they could bring the rest of their party on board, the party of Jackson, rather than its onetime enemies (a beleaguered Tyler and hotheaded Calhounites), could claim the glory and ascend to the regional and national prominence they had been accustomed to prior to 1840. Already Democratic congressman Robert Walker—a Pennsylvanian-turned-Mississippi-representative—had done more to aid the annexation cause than Calhoun. In a twenty-six-page open letter written in January 1844, Walker appealed to northern racial anxieties, economic interest, and concern over social conditions to defend annexation as a policy in the North's best interests.[128]

Relying on the same census data that Calhoun had invoked, Walker foretold the outbreak of racial and class warfare in the northern cities unless something was done to remove surplus slaves and free blacks. The annexation of a large tract of land like Texas would provide precisely the "safety valve" necessary to ameliorate social tensions in the North. While Walker—diplomatically though not necessarily disingenuously—suggested that diffusion westward might enable slavery to die out naturally, he also lambasted abolitionists, pointing out to potential northern allies that freeing slaves in the South would ultimately swell free black populations in the North. In addition, Walker quoted British officials and abolitionists discussing the great potential of Texas for cotton cultivation, reminding northern merchants that "to lower the flag of the Union before the red cross of St. George" would be "to surrender the Florida pass, the mouth of the Mississippi, the command of the Mexican gulf, and finally Texas itself, into the hands of England." Sympathetic newspaper editors—including those who had already promoted Green's musings, like *New York Herald* editor, James Gordon Bennett, and Tyler's official organ, John B. Jones of the *Daily Madisonian*—reprinted and distributed Walker's letter to hundreds of thousands of eager readers.[129]

Walker's appeal to interest, racism, and patriotism immediately impacted northern Democratic sentiment. Pennsylvania senator James Buchanan called for immediate annexation for the sake of commerce and hoped that it might even "convert Maryland, Virginia, Kentucky, Missouri, and probably others of the northern slave states into free states." Other northerners, including *Democratic Review* editor John L. O'Sullivan, highlighted recent legislation that demonstrated northerners' unwillingness to accommodate free blacks within their borders. An Ohio law, he pointed out, continued to limit entrance of free blacks into the state to those capable of posting a bond that protected that state "against the risk of his becoming a pauper"; Pennsylvania's constitution precluded the possibility of any free black becoming a full citizen. Such comments wisely catered to nominal antislavery sensibilities, but more importantly they exploited procommercial sentiments and contemporary racist fears shared by northerners and southerners alike.[130] When these appeals inspired only lukewarm support from the Democrats' presumptive nominee for the White House, Martin Van Buren, Walker and his allies worked behind the scenes to find another candidate. At the national convention in May, he and a group of proannexationists artfully used Tennessee planter-politician James K. Polk's connections with Andrew Jackson to forward him as the party's candidate on a proexpansion platform.[131]

One can speculate whether an entirely different history might have transpired had this not happened. As history would have it, Polk and his campaign managers' scheme proved a mark of electioneering brilliance, albeit one that had great cost to the nation. Pitted against a candidate on the record as opposing annexation and tapping into every ideological vein of "Manifest Destiny" he could, Polk won an impressive victory over a far-better-known statesman. Revealingly though, he did not win every slave state. Clay, the Whig nominee, achieved victories in his own state of Kentucky and Polk's home state, Tennessee, as well as North Carolina, where his American System still resonated much more powerfully than in cotton areas so utterly committed to international free trade. If election results can also be seen as a referendum on annexation—and at least some contemporaries thought they should—voters in the Upper South proved less enthusiastic than elsewhere. Polk and expansionism, on the other hand, played very well in the Cotton States. Voters there certainly had many reasons to love Texas. From a political perspective, it offered at least one more slave state. Economically, it allowed yeoman farmers and planters, familiar with cotton's heavy demand on the soil, to envision cheap and more fertile lands for their progeny and surplus slaves. In addition, by extending the Lower South's dominance of the raw cotton supply, it would force consumers to recognize and respect their long-term dependence on slave-grown produce. Polk's sweep of the Deep South and more narrow victories in the West, New York, and Pennsylvania gave him a slight edge in the popular vote and a 60 percent majority in the Electoral College. Polk's victory paved the way for Southern Democrats, with Tyler and Calhoun's help, to narrowly ratify Texas annexation through a somewhat unorthodox joint congressional resolution.

The Polk administration consolidated its political victory by quickly replacing Whig policies with Democratic ones that western and southern majorities found attractive. Walker reaped the political benefits of his scheming and accepted leadership of the Treasury Department. Using his position, he pushed Democratic majorities in both houses of Congress to reject distribution in favor of a graduation bill—a policy favorable to western settlement, northern laborers, and southern sensibilities—and to pass a warehousing system believed to be beneficial to commercial agrarians.[132] Perhaps most impressively, at least from the perspective of cotton planters and merchants, freer trade became national policy. Consistent with his party's platform to further liberalize commerce, Walker urged the repeal of the 1842 tariff and passage of a revenue-only resolution. For good measure, that reduction eliminated the 3-cent tariff on imported cotton. Free trade, he promised, would facilitate more international markets and further enhance U.S. prestige by enhancing Europe's dependence on America for raw materials like cotton and wheat. Buoyed by signs that European nations might be ready for increased free trade, supporters of Walker's tariff marshaled just enough western votes— including Texas's Democratic newcomers—to pass.

News from abroad sweetened the victory even more as British officials finally bent to political pressure from commercial and manufacturing centers. In 1845 the previously protectionist Peel government and Parliament refused to discriminate against slave-grown produce and even abolished all discrimination against foreign raw cotton.[133] George McDuffie joyfully wrote the president of the Anti–Corn Law League thanking him for an honorary copy of the organization's journal and noting that the league's early success was "destined to produce a fundamental change in the commercial policy of Great Britain." Free trade successes there, he continued, would ripple elsewhere as "the banner of free trade shall wave in triumph over the whole world, & beneath its ample folds 'the nations of the earth may pitch their tents in peace.'"[134] In light of the hawkish rhetoric from just the previous year, the words reflected sincere and newfound optimism from a longtime free trade warrior. As Americans reduced their tariff to approximate revenue levels, a Tory-led Parliament sacrificed the golden calf of British protectionism: the Corn Laws that had long discriminated against foreign grain growers. McDuffie and Lower South planters were not the only ones who commemorated what former Georgian governor Wilson Lumpkin praised as "the wise commercial policy of Sir Robert Peel."[135] One British merchant in Charleston literally etched the dual victory in stone and proudly forwarded busts of McDuffie and Calhoun to the Anti–Corn Law League to take their proper place among the champions of a transatlantic free trade movement.[136] Cosmopolitan free traders in the Lower South believed the near simultaneous repeal of American protection and the British Corn laws had marked an epochal moment in world history, one that would greatly further Anglo-American peace.

Success became all the more significant to the Lower South in light of the political and economic alterations that resulted. The moment practically ended what little backing for federal protection had existed in the cotton belt. Support for manufacturing continued to expand, even bringing a previous opponent, James Hammond, partly into the fold, but after 1846 only someone seeking political suicide would strongly support a federal protective tariff within the Cotton States.[137] Cotton prices jumped from 5.63 cents per pound in 1845 to 7.87 in 1846 to a decade high 11.21 in 1847, further convincing planters and farmers in the Lower South of the beneficence of free trade. Western farmers, by and large, had supported Walker's tariff levels, revealing cracks in the alliance between western farmers and northeastern protectionists. Future access to British mouths, Cotton South free traders hoped, would ensure that things continued to head in that direction. Southern Democrats seemed to have achieved the long-coveted alliance with the West and to have done so on traditional "southern" issues: free trade and, they hoped, slavery's expansion.

The situation could scarcely look bleaker for Whiggery in the Cotton South. While their counterparts in the North and even the Upper South predicted economic ruin and held out hope for a rebound during the 1846 midterm elections, Cotton South Whigs' spirits sank in the face of quite public and resounding defeats. The partly sectionalized, partly nationalized nature of Texas annexation had painted them into a dark and lonely corner. The voices of Calhoun and others had urged acquisition as a vital regional interest. Southern Democrats' success in nationalizing the question had brought northern Democrats but not northern Whigs in line. From either perspective, northern Whigs' repeated denunciations, especially during the final annexation push in early 1845, made them appear out of touch or openly hostile to Lower South interests. As Toombs had warned Berrien, "Once Texas became purely a sectional issue" its opponents "must be swept from the political boards." Only a last-minute Democratic amendment giving Polk complete control over implementing annexation provided Lower South Whigs political cover to oppose the final bill, though less on the wisdom of the policy than on grounds of potential executive abuse.[138]

The perceived triumph of free trade and King Cotton in 1846 against the cries of northern Whigs tarnished the party even more. Not surprisingly, Whigs in Georgia and other Cotton South states hoped to confine political campaigns "exclusively to state issues" so "that no allusion will be made in any way to national politics."[139] Even retreat into local issues could not stave off political disaster as election returns reflected Democratic dominance in the Lower South. In Mississippi, Whigs had won 43.4 percent of votes in 1844; by 1845 that figure had fallen to 35.2 percent and by 1847 to 33.6 percent. In Alabama they had claimed 41 percent of the vote in 1844 but in 1845 would not even field a candidate for governor, as they failed to do in Arkansas the following year. Only in Georgia, a traditional Whig stronghold, would things remain remotely competitive, and even there Whigs were on the defensive, falling from 51.1 percent in 1845 to 46.9 percent the following year.[140] Loyal Whigs in the Cotton South remained and made a brief resurgence during the secession crisis of 1850; they remained exceedingly weak, however, and spoke quietly as free trading expansionists had maneuvered themselves to the center of regional and national power. The Democrats' manifest design aided Lower South voters' confidence in them while putting Whigs in the region on life support.

Developments even briefly raised the spirits of a normally dour Calhoun, who in July 1846 informed another son-in-law, Thomas Clemson, that a western alliance might yet be secured. Though his personal political fortunes had been subsumed by southern Democratic dominance, the "recent course of events" had been almost in complete "conformity to his views," he told Clemson, who was serving as minister to Brussels. By the summer of 1846, he proclaimed that "the South & the West have never been so strongly united before; not only in reference to the Tariff, but the publick lands, the warehousing policy; and all other questions." Only three questions remained that prevented him from complete comfort.[141] First, the Oregon boundary, which he believed "would soon disappear." Second, Calhoun remained concerned that southern support for federally sponsored internal improvements continued to lag behind western demands, an issue he mistakenly believed he had remedied in a highly publicized speech before a Memphis railroad convention the previous November. There he had renewed his appeal for land cession to states for public works. The measure, however, would go nowhere, again failing to close the gap between southerners and westerners when it came to internal improvements.[142]

The final, and by far the most critical, issue threatening Calhoun's newfound optimism was the "unfortunate" Mexican War that had just erupted. Part of a minority within the Lower South who opposed the conflict, Calhoun feared its domestic and foreign policy implications. In addition to fearing he might have to share his "lily white" republic with Mexican residents whom he loathed, Calhoun believed that land acquired from the conflict would necessarily raise the question of slavery and thus undermine recent political gains with westerners. Less than a month after Calhoun had praised the progress made in bringing the West and South into natural alignment, his fears about the domestic landscape came true. Pennsylvania Democrat David Wilmot, part of a group of northeasterners frustrated by Van Buren's treatment at the hands of slave expansionists, sought to ensure that any new lands that seceded from Mexico remain closed to slavery. The fireworks Wilmot's Proviso generated offered a prelude to future battles. As the debate became fully engaged, Calhoun forcefully argued that slaveowners' constitutional rights mandated they be given unrestricted access to the territories. Most Democrats, North and South, decided to kick the question down the road and allow local constituencies to decide it. Rallying under congressional nonintervention, or what would eventually become known as "popular sovereignty," the Democratic Party temporarily pushed the issue out of the national spotlight. The story, as subsequent histories have thoroughly demonstrated, would not conclude happily, eventually confirming Calhoun's fears.[143]

Calhoun's less well-known worries about the conflict's international impact ultimately proved unfounded, for reasons which demonstrated to his contemporaries just how powerful cotton had become abroad. Calhoun feared that war with Mexico might "arrest, and even probably, defeat the arrangement of the Oregon question and invite the interference of the Great European Powers."[144] More-virulent expansionists, however, read recent developments in a way that precluded such anxiety. Commenting at the height of both crises in early 1846, Mississippi's Jacob Thompson urged that because the United States now controlled "nine-tenths of all the cotton-growing interests throughout the world," Britain must "keep the peace."[145] The United States' chief negotiators during the Oregon controversy, U.S. minister to Britain George Bancroft and Secretary of State James Buchanan both admitted that British dependence on cotton had been useful leverage in finding a satisfactory peace by June 1846.[146]

Interest, Clemson assured Calhoun, would also prevent Britain or France from trying to exploit the Mexican-American conflict, as they would "do all in their power to bring about a state of peace as speedily as possible not because either of those countries have the least affection for us as a nation or admiration for our institutions, but because their own prosperity appears to be dependent on a state of peace."[147] As Americans continued to accrue military victories, Bancroft confirmed such an assessment, telling President Polk from London that the British "do not love us; but they are compelled to respect us . . . England sees that California must be ours; and sees it with unmingled regret, but remains 'neutral.'"[148] In the end, these Democrats' assessments prevailed over Calhoun's temporary anxiety. British intervention remained limited to offers of mediation and first privately, and eventually publicly, British officials' acceptance of America's manifest design as a fait accompli.[149] With American military success imminent, British efforts turned toward securing peace, regardless of the geopolitical ramifications. In the Deep South and to some outside of it, Britain's continued hesitation meant primarily one thing: the British were unwilling to endanger the Anglo-American cotton trade, which they believed provided the lifeblood of both nations' economies.

Despite the ominous signs created by slavery's reemergence as a dominant domestic question, individuals who had urged Texas annexation reveled in the diplomatic leverage the acquisition had given them in Europe. In September 1847, Tyler attempted to revive his credibility by reminding the nation of the event which had allowed the nation to achieve greatness. Guided by his own judgment and the "opinions of other distinguished citizens," he had seen the wisdom in annexing Texas and securing "the virtual monopoly of the cotton plant to the United States . . . —a monopoly [with] more potential in the affairs of the world than millions of armed men."[150] For those inclined to see things in a broader perspective, subsequent events in Europe seemed to bear that decision out. Britain had accepted Texas annexation, freer trade, a favorable settlement in Oregon, and the United States' fulfillment of its continental destiny. Polk's European diplomats had also found continental Europe eager to accommodate more liberal trade. Belgium accepted reciprocal duties on March 31, 1846. Future Confederate commissioner, A. Dudley Mann, rapidly negotiated treaties with the German principalities, including Hanover, Mechlenberg, and Oldenburg. The Sicilians also came on board.[151] King Cotton, could, it seemed, sway the diplomacy of great powers. The calculated risk of adding Texas's cotton lands to the Union had paid off on the world stage.

Europe's, and particularly Britain's, nonresponse to Texas's annexation and cotton's perceived triumph also signaled the start of a hugely important transition in Lower South thought. Planters had entered the crisis believing they were engaged in a commercial war with Britain, one they feared had morphed into a more insidious assault on slavery. That Britain had stood idly by as annexation proceeded might have seemed success enough. In 1842 Green had told Calhoun that if America stood firm, Britain would have to accept free trade and, to an extent, American slavery. That Britain had largely acted and liberalized its trade policy and acquiesced to further land acquisitions infused the region with hope. By 1849, when lowcountry cotton planter and budding diplomat William Henry Trescot provided *A Few Thoughts on the Foreign Policy of the United States,* he credited cotton for creating cooperation between Britain and the United States, "the two great commercial nations of modern history." The best way to illustrate to someone that "the closest alliance" could exist between nations "sometimes antagonistic in their political theories" was "not surely by the history of governmental sympathies nor public treaties." Instead, he suggested, one should simply take

> him to the plantations of the South, and when he has seen in the whitening fields the result of immense capital, large experience and unwearied toil, let him follow the cotton to the warehouses of Liverpool, and the looms of Manchester, and when he has there witnessed the added capital, experience and labor requisite to its almost magical transformation, let him track the progress of this marvellous merchandize as American and British enterprise bear it to every distant land and hidden isle; let him see how both countries grow and prosper in this mutual labor; let him hear both speak one common language, and boast one common ancestry, and would it not be almost impossible to convince him that these two nations could be other than one people?[152]

Cotton and the Lower South's near monopoly of its raw form promised, Trescot believed, a new era of Anglo-American peace and prosperity.

Had those in the Cotton South remained content to simply accept and consolidate their victory of the mid-1840s and continue producing copious amounts of cotton for domestic and international markets, international and intersectional peace might have prevailed. Marginalized opponents to the Mexican War, including some South Carolinians and Whigs, gestured toward such a possibility. Yet emboldened by the political and diplomatic gains of the mid- to late 1840s, ascendant Democrats were not content with their economic or political situation within the Union. They insisted that slavery have equal access to new federal lands, including those in California, where gold had been discovered. The depression of the early 1840s had only temporarily humbled them, leading many to recognize the widening economic gap between their region and the rest of the nation. Economic reformers of a variety of political persuasions demanded that the geographic source for cotton's global wealth should be seeing more of its profits. More befuddling to all in the Lower South, cotton's recent demonstration of its economic and diplomatic benefits to the nation made northern antislavery gestures like David Wilmot's all the more inexplicable. As the political battles sparked by debate over California became ever more strident, observers and actors in the Lower South began pondering who could be counted upon to protect and expand their diverse interests, the most important of which remained King Cotton and the slave labor upon which its throne had been built.

# CHAPTER FIVE

# An Unnatural Union

King Cotton and Lower South Secession, 1849–1860

The debate over slavery's expansion, along with concerns over its political and economic security in the Union, propelled the Cotton States toward secession. Early advocates of secession urged that the drastic step needed to be taken at the first sign of defeat: California's entrance as a free state. That event led William Trescot to declare in 1850 that a "political revolution" had been inaugurated and "the only safety of the South is the establishment of a political centre within itself; in simpler words, the formation of an independent nation."[1] Others in the Deep South agreed, as southern rights associations sprang up throughout the Lower South, many threatening secession unless Congress protected southern interests. In the spirit of John C. Calhoun and at the behest of Governor John Quitman, the Mississippi legislature called for a southern convention to ensure the return of fugitive slaves and to guarantee slaveholders' access to new lands. Observers braced for a possible secessionist triumph when delegates elected vocal South Carolina secessionist, Robert Barnwell Rhett, president. This first secession crisis, and particularly Trescot's arguments, disseminated as a pamphlet entitled "The Position and Course of the South," provide insights into Cotton South secessionist thought and a template, albeit a premature one, for future action. It exhibited some of the defensiveness and irrationality historians have typically attributed to alleged "fire-eaters." Yet early secessionists also used domestic and international developments to provide a surprisingly pragmatic, and material-driven, argument for southern independence.

In explaining the origins of domestic conflict, Trescot prioritized allegedly universal laws of political economy, proposing that slavery had given the struggle between labor and capital (modernity's "vital principle of political organization") an ominous sectional tone. "At the North," he explained, "labour and capital are equal; at the South, labour is inferior to capital. At the North labour and capital strive; the one, to get all it can; the other, to give as little as it may—they are enemies. At the South, labour is dependent on capital, and having ceased to be rivals, they have ceased to be enemies." Race-based slavery had permanently subordinated the South's primary labor force and thus, according to Trescot, muted class conflict and left slaveholding capitalists to dominate southern politics. By contrast, northern working-class whites composed the Democratic Party's rank and file, especially in eastern cities and western farms. "Can a more violent contrast be imagined?" he retorted. "Free labour hates slave labour—capital, at the mercy of labour, is jealous of capital owning labour—where are their points of sympathy?" There were none, Trescot concluded: "The North and the South are irreconceivably hostile . . . their social and political systems cannot co-exist . . . the one in the nature of things wages internecine war against the other." Contrasting social systems impacted almost every aspect of politics, creating "competing systems of representation and taxation" and even divergent foreign policies.[2]

Proponents for secession drew richly from international developments and converted earlier free traders' calls for U.S. and British global cooperation into an imagined alliance between the South and Europe. As events suggested that the North was "in fact, a foreign power," Trescot placed almost infinite faith in cotton's power to ensure cooperation from allegedly more natural allies abroad. Quoting a September 1850 *London Times* article that highlighted the significance of the cotton trade, Trescot noted that Britain's trade "with America transcends all others." "Does it not follow," he arrogantly claimed, "that the industrial economy and the system of foreign relations of the nation, so far as based on commercial principles, should spring from, and be controlled by the cotton growing States?" A southern Confederacy, "cultivated by a slave population—supplying the staple of the world's manufacture, and ranged in imposing strength around the Gulf of Mexico, so as to command the trade of the Isthmus connection," would have "a close alliance with the few great manufacturing nations" and possess an "unchangeable resolution to leave the interior affairs of other nations to their own discussion." Trescot predicted that "the most selfish interests of the foreign world" would prompt "a speedy recognition of [the South's] national independence" while perpetuating selfish northern merchants' and manufacturers' "active diplomatic rivalry with Great Britain."[3] "Out of the union," another South Carolinian commented, "there may be some hope of safety for our institution, in it there is none."[4] According to Trescot, the "destructive energy" emanating from antislavery forces in the federal government made it "as wise, as safe, as honourable, to trust our domestic institutions and foreign interests to the Parliament of Great Britain as to a Congress with a northern majority. Nay, wiser and safer, for her colonial experience has taught England never again to sacrifice her profits to her philanthropy."[5] Only half jesting, Robert Barnwell Rhett presented just such a possibility. If other states refused to join South Carolina in seceding, then, he suggested, she could revitalize her commerce by embracing complete free trade and becoming in effect a British protectorate.[6]

Secessionists in 1850 drew extensively from the previous tirades against northern exploitation levied by free trade cosmopolitans like George McDuffie but repudiated the pacifist utopianism often underlying such arguments. John Quitman, a prominent general during the Mexican-American War and future filibusterer, accepted war as a way of life and in 1850 ordered an inventory of military supplies in the event of another one.[7] Even for the future diplomat, Trescot, "the marked characteristic of political life is the violent and uncompromising antagonism of great interests."[8] Like future Marxist and Progressive historians and their intellectual heirs, Trescot and late antebellum secessionists assumed that conflict, rather than peace, reflected the natural state of political affairs.[9]

Unlike later interpretations that pitted a mighty capitalist and modernizing North against a traditional agrarian society, contemporaries like Trescot, one of the nation's first historians, assumed slaveholders to be a superior type of "capitalist." Having used slavery to win the historic class struggle, he saw them as operating from a position of political and economic strength. Once "mature" the Lower South's "command of the Gulf and the cotton trade" would make them "the guardian of the world's commerce."[10] "The formation of an independent Southern confederacy would," in Trescot's view, not only defend against real or perceived northern antislavery gestures but also "give to the South the control of its industrial policy and its commercial connection; thus arming it, at the very outset of its national career, with diplomatic power, and at the same time, from the character of those interests propitiating all foreign jealousy, and inviting the cordial alliance of European powers." More than honor was at stake for Quitman, who proclaimed that the South must not "quietly submit to be robbed of her share in the broad harbours of the Pacific coast, and the vast territories," which they had helped win.[11] For these men sectional conflict had become inevitable because both the North and the South sought progress and were determined to pursue their respective interests within a rapidly changing and increasingly interconnected world.[12]

After much thought, majorities in the Cotton South rejected the secessionist appeals of Trescot, Rhett, and Quitman. They accepted instead the contentions of self-proclaimed "unionists" that northern allies remained numerous and powerful enough to serve Lower South interests. Their evidence came from the actions of western Democrats and "Cotton Whigs" who joined just enough southern Whigs and procompromise Democrats to secure a stronger federal Fugitive Slave Act, an acceptable western boundary to Texas, and nonrestriction of slavery into the remaining former Mexican provinces. Though the loss of California kept many Cotton South politicians yearning for secession, the compromise, as affirmed by Georgia voters in November 1850, blunted the independence movement. A Georgia platform, later endorsed by Mississippi and Alabama legislators, asserted the right to secede but promised to "abide by" the compromise "as a permanent adjustment of this sectional controversy" only so long as fugitive slaves were returned and slavery permitted to extend into new territories. Southern protonationalists had gained more adherents than when Thomas Cooper first proposed disunion two decades earlier, but by spring 1851 Mississippian Albert Gallatin Brown declared that "the Southern movement was dead."[13]

In reality it had helped redefine regional politics before going into hibernation, only to emerge with vengeance after domestic and foreign developments provided secessionists a more convincing case that regional interests would be better served outside of the Union. This need not have been so. Slaveowners seeking merely to preserve a traditional society might have sacrificed free trade or economic development, saving political capital to cultivate stronger northern alliances capable of protecting slavery. They might have dropped the question of slavery's expansion westward, threatening and compromising their way to a stronger Fugitive Slave Act and amendments protecting slavery in the states. Future efforts suggest that a majority of northerners, perhaps even Free Soil Republicans, would have accommodated such demands. Yet, constituencies in the Cotton States did not merely seek to hold on to the old. They sought the economic and political progress so closely identified with the modern experience. In fact, they firmly believed their central place in the global cotton business entitled them to it. Consequently, they aggressively fought to develop local and regional economies and to preserve their perceived rights in the federal territories.

Slaveholders' ambitions during the 1850s placed them squarely at odds with previous northern allies over major policy areas, including western homesteading, the meaning of popular sovereignty, long-cherished navigation acts, the Pacific railroad, and to a far lesser extent, the tariff. As fierce debates and eventual gridlock ensued over these substantive issues, antislavery Republicans in the North grew stronger after each battle. A majority of Cotton South politicians came to the conclusion—first offered by Turnbull in the 1820s, then by secessionists in 1850, and repeatedly by Free Soil Republicans—that free labor and slave capitalists represented separate civilizations incapable of peaceful coexistence. Reports of actual bloodshed, from the Kansas plain to the Senate floor to the streets of Harper's Ferry, provided tangible evidence. In the meantime, careful and successful diplomacy over potentially catastrophic disagreements (the arrest of American and British sailors, expansion into the Caribbean rim, and the illicit slave trade) along with the perceived centrality of King Cotton, kept hope alive for an imagined partnership with European nations, a development central to secessionist aspirations. While solid majorities in the Upper South, sugar planters in the Mississippi Delta, and many yeoman farmers outside of the black belt hesitated before secession, residents of the Cotton South generally welcomed it with a mixture of concern, relief, and optimism. Though certainly not all cotton planters and farmers supported secession, systematic voting studies suggest they disproportionately did so.[14] This was no mere coincidence.

## Economic Advancement in an Age of Democratic Ascendance

The marriage that propelled the compromise forward and thwarted secession in 1850 altered the political landscape, especially in the Cotton South. The entire ordeal had put the second party system under severe strain everywhere, but only in the states of Georgia, Mississippi, and Alabama did the Compromise of 1850 almost completely obliterate traditional party divisions. Most northern Whigs' resistance to accommodation tainted that party with the charge of hostility to the South, a problem deepened when Massachusetts voters summarily replaced sympathetic "Cotton Whigs" with antislave "Conscience" ones like Charles Sumner in 1851. Never particularly strong, Lower South Whigs faced difficult choices:

make their alliance with unionist Democrats permanent or work to preserve their ties with the national party. Brokering deals with unionist Democrats and riding the antisecessionist pendulum enabled many to stay in office in 1851. The presidential election of 1852, however, punctuated the party's slow and painful death. In Alabama and Mississippi, the Whig nominee, Virginia-born Winfield Scott, collected less than half the total votes received by Taylor four years earlier. Only 26.2 percent of Georgia's popular vote went to the party. While the Whig Party remained viable in the Upper South, the Compromise of 1850 killed it in the Lower South, where voters had long been skeptical of the American System. Those Whigs unable to tolerate a permanent alliance with Democrats unsuccessfully searched for an alternative, many placing faith in the short-lived American Party. Their failure meant, as Michael Holt has argued, that "there was no institutional check to extremism in the Lower South."[15]

Conversely, events strained but did not break local ties to the national Democratic Party. Following the lead of many South Carolinians, some secessionists and states' rights advocates remained virulently antiparty men in the wake of their defeats. Many others, however, returned to the national Democratic fold, in most cases supporting New Hampshire's Franklin Pierce's successful 1852 bid for the White House. Only slightly taken aback by their failure, these states' rights Democrats loudly insisted that the national party preserve the Georgia Platform and sought to transform it into a generally sympathetic body. Though failing to achieve their goals nationally, secessionists and states' rights efforts had redefined regional politics around sectionalized issues rather than competing national economic agendas and had moved the dichotomy of "secession" versus "union" to the forefront of discussion and political choice.

Within the context of this political realignment and an emboldened but eclectic Democratic Party, politicians and residents pursued an array of state policies aimed at advancing their own and their regions' economic and political interests. They did so under greatly improved economic circumstances fueled by a thriving global cotton market. European revolutions in 1848 proved less disruptive than anticipated. Britain furthered its commitment to breaking down trade barriers, even allowing increased foreign participation in its coastal and intercolonial trade. Planters who had awaited the blessings of freer international trade rejoiced when cotton prices spiked from 7.87 cents per pound to 11.21 in 1847. Two years later prices rose again to over 12 cents per pound, reaching average levels as high as those seen in the mid-1830s. Unlike that earlier boom, however, this one lasted, and prices remained relatively high even after the Crimean War and Panic of 1857.

With the exception of 1855 and 1856, global demand for raw cotton outpaced supply throughout the decade. Just to keep up, planters and ginning companies installed larger gins and presses, many of them steam powered.[16]

Observers attributed the spike in trade and prices to tariff reductions throughout the Atlantic and increased manufacturing on the European continent. By the mid-1850s, Europe's seemingly unquenchable demand for raw cotton convinced many in and outside of the region of cotton's power and slavery's necessity. According to Cincinnati editor David Christy, "HIS MAJESTY, KING COTTON . . . is forced to continue the employment of his slaves; and, by their toil, is riding on, conquering and to conquer! He receives no check from the oppressed, while the citizens of the world are dragging forward his chariot, and shouting aloud his praise!"[17] The large wealth accrued in the 1850s—a result of cotton and the slaves used to cultivate it—infused the region with optimism that the triumph of free trade and the end of war in 1848 had ushered in lasting peace and prosperity. Those comfortable merely remaining agricultural suppliers for the most vibrant global trade remained lukewarm supporters of government-assisted economic programs.

Yet the depressed cotton prices of the early 1840s and the angry political debates that followed created great concern about overdependence on agriculture and northern commerce. Economic reformers accelerated their calls for diversification and modernization, variously urging municipal and state governments to support direct European trade, internal improvements, and increased industrial capacity. Virtually no reformer doubted the supremacy or value of cotton cultivation; the prices of the 1850s made it difficult to do so. But King Cotton, the pages of J. D. B. De Bow's *Review* and the thousands who attended local and regional conventions argued, must serve broader and more egalitarian economic development. Each new national political battle, generally over slavery, further belied the claims of agrarian pacifists, suggesting the wisdom of regional economic diversification and modernization. Even as the reformers' preferred Whig Party melted away, sympathetic state politicians, often of a Democratic ilk, provided growing political support for these efforts.[18]

The cacophony of voices and perspectives rarely provided politicians a coherent agenda with which to define clear policies. Debates over how best to direct individuals' and states' limited liquid capital, how much to rely on the federal government, and how to view the fit between slave labor and industry continued to rage. But planters, manufacturers, merchants, and shopkeepers of all economic outlooks agreed that regional hopes depended on embracing what one upcountry planter referred to as "the ruling Mania of the day": constructing more railroads.[19] Early planning paid off by decade's end. In 1860 the number of railroad companies operating within South Carolina had grown from just one, operating 248 miles of track in 1850, to eleven with nearly 1,000 miles of track and a total capital investment of over $22 million.[20] The model for regional railroad construction remained Georgia, which had continued building through the early 1840s. In addition to expanding the Western-Atlantic lines, new projects sought to connect the Gulf of Mexico and the Atlantic and to link commercial centers with new and potential mining and industrial centers in northern Georgia and Alabama. From 1846 to 1860 the Georgia legislature passed eighty-eight special acts for railroad projects. By 1860 over $25 million in capital had been poured into state railroads, half of which came from state and municipal governments, the rest from native and foreign private investors.[21]

As the southwestern cotton economy rebounded, governments and their citizens responded with what can only be described as a regional "transportation revolution." In Alabama, the miles of usable track grew from only 130 miles of dilapidated road in 1850 to almost 330 miles by 1855. By 1860 over 730 miles of new track crisscrossed the state, with hundreds more planned.[22] Mississippi, still heavily burdened by defaulted loans from railroad projects in the late 1830s, had little public money to spend. Yet legislators overcame a long-standing aversion to granting new corporations, and both states' rights and unionist legislatures chartered a total of seventeen railroad lines between 1850 and 1857. Some companies sought to siphon trade from the Ohio, Mississippi, and Tennessee River Valleys. Others focused on creating an interlinked state economy, following the advice of an 1852 contributor to the states' rights *Mississippian and State Gazette* in Jackson who believed that railroads concentrated "wealth at home" and diffused "among the masses a higher degree of comfort, intelligence, and independence."[23] Regardless of their intended goal, Mississippi citizens helped ante up the capital and labor necessary to launch these projects.

The cotton trade provided some of the incentive and much of the capital, opening up new opportunities at the local level. Planters like Quitman, Thomas Butler King, and hundreds more, invested considerable time and money in railroad ventures, many of which directly benefited their agrarian pursuits while diversifying their portfolios. Planters who previously had to sell and transport crops to factors on the coast—factors who generally represented northern or European firms—could now sell their crops to local merchants or storekeepers empowered by easier access to wider markets. Doing so enhanced local pride while saving planters the transportation costs and ensuring that at least the initial commission, generally 3 percent, remained at home, creating more capital for local investment. If prices were deemed low in new inland towns like Milledgeville, Macon, Atlanta, and Montgomery, planters could and did send their crop forward in hopes of better prices. The fact that, by the end of the 1850s, larger commercial houses began sending purchasing agents deeper inland or opening their own company stores in small southern towns suggests that railroads had, at least partly, altered the nature as well as the quantity of trade within the region.[24]

Railroad entrepreneurs did not, however, suppose their projects served only, or even primarily, agricultural interests. Local merchants, industrialists, farmers, and storekeepers joined the frenzied competition for advancement. The breakdown of directorships for South Carolina railroads reveals that planters held only 40 percent of leadership roles, while merchants and lawyers each controlled 20 percent and industrialists and bankers combined for 8 percent.[25] Projects through the Georgia and South Carolina upcountry advanced development by linking manufacturing, livestock, and grain regions to more commercialized towns in the cotton belt. Boosters hoped to turn profits by increasing merchants' and planters' marketing options, raising real estate prices, and reaching groups not yet part of the market economy. These projects also tapped a deep well of civic-mindedness, as most residents knew that bringing a railroad to town immediately enhanced community prestige and accelerated the local economy.[26]

Profits and local boosterism provided the main incentive, but visionaries continued to believe that railroad expansion would increase the possibility of more direct trade with Europe. The presence of several European trading houses in the Lower South and unusually high percentages of foreign investment in local bank capital and state bonds further fueled their hopes.[27] Much of the money and business came from Britain, by far the primary destination for raw cotton, a good portion of which subsequently found its way to the European continent. The rapid expansion of industrial capabilities in northern and western European nations also led many to hope that "direct trade" would curtail both Britain's and the North's dominance in the cotton trade. Recognizing "the importance of extending our markets, consumption and creating competition," an 1851 Cotton Planter Convention in Macon, Georgia, invited the U.S. consul to Amsterdam, C. G. Baylor, to discuss "the proposition of the Merchants of Amsterdam, Holland, for opening 'Direct Trade' with the mouth of the Rhine and the Continent of Europe generally." Before the convention and later before Georgia legislators, Baylor proposed an ambitious scheme to link southern cotton producers with merchants and textile manufacturers in north-central Europe. Baylor admitted that European investors would have to be compelled away from existing capital and commercial flows through Britain and New York, but he urged southern planters to see that "direct trade is the cause of the *South*—the interest of the planter" and expedient regardless of the region's political future.[28]

Railroads and direct trade did not seem sufficient to others, including South Carolina planter James Hemphill, who demanded "there must be something else to enlarge and enrich towns—There is need of manufacturers."[29] William Gregg's calls for increased industrialization gained new attention, as manufacturers appealed to local and sectional identities to prod more conservative minds to action. Such calls echoed the language of earlier nationalist Whigs but argued for a southern "home market." According to one Louisiana commentator: "Every improvement in the agricultural and manufacturing sciences, produces a corresponding movement in the political and social world, we must perforce read of the rise and fall of ancient powers, and watch the onward march of the present age with an intense interest, with a feeling which is strengthened in proportion to our *amor patriae*, deepened in proportion to the keenness of our perceptive powers."[30] In short, economic and political progress required manufacturing; the South could and must inaugurate its own industrial revolution.

While twentieth-century economists saw the simultaneous call for free trade and manufacturing as incompatible, contemporaries often saw them as mutually reinforcing. By decade's end even supporters of industry like William Gregg and De Bow had joined arch–free trader James Hammond to support the pursuit of both direct trade and industrial development. By Gregg's account, a chief obstacle to southern manufacturing remained the region's continued dependence on northern importers and exporters, especially in New York, who allegedly siphoned off capital that could go toward southern industrial development. Direct importation would keep that money at home, pooling resources for potential manufacturing. Free trading industrialists also believed that direct trade with Europe would help develop southern shipbuilding and support industries while allowing the region access to other goods necessary to create more manufacturing establishments. Free traders in the Lower South calculated, though often vaguely and with political overtones, that direct and nonexploitative international trade (as opposed to what was seen as exploitative trade with the North) could provide the capital necessary to develop southern industry. Strong divisions remained over whether factories should employ free whites, enslaved blacks, or some combination, but few shared the older assumption that slave societies were incapable of successfully embarking on nonagrarian pursuits. William Harper's theorems and applications of slaves to tasks ranging from mining to mill-work increasingly suggested slavery's flexibility for a more industrialized society. But regardless of what labor was used, a growing number of planters, farmers, and merchants in the Cotton South placed their limited liquid capital and more boun-tiful rhetoric into new businesses and increased manufacturing, especially in textiles and ironworks.[31]

Such efforts belie the rustic agrarianism offered by southern writers and politi-cians, who promoted regional distinctiveness or denigrated their northern coun-terparts for their greedy acquisitiveness. Though admittedly lagging behind their northern counterparts in results, residents of the Cotton South were perhaps not so far behind in spirit. Beginning in the late 1840s, state politicians embarked on a chartering bonanza to encourage new financial, commercial, and manufactur-ing businesses. South Carolina overcame its traditional fiscal stinginess, increased state expenditures nearly threefold in the 1850s, and granted business charters more liberally.[32] One study of interior counties in South Carolina persuasively argues that by 1860 "corporations . . . as well as the rambunctious merchant class . . . had spent thirty years successfully sculpting the agrarian landscape in the interests of [commercial and corporate] capital."[33] The story was even truer in Georgia, where between 1846 and 1860, legislators incorporated numerous public work projects and more than 339 new private businesses, over two-thirds of the entire number that state had chartered since the Revolution! Included in those were thirteen insurance companies, thirty-five banks, twenty-four building and loan companies, fifteen steamboat companies, fourteen textile manufacturers, seventeen iron and metal works, and sixty-three mining companies.[34]

Unlike earlier times, the developmental spirit even extended into newer Cot-ton States, which overcame anticorporation proclivities in an attempt to diversify their economies. In Alabama, politicians increased the annual number of busi-ness charters from under twenty in 1846 to over fifty in 1849. The pace slowed slightly in the 1850s, but Democratic-controlled legislatures still chartered dozens of municipal companies and nearly 350 new private businesses during that decade (almost 35 per year).[35] Wealthy planters from the Broad River region pumped money into not only a telegraph line and railroad company but also a gaslight business, an insurance company, and the rather extensive Tallahassee textile mills. By 1860 Alabama's fourteen textile mills earned their description as "emi-nently successful" by producing three times the value of finished cloth they had in 1850 and returning as high as 12 percent annual profits. The 1850s were, a leading state historian has argued, "singular because other Alabamians began to seek outlets for their money in addition to the usual land and slaves," meaning that "at the time she seceded, the state had clearly reached the industrial takeoff point."[36] The economic situation remained less sanguine in Mississippi, but even there iron, brass, and, of course, textile manufacturing had been introduced and "attained substantial dimensions." Though the least industrialized Cotton State, Mississippi's economy by 1860 "unquestionably possessed the essential elements for developing a balanced agricultural and industrial economy."[37]

From a historical and contemporary perspective, there are three points of comparison for the cumulative efforts of planters, new mercantile businesses, shopkeepers, and industrialists. Compared to the U.S. North, Western Europe, and the Upper South—with their port cities of New York, Liverpool, or Baltimore and the mill towns of Lowell, Manayunk, and even Chillicothe, Ohio, or Petersburg, Virginia—these efforts seem wholly insufficient. Many southerners even prided themselves on the contrasts. Compared to contemporaneous societies in Asia, Africa, Eastern Europe, and South America, however, the Cotton South's economy appears quite developed, diversified, and unquestionably modern. Taken in the context of the region's own history and early agrarian assumptions, these commercial and industrial efforts and their fruits, in cities like Graniteville, South Carolina; Montgomery, Mobile, and Huntsville, Alabama; Columbus, Athens, and Atlanta, Georgia; Vicksburg, Natchez, and Jackson, Mississippi, showed unprecedented growth and heightened levels of excitement about future progress. The fact that all three reference points informed regional self-perception has made understanding these dynamics difficult. Lower South residents prided themselves on the uniquely advanced civilization that slavery and cotton had created even as they brooded over their relative backwardness in the face of superior northern economic power. The angry political debates of the 1850s only exacerbated the countervailing pressures within an already muddled political economy.

At the center of these contradictory feelings remained the fact that, directly or indirectly, the cotton trade and much of its profits continued to flow through the hands of northern merchants, financiers, and shippers. A few staunch unionists—especially those on good terms with northern agents—cast these connections as a regional and national blessing made possible by the Constitution's preservation of free interstate trade. In increasing numbers, however, politicians and commentators lamented what Mississippian John Forsyth called the "chain of commercial thralldom" binding the South to New York and other northern cities.[38] Higher cotton prices had heightened expectations and despite more successful state and local concentrations of capital for internal improvements, Cotton South planters and politicians lamented their region's continued dependence.

The issue of dependence gained enhanced political significance as both the Nashville Convention and individual states considered nonimportation of northern goods during and after the crisis of 1850. Advocates for economic coercion argued that such measures would curb northern antislavery by teaching northerners the "money value of the Union" while also promoting commercial and industrial independence. Despite repeated and serious discussion, however, little came of these proposals. Opponents argued that southern consumers would suffer and that such policies hypocritically violated long-heralded free trade axioms. Equally important, discriminatory import or sales taxes violated the commerce clause, highlighting the obstacle that the U.S. Constitution presented to those looking to settle political scores or foster more regional self-sufficiency.[39]

These debates, though bearing little fruit, were revisited regularly in response to subsequent northern personal liberty laws. They elevated sectional rhetoric while furthering the belief that federal policy harmed rather than helped regional advancement. While free trade within the Union continued to ensure that northern comparative advantage would impede southern development, politicians continued the steady drumbeat against federal economic policies they believed advantaged northern interests. In contrast to Upper South politicians and a number of Louisiana sugar planters who remained optimistic about the national government's potential for serving their interests, the Cotton South united against federal tariffs, bounties, and internal improvement projects they believed continued to redistribute wealth to the North.

These resentments forcefully cohered against the Rivers and Harbors Bill debated during Congress's otherwise calm 1852 summer session. The bill allocated more than $2 million for improvement projects primarily in the Great Lakes region and the Upper Mississippi, Missouri, and Ohio Rivers. Apparently fearing that the measure would divide the Democratic Party over the question of its constitutionality, Stephen Douglas and Missourian David R. Atchison suggested an alternative plan first proposed by Robert Barnwell Rhett in the late 1840s. State and local governments, rather than the federal government, would levy tonnage duties for their own river or harbor improvements. Though Douglas eventually dropped the matter, Lower South senators ranging from South Carolina states' righter Andrew Butler to Mississippi unionist Walker Brooke threatened to filibuster if not allowed to debate the alternate measure.

Proponents like Georgian Robert Charlton argued that entrusting such matters "to the energies of the States" would take things out of the hands of an "inefficacious" general government and decouple federal tariffs from public works. Butler believed it would cease the redistributive nature of a general system which he equated to "burning the cotton of the South" in order to "cut a ditch" to Lake Superior. Less prone to exaggeration, Brooke simply hoped that tonnage duties would provide funds for Mississippi's long-neglected smaller rivers. Whether out of constitutional scruples, a desire to further shrink federal tariffs, or a need to fund state-level projects, Lower South congressmen united to replace a general system they believed had offered little benefit and considerable harm to their region with a locally controlled system that they thought might benefit their burgeoning state efforts. Understandably, representatives outside of the Lower South, including those from inland states and northeastern manufacturing states, berated the idea and united to pass an unprecedented federal allocation for internal improvements.[40]

Having lost the measure and the principle, Lower South delegates again had to calculate whether to obstruct further federal works or to attempt to draw some benefit to their region from future apportionments. The possibility of transportation between the Pacific coast and the Deep South partially reinvigorated the idea that federal economic policy might still serve regional commercial interests. The desire for a southern railroad to California predated the Mexican-American War and had been forcefully advocated by John C. Calhoun at the Memphis Railroad Convention of 1845. Calhoun hoped his beloved South would take advantage of the expiration of the British East India Company's monopoly and the new commercial treaties with China that he had helped oversee as Tyler's secretary of state. Supported by a committee report drafted by South Carolina railroad promoter James Gadsden, the convention urged Congress to use federal land grants to pay for a road that would make the Mississippi River the center of world commerce and New Orleans the South's Liverpool.[41]

The cries for a Lower South terminus increased after the Mexican-American War raised the issue of slavery in the territories, though southern commercial conventions continued to stress the economic benefits the region would gain from a Pacific railroad. While self-interest led to disagreements over whether Memphis, Natchez, or New Orleans provided the best eastern terminus, insistence on a route with a "genial and temperate climate" united the parties in opposition to any federal measure likely to result in a more northward route.[42] The high point of Lower South optimism came in 1853, when boosters believed that a southern-led congressional committee, a sympathetic secretary of war, Jefferson Davis, and the pending Gadsden Purchase of land around the Gila River had paved the way for a southern route. Earlier that year a bill supported by a number of Lower South delegates emerged from committee and would have appropriated $20 million in U.S. bonds and empowered the president to designate the route and oversee a blind bidding process for construction. A congressional land grant for an Arkansas railroad led that state's representative, Albert Pike, to tell a Memphis railroad promoter that "we regard this as settling, in point of fact, the Pacific Rail Road question, and as securing the ultimate adoption of the southern route."[43] Observers believed passage imminent until supporters of a Chicago terminus, led by Douglas's Illinois colleague Senator James Shields, pushed through an amendment expressly forbidding the use of U.S. bonds within existing states.

The measure might have been motivated by real constitutional concerns (several southern critics had long made similar points), but southern supporters of the original bill believed it a ploy by advocates for a northern route. Arkansas senator Solomon Borland angrily noted that Shields's amendment "excludes the whole range of Southern states from participation in the Bill." Whereas the two most discussed northern routes would travel through only one existing state (Missouri or Iowa), the southern routes would have to travel through either Arkansas or Louisiana *and* the expansive but unsettled state of Texas. Barred from receiving bond money and lacking federal public lands, due to the unique nature of Texas's annexation, most of the burden of a southern route would fall on the individual states, while a northern route would come primarily at federal taxpayers' expense. Borland's southwestern colleagues and six senators who had favored the legislation prior to Shields's amendment withdrew their support. South Carolinian Andrew Butler, who had opposed even the initial measure, cynically retorted that though "there is a concurrent opinion that the Gila route is best, the road will go to the lakes."[44]

This development, along with northern opposition to appropriating funds to implement the Gadsden Purchase, led the previously hopeful Pike to despair. At an April 1854 convention in Charleston, Pike urged his fellow southerners to negotiate directly with Mexican officials and begin building their own railroad in what would amount to "a sort of declaration of independence on the part of the South."[45] Not all railroad advocates lost hope, however, especially when Davis was assigned to oversee surveys of proposed routes and President Pierce signed the Gadsden Purchase in June 1854. A few ardent supporters hoped that movement on Arkansas, Texas, and California state projects might make a southern route appear more practical by limiting direct federal expense to the already organized territory of New Mexico. More northern routes, in contrast, would require more funds, suffer from harsher winters, and travel directly through Mormon-controlled or unorganized Indian territories.

The distinct possibility of a southern Pacific railroad provided the sometimes overlooked context for the ill-fated Kansas-Nebraska Act. In early 1853, Douglas's deep desire for a Chicago route had led him to use his chairmanship of the Senate's committee on territories to push hard for organizing the Nebraska Territory. Having failed in that effort, he forwarded a bill the following year that would allow the region's inhabitants to decide if slavery would be permitted. When pressed by proslavery Missourian David R. Atchison and southern representatives to acknowledge that the new bill repealed the Missouri Compromise, a somewhat reluctant Douglas complied. He and other northern Democrats supported the measure, claiming that it did not ensure slavery's expansion but instead advanced congressional noninterference and self-government, "the principle to which all our free institutions owe their existence, and upon which our entire republican system rests."[46] Applied now to all remaining territories, "popular sovereignty" would, they envisioned, remove the issue from the national debate and allow it to be settled at the local level. It did not.

Southern slaveowners appreciated the opportunity, and many praised Douglas's foresight. Their support, however, added momentum to a northern route, much to the chagrin of southern promoters like Pike and Gadsden. Few southerners viewed the Kansas-Nebraska Act as a favor, and certainly not one that warranted ceding the railroad question. What northern Democrats believed to be a final settlement, a contributor to the *Charleston Mercury* saw as a bill that inaugurated "the last, final struggle between the sections of the Union, a struggle in which there will be no compromise."[47] Unfortunately for moderate Democrats who had rallied the votes and pressured Franklin Pierce to sign the bill, both southern and northern extremists believed the battle lines set for Trescot's "violent and uncompromising antagonism of great interests."[48]

Some voices in the Lower South, particularly in South Carolina and former Whig circles, believed slavery's expansion a chimera perpetuated by opportunistic Democrats. Diverse reasons led many more to the conclusion that southern society and regional interest actually depended on what a Jackson, Mississippi, man called an "almost unanimous" desire for more land suitable for slavery.[49] Simple political arithmetic suggested that a contained Slave South might not survive an expanding free soil American empire. Amateur demographers, especially

in the black belt, argued that without a vent for rapidly reproducing slave populations the region would soon be on the brink of racial warfare. Proud men, and not
a few women, believed on principle that taking their property anywhere in federal
territories remained a natural right, the relinquishing of which would make them
second-class citizens. Others just wanted to prop up their proslavery belief that
race-based slavery could adapt to all climates and businesses. To this traditional
list must be added slaveholders' desire, largely economic in origin, to ensure that
their progeny would have the cheap land, labor supply, and access to commercial
opportunities necessary to fulfill the Lower South's version of the American
dream. Less clear, however, remained what policies and partners would best help
them and their region achieve political survival and economic greatness.

## Converting Friends to Enemies and Enemies to Friends: The Search for Natural Allies

The quest for slavery's expansion into either the Great Plains or the Caribbean
rim and the related need for more labor threatened to destroy domestic political
alliances that were decades in the making. They also heightened the possibility of
conflict with European partners. Recognizing these potentialities, many former
Whigs and some South Carolina pragmatists tried to blunt their neighbors' enthusiasm. They fought an uphill battle, however, as regional political economy,
honor, and rights had been redefined around grander economic ambitions and
the ability to take slaves south and west. Triangulating between perceived regional interests, a domestic situation seen as increasingly hostile, and foreign developments they interpreted as favorable, many Cotton South politicians and
commentators came to Trescot's 1850 conclusion: the region possessed more clout
internationally than domestically. Its true allies were to be found not at home but
abroad.

The Pyrrhic nature of their political victory in the Kansas and Nebraska Ter-
ritories became increasingly clear as practically no slaveholders migrated to the
Plains and as political events unfolded in the North. Disillusioned northern
Democrats defected from the party en masse, joining similarly angry Whigs to
form a Republican Party based on free soil principles. An American, or Know-
Nothing, Party provided an alternative with only limited appeal. Reaction to the
Kansas-Nebraska Act quickly bled into other issues as seven northern states passed
or revised personal liberty laws that withdrew, to varying degrees, state coop-
eration in enforcing federal fugitive slave laws. Southern slaveholders perceived

them as clear evidence that free soil parties and the people who elected them held a new level of disregard for southerners' constitutional rights and regional security. Secessionist minorities claimed the measures violated the Constitution and thus warranted drastic action. More moderate southern legislatures again discussed nonimportation of goods from offending states, but to no avail. Informed by such discussions, one *De Bow's* contributor argued that the direct trade with Europe was "much more natural than that which now prevails" through northern agents and cities.[50] By 1856 reports of open violence from the Plains to the Senate floor filled newspapers. Some praised, most lamented, the horrific tales of canings and massacres. Many feared that the political war between free soil and proslavery factions was fast giving way to an actual one.[51]

The heated language prompted by northern political realignment contrasted sharply with the cotton-conscious diplomacy of European officials seeking to repeal the Negro Seaman's Acts that, when enforced, targeted their citizens. In October 1850, frustrated with the inactivity of the national government, the Foreign Office instructed British consuls to seek redress through direct "negotiations . . . with the several State Governments."[52] The first attempt ended in disaster, as Charleston consul George Mathews's conversations with South Carolina officials only attracted suspicion that the parties had violated the federal government's exclusive right to negotiate with foreign powers. The British foreign secretary, Viscount Palmerston, and South Carolina's governor defended the right to direct dialogue, but a frustrated Mathews took the matter back to federal courts, an action that angered state officials and the local press.[53]

Having learned that tone and process mattered, British officials retreated and turned to comforting words rather than official bluster. The new secretary for foreign affairs, Lord Clarendon, withdrew the court appeal, a move the *Charleston Courier* praised as representing the "good sense and the good feeling" of the new administration. Subsequent newspapers reported that the British chargé d'affaires in Washington, John F. Crampton, had informed two South Carolina congressmen that the legal actions had been in defiance of the wishes of the British government. Such rumors gained legitimacy when Mathews was replaced with Philadelphia consul Robert Bunch in 1853. Bunch modeled his behavior on other consuls in the Deep South who had achieved partial successes elsewhere. In 1852 New Orleans consul William Mure had used private connections to convince Louisiana's legislature to amend its act and allow free blacks to stay on board their ships or receive special permits to work on the docks. Two years later longtime Savannah consul Edmund Molyneaux worked alongside the president of Georgia's senate (who was, conveniently, a relative of the consul's wife) to pass a similar measure. Bunch privately circulated copies of these laws and cultivated personal relationships by hosting dinners and attending Race Week celebrations. He assured Carolinians that Britain had no desire to attack slavery in the United States or to "Africanize" Cuba. Understanding how closely South Carolinians monitored British politics, Bunch repeatedly instructed his superiors to prevent denunciations of the acts in Parliament or the British press, believing they would be fatal to his efforts.[54]

By 1854 Bunch's charm offensive began to pay dividends, first in the governor's office and eventually in the state legislature. Noting Britain's turn toward an "entirely proper and respectful" approach to the subject, Governor John Manning requested that the state legislature repeal the most onerous sections of the law, those imprisoning sailors and forcing shipmasters to pay expenses. The bill passed one house but narrowly failed in the other—something Bunch attributed to the long shadow cast by Mathews's earlier indiscretions. Manning's successor, J. H. Adams, encouraged him to submit another request, and in 1855 Bunch traveled to Adams's plantation to review an official letter before a formal submission was made. The remarkable document was conciliatory in tone and called for a mutually agreeable solution. Bunch admitted the necessity of the original 1822 act but argued that the possibility of slave insurrections had become remote. Free black sailors, he contended, would be less inclined or able to denounce slavery publicly if permitted to remain on their ships rather than being arrested. Bunch assured his audience that Britain, "bound to South Carolina by a thousand ties, entertains no wish but for her prosperity" and "would neither ask nor expect that the safety or well-being of a friendly State should be made subservient to their advantage." The carefully scripted missive resulted in a cordial reply from Adams praising the consul's judicious approach to this "delicate and, as *heretofore conducted,* irritating question."[55]

Frightened that anger over Kansas, northern personal liberty laws, and Massachusetts lawsuits might thwart his plans, Bunch assured Adams in September 1855 that he and his government were alarmed by northern hostility toward South Carolina. He earnestly hoped his own nation's "conciliatory conduct" would ensure that "Great Britain and Massachusetts would not be placed by South Carolina in the same category" as their actions were "as opposite as light is from darkness."[56] Adams, previously an adamant supporter of the act, accepted Bunch's logic and asked the state legislature to amend the law, though only for citizens of "foreign nations." Legislators did not take immediate action, but the following year they amended the law to exempt all free black sailors from imprisonment, provided they remained on board their vessels. Though the amendment failed to recognize equality between British black and white subjects, Bunch communicated success to his superiors, noting that the new bill was "really not oppressive and involve[d] no violation of international law." In 1857 he happily informed them that not a single British subject had been imprisoned.[57]

Though John Brown's 1859 raid on Harper's Ferry sparked some discussion about tightening the act, no such measures were taken, largely out of concern that "on the verge of a disruption" and overthrow of "a great empire," it would "declare cause against England . . . our natural ally—our very best Customer, & our most reliable carrier & consumer."[58] While British officials like Bunch treated the 1856 law as resolving the matter, in 1859 a Massachusetts federal court, for the second time, declared Louisiana's port law to be in violation of the federal Constitution's commerce and privileges-immunities clauses. Few Cotton South officials were naïve enough to believe that Britain would drop its antislavery convictions. Especially in light of polarized domestic politics, however, they welcomed the calm dialogue and Britain's apparent willingness to accommodate southern sensibilities.[59]

Lower South politicians remained divided over Europe's likely response to more aggressive regional goals, including slavery's expansion into tropical lands and the reopening of the international slave trade. The drumbeat for expansion into the Caribbean and Central America began almost immediately after the Compromise of 1850 and reached a fevered pitch by middecade. Hoping to bounce back from financial and political setbacks, ex-Mississippi governor John Quitman and former *New Orleans Crescent* editor William Walker, amongst others, fueled the imaginations of Lower South residents by asserting that American control of the Gulf region would restore political parity and provide merchants and planters with critical trade routes and valuable land. More peaceful—and thus more popular—efforts to annex land remained central components of the Lower South's political agenda throughout the 1850s. Though many northerners, especially northern Democrats, supported the idea of expansion into the Caribbean, the Lower South's insistence that slavery extend as well could not help but make the issue a sectionalized one.

Expansion southward, however, placed the region on a path toward potential conflict with European powers, especially Britain, which retained significant commercial interests and some territory in the region. A number of regional commentators, especially in South Carolina, feared precisely that. They argued that expansionism, especially violent expansionism, harmed rather than helped regional efforts and might antagonize otherwise natural allies. South Carolinian William Boyce, for example, feared that land hunger might create costly wars and conflict with European powers at a time when relations had seen such marked improvement. Consecutive U.S. ministers to Mexico from 1853 to 1858—railroad promoter James Gadsden and the owner of the *Mobile Register,* John Forsyth— came to the conclusion that filibusters thwarted peaceful efforts to acquire land and build railroads that would benefit the South.[60] These voices of moderation would eventually prevail when secession became a real possibility. For the time, however, these dissenting voices represented the minority view and most seemed to agree on the desirability of a "Southern conquest" of tropical lands in Central America and Cuba.[61] For some the threat of British or French cooperation to end slavery in Cuba served as an impetus for action, as it had in the Texas annexation crisis.

Yet renewed faith in cotton's power after its victories in the late 1840s, along with the outbreak of war in Europe, led other expansionists to argue that Europe would accommodate U.S., and possibly even slavery's, expansion around the Caribbean rim. In 1854, Pierre Soulé, minister to Spain and participant in the Ostend Conference, boldly informed secretary of state, New Yorker William Marcy, that should the United States forcibly seize Cuba "neither England nor France would be likely to interfere with us." "England," the French-born New Orleans resident believed, "could not bear to be suddenly shut out of our market, and see her manufacturer paralyzed, even by a temporary suspension of her intercourse. And France, with the heavy task now on her hands . . . would have no inducement to assume the burden of another war."[62] Marcy and President Pierce— still reeling from the aftermath of the Kansas-Nebraska Act—decided differently and for domestic and diplomatic reasons disavowed the Ostend ministers' suggestion of coercion. The South's adopted son immediately resigned his post. Returning to his law practice in New Orleans, Soulé devoted the rest of the decade to supporting Quitman and Walker's filibustering efforts and lamenting the timidity of national leaders.[63]

Westminster's tentativeness, missteps by British diplomats, and newspaper editors' repeated exhortations for Anglo-American cooperation further muddied southern understanding of Britain's likely response to expansion. While some officials warned American counterparts that U.S. aggrandizement "would in the opinion of many Countries render you dangerous to the peace of the World," higher officials and the press swore off actions that could be interpreted as provocative to the United States or its citizens.[64] After William Walker seized

Nicaragua in the summer of 1855, Foreign Secretary Clarendon proceeded cautiously. Rejecting bellicose talk, he told Prime Minister Palmerston that direct intervention would get "no backing at home if we frightened the Cotton Lords."[65] The end of the Crimean War, along with the Pierce administration's insistence on Crampton's recall and recognition of Walker's government in Nicaragua, led officials to posture more forcefully. Their efforts, which included sending a regiment to Canada and a small fleet to the Caribbean, generated a groundswell of opposition. The *Times* announced "fright at the warlike preparations," and opposition groups in Parliament stressed the centrality of Anglo-American trade, especially in cotton, as they argued against hostile action. Seeing few options, the prime minister refused to retaliate against the American minister and announced his determination to avoid a breach with the United States over the Central American question.[66]

Though determined to protect their regional interests, especially transit across the isthmus, Palmerston, Clarendon, and his successor as foreign secretary, the Earl of Malmesbury, became increasingly glum about their chances of containing slaveholders' hemispheric ambitions. If filibusterers like Walker defeated Latin American forces, Palmerston predicted in late 1857, Britain would have to "give way Step by Step to the North Americans on almost every disputed matter . . . except the maintenance of our own Provinces and of our West Indian Islands." It would be "in short Texas all over again." To excuse British passivity, Clarendon blamed "the Indifference of the Nation as to the Question discussed" and "its strong Commercial Interest in maintaining Peace." Revealing the pervasiveness of scientific racism on both sides of the Atlantic, Palmerston even suggested that "commercially no doubt we should gain by having the whole American continent occupied by an active enterprising race like the Anglo-Saxons instead of the sleepy Spaniards."[67] To prevent problems with Spain, however, Palmerston conceded, "it is for our Interest that this should not happen until the swarms are prepared to separate from the Parent Hive."[68]

Crampton's replacement in Washington, Lord Francis Napier, acknowledged his nation's reluctance to challenge the United States, even—it seemed to some— if that meant slavery's expansion. Though Napier told Buchanan that he "believed" Her Majesty's government desired to see slavery removed from Central America (a conclusion supported by Palmerston's insistence that Honduras exclude slavery from lands ceded to it by Britain), Napier privately and publicly revealed a far less rigid stance, one closer to a northern Democrat than a Republican desiring to stop slavery in its tracks. In May 1857—as southerners defended slavery's expansion based on the controversial Dred Scott decision—Napier penned a revealing letter to his superiors rejecting the desirability of preaching abolitionism and offering eight reasons why Britain should support U.S. annexation of Cuba.[69]

Repeated socializing with southern congressmen and a dinner invitation to William Walker (even after his self-proclaimed republic had legalized slavery) led the frustrated French minister to nickname Napier "le Lord Filibustier." Similarly, Charles Sumner, still recovering from the caning delivered by South Carolina's Preston Brooks, complained to one British noble that his chief diplomat in Washington "accepts the Democratic doctrine . . . & talks as glibly as the President on popular sovereignty & the right of Settlers to establish Slavery if they see fit." When superiors forced Napier to confront such accusations, after Napoleon III requested explanation for his "pro-American" behavior, he responded that efforts to paint him in that light did "not make the Americans dislike me." Moreover, he argued, though he was not a "propagandist of the Expansion Doctrine in the filibustering sense," he still "believed that it would be advantageous to England that the U.S. should possess Mexico and those parts of Central America which do not intercept the Transit . . . [as well as] Cuba," areas he thought they would peacefully acquire within a generation.[70] A vacillating and often ill-expressed British policy allowed hundreds of Lower South expansionists to continue envisioning the realization of a slaveholding empire without risking war with their chief trading partner.

Proponents of slavery's expansion sometimes joined others who believed that international circumstances might even allow the South to meet another critical need: African labor. The movement for reopening the international slave trade had supporters as early as the 1830s but gained new impetus when Governor Adams, having just successfully resolved the Negro Seaman's controversy, used a November 1856 address to ask South Carolina legislators to repeal state laws that closed the trade. Developments in the British West Indies and the perception of European accommodation appear to have been foremost in Edward B. Bryan's mind as he drafted the state's 1857 majority committee report that recommended going forward with Adams's proposal. After the proposal narrowly failed, Bryan took his appeal to the broader public, highlighting the wider economic and geopolitical context for a movement mistakenly seen by historians as delusional or motivated by disunionist motives. Bryan opened each of his twelve "Letters to the Southern People" with quotations from the *London Times* and *Paris Constitutionalist* that characterized emancipation as misguided "philanthropy." Believing that slaves were necessary for southern and global economic development, Bryan argued that a "COTTON PARLIAMENT" would not let "abolitionist influence" stand in the way of further profits and would concede to economic interest: "Commerce now rules. *It* is king; cotton is heir-apparent, and slavery is queen-dowager." Subsequent quotes cherry-picked from the European press and parliaments to highlight the political and economic weakness of the West Indies compared to slave economies in Cuba, Brazil, and the United States.[71]

By 1858 such comparisons had become standard fare for a southern press that carefully followed debates in Britain and France over how to revitalize their postemancipationist societies in the West Indies. Since 1846 the strength of the free trade movement had thwarted British abolitionists' efforts to retain special protection for sugar and cotton produced in the empire by free labor. In 1853, the noted literary figure Thomas Carlyle attached his name to an "Occasional Discourse on the Negro Question," which argued that emancipation had ruined the West Indies and its residents, white and black. Such views continued to find frequent expression in business-centered newspapers, including the *Times* of London. Private and official accounts highlighted the depressed economy of Jamaica and other West Indian colonies, generally blaming allegedly lazy blacks for their unwillingness to work without coercion. Despite sympathetic missionaries who trumpeted the real progress made by Caribbean blacks, large segments of the press and a number of British officials openly questioned whether the moral gains of emancipation had been worth the financial cost. "The tide," one historian has suggested, "was running against abolitionist truths."[72]

France and Britain's desperate search for ways to restore West Indian profitability buoyed Lower South confidence in slavery and its global importance. A need for labor led Britain to resume and extend the East Indian coolie trade. By the mid-1850s it also lengthened the term of contracts to a mandatory ten years before allowing free transit back home.[73] By the decade's end the challenges of recruiting labor from East India, especially after the Sepoy Rebellion of 1857, led both Britain and France to turn to larger numbers of African indentured servants. According to one editorial in the *Charleston Mercury,* the "return to the old locality with the old instrumentality" of "imported negroes" proved "that the furor of the British Government for the abolition of slavery and the suppression of the African slave trade, was more political than philanthropical."[74] More charitable, and accurate, sources admitted benevolent intentions but noted fiscal conservatives' outcry at the millions of pounds and francs being expended. These observers concluded that both nations would think twice before again placing morality above profits. In early 1858 the U.S. minister to France, Virginian John Y. Mason, informed the State Department that the French and British governments had collaborated to ensure that vessels transporting contracted or indentured Africans and coolies would not be stopped under the slave trade conventions. Mason's letters to the State Department, later submitted to Congress and made public, asserted that "judging from the tone of the public press, and reasoning *a priori,* I feel quite confident that in future we will see the fanatical denunciations of American slavery greatly moderated, if not silenced, in France, perhaps in England."[75] Rather than serving as a model for an alternative course, Britain and France's decision to turn to coolie and African contracted labor encouraged Lower South slaveholders' perception that agricultural productivity in warmer climates required coerced labor and that permanent bondage remained the most steady and economical way to achieve that.

What some American papers uncharitably called the Europeans' "revival of the slave trade" also provided the context for other Lower South states' efforts to increase the region's labor supply by reopening the international slave trade. Napier identified the connection, blaming the "French project" and "our coolie trade" for the "revival of the slave trade" movement amongst "certain parties in the United States."[76] These efforts reached their apex, not in South Carolina, but farther west. In March 1858 Louisiana's house passed a bill to import 2,500 African "apprentices" by a vote of 46 to 21. One New Orleans observer excitedly commented that slavery was "daily rising from its ancient and petrified fixedness to feel the power of illimitable expansion."[77] Proponents of the measure, especially in southwestern states, believed African labor necessary to capitalize on higher cotton prices, expand into new lands, and diversify economically. "Give us," Mississippian I. N. Davis argued, "more and cheap operatives and we would not only have the will, but be enabled to diversify our labor, and improve our country. We would build our own vessels and steamboats, railroads . . . erect manufactories and foundries, build our levees and dikes."[78] The most ardent supporters of reopening sought to accomplish more than simply removing the "mark of Cain" surrounding slavery or destroying the Democratic Party.[79]

Ardent expansionists and economic reformers worried less that the region had too many slaves and more that they did not have enough. They thought Upper South opposition was designed to keep the price of slaves high. They viewed northern and European critics as hypocrites who sought to suppress southern growth and development even as they relied on cheap white labor ("white slaves") to work their mills or on semibound persons of color to labor in their plantations.

A tie-breaking senate vote by the lieutenant governor would have begun shipments of Africans, but four days later a wavering senator changed his mind and the project ceased. The debate, however, did not.[80]

Those seeking to repeal the federal ban on the slave trade transformed the Montgomery 1858 Southern Commercial Convention into an extended and revealing discussion of the issue, demonstrating again the divisions between Cotton and non-Cotton Slave States. Virginia representatives led by Roger Pryor opposed reopening, claiming that a fresh supply of more slave "barbarians" would undermine party unity and southern white labor while offending "the sentiment of the Christian world." Delegates from the Cotton South, led by William Yancey, retorted that the prohibition of importations violated free market principles, kept slave prices artificially high, and deprived those in the region, especially non-elites, of the resources necessary for economic development.[81] After three days of arguments, Yancey's efforts had radicalized the entire convention movement. A year later at Vicksburg, delegates from the Lower South states voted 40 to 7 to declare that "all laws, State and Federal, prohibiting the African slave trade, ought to be repealed." Those few Upper South delegates in attendance opposed the measure 12 to 4.[82] In November, Georgians' effort to repeal that state's 1797 ban on the international trade failed by merely one vote.[83]

Unlike any previous event, the Montgomery Commercial Convention of 1858 had brought the issues of slave trading and southern expansionism together into a platform for disunion. Though he was not a delegate, William Walker's presence in Montgomery as part of his recruitment efforts had generated considerable enthusiasm. Fresh off of his "victory" against Pryor and angered by northern Democrats' "betrayal" in refusing to accept Kansas's proslavery Lecompton Constitution, Yancey worked to create a "League of United Southerners," freed from "party influence" and "pledged to resistance at the proper time." Seeking to promote the league and harkening to the language of revolution, Yancey wrote to Alabama newspaper editor James Slaughter to inform him that "no National Party can save us; no Sectional Party can do it. But if we could do as our fathers did, organize Committees of Safety all over the cotton States, (and it is only in them that we can hope for any effective movement) we shall fire the Southern heart—instruct the Southern mind—give courage to each other, and at the proper moment, by one, organized, concerted action, we can precipitate the cotton States into a revolution." Reprinted throughout the nation, Yancey's letter, followed by subsequent speeches, sparked excitement from secessionists and hostility from unionist Whigs and Democrats, especially in the Upper South. Northerners publicly excoriated Yancey and other "reopeners" as secessionists and called the movement an affront to the Constitution, past compromises, and humanity.[84]

Though British officials were equally appalled, circumstances dictated that they remain diplomatic for fear that political moderates might use missteps to unite the country behind war with Britain. Such an event nearly occurred in early 1858, when British naval officers patrolling the Caribbean searched several American-owned vessels suspected of trafficking in slaves. The resulting "crisis" harkened back to the issues and rhetoric that had defined the Jeffersonian period and prompted a rare (and final) moment of national unity. Republicans in Congress joined Stephen Douglas and Robert Toombs in support of Buchanan's forceful reply. Even the solidly antislavery paper, the *National Era,* demanded that the United States must "resist to the death the insolent assumption of any foreign power to subject our ships to detention and examination."[85] Secretary of State Lewis Cass and U.S. minister to Britain George Dallas insisted that Britain immediately cease visitations of vessels flying the American flag. Initially disinclined to concede to these demands, British officials again faced challenges to a forceful policy. Alarmed British editors cautioned against escalating the situation, claiming that "it is no business of ours to drill them into virtue."[86] Informed by these sentiments and Napier's repeated warnings that any perceived aggression would rally a public deeply divided over the Lecompton Constitution, the new Conservative government backed down and settled the issue largely on American terms. After receiving a pledge that the United States would expand patrols, Westminster disavowed aggressive action, relinquished the right of "visit" of American-owned ships, and defused the situation by explaining that the naval commanders had acted beyond their orders.[87]

Lower South politicians and commentators remained divided over how to interpret the events of 1858 and the larger significance of the international slave trade. Deeming the free trade in Africans as necessary for achieving the region's ambitious economic and political agenda, some perceived Britain's retreat as further evidence of that nation's weakening antislavery commitment. Believing he needed more slaves for his dream of a Nicaraguan republic, William Walker claimed in 1860 that "the frenzy of the British public against the slave-trade has exhausted itself, and men have begun to perceive that they were led into error by the benevolent enthusiasms of parsons, who knew more about Greek and Hebrew than they did about physiology or political economy."[88] By contrast, South Carolinian William R. Smith, eyeing the formation of a southern Confederacy, pleaded that any attempt to permit the slave trade "bid defiance to the whole civilized world" and would "bring down upon our earliest deliberations the anathemas of all Europe."[89] Responding to these sentiments and, equally significant, the divisions created by the issue within the Slave South, some advocates backed away. Among them was the influential editor of the *Charleston Mercury* Robert Barnwell Rhett, who decided the issue would have to rest until a southern Confederacy had been formed. Even then, after considerable debate, and much to Rhett and others' chagrin, the need to cajole the Upper South's cooperation and concern about alienating Europe led the 1861 Confederate Constitution to prohibit the international slave trade even as the South abdicated responsibilities to enforce antislave trade treaties.

Perhaps the most revealing feature of the 1858 crisis and its denouement, however, was the faith that Lower South politicians had in cotton's ability to preserve peace between the two nations. Rebutting Stephen Douglas's call for additional U.S. gunboats, Jefferson Davis confidently asserted that he expected "that we shall have no occasion for anything but peace because it is not every little collision . . . which means war between two Powers tied together by their commercial relations to such an extent that neither Government can desire war with the other."[90] The Savannah *Daily Morning News* agreed and then proceeded to blame northern shippers and politicians for stirring up the trouble, claiming that "even the nationality for whose honor she is ready to engage, exists only in name." Drawing comparisons reminiscent of early secessionists like Trescot and British officials like Bunch, the editors claimed that "the fraternity known as the 'underground railroad' . . . have committed more outrages upon the South than all the British cruisers in the Gulf."[91] After the crisis passed, a Mississippi editorial downplayed the entire ordeal, noting that "every consideration of interest and sound policy demands the perpetuation of peace between the two governments. They are allied to each other by the ties of kindred and by the yet stronger bonds of mutual dependence. The Cotton of America keeps in motion the looms of England. Let peace be cultivated."[92] Anglophobia did not disappear from the region, but it had subsided considerably.[93]

Whether thankful for peace or eager for a more aggressive policy, Lower South politicians based their attitudes on the belief that cotton gave the region remarkable leverage and powerful allies within international politics. The region's relatively quick rebound after panics hit financial circles hard led politicians like James Hammond to proclaim that "Cotton is King. Until lately the Bank of England was king; but she tried to put her screws as usual, the fall before last, upon the cotton crop, and was utterly vanquished. The last power has been conquered.

Who can doubt, that has looked at recent events, that cotton is supreme?" Statistical data provided by an 1858 Department of Interior report lent some credence to these bold assertions. Drawing from a variety of foreign trade secretaries, chambers of commerce, and American consuls, Natchez native and New Orleans resident John Claiborne concluded that "it would be difficult to overestimate the importance of cotton in the movement of the industry and commerce of the civilized world."[94]

Quantitative data demonstrated Britain's failure to find alternative supplies, but Claiborne also found rhetorical support from one of the leading socialist minds of the time. According to Friedrich Engels, "*England and the United States are bound together by a single thread of cotton, which, weak and fragile as it may appear, is, nevertheless, stronger than an iron cable.*"[95] Claiborne's report also highlighted the opportunities afforded by industrializing continentals. After a slow initial start, "since 1851, the march" of France's cotton textile industry had "been rapid." Centered largely on delicate tissues, muslin prints, and lace, it promised to remain "highly prosperous and remunerative."[96] The Hanse towns, Switzerland, Russia, the Zollverein States, Spain, and the Austrian Empire: all had recognized the centrality of textile manufacturing and all relied heavily on raw cotton, directly or indirectly imported from the United States. What had begun in the early nineteenth century as a partnership between Britain and the United States had become a much broader phenomenon, offering cotton planters more vibrant alternate markets and higher prices.[97]

A more comprehensive review of Euro-American trade would have highlighted the importance of northern wheat growers and consumers of European goods, but all too frequently Cotton South commentators saw their raw cotton as the tie that bound Atlantic commerce together. In their estimation, the growth of the trade and heightened demand for raw cotton placed their region in an enviable position. According to Claiborne, cotton had "created sympathies and ties of common interest, which makes the policy of peace and its attendant blessings one far more easy to maintain," adding to national and international wealth.[98] Even De Bow, though not wishing cotton to remain the only engine of growth within the Lower South's economy, proclaimed that cotton was dominant, concluding that "any considerable diminution in the crop of the United States, would cause the gravest inconveniences" in Europe and that cutting off southern supplies "would be followed by social, commercial, and political convulsions, the effects of which can scarcely be imagined."[99] *Blackwood's Magazine* frustratingly lamented that the Lower South's near monopoly on raw materials placed the subsistence of "millions in every manufacturing country of Europe within the power of an oligarchy of planters."[100] Even after the 1858 bumper crop, Lower South newspapers forecasted that seemingly insatiable European demand would keep supplies short. As one Mississippi newspaperman reported: "A contemporary aptly says that the temporal ruler of the globe *par excellence* is the American cotton plant. It speaks cities into existence, constructs railroads across barren desserts and through sky-capped mountains, encompasses civilized States with magnetic wires, whitens every sea with the sails of ships, enters alike the palace and the hut for the dispensation of blessings. In short, the world would be 'a mighty maze, and without a plan,' were it not for the cotton fields of the South."[101]

Cotton's prospects and northerners' postpanic struggles again spawned efforts to reorient international trade in a way that would aid regional political and economic goals. In a possibly positive indicator, the North's most respected commercial journal, *Hunt's Merchants' Magazine,* noted disapprovingly that the 1857 panic had given the South a higher percentage of national specie than previously.[102] But Lower South supporters of increased trade with Europe remained proactive and, in a profoundly revealing move, Cotton South congressmen led a political assault on the most sacred of national economic policies: navigation acts that dated back to the Jeffersonian era. By seeking to abolish northern shippers' legally aided monopoly of the coastal cotton trade, they hoped to increase competition, drive down prices, lessen dependence on northern carriers, and potentially provide a path toward direct trade with Europe.

The opening salvo was fired in spring 1858, when—in the midst of a prolonged debate over the Pacific railroad—South Carolinian William Boyce submitted a special committee report demanding complete abandonment of any form of commercial protection, including those aiding northern merchants and fisheries. Guised as a "revenue bill" (perhaps explaining historians' neglect), Boyce's proposal overtly challenged the highly discriminatory duties against vessels not built, owned, or operated by U.S. citizens. Such laws, he argued, had given "American ship-builders a perfect monopoly" by excluding foreign vessels from participating in the coastal trade. The report asserted that such measures violated free trade precepts and unnecessarily harmed American producers and consumers by limiting competition.[103]

More private conversation between Cotton South colleagues revealed the overtly sectional nature of the proposal. According to Alabama senator C. C. Clay, the measure sought to eliminate the "ship-building, coast-wise trade, and other monopolies now enjoyed to the wrong of the South."[104] In addition to precluding greater competition in the cotton shipping business from British, Dutch, French, and Belgian vessels, the insistence on American-built ships (and the practical nonexistence of shipbuilding in the region) severely hindered the Lower South's own commercial empowerment by preventing capitalists or cooperatives from purchasing and manning foreign-built vessels. The bill, however, had no chance of passage, a reality acknowledged by committee members and the Lower South press. The North remained united behind measures so clearly beneficial to merchants, shipowners, and sailors in northeastern ports and the Great Lakes. Reportedly even many Virginians, including Muscoe R. H. Garnett and Matthew Maury, could not concur with Boyce's report, apparently believing it threatened shipbuilding interests in Norfolk.[105]

A more minor success nearly occurred when Clay proposed repealing decades-old bounties for fisheries. "Since 1792," he argued, "there have been paid to the cod-fisheries the sum of $12,128,532 . . . a purely local interest confined to a very small section of the United States." Repeating the rhetoric and substance of the tariff debates, Clay demanded that the "unequal, unjust, and unconstitutional" bounties—"the extremist, greatest, and worst kind of protection . . . taking money derived from taxing the many, and giving it to the few"—be revoked.[106] Not all southern Democrats chose to stress these overtly sectional concerns, but all did oppose the bounties, believing in Jefferson Davis's words, that they had "the character of class legislation."[107] Clay's efforts paid off in the Senate, which repealed the bounties by a 30 to 25 vote. Among Lower South delegates, only Texas's Sam Houston (claiming allegiance to the American Party) opposed the measure, joining all Republican senators and four northern Democrats. Nevertheless, the bill stalled in the House when northern Democrats from coastal regions united with Republicans to prevent victory, despite unanimity amongst the fifty-seven southern Democrats.[108] The failure of this more modest attack on American shipping did not bode well for the Lower South's bolder plans to place European merchants on equal terms with American ones.[109] What had been intended, according to Mississippian William Yancey, as inaugural battles in the larger war against "that series of Congressional acts which have tended to increase the power of the North, and to cripple and stigmatize the South" only served to further alienate northern merchants who carried the Cotton South's goods to market.[110]

The substance and tone of the Lower South's frontal assault on commercial laws starkly revealed how drastically regional political economic goals had changed. Boyce and Clay's efforts directly challenged the principles behind Jefferson's Reports on Fisheries and Commerce, the foundations for Jeffersonian

Republican national political economy. They not so subtly dismissed the sacrifices that Americans had made to protect sailors' and merchants' rights against Britain during "Mr. Madison's War," and rejected outright the postwar attempts to further integrate southern planters and northern merchants by providing American ships a monopoly on the coastal trade. Even during the height of arguments between free traders and protectionists, these laws had remained something of a sacred bond uniting American interests. Now amidst the growing concerns over slavery and the rising hopes for direct trade with Europe, cotton planter-politicians sought to cast them off in exchange for easier access to British and other European shippers. Though some accurately blamed their own ancestors' complicity in these acts, others' logic generally perpetuated the victim mentality fast becoming pathological. Ignoring the circumstances surrounding the acts—namely, southern Anglophobia and self-interest—self-conscious sectionalists blamed exploitative northerners and soft Virginians for erecting an artificial monopoly in place of a supposedly more natural direct trade between Europe and the South.

Adding insult to injury, Lower South planters and politicians followed up these political jabs with concerted state and local action aimed at cutting out northern middlemen. In late 1859 the Chamber of Commerce at New Orleans, the major cotton port, gave an enthusiastic endorsement of the British American Southern Steamship Company's plans to charter a joint-stock company in Great Britain to pursue direct trade.[111] Backing its words with actions, Louisiana's legislature offered a bounty of $5 per ton for every ship over one hundred tons built in the state. In early 1860 Alabama also "broke ground in a practical shape on the subject of *Southern Direct Trade* and displayed the most enlightened and liberal spirit" by granting state and local tax exemptions to the sale of "all goods imported into the Southern States *directly* from foreign countries."[112] Potential allies in northern mercantilist circles—whether or not they cared about slavery—did not look favorably on attacks so clearly aimed at undermining their interests.

These efforts not only actively damaged national economic partnerships; they also revealed just how narrow regional views of the federal Union and Constitution had become. When pressed by a New York senator to explain why a law that operated unequally was unconstitutional, Clay barked that the Constitution had been framed "to establish justice" measured by "imposing equal burdens upon all the States, and all classes of citizens within the States."[113] Skirting the Founders' desire to "form a more perfect union" and achieve mutual economic advancement, Clay's definition of justice and constitutionality might have baffled the

Founders. In one fell swoop he and others rejected the idea that the federal government could pass any legislation that operated unequally on the nation's different parts. In place of any "generous sympathy" between citizens, which Calhoun had claimed was natural and essential in 1814, southern sectionalists helped create a paralyzing hostility, declaring even the smallest allocation of federal funds to northern interests unconstitutional.[114]

Lower South unwillingness to aid northerners expressed itself even more forcefully, and in northerners' eyes with marked hypocrisy, as the debate over fugitive slaves and westward expansion continued to rage. By the late 1850s, southerners challenged northern states' personal liberty laws and demanded more direct federal intervention to assure the return of their uniquely mobile slave property. Of critical importance, their inability to guarantee slavery's expansion within or outside present national borders enhanced pressure on Lower South politicians to thwart free soil expansion within the Union. As a result they united against a pragmatic homesteading policy fast growing in popularity amongst northern Republicans and Democrats alike. The idea of homesteading, or granting small and inexpensive tracts of land to individual settlers and families, had historical roots in Jefferson's idealized yeoman republic but had gained special attention amongst western Jacksonians in the 1830s. Until the late 1840s, easterners, and especially Whigs, had generally opposed it and other measures supporting expansion, out of fear that it would reduce government revenue and drain labor and capital to the west. Southeasterners had not been especially fond of the policy but used their support for devaluation and cession of public lands to claim that they sought to empower rather than hinder western farmers.

By the late 1850s, however, northerners' concerns about urban poverty and southerners' alarm about slavery had almost entirely reversed the political calculus. New York Whig and future Republican Horace Greeley had helped inaugurate the change, arguing as early as 1846 that opening cheap or free "small tracts (not over 160 acres) to actual settlers only" would relieve urban class tensions and prevent the wasteful speculation encouraged by recent devaluation policies.[115] Greeley's conversion, broadcast through his influential *New York Tribune* editorials, reflected a key, if gradual, turn in northeastern thought regarding western lands. As a safety valve, settlement of the West would reduce overpopulation and increase wages while also providing consumers for manufacturers and merchants carrying goods over an ever-expanding infrastructure. Given its popularity amongst northern immigrants, workers, and farmers, homesteading remained a major policy goal of northern Democrats. It quickly, however, became a central plank of Free Soil Republicans as a way to fight slavery's expansion and to attract voters. In 1858, Galusha Grow, the representative from David Wilmot's Pennsylvania district, proposed a measure that narrowly failed in the House. The following year, however, Republicans (supporting the measure 87 to 1) almost unanimously pushed a homesteading bill through the House before powerful southern senators, Robert Toombs and Virginia's Robert Hunter, used Treasury Secretary Howell Cobb's gloomy revenue forecast to torpedo it.[116]

A closer examination reveals that more than simple concerns about the federal government's finances informed southern Democrats' opposition to cheap or free lands. An 1852 House vote on homesteading reflected a traditional East-West divide within the Lower South; Georgia and South Carolina unanimously opposed it, and southwestern states favored it 11 to 1.[117] The application of the principle of popular sovereignty in the Kansas-Nebraska Act of 1854 radically changed the outlook of previously supportive southwestern representatives. By deciding the question of slavery at the ballot box rather than by a predetermined geographical line, the act turned future homesteaders into constituents who would determine slavery's fate in the West. Showing the power of proslavery thought, in spring 1854 representatives of southwestern states evenly split on a measure that Alabama's Richard Johnson noted was "too strongly tinctured with abolition."[118] Cotton State concerns reached new heights after Republicans and Douglas Democrats refused to accept Kansas's proslavery Lecompton Compromise and Douglas's 1858 Freeport Doctrine suggested that Free Soilers might prevent slavery by not passing supporting legislation.[119] By February 1, 1859, all but one southern Democrat opposed homesteading. The following year, with the Democratic presidential convention in Charleston on the horizon, not a single southern Democrat voted for a new version of the Homestead Bill. By contrast all but four northern Democrats and every Republican supported it, along with a handful of Upper South "Americans," including John Bell. Only a southern-inspired veto by Buchanan, under tremendous pressure from southern advisors in his cabinet, prevented the bill's passage. Northern Democrats felt angry and betrayed. Republicans had found further evidence of southern obstructionism to use as campaign material against the "Slave Power."[120]

The Kansas-Nebraska Act and the homesteading debate also ensured gridlock over the Pacific railroad. Southern supporters of a Pacific railroad had found some hope after the Senate ratified the Gadsden Purchase in 1854 and Secretary of War Jefferson Davis's reported preference for a Gila River route. Objections by northerners and southern fiscal conservatives, however, again postponed the project. The legislative session of 1858–1859 witnessed the most extensive debate on the railroad measure and its ultimate antebellum demise. Georgia's senator Alfred Iverson proposed that both a northern and a southern route should be built, particularly in light of the perilous break he thought increasingly likely. "What I demand," he insisted, "is that the South shall be put upon an equality with the North, whether the Union lasts or not; that in appropriating the public lands and money . . . the South shall have an equal chance to secure a road within her borders to insure to her benefit whilst the Union lasts, to belong to her when, if ever, the Union is dissolved."[121] Such language made northern Republicans, then holding a narrow House majority, even less likely to consider a southern route, though they themselves remained divided about the best northern route. Though southern political and fiscal sensibilities had largely prevented passage of a Pacific Railroad Bill, southern secessionists utilized its failure to further demonstrate that a northern-dominated federal government (whether Democratic- or Republican-controlled) would do the region no favors. Far from a mere abstraction, the issue of slavery in the territories short-circuited important and tangible national economic policy and party alliances.

For national Democrats, averting calamity meant mobilizing support for the annexation of Cuba, a policy they hoped could garner northern support while offering the South a tangible success. President Buchanan, though now privately embarrassed by the Ostend Manifesto, redoubled diplomatic efforts to purchase the island in early 1859. During the lame duck winter session, Louisiana senator John Slidell pushed legislation to grant Buchanan the $30 million he requested to negotiate the purchase of the island. Outside of South Carolina most Lower South delegates and newspapers waxed enthusiastic about the measure, some asserting that loyalty to the Union required the slave island. Only one Palmetto congressman, however, supported Slidell's bill. Senator James Hammond described it as an "evil political measure," a belief forwarded by another Carolinian, who described Cuba as "the bait which the Democratic Party holds out to the South."[122] Boyce's well-circulated antiannexation congressional speech cited, amongst other things, a belief that the presence of some 200,000 free blacks would threaten slavery, benefit northern commercial interests more than southern ones, and possibly alienate European powers "upon the eve of a great struggle with a hostile majority of the North."[123] Boyce may have been right. The man responsible for negotiations, ambassador to Spain William Preston, made little headway. Spanish politicians remained firm, and the British and French officials he hoped would pressure them to sell refused.

Preston's failures overseas, however, were upstaged by the political controversy Slidell's bill generated at home. When less-than-savvy Lower South delegates Judah Benjamin of Louisiana and Stephen Mallory of Florida infused proslavery arguments into the Senate discussion, Republicans retorted that they would never permit a slaveholding Cuba to enter the Union. Petitions opposing the annexation of Cuba poured into Congress. As the February debate raged, northern Democrats, who had suffered huge losses in the fall 1858 midterm elections, found themselves forced to the sidelines lest they be seen as in the pockets of a slave power responsible for torpedoing so much recent legislation. The likelihood of a bill passing became even more remote after March, when Democrats lost their House majority and Republicans gained six Senate seats. Heading home in the summer, expansionists could vent their spleen on "Black Republicans" and suggest, as Jefferson Davis did to a Mississippi state Democratic convention, that "the inevitable end of continuance in such hostility between the States must be their separation."[124] Hopeful expansionists and proponents for economic development continued to envision scenarios where the region could acquire more land for slavery and gain a firmer grasp over its commercial destiny, but only, many argued, once freed from unaccommodating free soil forces in the Union.[125]

By the summer of 1859, secession-minded individuals outside of Washington, including Rhett in the East and Yancey in the West, offered generally reinforcing accounts for why the Union had failed the South. At an Independence Day gathering in Grahamville, South Carolina, Rhett drew direct parallels to the challenges facing the South and those facing revolutionaries who opposed "unconstitutional taxations" and British tyranny. His revisionist history began by arguing that a bifurcated understanding of the Constitution had emerged. Northerners seeking a "consolidated democracy" believed that "nothing was easier than to establish the government of the United States." Rejecting such images of a natural union, Rhett contended, "that the formation of the Constitution of the United States was a most difficult enterprise," the convention coming to a "dead stand from an impossibility of agreement" on most issues. "The great leading motive" that overcame the challenges "was the fear of foreign powers," as weak and impoverished states "united as to *be one people,* in relation to foreign nations for self-protection."[126]

The Constitution successfully fulfilled this purpose until the War of 1812, which Rhett believed had been "produced by northern interests," "demonstrated . . . our ability to protect ourselves from foreign nations" and thus removed the "apprehensions which drove us together into a Union." Ignoring the complexity of Jeffersonian-inspired navigation acts and tariffs, Rhett told his receptive audience of farmers, merchants, planters, and artisans that the "northern people" subsequently "turned to the internal operations of the government" and "sought by its instrumentality to make the South tributary to their enrichment and their power." Overlooking South Carolinians' early complicity with events, Rhett argued that the tariff of 1816 and the initial rejection of Missouri's constitution by northerners "showed the two great points on which they could best, and intended, to build up a consolidated democracy for the predominance of the North over the South": slavery and economic policy. Neither Jefferson nor Calhoun, "greater than Jefferson in intellect and his equal in patriotism," successfully resolved the issues. His beloved state had first recognized the consolidationist threats in the 1820s. The North's "renewed interference and aggression on the institution of slavery" had finally awoken the rest of the Slave States, who finally appeared ready to act as their forefathers had and commence the struggle for independence.

The future looked certain, exceedingly bleak, and suggested that the Constitution no longer served southern interests. "The sectional majority from the North grows stronger and more resolute every day," and Republicans hostile to the South would soon have the power "to sweep away every obstacle to their sectional domination and the consolidation of the government." Manufacturers and "internal improvements and national railroads" would justify higher tariffs and "a greater tribute shall be wrung from the South." Under a new homestead policy justified as "land for the landless . . . the northern and emigrant population shall take all the common territories and make free States of them." Whether such policies were "consistent, with the Constitution of the United States or not, is of no sort of consequence. If it is, then the constitution established a sectional despotism over the South. And if it is not, then the constitution is abolished by the North, the only power which can maintain it." Then again, he concluded, it may never have served regional interests. Prosperity, he believed, had been "the result of our State governments and of our magnificent staples." "We know," he claimed, "the general government only by its taxation." At best, the Constitution had lost whatever relevance it had; at worst, it had become a tool for the South's oppression.

A few days later, William Yancey traveled to South Carolina to lay the groundwork for agitation at the following year's national Democratic convention in Charleston. While there he offered his own view of the past, echoing Rhett's arguments while shifting the emphasis to elevate southwestern concerns. Yancey encouraged slightly more faith in prosouthern possibilities under a properly understood Constitution. Though mentioning the tariff as significant, Yancey feared it to be divisive within the Slave South and trusted that South Carolinians fully appreciated "the greater question of slavery" and particularly its expansion westward. Alabamians, he informed South Carolinians, stood ready to join the secession movement if slaveholders' rights were not positively protected in the territories, something he doubted Douglas Democrats or "Black Republicans" would do. Whatever their expressed reasons, both Yancey and Rhett believed that the 1860 election would be the climactic political battle.[127]

They and other speakers of that day also concluded that secessionists must accept a lack of unanimity as they moved forward. To accomplish this they drew very favorable comparison between their own situation and those who advocated American independence in the 1770s. Unanimity, of course, would remain elusive, South Carolinian Thomas Hanckel told the Cincinnati and Seventy-Six Association. The patriots of 1776 also had "chilling doubts" and "gloomy apprehensions."[128] "When our fathers resisted the whole might of England, they were scattered along the seaboard," Yancey noted, "possessed no such good governments . . . had no system of revenue . . . had no such arms or means of manufacturing arms. They were but three millions in number; they were divided even amongst themselves as to the propriety of their resistance." Yet, he continued, "for eight long years they maintained the contest with England, and maintained it triumphantly." In Yancey's mind the South was more than able to protect herself from aggression: "We have eight millions of people . . . we have unity of production, unity of institutions and a compact country. We have the great product without which the world cannot do. We are rich in the elements of prosperity."[129] Cotton featured prominently in even these early efforts to steel Lower South resolve.

Such arguments reflected the heightened faith that, internationally if not domestically, King Cotton would trump any lingering antislavery efforts and help secure slavery's permanence, regardless of the political situation in Europe. The proposition occasionally seemed to have been reinforced by powerfully positioned acquaintances in Europe. In 1857 Liverpool shipping magnate George Holt visited business partners in the Georgia and South Carolina lowcountry. His encounters, and perhaps more importantly his interest in cotton, led him to conclude that "the abstract principle of slavery is no doubt to be utterly condemned & abhorred, but as seen in this country, fixed in a long existence it is not an easy matter to see the way to its abolition."[130] In early 1860 William Gregory, an avid free trader and Conservative MP who had recently shared lodging with a group

of southern congressmen and future secessionists, went a step further by informing South Carolina representative and secessionist William Porcher Miles that
the last several years had witnessed "a great alteration of opinion" about slavery
in Britain. Though "abstractly, of course, all we Englishmen are opposed to Slavery," Gregory stressed that "the working of abolition in the West India islands,"
had widened the "gulf between us and your own abolitionists."[131]

At least one prominent abolitionist agreed. In 1859, after returning to Britain
for the first time since his visit in 1846, Frederick Douglass expressed alarm at the
"prejudice" "in nearly all . . . commercial towns." In contrast to his earlier visit, he
found "pro-slavery ministers" welcomed and "contemptuous sneers all originating in the spirit of slavery." Douglass and other American abolitionists feared that
Britons, after successfully emancipating slaves in their own empire, were retreating from the abolitionist cause. Gregory assured Miles of precisely that: "Rely on
it, Englishmen are not traveling with closed eyes, and in spite of Mrs. Beecher
Stowe, Wendell Phillips, O' Exeter Hale at home, we are beginning to see that the
Southern Americans have something to say, quite as much as the New Englanders."
Demonstrating the sincerity of his convictions, he forwarded his "southern
friends" a copy of a new book, which argued "for the necessity of a black separate
creation and that Adam was not the ancestor of Sambo and Gambo as well as of
John & Jonathan." Not surprisingly, Gregory would become one of the leading
proponents of recognizing the Confederacy.[132]

Lower South periodicals and sectionalists closely followed political developments, often reading positive signs into what they saw. The formation of a Conservative government in late 1858 with a political agenda similar to the Cotton
South's—free trade and the prevention of democratic excesses—heightened expectations that allies could be found amongst Britain's ruling elite. The return of
Palmerston to power at the head of a newly formed "Liberal" government in June
1859 hinted at a rebirth of democracy, but the place in it for peoples of African
descent remained uncertain at best. Furthermore, Miles and his extensive network of prosecessionist contacts retained hope that they had at least one prominently placed friend in the new administration. Palmerston's personal private
secretary, Evelyn Ashley, had recently returned from an extended tour of the
United States and fondly recalled to Miles the "delightful hours" he spent with
that "pleasant quartet" of southern congressmen that he had roomed with while
in Washington.[133] That quartet included four archsecessionists, and no doubt
each had considerable faith that his personal relationship with Ashley and cotton
would help usher in a new independent Confederacy.

Had Cotton South secessionists been forced to, they could easily have found evidence that British antislavery sentiment remained fairly deep. Gregory proudly admitted to Miles that his "southern propensities have brought such a storm on my head at home."[134] When the Prince of Wales made the first royal visit to North America in the fall of 1860, he politely declined an invitation to the Lower South, instead gracing the Slave States with only a brief visit to Richmond and the home of George Washington.[135] Yet even southerners who experienced direct rebukes retained great faith in the power of cotton. A summer 1860 "Statistical Congress" turned into an embarrassing moment for Georgia author and university president, A. B. Longstreet. At the event's opening, former lord chancellor and abolitionist warrior Lord Brougham pointedly observed that the U.S. minister, representing a slave power, shared the platform with a "negro" doctor from Canada. Taking the stirring applause for the doctor as an insult, Longstreet walked out, subsequently penning a spirited defense of his actions. After charging Londoners with hypocrisy and bidding the city "farewell forever," he closed by telling his newspaper audience in Britain (and at home) that he was proceeding to Liverpool, claiming he "liked her better . . . because she likes my people better." Even Longstreet's literary-inspired mind found comfort by retreating into commercial determinism, claiming that "Interest!" and "Cotton!" dictated actual policy.[136]

Lower South planter-politicians continued to debate how far British antislavery opposition could be tested on land or sea. By surviving the late antebellum crises over free black sailors, territorial expansion into the Caribbean, and the international slave trade, however, Lower South faith in enduring peace and economic partnership with Europe had actually grown stronger. British officials voiced their displeasure with the idea of slavery or the slave trade expanding in the Caribbean but made it equally clear that they would not risk war with the United States to curtail either development. Southerners attributed that reluctance to cotton. Critically, British consuls in the Deep South had finally approached the subject of the Negro Seaman's Acts in a way that recognized state sovereignty and demonstrated sensitivity to the needs of slaveholders by limiting contact between slaves and free black foreigners. Especially after John Brown's October 1859 raid on Harper's Ferry, those eager for southern independence scarcely doubted that slavery would be safer outside of the Union than within it. They placed considerable faith in the belief that similar racial assumptions and a cotton-centered commercial worldview could roll back abolitionist efforts overseas and pave the way for cordial relations with European powers.

At the same time, gridlock over domestic debates ranging from homesteading, to navigation acts, to annexation of Cuba, to the Pacific railroad suggested that domestic politics had devolved into bitter sectional rivalry. Motivated by visions of economic greatness and a compulsive desire to preserve their slave society, Cotton South politicians refused to concede anything to northern politicians, friend or foe. Unlike their Upper South neighbors, they had concluded that the Union could only be of benefit to southern interests if it "protected" the rights of slaveholders through a stronger Fugitive Slave Act and guarantees for slavery's expansion westward. The position directly contradicted the states' rights rhetoric often heard from the same circles. The rapid ascendance of a Republican Party that trumpeted free soil and free labor principles stood in their way while also providing compelling evidence that southern slave capitalists and northern free laborers were headed toward a political Armageddon. By the close of 1859, many in the Lower South had come to reject even the possibility of a harmonious union of interests.

## Realists Decide: Election and Secession

Unlike Rhett and Yancey, most voters in the Cotton South did not approach the election of 1860 believing secession was inevitable or desirable. They did, however, enter the contest celebrating politicians who confidently asserted "southern" rights and interests on the national and international stage. The Panic of 1857, mutinies in India, the turn to African and coolie labor in the West Indies, and Europe's seemingly malleable foreign policy elevated faith in cotton and, by extension, slavery's power abroad. A bumper crop at relatively high prices created significant economic optimism, leading Godfrey Barnsley, a British-born New Orleans factor-turned-slaveowning-planter, to exclaim that "the receipts of cotton are astounding, I hardly know what to think."[137] Yet a bleak political forecast at home clouded any bright economic forecast. The rejection of the Lecompton Constitution, John Brown's raid at Harper's Ferry, and Stephen Douglas's Freeport Doctrine had eroded faith that northerners, Democrats or Republicans, would continue to serve the diverse and ambitious interests of the Cotton South.

As Congress convened in early 1860, Jefferson Davis brought the debate over slavery in the territories to a head by proposing a resolution that would make it the "duty of Congress" to intervene if "the judiciary does not possess power to insure adequate protection" for slaveowners.[138] Opportunistic South Carolinians rallied behind Davis's proposal for congressional intervention.[139] The most forceful advocates, though, came from newer cotton states, including Mississippian Albert Gallatin Brown and Alabamians C. C. Clay and William Yancey, whose constituents would be more directly affected by exclusion from the West. Newer but still insecure planters and slaveholding farmers in the southwest cotton areas had great expectations but also grave concerns about their future and that of their children should slave territory not spread.[140] Though many fervently denied it, backers of so-called positive protection lacked faith in popular sovereignty. Their new demands promised to fracture the Democratic Party.

Northern Democrats, still stinging from defeat at the polls and the selection of a Republican speaker of the House, rightly perceived the proposed legislation as a betrayal of congressional nonintervention. The issue ground congressional politics to a halt, leading recently returned representative James Hammond to tell a relative in April that "no two nations on earth are or ever were more distinctly separated and hostile than we are. Not Carthage and Rome, England and France at any period. How can the thing go on?"[141] After blocking Davis's bill, which Stephen Douglas compared to the "doctrine of the Tories of the Revolution," northern Democrats prepared for the national party convention, ready to reaffirm congressional noninterference and nominate Douglas, its chief proponent. Some noteworthy politicians in the Lower South, including Alexander Stephens and Douglas's eventual running mate Georgian Herschel Johnson, angrily blamed Davis and others for manufacturing a controversy that threatened to undermine the Union.[142] They did not, however, have the sway to stop more aggressive majorities from composing the state delegations headed to Charleston in May.

Instead, slave expansionists played to regional pride and interest, claiming that the region's economic, political, and social viability necessitated access to new lands and arguing that northern Democrats could no longer be trusted. "Python" raised the pointed question in the March issue of *De Bow's Review*: "Of what advantage is it to the South to be destroyed by Mr. Douglas through territorial sovereignty to the exclusion of Southern institutions, rather than by Mr. Seward through congressional sovereignty to the same end? What difference is there to the South whether they are forcibly led to immolation by Seward, or accorded, in the alternative, the Roman privilege of selecting their own mode of death, by Douglas? Die they must in either event."[143] South Carolina's Alfred Huger agreed, emphasizing that at least Republican policy framed the matter honestly: "If there be any difference so far as the South is concerned between the Squatter Sovereignty of Mr. Douglas and the 'irrepressible conflict' of Mr. Seward, *that* 'difference' is in my poor judgment, in favour of the latter! It is more natural, & it is farther off—the one is abolition *eo nomine* the other is abolition in an offensive disguise! and therefore the more alarming."[144]

Exploding the logic of popular sovereignty, pessimistic and powerful Cotton South leaders, generally supported by their constituents, concluded that only a candidate and platform favoring slave expansion could ensure that the federal government preserved regional honor and interest. Alabama firebrands, led by William Yancey, carried this ultimatum to the Charleston Convention in 1860. When northern Democrats refused to bow to the request, Lower South delegates bolted, thus fracturing the only national party that had deep roots in the region. Finalized a month later, when Southern Democrats put forward John Breckinridge on a platform of positive protection, the dissolution of the Democratic Party along almost purely sectional lines suggested that the free labor of the North and slave society of the South had reached the crossroads.[145]

Cotton South residents who rejected such a fatalistic assessment turned, not primarily to Douglas, but to a hastily formed political newcomer. The Constitutional Union Party had its roots in a number of earlier movements but claimed as its birthplace Massachusetts, where "Cotton Whigs" and "Americans" had struggled to find a conservative alternative to Republican antislavery views and Democratic incompetence. John Brown's raid on Virginia provided them an opportunity to nationalize their efforts by making overtures to the South. Five days after Brown was hanged, conservatives met at Faneuil Hall to form the Constitutional Union Party, express sympathy to Virginians, and convey their desire to preserve and protect the Union and prosperity for all white Americans. They found many prominent partners in the Upper South, where opposition groups had continued successfully to challenge Democrats for state and national office. Former Whig senators, Kentuckian John Crittenden and Tennessean John Bell, welcomed a national umbrella for their efforts; in fact Bell was pegged as the party's presidential nominee on a ticket with famed orator and former Cotton Whig, Edward Everett.

Farther south, however, where the bonds of cotton were supposed to generate support, they had far less success. Democratic dominance had marginalized opposition parties, many of whom continued to run under the "American" name, but with very little success. Playing the politics of slavery endemic to the region, many had embraced advanced proslavery positions not easily conformable with the Constitutional Unionists' desire to downplay the issue.[146] The Unionist ticket continued to be dogged by charges that Bell and Everett's assertions of congressional supremacy over Washington, D.C., and interstate commerce threatened slaveholders' access to the capital and the continuation of the domestic slave trade. As critically, the claim that cotton and commercial interests could preserve the Union failed to resonate fully with Lower South voters, many of whom were frustrated by their region's continued dependence on northern merchants and financiers.[147]

Whereas Constitutional Unionists mistakenly hoped that cotton would preserve the Union, Republicans rarely mentioned the crop, and when they did so it was rarely in a positive light. Indeed, recent developments suggested to them that King Cotton and the "Slave Power" needed humbling. The Cotton States, in particular, had refused to support free state interests, defined by many to include protective tariffs, homesteading, and internal improvements. Now they demanded that the federal government ensure slavery through an even more intrusive fugitive slave law and possibly a federal slave code for the territories. Such policies, Republicans like Minnesota's William Windom argued, unmasked the hypocrisy of those claiming to favor states' rights and supposedly committed to laissez-faire economic arguments. They also undermined the very meaning of America: "The early theory of the founders of this Republic was that it should be an asylum for the oppressed of all nations." The country's "spacious arches were broad enough to protect every human being . . . [in] whose soul the Creator had planted a love of liberty." Southern Democratic foes, who continually "thrust the slavery question upon us, and proved their love of slavery," prevented the fulfillment of America's destiny.[148] Delegates to the Republican Party's June nominating convention arrived angry and confident, believing they could and must win in order to thwart slaveholders' complete dominance and to preserve their own understanding of the Republic.

Victory, Republicans also knew, would require attracting a larger number of traditionally Democratic voters. In April, *New York Tribune* editor and Republican mouthpiece Horace Greeley confided the new strategy to a female confidante: "I want to succeed this time" and "yet know the country is not Anti-slavery. It will only swallow a little Anti-Slavery in a great deal of sweetening. An Anti-Slavery man *per se* cannot be elected; but a Tariff, River-and-Harbor, Pacific Railroad, Free-Homestead man *may* succeed *although* he is Anti-Slavery . . . I mean to have as good a candidate as the majority will elect."[149] Embracing this approach and drawing upon continued northern frustrations after the Panic of 1857, Republican leaders in Chicago provided a moderated national platform broadly appealing to diverse groups in the Northeast and Northwest and even a few lonely individuals in the Upper South. After reaffirming the party's commitment to preventing slavery's expansion and demanding Kansas's immediate entrance as a free state, it pledged to maintain "the right of each state to order and control its domestic institutions."[150]

Chicago conventioneers then trumpeted specific policies beneficial to a variety of northern constituencies. A homestead policy desirable to westerners, newly naturalized citizens, and northeastern workers easily passed, as did a plank calling for the immediate construction, with federal support, of a Pacific railroad, presumably on a northern route. Farmers who claimed wheat was king found much to like in this platform. So, too, did manufacturing and merchant groups when the Republicans unabashedly affirmed the constitutionality and desirability of federal expenditures to improve rivers and harbors. In a decision carefully calculated to attract manufacturing groups and workers in swing states (like Pennsylvania) without alienating western free traders, the convention endorsed a moderately protective tariff, reportedly evoking "spasms of joy" from the Pennsylvania delegation. Understandably, the interests of cotton planters received scarce mention and the importance of the cotton trade was expressly downplayed, a fact southerners duly noted.[151]

The Chicago Platform represented both the fruits of Cotton South policies and the sum of the region's fears. Southern sectionalists were aware of what Republicans offered to the rest of the nation. This was not least because Lincoln Republicans were accomplishing the same type of coalition building that Jeffersonian Republicans had successfully achieved in 1800 and that southern compromisers had been trying, with only limited success, to revitalize since the 1830s. In a striking, and for the Deep South horrific, parallel, northern free soil forces in 1860 stood on the brink of their own "Republican Revolution," one brought about largely because of northern fears of a "Slave Power Conspiracy."[152] Victory in the Electoral College was not a foregone conclusion, but informed observers knew that Lincoln and his running mate, Maine senator Hannibal Hamlin, would receive the most votes.

Those ready to carry the mantle of secession forward observed the chaos with a sense of perverse pleasure, taking every opportunity to highlight the apparent incompatibility of southern and northern society. Rhett used the *Mercury* to attack "cooperationists" at the Charleston Convention and proudly claimed credit for its dissolution.[153] In July, with the party conventions over, citizens of St. John's Colleton joined other South Carolina assemblies to celebrate the end of the national Democratic Party and suggest that "it will be the highest interest of the Southern States to take their destinies under their own control, and prepare, without delay, to organize for themselves a separate and independent Confederacy." The meeting's resolutions and featured address by eminently successful low-country cotton planter John Townsend updated long-rehearsed arguments. Slaveholders could never entrust their rights or interests to "Party Hacks." The South needed to "brush away those cobwebs" of "sophomoric sentimentality" and "look at the subject clearly, like practical and sensible men." A Union promoting the "interests," "peace," and "honor" of its constituent parts had "long since ceased to exist," transforming instead into "the forced, and unnatural *herding together* of two *sections*—spiteful to each other—hating each other more and more every day—with interests opposed—and the stronger section making laws which operate with merciless severity upon the weaker section."[154] Townsend's background added gravity to his words. In addition to boasting a Princeton degree, he owned some 270 slaves and prime cotton lands estimated to have been worth half a million dollars. European lace makers coveted his award-winning Sea Island cotton. He was known as a moderate, and both his earlier opposition to nullification and his cooperationist stance in 1850 made Townsend's demands for immediate state secession all the more noteworthy.

The *Charleston Courier*'s account of Townsend's address focused on the portion clarifying any misconception that "England, France, Germany, Russia, and other commercial manufacturing nations of Europe, are hostile to our African slavery." Recasting recent developments to serve his larger purpose, Townsend concluded that Britain had agitated "not to abolish slavery, but to break up the Union." "John Bull's" "humane" pursuit for "mastership in *commerce* and *manufacturers*" had placed him in an economic rivalry with the "*Northern Section* of the United States," whose legalized exploitation under the federal Constitution had provided it with "preponderating advantages as to turn the scales of victory." At first Great Britain had sought to "*cripple her rival*" by "setting her agents at work, both at home and at the North, to agitate and agitate, on the slavery question." But realizing the "folly" of her own emancipation and unable to "*obtain the raw material without depending on others* for it," Britain no longer believed abolition possible. Instead, her politicians eagerly anticipated disunion as a development that "strips her rival of all his fortuitous advantages, and so secures to herself an unbounded ascendency . . . in commerce and manufacturers."[155]

Though not an accurate characterization of British officials' true wishes, Townsend's distorted economic determinism transformed earlier fears about British meddling into a central reason for why secession would be favorably received abroad. "Be assured, then, fellow citizens," he told his receptive audience,

"Great Britain is too deeply interested in slave-grown productions to desire the abolition of slavery." Indeed, Europe's dependence on a politically independent South would create "*jealousy and unfriendly* rivalry between the Northern section of this Union, and the chief commercial nations of Europe and, on the other hand, kindly relations between them and us." The relatively moderate *Charleston Courier* editor summarizing the piece agreed. Independence would free the Cotton States "from any further disturbances on the subject of slavery" and render it "the strongest and most flourishing section" of North America.[156] Fear of increased attacks against slavery within a Republican-controlled Union drove individuals like Townsend to see secession as necessary. A deeply held conviction in cotton's international power gave them the courage to see it as possible, and even beneficial.

The printed version of Townsend's address, published under the title *The South Alone Should Govern the South,* featured haunting descriptions of slavery's future under "Black Republican" rule but then relied heavily on recent articles from the *London Times* and Thomas Kettell's recently published *Southern Wealth and Northern Profits* to highlight the centrality of King Cotton. Kettell, who had founded the *United States Economist* and edited *Hunt's Merchants' Magazine* (arguably the nation's two most prominent commercial periodicals), intended his treatise as an appeal for northern concessions to the South. It instantly became a tool for Cotton South secessionists, who joined Townsend in suggesting that Kettell's tract should be "in the hands of every southern man."[157] In the hands of secessionists, a cotton-centered argument aimed at making northerners accommodate southern demands in order to preserve northern profits became further evidence for how unequally the Union had operated. Kettell's catalogue of the South's real and growing wealth, including recent advances in southern manufacturing (equal he argued to the West), morphed into statements that the South would survive and even benefit from independence. For Cotton South audiences, the lengthy treatise validated the region's victim mentality while more confidently asserting cotton's paramount importance.[158]

Townsend also drew richly from *London Times* articles, including one that excoriated Lord Brougham for seeing "only the black laborers" and ignoring "the free and intelligent English families who thrive upon the wages which those cotton bales produce." "Even Lord Brougham would not ask us to believe," the *Times* argued, "that there is any proximate hope that the free cotton raised in Africa will, within any reasonable time, drive out of culture the slave-grown cotton of America." Collectively, Kettell's analysis, *Times* editorials, and secessionists' use of both suggested that while the North's need for cotton no longer blunted its attacks against slaveholders, Europeans, and certainly Britons, had come to understand that without slavery the cotton trade would shrivel and that without the cotton trade Europe would be brought to its knees.

Robert Gourdin appreciated the rationale and saw the political promise of this type of argument. By day Gourdin and his brother Henry ran one of Charleston's largest import-export firms, Gourdin, Matthiessen and Company. The firm had offices in Charleston and Savannah and boasted vast connections to Europe's cotton markets, including sales to the McConnel & Kennedy firm. The Gourdin brothers spent considerable time with George Holt during his visit to the area and one had traveled to England as recently as 1859.[159] They were, in short, men of the business world. By night, Robert coordinated the semiclandestine efforts of the "1860 Association," a committee of correspondence dedicated to mobilizing the Cotton States for secession. With the help of Isaac Hayne, William Dennison Porter (president of the state senate), Judge Andrew Magrath, and sympathetic printers, Gourdin helped distribute over 200,000 pamphlets in the two months prior to the November election, including an estimated 165,000 copies of two of Townsend's pamphlets, *The South Alone* and *The Doom of Slavery*.[160] The impressive propaganda machine generated remarkable results. On October 8, nearly a month before Lincoln's election, South Carolina voters overwhelmingly elected an aggressively prosecessionist state legislature, all but assuring dramatic action should Lincoln win.[161]

Farther west, cotton also factored into political calculations, though voices of disunion, including Yancey, posited that a Union preserved strictly on slaveholders' terms might yet serve Cotton South interests. In a six-week speaking tour, the man most responsible for breaking apart the Charleston Convention insisted that the fate of the Union rested in northern hands, claiming that only a Republican defeat, a stronger fugitive slave act, and federal protection for slaveholders' property in existing and new territories could preserve the Union. Despite consciously moderating his language and occasionally disavowing the label "disunionist," Yancey could not help but attract as many jeers as cheers. At New York's Cooper Institute he derided William Seward and insisted that northerners would need to "enlarge your jails and penitentiaries, re-enforce and strengthen your police force, and keep the irrepressible conflict fellows from stealing our negroes." At Faneuil Hall in Boston, the heart of abolition and textile manufacturing, Yancey mocked the state for giving blacks voting rights, gave a virulent proslavery speech, and insisted that cotton mill owners and workers ought to be more respectful of slaveholders' rights. The jabs highlighted a conviction that Yancey conveyed to many of his audiences: the North needed the Union more than the South did. As he had told an audience in the federal capital: "The Union is everything to New York, Boston, and Philadelphia. The Union is much to the South." In a statement revealing an inflated estimation of southern manufacturing and the value of its chief staple, Yancey declared that a South freed from the Union would be economically "independent of the world; we have the great peace-maker, King Cotton, within our midst." Unless northerners "want to go naked, and show their nakedness," he closed, "they had better come and solicit the support of our cotton planters."[162]

As he retreated back into the South, his discussion of the political situation revealed more nuance but even less accommodation. After mocking Bell supporters' habit of ringing small bells before a Louisville audience, he suggested that the well-meaning party was ill suited for the challenges ahead. Ascending a Nashville stage that Stephen Douglas had spoken from the night before, he accused the "Little Giant" of lying. After traversing nine states and giving twenty speeches, Yancey ended his broadly covered tour in parade-like fashion at New Orleans just a week before the election results were announced. There he eliminated much of the ambiguity that his entire tour had created for some archsecessionists who pondered why the "fire-eater" had even bothered. After lauding New Orleans for her superiority to New York in uniting the products of western free and southern slave labor, Yancey informed an estimated crowd of 30,000 that his tour had taught him a couple of things. For one the North had a "unity of purpose," and though there remained "many true friends of Constitutional government," early returns from Pennsylvania suggested they were not strong enough and that a Republican victory was likely. Secession would then be necessary. To allay his Louisiana audience's concern about that possibility, Yancey assured them that his tour had convinced him that, contrary to his earlier assumptions, secession would be peaceably and profitably achieved. The North would be disinclined to make war on cotton. If they did, however, Yancey "was now well satisfied the border states would never permit a hostile army, marching on the cotton States, to pass over their territory." In addition, "England needs our cotton and must have it."[163] As he had alluded in Washington, D.C., over a month earlier, Yancey insisted that an independent southern republic would allow for the commercial takeoff of southern coastal cities. Having succeeded in tapping into Lower Louisiana passions and bolstering its confidence, Yancey returned home, where he and others awaited news of the election returns.

The rhetoric of the campaign and its results confirmed Lower South secession-ists' assertions and unionists' fears, while portending the likely end of any southern-western political alliance. Republicans extended their margins of vic-tory in Michigan, Minnesota, and Ohio by capturing majorities of 57, 63, and 52 percent, respectively. Though not winning pure majorities, they carried the Democratic states of Indiana and Illinois by adding 76,000 and 45,000 voters to their 1856 tallies. The picture remained even more troubling in northeastern commercial and manufacturing states allegedly bound to the South by cotton. In Pennsylvania, the home state of one of the region's most loyal northern allies, President Buchanan, the Republican Party won an outright majority, gaining a shocking 120,000 votes more than it had in the previous election. Even greater gains were made in the Northeast. Massachusetts voters, one New Orleans paper noted, had handily rejected the "conservative elements" and "the pure, the wise, the peerless Edward Everett, by over a seventy thousand majority."[164] In New York City, despite the best efforts of cotton financier and close friend of many Geor-gians, August Belmont, Republicans made inroads into the Democratic ma-chine.[165] As ominously, the Republicans had "even displayed unexpected and growing power in some of the slaveholding States themselves," a clear reference to notable Republican minorities in the slave states of Delaware (23.7%) and Mis-souri (10%). Cotton's power could not prevent the rise of antislavery politics within the Union.

Secessionists used Lincoln's resounding victory to highlight for Cotton South residents the weakness of potential political allies in the North and to suggest that the Union had devolved into two irrevocably hostile sections. "Why has the elec-tion of Lincoln so altered the opinion of conservative Southerners in favor of Secession?" the *New Orleans Bee* rhetorically asked and then answered: because, even with Democratic successes in some key congressional races, "the result . . . showed the tremendous power and popularity of Black Republicanism . . . With what shadow of reason could Southern men be advised to submit and await the possible events of the future when abolitionism had swept every Northern Com-monwealth?"[166] Editors for Augusta, Georgia's, *Daily Constitutionalist* agreed that the "'ties of Union,' if by the term is meant ties of fraternal sympathy, can never again be strengthened, for they no longer exist to bind the two sections together. They are broken—utterly sundered between portions of the South, and portions of the North." Not even the most conservative Republican or northern Democrat, the paper continued, could change that.[167]

Individuals continued to believe that free labor might safely be incorporated within a slave society, but both Republican and secessionist campaigning had sensitized observers to an allegedly irrevocable conflict between free labor "Black Republicanism" and a "Slave Power." According to Alabamian S. D. Moore, William Seward had been right to argue that an "irrepressible conflict between the institutions of the North and South" existed. The tendency was for a "conflict between capital and labor." Though Moore hesitated to call northern wage labor "free," he believed that in the "social and political power their slaves [northern laborers] possess may be found the true cause of the conflict." Northern laborers' desire (bolstered by the influx of radical-minded Europeans) to "control the governments of the North" through the ballot box, unless prevented, would ultimately succeed. The northern assaults on the South, Moore continued, had "averted the tendency to a conflict" between northern capital and labor by turning it instead into a "conflict between the institutions of the North and South." "Unless checked," and Moore offered no tangible way of doing so, the conflict was destined "to drench this fair land of ours in fraternal blood."[168] The Union had devolved into a disharmony of interests in which the Lower South no longer had politically viable natural allies. Natural enemies might even be making inroads into the slave states.

At the heart of these arguments lay the conviction that Lincoln's election reflected northern antislavery or at least antisouthern sentiments that would eventually doom slaveholders should they remain in the Union. Shortly after announcing his resignation as treasury secretary, Georgian Howell Cobb began his "letter to the people of Georgia" by noting that Black Republicans had managed to unite "men of all previous parties": "Free-trade Democrats and protective-tariff Whigs, internal improvement and anti-internal improvement men, and indeed all shades of partisans in cordial fraternity upon the isolated issue of hostility to the South" and slavery.[169] That northerners would do that, despite the apparent benefits they had received (or, some argued, stolen) from slaveholding cotton planters suggested that, as Trescot had predicted in 1850, economic calculation had given way to "moral strife."[170] Moore, Cobb, and other secessionists repeated many of the same arguments Trescot had proposed in 1850. This time, however, they had a decade of political gridlock, actual violence, and now election results to support those conclusions.

This was more than a war of words. Secessionists determined their course of action by directly calculating what they thought to be the value of union and disunion. In particular, they feared that the inability to move their slave property to new territories or to adequately protect it in existing ones would undermine the South's greatest economic asset: the estimated $3 billion invested in some 4 million slaves. Since the nation's Founding—and especially after cotton had transformed the southern economic and physical landscape—slaveholders' economic livelihoods and political power had been largely measured by their ability to move their slave capital to new lands and to buy and sell it amongst themselves. A future union dominated by Republicans, even relatively moderate ones like Lincoln, would increase the chances of costly and deadly insurrections. With slavery bottled up, as it assuredly would be, slave prices would drop and the region's primary capital investment and source for profits would begin to dry up. Dreams of future greatness would give way to bankruptcy.[171] By contrast, secessionists of every occupation, much like their revolutionary forefathers, eyed political independence with near limitless economic possibility.

Plunging the nation toward the precipice, they enlisted King Cotton's aid with tremendous effect. Kettell and Townsend's tracts rapidly became favorites and were disseminated throughout the broader Cotton South. Alabamian Jabez Curry enlisted Kettell's work, telling a Talladega crowd that "every man who wears a shirt is interested in slave labor, because cotton cannot be produced sufficient for the world's wants without African slavery."[172] One "well-cultivated man of the South," quite likely South Carolinian W. H. Campbell, boldly informed the editors of the *New York Express* that cotton's primacy would mean "secession of these States must necessarily be a peaceful one, because England, France, and the rest of commercial Europe, and the Western and Northwestern States require that it should be." Should northerners unwisely choose coercion, "the first demonstration of blockade . . . would be swept away by the English and fleets of observation hovering on the Southern coasts to protect English commerce, and especially the free flow of Cotton to English and French factories."[173] Whether their future held war or peace, nearly all agreed that cotton would be a, perhaps the, key for achieving success. "King Cotton" could be heard everywhere, and after George P. Morris's poem by that title was put to music during that summer, the cry became even more melodious.[174] For secessionists all that remained was to lay the political and diplomatic groundwork for cotton's ultimate victory.

Almost immediately after Lincoln's election was confirmed, officials and citizens from Cotton States began making overtures to foreign governments. As early as the first week in November, the New York media reported rumors of an "informal meeting" of secessionists from the "Cotton and Gulf States," who sent instructions to "a distinguished Southerner now in Paris" in hopes of extracting the "promise of friendly recognition from Louis Napoleon." Though the incumbent U.S. minister to France, Virginian Charles Faulkner, would lobby France for recognition, the existence of these "instructions" has never been substantiated. Other early exchanges between secessionists and foreign officials, however, can be clearly demonstrated.[175] On December 4, weeks before he resigned his House seat in anticipation of South Carolina's secession, William Miles forwarded letters to the representatives of foreign governments informing them that secession was "almost a certainty" and warning them that "Foreign Powers may soon be called upon to form treaties with the Seceding States." Claiming secession as a "right" under "our Federative System" rather than as an "act of rebellion," Miles hoped to present recognition of independent southern states as automatic, under a strained assumption that the 1783 treaty had recognized the thirteen independent states, not one United States of America.[176] To help make his tenuous case, Miles enclosed copies of South Carolina's senate president (and president of the 1860 Association), William D. Porter's tract challenging Stephen Douglas's assertion that secession was illegal.[177]

Just days before South Carolina's secession convention, Robert Barnwell Rhett embarked on an extraordinary mission of personal King Cotton diplomacy, visiting Consul Bunch to inquire about Britain's likely response. According to the account Bunch forwarded to Foreign Secretary Lord John Russell, Rhett "stated that the wishes and hopes of the Southern States centred in England; that they would prefer an Alliance with Her to one with any other Power." Not surprisingly, commerce would serve as the glue because "with Great Britain dependent upon the South for Cotton ... and the South upon her for manufactured goods and shipping, an interchange of commodities would ensue which would lead to an unrestricted intercourse of the most friendly character." A Confederacy of "Cotton States," which Rhett promised would form within sixty days, would pursue a policy of free trade and work for "direct communication, by steam, between the Southern and British Ports." Rhett recognized that "the feeling of the British Publick was adverse to the system of Slavery" but also "saw no reason why that sentiment should stand in the way of commercial advantage" derived from continued relations with its longtime and chief source of cotton.[178]

The visit served two purposes. First, Rhett transmitted the friendly intentions of South Carolina—as a representative of the entire seceding Cotton South—to the most senior British official in the region. Second, Rhett sought to probe the consul about "the probable action of Great Britain and other foreign Nations" following secession. In particular, Rhett desired to know how Confederate ships arriving in British ports without U.S. customs clearances would be received, a hypothetical situation which became very real with South Carolina's seizure of Charleston's custom house on December 27. Embedded within this practical question, however, was a more important one: would these ships be legally recognized, a de facto recognition of the Confederacy? After stating "in the most explicit manner" that he had no authority to speak for the government but only as "one friend might to another," Bunch gave Rhett encouraging news. "There seemed to be no reasons why his ideas should not be carried into practice," especially if the new government would "open their Coasting trade to British ships." Furthermore, "as regarded the question of Domestick Slavery," Bunch "really saw no reason to apprehend an interference with it on the part of the British, as it was a matter with which they had no direct concern" beyond hoping that the example of their own colonies might "act favourably upon the South in its estimate of the moral wrong of such a system of labour."[179] Indeed, in Bunch's opinion only the possibility of reopening the African slave trade would serve as an obstacle to entering "cordially into communication" with the new Confederation.

Rhett's obstinate response to this last statement reflected the position of strength he believed the new Confederacy would operate from. Taking "a very decided stand," he argued that "no Southern State" would ever negotiate on the subject of the slave trade because doing so would deny the belief that slavery was "a blessing to the African Race and a system of labour appointed of God." Germany and France, he confidently asserted, would "gladly avoid the question of revival of the Slave trade" in exchange for "commercial advantages of the most liberal character." When Bunch resisted such a proposition and refused to back down, Rhett, who had publicly abandoned the policy two years earlier, stressed that "he felt assured that the newer States . . . such as Mississippi, Arkansas, and Louisianna [sic], would insist upon the revival of the traffick" because "they required fresh labour, in view of the increasing demand for cotton." He concluded, however, that a compromise could possibly be worked out so that the new Confederacy would be allowed to import slaves for a period of five years and then cease the trade. The echoes of compromises born in 1787 could be heard again. Bunch ended the conversation, suggesting only that "some satisfactory arrangement . . . would be essential to the recognition of the new Confederacy." To Russell he noted that, given Mr. Rhett's position, he "deemed it wise not to discourage his approaches."[180] Five days latter Rhett signed the ordinance of secession he had long desired.

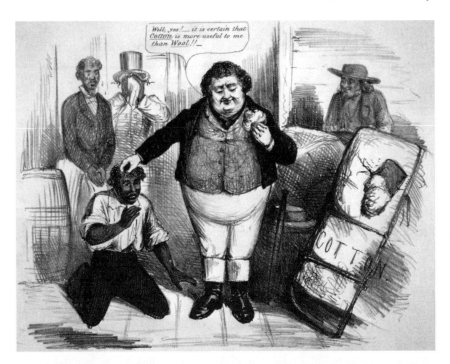

"John Bull Makes a Discovery" (New York: Currier & Ives, 1862). This cartoon from the height of the cotton famine reflected just the type of interest-based choice that secessionists in the Cotton States, as well as many outsiders, anticipated Britain and the rest of Europe making. John Bull examines the hair of a slave and a bale of cotton declaring, "Well yes! . . . it is certain that *Cotton* is more useful to me than *Wool*!!" Courtesy of the Library Company of Philadelphia.

Bunch was not the only British official to convey sentiments that could be construed as favorable to southern independence. In early December secessionists in New Orleans approached the British consul there, William Mure, to inquire about his nation's likely view of a Cotton Confederacy. Mure indicated that he thought his country would "recognize any '*de facto*' Government, especially with a people, whom it was her interest to cultivate the most intimate commercial relations."[181] Efforts to foster secession and curry international favor sped along even more publicly in Georgia, a state in which separate state action remained in doubt until early January. On the heels of Lincoln's election, Unionists there hoped to stall the secession movement. The so-called Empire State seemed the best place to do it. Of the Deep South states, Georgia had the largest population and the most land. It had the most diversified economy, the most railroad mileage, and a relatively stable financial system. Only the nominally cotton states of Florida and Louisiana had a Whig presence as strong or enduring. Before the state's legislature, former Whig and Douglas Democrat Alexander Stephens offered one of the most powerful and famous unionist speeches in the region. He appealed for calm, arguing that Lincoln did not have the power to attack slavery and should be given the chance to allay southern concerns. Out of necessity, Stephens downplayed the issue of slavery's expansion, central to secessionists' argument.

Instead, he engaged the claims made by former friend-turned-archsecessionist Robert Toombs that the "evils of this General Government" had included fishing bounties, tariffs, and navigation laws. In methodical and sound logic, Stephens argued that, since 1846, tariff policy had favored free trade and that the 1857 tariff had largely removed the protection issue from national public debates: "Massachusetts and South Carolina. The lion and lamb lay down together." Regarding the fishing bounties and navigation acts, Stephens would not defend their continuation but noted that both policies had been passed and continued under "Southern Presidents who ruled so well." He credited the first with helping to develop an American navy and the second with helping American shipping compete with British rivals. Finally, reminiscent of earlier federalist arguments, Stephens contended that the South had benefited from the security that union had afforded and had "grown great, prosperous, and happy under its operation." Secession would, he contended, risk that wealth for the unknown.[182] Stephens's plea for moderation *may* have, as has been argued, briefly restrained the secessionists' advance in the fall of 1860. Had enough Georgians supported his conclusions when they went to the poll on January 2, they *might* have voted against immediate secession and slowed resistance by calling for a southern convention.[183]

Fear of precisely that drove immediatists like Toombs, the Cobb brothers, and others to redouble their campaigns for immediate disunion. Fortuitously, the region's long-anticipated annual Cotton Planter Convention in Macon on December 10 provided them with an ideal platform from which to counter Stephens's claims and assure voters that independence would serve the Cotton South's interests. Belgium's consul to Savannah, Laurent de Give attended, as did Georgia's governor, delegations from both houses of Georgia's legislature, and representatives from surrounding states. The convention, which boasted Howell Cobb as its president, had planned a grand three-week affair to begin with three days of meetings and speeches, to be followed by an extended exhibit of goods, including those of European merchants who had been recommended by Consul Baylor in Amsterdam and de Give. Almost immediately the convention transformed from a call for economic development and encouragement of direct trade with continental Europe into a ringing endorsement of secession.[184]

Three weeks before Georgia voters were set to elect a convention, attendees heard an opening speech from Alabama secessionist, lawyer, and state supreme court justice, George Washington Stone. The high point of the convention was a rousing prosecessionist address by Professor of Medical Chemistry Joseph Jones. A practical man who had just completed a detailed three-hundred-page report on Georgia's resources, Jones assured his audience that despite the unequal partnership with the North, southerners had all the wealth, natural resources, and industrial potential necessary to thrive as an independent nation. Indeed, Jones lamented, the "North has grown brutal upon the generosity of the South," which had allowed Yankees to dominate the carrying trade. She had "become inflated, inflamed, drunk, and maddened by her success," failing to recognize that slavery and cotton had served as the source of that wealth. Jones promptly called for "decided action" to assert Georgia's rights, protect slavery, and end its "degrading association under a common government with those who have plundered and insulted her."[185]

What had begun as an appeal for more agricultural development and direct trade concluded with assurances that the "three-hundred and fifty million dollars invested in cotton manufactories," "the four million interested in the cotton trade," and the "fruitless experiments . . . to supply herself with cotton from . . . Asia, Africa, and South America" would ensure that Britain "must forever remain the firm ally and defender of the South, and the natural and uncompromising rival of the North." Jones then rehearsed Claiborne's and Kettell's reports about the "progressive increase of the consumption of cotton in France, Belgium, Holland, Germany, and Spain." "These well established facts," Jones confidently argued, "will prove that their great staple will prove the greatest blessing to mankind" and "will ever prove the strongest defense against lawless oppression, and will ever command the navies and armies of the world."[186] Upon return from the fair, de Give informed his nation's foreign minister of the "abundant proof of the cordial sentiment and of the importance which Georgia attaches to trade with us—the other [southern] states think the same."[187] He added that the state legislature had taken positive action to foster direct trade by unanimously passing two laws: "one guaranteeing a minimum of 5 percent interest on the Belgian-American's capital of ten million francs; the other offering a subsidy of 520,000 francs ($100,000) to a company which shall establish a steamship line to Savannah. Although Antwerp is not mentioned in the law, I have reliable information that the legislatures had our commercial capital in mind."[188] According to De Bow, who predicted the Macon Convention would "be the most brilliant, probably ever held upon Southern soil," such fairs were "doing much for the enfranchisement of the South."[189]

Longtime Savannah consul Edmund Molyneaux seemed to agree. On the same day as Jones's speech (and perhaps not entirely unrelated to it) Molyneaux amended his earlier prediction that Georgia would not secede, writing to tell Lord Russell that the "secession party is gaining ground" and disunion would, in all likelihood, peacefully occur.[190] Already in late November, the state had retained the services of a U.S. Army commander and appropriated $1 million for arms purchases in Europe. On the second day of the new year, Georgia voters elected delegates who two weeks later followed the path that South Carolina, Mississippi, Florida, and Alabama had taken. They dissolved their connection with the United States and immediately began pursuing new relationships with Europe. Following up informal contacts made prior to secession by what one *New York Herald* reporter described as a "direct trade party" centered at Macon, Governor Joseph Brown, sanctioned by the secession convention, commissioned Thomas Butler King to lobby the governments and peoples of British, French, and Belgian governments on behalf of recognition and direct trade.[191]

Why did majorities in the Lower South prove to be less reluctant secessionists than their Upper South brethren? No one answer exists. Simple geography allowed them to envision themselves as more isolated from the North and to see their ports as gateways to the world. Lower South politicians also retained a historical memory that, unlike Virginians', had placed them on the geographic and political periphery of the great American empire. The lack of a healthy two-party system in the 1850s increased the possibility of extreme political action.[192] More recent answers suggest, with considerable accuracy, that a deeper commitment to slavery made all the difference. Living among denser populations of African Americans heightened racial anxiety and perhaps the need for uncompromising positions on political questions related to slavery.[193] Higher proportional investment in slave property made protecting slavery's economic and political power and mobility absolutely essential.[194] Indeed, the primary cause of southern secession *was* the Deep South's unabashed commitment to a system of slavery it thought necessary for its economic success, social stability, and political power.[195]

Yet the depth of this commitment to slavery, it must be remembered, traced directly back to the centrality of cotton. Whereas more rapidly diversifying Upper South states could envision a day (some even hopefully) when slavery might

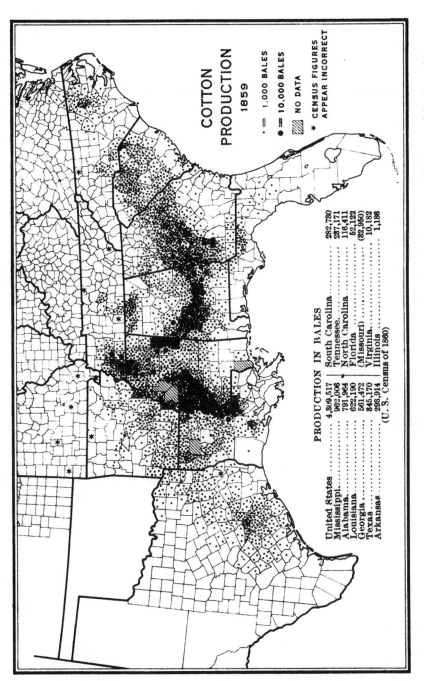

U.S. cotton production in 1859. From U.S. Department of Agriculture, *Atlas of Agriculture,* pt. 5: *The Crops of the United States,*
*Advance Sheets* (December 15, 1915).

recede from their borders, the Lower South's unwavering commitment to growing and selling cotton—cotton it believed had to be harvested by "enslaved
Africans"—prevented it from contemplating even a long-term future without
cotton and slavery at the center of economic activity. Thus, not just slavery, but
slavery directed toward cotton production best explains why arguably the most
sophisticated quantitative examination of secession in Alabama, Mississippi, and
the more mixed economy of Louisiana has concluded that "the secessionists
tended to be strongest in the Black Belt counties, but evidently only in those where
cotton was the primary crop."[196]

To be sure, reluctant Confederates existed in the Lower South. They were
strongest in mountainous regions ill suited for cotton cultivation or dense concentrations of plantation slaves. A sizable minority of individuals in cotton-
growing regions expressed reservations about secession, but the rhetoric and political realities of the last decade gave their secessionist opponents a decided edge.
Unable to guarantee slavery's future growth under Republican rule, Unionists
had to construct an argument based primarily on historical memory and economic profitability. The task proved surprisingly difficult in a region that had
developed a dual consciousness as the source of international wealth and the victim of economic inequality within the Union. Unionists argued with considerable justification that the slaveholders had benefited from the Constitution. Secessionists retorted that southern profits had come "in spite of it." While hardly
ever asserting protective tariffs or navigation acts as a cause for secession, they
reminded voters of their supposed interest in free trade and advanced the widely
shared assumption that federal economic policy offered them little and had always disproportionately benefited the North.[197] Those favoring economic diversification added that the Union had actually stalled industrial and commercial
development. Unionists could claim that natural affinities still existed within the
Union. Secessionists pointed to the last decade of political hostility and derided
such a view as naïve and bordering on submission.

With the die cast in favor of independence, even Stephens (who had been
elected vice president of the Confederacy) inverted his earlier calculus, using his
so-called cornerstone speech to encourage Upper South states to join their new
southern Confederacy, a Confederacy allegedly representing a more naturally
aligned union of interests. This would be a union, Stephens maintained, that "put
at rest *forever*" the questions surrounding slavery and "*the immediate cause of
the late rupture and present revolution,*" the "erroneous" idea of "*the equality of
races.*"[198] In this sense, then, white southerners accepted war as a necessary means

to preserve their doctrines of racial supremacy. Ironically, of course, by so doing they opened the door for perhaps the only means by which the institution of race-based slavery could have been destroyed in the United States, a catastrophic war that provided slaves the opportunities for self-emancipation, ultimately leading to the Emancipation Proclamation in the North. Yet after his conversion, Stephens suppressed his fears of war, holding out hope that cotton would prevent it: "In olden times the olive branch was considered the emblem of peace; we will send to the nations of the earth another and far more potential emblem of the same, the cotton plant." Cotton did not achieve what Stephens hoped, but it had eased his transition from unionism to secession.

William Trescot, one of the earliest proponents of King Cotton diplomacy and secession, had observed and participated in these events from his precarious position as assistant and, for a few fateful days after Lewis Cass's resignation, as acting secretary of state. His renowned diplomatic histories and service as a secretary to Buchanan's British ministry had helped earn him the appointment in the summer of 1860. As friends at home moved South Carolina toward secession, a tormented Trescot placed his personal loyalty to Buchanan aside. On December 14 he counseled the governor of South Carolina to "definitely, clearly, and irrevocably declare the State of South Carolina out of the Union," an event he thought would compel the rest of the Cotton States and eventually the entire South to join them in a southern Confederacy that he had first articulated in 1850. He used his last remaining days in office to counsel Buchanan against reinforcing Fort Sumter or taking aggressive action elsewhere in hopes, he informed his secessionist friends, of avoiding a "collision," at least "until the action of other Conventions in January places other States in the same position."[199] Fortunately for him and South Carolina, Buchanan obliged.

Returning to his lowcountry cotton plantation after that eventful winter, Trescot found comfort, as many of his secessionist brethren would, by casting aside personal responsibility and suggesting that inescapable material interests and historical processes, not people, had destroyed the Union. "It is the inevitable result of our history," he contended, "which in its results has now proved that the Union was only a state of transition and that the U.S. were in no true sense ever one nation." Trescot brazenly reduced America's grand federal experiment to an unnatural anomaly in history's never-ending clashes between competing interests. In its place, he hoped, "the real homogeneity in the sentiment and interests of the South . . . will find its expression in unity of national feeling and centralization of national Government," a process formally inaugurated in February 1861.[200]

The events culminating in the secessionist winter of 1860 and 1861 have been often told and much debated. Contradictory histories attribute the Lower South's motivation to various impulses: "a crisis of fear" or an abundance of arrogance; a grand "honor" affair to save public face or a paranoid minority's "dishonorable" overthrow of a supposedly unionist public; the culmination of a slaveholding "counterrevolution" or the climax of a second American Revolution. Yet secession represented much more than simply the hasty reactions of an insecure people. The decision reflected a strongly held conviction, based on years of political calculation—or rather miscalculation—that the federal Union no longer served regional interests. This conclusion derived largely from the belief that northern partners were unable or unwilling to continue protecting slaveholders' rights. Those in the Cotton South had also concluded, however, that international economic and political developments afforded them considerable opportunities for advancement outside of the Union. Assisted by high cotton prices and growing European markets, Lower South elites looked across the Atlantic and saw reason for optimism.[201] Secessionists in the Lower South were not simply fleeing a system they believed would fail their slave society; they were also creating a new one that they believed would have powerful partners abroad.

The trajectory of Lower South self-perception from 1787 to 1860 demonstrates how far regional perspective had come. South Carolinians and Georgians had embraced the federal Union from a position of weakness because they believed it provided the best option for their interests in stabilizing a society reeling from the aftershocks of revolution. Pierce Butler, the Rutledges, the Pinckneys, Joseph Clay, and Joseph Habersham all believed that a stronger national government would protect a slave society and assist regional commercial interests. These hopes had found new life in a diverse Jeffersonian majority which cotton planters had thought would organize the nation's interests into harmony under a decentralized political system. By 1860, however, the decades-old debates over slavery and political economy led all but the most strident unionists to conclude that the federal Union had become an unnatural and unequal partnership. The prediction of Rawlins Lowndes, that the "sun, of the Southern States, would set never to rise again," reverberated throughout the region.[202] The political struggles of the 1850s suggested to most whites in the region, some more reluctantly than others, that the Union had outlived its usefulness and become a, perhaps *the,* major obstacle to protecting slavery and enhancing economic profitability. Driven by these calculations, aided by a reservoir of real and perceived grievances, and burgeoning with confidence from the commercial leverage they felt they had, the Cotton

States helped inaugurate a devastating war that eventually destroyed the very society and economic hopes they desired to protect and expand.

The region's commitment to cotton permeated nearly every aspect of this aggressive drive toward secession and, by consequence, the war that followed. Cotton had deepened and broadened the region's commitment to slavery and its extension, which was the overriding issue that politically fragmented the second party system and the Union. Cotton inspired in planters and politicians an abiding faith in international commerce and free trade, the defense of which alienated them from otherwise sympathetic northern merchants and manufacturers. Cotton hindered regional industrial development in some areas, though few contemporaries admitted it, and led to a deep (and generally misplaced) frustration over an allegedly exploitative federal Union that the Cotton South blamed for fostering regional dependence on a more populous and rapidly advancing North.

Finally, cotton's central place within the global economy drove planters and farmers, merchants and manufacturers, politicians and writers to imagine a better future outside the Union and gave them the confidence for bold action. Whereas many grain producers, artisans, and even hemp and tobacco planters in the Upper South hesitated and even rejected the call to secede, the Deep South seized the language of revolution and masculine honor, convincing regional majorities to create a nation founded "on the cornerstone" of slavery and protected, they assumed, by King Cotton. Rather than tightening the bonds of union, as Tench Coxe had hoped it would in 1787, cotton's internationally driven political economy had weakened the bonds by limiting the degree to which its growers would invest, intellectually, politically, and financially, in the idea of *a* United States. It is perhaps not too much of a stretch to say that, without cotton and the international demand for it, there would not have been secession or a Civil War.

# Epilogue, 1861

In February 1861 the first six seceding states formed their own provisional government and began drafting a new constitution. They chose as their meeting place and eventually their capital, Montgomery, an eastern Alabama town overlooking the Alabama River. The Confederacy's first capital reflected cotton's relationship to the region, and in many ways the story of the new "Old South." Reportedly called New Philadelphia by the first whites who settled there in the waning years of the War of 1812, it grew in the 1820s as a result of cotton and steam power, which allowed boats easy access up- and downriver. In the midst of the Panic of 1837 residents incorporated, renaming their home Montgomery, after the Revolutionary War general killed leading an American effort to take Canada. By the 1840s Montgomery and its surrounding area included thriving businesses, some manufacturers, and of course countless fields of cotton. Its prosperity and central location led the state government to move there in 1846. Gas lighting arrived in 1852, and by 1860 north-south and east-west railroads joined riverboats to make Montgomery a modest but thriving commercial center. The town's year-round population had steadily grown, consisting of 4,341 whites and 4,502 slaves.

With over $51 million worth of real estate, 130,000 bales of cotton sold per year, and millions in enslaved African Americans, some estimate Montgomery amongst the wealthiest per-capita areas in the South.

Alabama's state secession convention met there in early January, amidst rumors of slave plots attributed by many whites to the stirrings of Lincoln's election. Northern Alabamians outside of the cotton belt, along with one of Montgomery's own, former Whig Henry Hilliard, opposed immediate secession. Those in heavy cotton-growing regions, however, overwhelmingly supported it, drawing Bell voters to secession in large numbers. On January 11, after four days of sometimes fiery debate, the conventioneers voted 61 to 39 to remove themselves from the Union. As delegates rushed from the chamber wild with enthusiasm, they unfurled a 16-by-20-foot blue flag made for the occasion by Montgomery women and declaring the state "Independent Now and Forever." One side displayed the goddess of liberty holding a sword and Alabama's flag; the other featured a rattlesnake and a cotton plant, below them the words: "Noli me tangere." The warning, "Touch me not," applied as much to the nation's new symbol, the cotton plant, as it did the snake, a traditional image of resistance dating back to the colonial period.[1] Having destroyed their connections with the old Union, delegates from Alabama invited their sister states to peacefully create another one at this New Philadelphia.

As they arrived, mostly by train, the leaders of seceded states faced quite different circumstances from those that had surrounded the Philadelphia Convention they were emulating. More so than at the first national constitutional convention, time mattered. A government *had* to be formed. Lincoln *had* to be met with a fully functioning executive. The stubborn Upper South slave states *had* to be compelled to join their cause. The proliferation of newspapers, reporters, the telegraph, and photography as well as the delegates' comparatively more comfortable relationship with democratic politics ensured that the decisions made would be more public than those that had taken place in the stuffy confines of Independence Hall seventy-three years earlier. The first day of the convention, at the prompting of Robert Barnwell Rhett, delegates chose Howell Cobb as its president. No George Washington he, but Cobb's moderate reputation and long service to state and country made him an attractive choice. Like his predecessor, his election was unanimous.

As they framed their new government, Cobb and his fellow delegates had much to debate, though less than the original Founders. Confident that they already had the best model of government from which to work, they took little time to make long-desired remedies. While the text remained very similar to the 1787 U.S. Constitution, those changes reveal the scars of decades of political battle and the pragmatic necessity of securing a slave society and a developing commercial-agrarian economy. Though they ultimately rejected both reopening the slave trade and preventing non–Slave States from joining, the Montgomery delegates unanimously expressed their support for slavery and repeatedly protected it, using the term ten times in the document and even broadly insisting that no "law denying or impairing the right of property in negro slaves shall be passed."[2] The foundation for this new government, as its vice president Alexander Stephens soon announced to thunderous applause at the Athenaeum in Savannah, Georgia, "rests upon the great truth, that the negro is not equal to the white man; that slavery—subordination to the superior race—is his natural and normal condition."[3] Within the new Confederacy there was to be no challenging this racist idea or the institution, at least among her white citizens.

More divisively, delegates debated the appropriate tariff levels and constitutional boundaries for regulating commerce and raising revenue. After some debate Confederates expressly restricted the national government's ability to pay for internal improvements (except for "aids to navigation") and expressly empowered states to lay duties on "seagoing vessels, for the improvement of its rivers and harbors," a measure Rhett had proposed in the 1840s.[4] Some argued for the desirability and even necessity of offering incentives to manufacturing by permitting protective tariffs, also noting that such a policy would help attract Upper South states. When Rhett, an ardent free trader, proposed a constitutional prohibition on protective tariffs or bounties, to his "astonishment" he "found great opposition to this policy. Georgia, Mississippi, and Louisiana were opposed to it; South Carolina, Florida, and Texas were in favor of it." In the end, at least according to his autobiography, direct personal negotiation with the Alabama delegation resulted in that state's support, and a constitutional clause declared that "no bounties shall be granted from the Treasury; nor shall any duties or taxes on importations from foreign nations be laid to promote or foster any branch of industry; and all duties, imposts, and excises shall be uniform throughout the Confederate States."[5] Congress's actions did not please economic reformers who believed, much like Tench Coxe in 1787, that the national government must explicitly support industrialization. The narrowness of this vote, if not its outcome, reflected the continuing momentum for economic reform within the Cotton South on the eve of the war and demonstrates how far regional views on industry (and once out

"The Dis-United States of the Southern Confederacy" (New York: Currier & Ives, 1861). Contemporaries understood the degree to which cotton supported secession, as evidenced by this cartoon in which cotton bales, and in South Carolina's case, a slave, holds up prominent secessionists from Lower South states. Left to right: South Carolina's Francis Pickens: "South Carolina claims to be file leader and general whipper in of the new Confederacy, a special edict! Obey and tremble!" Floridian Stephen Mallory: "We want it distinctly understood that all the lights on the Coast will be put out, in order to facilitate wrecking business." Alabama's William L. Yancey: "Alabama proclaims that 'Cotton is King,' and the rest of the Confederacy *must obey* that Sovereign." Mississippian and eventual CSA president Jefferson Davis: "We came in, with the understanding that we shall issue bonds to an unlimited extent, with our ancient right of repudiation when they come due." Georgia governor Joseph E. Brown: "Georgia must have half the honors, and all the profits, or back she goes to old 'E. Pluribus Unum.'" An unidentified Louisiana man: "A heavy duty must be levied on foreign sweetening in order to make up for what we have sacrificed leaving the Union, otherwise we shall be like a 'Pelican in the wilderness'!" Despite their shared interest in slaves and cotton and desire for an antipartisan polity, disagreements immediately arose over important policy matters. Courtesy of the Library of Congress.

of the Union, even "protection") had come since the 1820s. One could reasonably assume that Rhett's amendment would have failed had more industrialized Upper South states participated in those initial constitutional deliberations.

Ultimately, though, the vote against protection demonstrated the degree to which the Confederacy believed free international trade would serve its diplomatic, political, and economic interests. As the convention's youngest member, Alabamian Jabez Curry, told a friend: "We have to change our tariff and navigation policy so as to make our commerce and trade as free as possible to all nations."[6] Rhett proudly declared that "for the first time in the history of the world, the great principle of Free-trade became a part of the fundamental Law of a People."[7] Further affirming free trade, the Confederate Congress pushed a tariff schedule designed primarily for revenue. In addition, representatives threw open the coastal trade, again hoping to attract a peaceful separation from the North and direct partnerships with European powers.

The northern press noted the constitution's new safeguards for slavery, but the public, especially the business sector, closely followed the Confederacy's commercial policy. Sympathetic Democrats saw free trade as a peace offering that would prevent bloodshed and allow northerners continued access to the cotton trade. Less sympathetic groups, including most Republicans, viewed the tariff reductions as an attempt to circumvent well-established trade routes through New York, thus undermining the North's economy. Both impulses may have been at work, though as tensions mounted at Fort Sumter, fewer and fewer believed peace possible. After Lincoln responded to the CSA's bombardment by declaring an embargo on April 19, the Confederate Congress banned trade with the United States and required all exports to travel through southern or Mexican ports, a policy indicating the rising importance of the cotton port of Matamoros just across the Rio Grande.[8]

Secession had been partly predicated on the assumption that cotton would preserve peace with the North. After fighting broke out, people and politicians fully expected news of King Cotton's triumph abroad. From the moment the Confederacy had formed, politicians and the public exuded great optimism that European dependence on the region's cotton made recognition imminent, even before Upper South states seceded. On February 19, delegate Thomas R. R. Cobb told his wife that there existed a "firm and universal conviction that Great Britain, France and Russia will acknowledge us at once in the family of nations."[9] Throughout 1861 Robert Bunch informed superiors back home of the almost "universal conviction entertained by the South that Great Britain will make any sacrifice, even of principle or of honor to prevent the stoppage of the supply of cotton."[10] When news of Lincoln's blockade came down, one North Carolina woman quipped that "the English will sweep Lincoln's navies away like dust."[11]

The official word from London and casual conversations from William Howard Russell, the *London Times* correspondent traveling through the region, occasionally reminded arrogant luminaries that more than just cotton guided Britons' actions. Yet overly enthusiastic or overly frank foreign diplomats and consuls intentionally or unintentionally offset such caution and played directly into Lower South assumptions and hopes. Rhett's encounter with Bunch remained so impressionable that he spent his entire tenure in Congress pushing the policies they had discussed. In April, despite having been instructed by the British minister to the United States, Lord Richard Lyons, to entirely avoid the subject of recognition, Bunch told South Carolina governor Francis Pickens that Prime Minister John Russell had informed him that a northern blockade "would immediately lead to the recognition of the Independence of the South by Great Britain."[12]

Word from the continent inspired further confidence. Thinking Napoleon III a sympathetic nationalist willing to do almost anything to get ahead of his British economic rivals, Confederates believed he could be swayed by King Cotton diplomacy. The French minister, Count Édouard-Henri Mercier, intimated to his friend, former U.S. senator and future Confederate diplomat, John Slidell, that French recognition could be expected. Indeed, after consulting with Lyons in Washington, Mercier recommended such a course to the French Quai D'Orsay, a policy he told Lyons would be appropriate based on "Right, of Politics, and of Commerce." Though holding to his government's policy of complete silence on the issue, Lyons privately described Mercier's dispatch as "very able" and acknowledged his agreement with its substance. He told Mercier and Russell that he believed any attempt to close the South's ports of entry would "force on a question of Recognition even more unavoidably than a regular blockade." In the end, as Mercier and Lyons had envisioned, France and Britain began discussing a joint response to the crisis in America. Joint action tied their diplomatic stakes together, formally announcing a declaration of neutrality in mid-May. The declaration thus granted belligerent status to the Confederacy, a policy that many believed made recognition imminent. Though it initially inspired hope in the Confederacy, Anglo-French cooperation prevented Confederate diplomats from playing the two powers off of one another, ultimately meaning that Britain, with her stronger navy and influence, would determine the fate of King Cotton diplomacy.[13]

The commissioners sent to convince Europe of the reality of southern independence arrived with the same confidence as the people who cheered their departure. Upon being chosen provisional president, Jefferson Davis almost immediately appointed a three-man commission to London to request admission "into the family of independent nations."[14] Despite the questionable qualifications of the three men—Yancey; Pierre Rost, a French-born Louisiana judge; and

Ambrose Dudley Mann, the only career diplomat—Lord Russell granted an un-official interview, and the queen's recognition of belligerent status indicated progress. It certainly angered the just-arrived U.S. minister to Great Britain, Charles Francis Adams, who placed tremendous pressure on the government to sever communication with the commissioners. Yancey and Rost remained hopeful, but when Russell refused a follow-up personal meeting in favor of written correspondence, they assumed that only after the English and French had "come to the conclusion that the North and South are irremediably separated . . . and . . . when the cotton crop is ready for market" will "their necessities . . . force them to conclusions favorable to the South."[15]

With immediate recognition thwarted, Confederate leaders were divided over how best to leverage cotton's power. In July congressmen floated two separate proposals for an official embargo policy meant to force Europe's hand. The first would have prevented cotton from leaving southern ports, a plan some—including Davis—feared would be construed abroad as bald-faced economic coercion. A more cunning plan forwarded by Louisiana representative Duncan K. Kenner proposed banning the shipment of inland cotton to port cities. The measure sought to create embargo-like conditions but mask them behind the need to prevent cotton from falling into U.S. hands. Davis and his supporters again suppressed the measure, perhaps fearing it might add legitimacy to the U.S. blockade.[16]

As the summer planting season continued and aspirations for immediate European recognition dimmed, merchants and planters decided to push a coercive cotton diplomacy, even without government support. In July 130 of the most prominent cotton merchants in New Orleans published a circular declaring that they wanted inland cotton withheld until the blockade was lifted. Given the un-likelihood of Lincoln doing that, the proposal clearly had France and Britain in mind. Cotton brokers in Mobile, Savannah, and Charleston issued similar circulars and editor after editor insisted economic coercion would best aid the diplomatic effort at recognition. In a remarkable display of self-restraint and peer pressure cotton planters kept their crop inland. By early August, Robert Bunch communicated directly to Russell that he was "sure that the planters of the South will retain upon their plantations every bale of cotton they may grow until the end of the blockade."[17] The widespread compliance with this policy reflected considerable faith in King Cotton diplomacy.

Yet, the voluntary embargo severely hindered cotton's ability to finance the war: the second great promise made on its behalf. The Confederacy's first loan of $15 million had been funded largely through stocks purchased by regional banks, state and local governments, and even a few sympathizers in New York.[18] Realizing the limited bank capital within the region and now forced to prosecute a war, Congress passed a produce loan asking planters to subscribe a certain portion of the profits from their future crop (or other goods) toward the purchase of government bonds. To perpetuate the scheme, congressmen were given promissory notes and pressured to sign up their planting and farming constituents. Many, including the Cobb brothers, actively propagandized the scheme, believing that it would sustain the government's credit and lead to advances from Europe. "Repeating the same operation every year," they claimed, "we can keep up a war for a century."[19] Though apparently attracting large subscriptions from the 1861 crop (417,000 bales, or about 10% of the entire 1859 crop), this so-called Produce Loan and subsequent extensions only brought in about $35 million over the course of the entire war, far short of the $50 million that Davis had envisioned the first loan would provide. This was largely due to the precipitous drop in cotton prices in the fall as communities, planters, and merchants began the voluntary cotton embargo intended to apply economic pressure on Europe for recognition.[20]

Despite these initial setbacks, faith in King Cotton diplomacy persisted and was nearly rewarded when the cotton famine finally hit and Lee's army pushed McClellan's out of Virginia in the summer of 1862. Even as late as 1864, economic interests, combined with concerns about the horrific loss of life, led British and French officials to offer mediation that could have ended the war and secured southern independence. Yet neither France nor Britain ultimately bowed to the lords of the loom, who managed to get just enough cotton from colonial dependencies or smuggled out of the South through Mexico or northern-controlled ports to survive, though certainly not to thrive. The war droned on endlessly, it seemed, to those affected by it. Military necessity led Union officials to embrace emancipation as a war aim. Their ultimate victory on the battlefield and the actions of individual slaves who seized freedom in the midst of battle subsequently transformed the nature of the global cotton trade and, perhaps, capitalism.[21] The failure of King Cotton diplomacy hastened the demise of the slave system to which cotton had been bound for over half a century. Few in the South or in Britain or in the North could have predicted such an outcome in 1860 or even 1862.

In the end southerners' faith in King Cotton had been misplaced, leaving its earlier proponents to debate the reasons for and significance of their miscalculation. After the war Robert Barnwell Rhett's self-serving autobiographical account fixated on the issue: casting blame on Jefferson Davis and southern "protectionists" for failing to entice European powers into recognition by tendering them "a mutual dependency" through special treaties.[22] The actual failure of Rhett's repeated congressional efforts to force such trade concessions reveals both the confidence most had in the region's "white gold" and the continued regional hopes for a more balanced economy. In May 1861, when Rhett proposed a uniform twenty-year reciprocal trade policy with low duties to encourage recognition, Mississippi, Florida, Georgia, and Alabama joined the newly seated members from Virginia and narrowly prevented it, believing it too long a time to subject the region's economic interests to a foreign power. Rhett, to his dying day, believed such efforts would have worked. Jefferson Davis's widow, Varina, used her 1890 memoir to defend her dead husband and blame Congress for cotton's failure.[23]

In the long run, southerners found less contentious understandings of cotton's long relationship to their past by transforming it into "Lost Cause" lore. Especially as the southern economy continued to struggle after the war, they shed cotton of its regal economic status, offering it instead as the cause of the region's economic backwardness. The northern economic juggernaut, some argued, had perpetuated the South's colonial status by duping it to permanently grow cotton and by abusing federal powers to retard southern economic growth. The war had originated, Lost Causers defensively claimed, not because of slavery but because a consolidationist North (some focused on the tariff as the main issue) had *forced* the South to secede to prevent further abuse. Confederate defeat came, they continued, not because of superior martial skill or stronger Union desire but because of superior northern wealth and power compared to an impoverished Confederacy that was simply unable to overcome such a gross disparity in resources. Cotton, late nineteenth-century southerners argued, had always held the South back economically. By the early twentieth century, sentimental whites, especially of a literary bent, contended that this may not have been all for the worst. The supposedly rustic cotton fields, virtuous chivalry, and paternal relations of Dixie provided a nostalgic haven for a nation adjusting to the rapidly changing capitalism of the Gilded Age. Confederate apologists and Progressives (including many of the first professionally trained historians) agreed, concluding that the nasty Civil War had sadly destroyed a less material-driven and more harmonious and honorable provincialism.[24]

For southerners and many northerners these explanations helped remove personal accountability for causing and losing a bloody war, while restoring the South to a desirable place within the nation's past. As this book has shown, however, these postwar explanations had little—if any—basis in historic fact. Antebellum residents of the Lower South had been inextricably materialist in their outlook, greedily looking for ways to protect their near monopoly in raw cotton and expand their commercial and industrial capacity. Far from a weakness, cotton had been, or so they thought in 1860, an asset strong enough to win European partners and defeat northern enemies. Much more than purely a defensive effort to protect abstract ideals, Lower South secession, in the final analysis, had been an offensive action eagerly embarked on by men and women seeking to advance their interests within a larger world.

# Notes

## Introduction

1. David Christy, *Cotton is King: Or the Culture of Cotton, and its Relation to Agriculture, Manufactures and Commerce and also to the Free Colored People of the United States, and to those who hold that Slavery is in itself sinful*, 2nd ed. (New York: Derby & Jackson, 1856), quotes from 62–63, 264–65; Edward B. Bryan, *Letters to the Southern People Concerning the Acts of Congress and the Treaties with Great Britain, in relation to the African Slave Trade* (Charleston: Press of Walker, Evans & Co., 1858), esp. 20. Quite appropriately E. N. Elliot's assemblage of proslavery pieces placed a slightly revised version of Christy's piece at the front: *Cotton is King and Proslavery Arguments* (Augusta: Pritchard, Abbott, & Loomis, 1860).

2. According to official values, in 1820 cotton yarn and manufactures were valued at £22,532,000 of the £38,400,000 in overseas trade. B. R. Mitchell, *Abstract of British Historical Statistics* (Cambridge: Cambridge University Press, 1962), 180, 282, 295; Stuart Bruchey, *Cotton and the Growth of the American Economy, 1790–1860: Sources and Readings* (New York: Harcourt, Brace & World, 1967), table 1.D. Cotton's global significance is expanded on in the geographically and chronologically capacious book by Douglas A. Farnie and David J. Jeremy, *The Fibre That Changed the World: The Cotton Industry in International Perspective, 1600–1990s* (New York: Oxford University Press, 2004). See also Sven Beckert's two recent articles: "Emancipation and Empire: Reconstructing the Worldwide Web of Cotton Production in the Age of the American Civil War," *American Historical Review* 109, no. 5 (December 2004): 1405–38, and "From Tuskegee to Togo: The Problem of Freedom in the Empire of Cotton," *Journal of American History* 92, no. 2 (September 2005): 498–526.

3. Historians of the South have been particularly drawn toward overly deterministic understandings of economics and politics, many of them informed by systems theory, including Immanual Wallerstein's classic, *The Modern System: Capitalist Agriculture and the Origins of European World Economy in the Sixteenth Century* (New York: Academic Press, 1974). See Eugene and Elizabeth Fox-Genovese, *Fruits of Merchant Capital: Slavery and Bourgeois Property in the Rise and Expansion of Capitalism* (New York: Oxford University Press, 1983). Even Harold Woodman's pathbreaking and invaluable examination of the cotton factorage system falls back into dependency as its major interpretive conclusion: *King Cotton and His Retainers: Financing and Marketing the Cotton Crop of the South, 1800–1925* (Lexington: University of Kentucky Press, 1968). Themes of dependency in Lower South thought are explored most forcefully in Joseph Persky, *The Burden of Dependency: Colonial Themes in Southern*

*Economic Thought* (Baltimore: Johns Hopkins University Press, 1992). Concerns about dependency (first on Britain and then on the North) did play an important role in shaping Lower South agendas, just as British manufacturers expressed similar concerns about overdependence on the South. Yet, especially within an age of commerce, participants stressed the positive as well as the potential negative effects of what many cotton planters saw as "mutual dependence." In any event, it would be inappropriate to assume that concerns over dependence paralyzed southern thought or action. A failure to appropriately integrate the Lower South into modern developments and a minimization of southern planters' agency during the antebellum period has set interpretations of secession on a course to see it as a defensive reaction to modern developments assumed to have threatened the South's traditional society. For more on this see the essay on sources.

4. Though cotton's role in shaping national and diplomatic agendas remains woefully understudied, some recent work has appreciated the agency of cotton planters at the local and state level, especially in the early national period. See, for example, the work of Joyce Chaplin: "Creating a Cotton South," *Journal of Southern History* 57, no. 2 (May 1991): 171–200, and *An Anxious Pursuit: Agricultural Innovation and Modernity in the Lower South, 1730–1815* (Chapel Hill: Institute of Early American History and Culture, Williamsburg, Virginia, by the University of North Carolina Press, 1993). A few studies have taken cotton as a serious factor in shaping isolated national policy decisions: Thomas Hietala's, *Manifest Design: Anxious Aggrandizement in Late Jacksonian America* (Ithaca: Cornell University Press, 1985); Roger Kennedy's *Mr. Jefferson's Lost Cause: Land, Farmers, Slavery, and the Louisiana Purchase* (New York: Oxford University Press, 2003); and Adam Rothman, *Slave Country: American Expansion and the Origins of the Deep South* (Cambridge: Harvard University Press, 2005). Gavin Wright's classic book points this conversation toward the Civil War, but its narrowly economic approach unfortunately limits its explanatory power: *The Political Economy of the Cotton South: Households, Markets, and Wealth in the Nineteenth Century* (New York: Norton, 1978).

5. This project has drawn inspiration from the calls of David Brion Davis and Daniel Walker Howe to take a "big picture" approach to studying slavery and the history of the nineteenth-century United States: David Brion Davis, "Looking at Slavery from Broader Perspectives," *American Historical Review* 105, no. 2 (April 2000): 452–66, and Daniel Walker Howe, *American History in an Atlantic Context: An Inaugural Lecture Delivered before the University of Oxford on 3 June 1993* (Oxford: Clarendon Press of Oxford University Press, 1993). There is increasing evidence that historians are taking such calls seriously, as evidenced by recent works including Michael O'Brien, *Conjectures of Order: Intellectual Life and the American South, 1810–1860,* 2 vols. (Chapel Hill: University of North Carolina Press, 2004); Michael Gomez, *Exchanging Our Country Marks: The Transformation of African Identities in the Colonial and Antebellum South* (Chapel Hill: University of North Carolina Press, 1998); and the collection of essays in David Carlton and Peter Coclanis, *The South, the Nation, and the World: Perspectives on Southern Economic Development* (Charlottesville: University of Virginia Press, 2003), and Susanna Delfino and Michele Gillespie, eds., *Global Perspectives on Industrial Transformation in the American South* (Columbia: University of Missouri Press, 2005). This study joins these approaches.

6. My approach to American nationalism has been informed by David C. Hendrickson's *Peace Pact: The Lost World of the American Founding* (Lawrence: University Press of Kansas, 2003) and Cathy Matson and Peter Onuf, *A Union of Interests: Political and Economic Thought in Revolutionary America* (Lawrence: University Press of Kansas, 1990). The influence of the conceptual and interdisciplinary work of Nicholas and Peter Onuf will be readily apparent throughout this project: see *Federal Union, Modern World: The Law of Nations in an Age of Revolutions, 1776–1814* (Madison: Madison House, 1993) and *Nations, Markets, and War: Modern History and the American Civil War* (Charlottesville: University of Virginia Press, 2006). Also helpful have been David Waldstreicher, *In the Midst of Perpetual Fetes: The Making of American Nationalism, 1776–1820* (Chapel Hill: University of North Carolina Press, 1997); Peter B. Knupfer, *The Union as It Is: Constitutional Unionism and Sectional Compromise, 1787–1861* (Chapel Hill: University of North Carolina Press, 1991); and for later chapters, John McCardell, *The Idea of a Southern Nation: Southern Nationalists and Southern Nationalism, 1830–1860* (New York: Norton, 1979). On the significance of "rhetorical modes," see Elizabeth R. Varon, *Disunion!: The Coming of the American Civil War, 1789–1859* (Chapel Hill: University of North Carolina Press, 2008), 14. It is well worth recalling David Potter's definition of nationalism as resting "on two psychological bases rather than one—feeling of common culture on the one hand and feeling of common interest on the other." "The Historian's Use of Nationalism and Vice Versa," in Don E. Fehrenbacher, ed., *History and American Society: Essays of David M. Potter* (New York: Oxford University Press, 1973), 84. For historians of the early American Republic's recent fascination with the idea of "political economy," see James L. Huston, "Economic Landscapes Yet to Be Discovered: The Early American Republic and Historians' Unsubtle Adoption of Political Economy," in John Lauritz Larson and Michael A. Morrison, *Whither the Early Republic: A Forum on the Future of the Field* (Philadelphia: University of Pennsylvania Press, 2005). Useful studies of specific political economic policies can be traced in individual chapters and the notes on sources. For evidence of the widening breech between political history informed by ideas and the new institutional history, compare Gordon Wood, *The Radicalism of the American Revolution* (New York: Knopf, 1991), and Robin Einhorn, *American Taxation, American Slavery* (Chicago: University of Chicago Press, 2006).

7. See *Federalist* 10 and 11, in Jacob E. Cooke, *The Federalist* (Hanover: Wesleyan University Press, 1961), esp. 62–64, 68–71. Also Lacy K. Ford Jr., "Inventing the Concurrent Majority: Madison, Calhoun, and the Problem of Majoritarianism in American Political Thought," *Journal of Southern History* 60, no. 1 (February 1994): 19–58.

8. See, for example, Rachel Klein, *The Unification of a Slave State: The Rise of the Planter Class in the South Carolina Backcountry, 1760–1808* (Chapel Hill: University of North Carolina Press, 1990); Jeffrey Robert Young, *Domesticating Slavery: The Master Class in Georgia and South Carolina, 1670–1837* (Chapel Hill: University of North Carolina Press, 1999); J. Mills Thornton III, *Politics and Power in a Slave Society: Alabama, 1800–1860* (Baton Rouge: Louisiana State University Press, 1978); Daniel S. Dupre, *Transforming the Cotton Frontier: Madison County, Alabama, 1800–1840* (Baton Rouge: Louisiana State University Press, 1997); James Oakes, *The Ruling Race: A History of American Slaveholders* (New York: Knopf, 1982); Chaplin, "Creating a Cotton South," 171–200; William Cooper, *The South and the Politics of Slavery,*

*1828–1856* (Baton Rouge: Louisiana State University Press, 1978); Vicki Vaughn John-son, *The Men and the Vision of the Southern Commercial Conventions, 1845–1871* (Co-lumbia: University of Missouri Press, 1992); Robert Royal Russell, *Economic Aspects of Southern Sectionalism* (New York: Russell & Russell, 1960); McCardell, *Idea of a Southern Nation.*

9. This account challenges many deeply rooted assumptions regarding the devel-opments and motives which led to the Civil War. These are discussed in greater depth in the essay on sources. The perspective offered here joins James L. Huston in high-lighting southerners' aggressiveness on the eve of the Civil War: Huston, *Calculating the Value of Union* (Chapel Hill: University of North Carolina Press, 2003). It also concurs with Michael O'Brien's useful but underdeveloped idea that southern intel-lectuals had embraced philosophical realism as they viewed their world. O'Brien, *Conjectures of Order,* 2: 1161–1202.

## Prologue, 1787

1. Delegates of Georgia, *Observations Upon the Effects of Certain Late Political Suggestions* (Philadelphia: R. Aitken, 1781), 3–4, 8, in Evans, *Early American Imprints,* 1st ser. (New York: Readex Microprint, 1985), no. 17419.

2. Don Higginbotham, *The War of American Independence: Military Attitudes, Policies, and Practices, 1763–1789* (New York: Macmillan, 1971), 375.

3. On the uncertainty created in the Lower South by the Revolution, see Sylvia Frey, *Water from the Rock: Black Resistance in a Revolutionary Age* (Princeton, N.J.: Princeton University Press, 1991); Robert Olwell, *Masters, Slaves, and Subjects: The Culture of Power in the South Carolina Lowcountry, 1740–1790* (Ithaca: Cornell Uni-versity Press, 1998); Ronald Hoffman, "The 'Dissaffected' in the Revolutionary South," in Alfred E. Young, *The American Revolution: Explorations in the History of Ameri-can Radicalism* (DeKalb, Ill.: Northern Illinois University Press, 1975), 273–318. For broader, and at times competing, versions of the frontier's meaning as well as African and Native Americans' role in shaping the revolutionary era, see François Fursten-berg, "Beyond Freedom and Slavery: Autonomy, Virtue, and Resistance in Early American Political Discourse," *Journal of American History* 89, no. 4 (March 2003): 1295–1330; Patrick Griffin, *American Leviathan: Empire, Nation, and Revolutionary Frontier* (New York: Hill & Wang, 2007); Gary Nash, *The Unknown American Revolu-tion: The Unruly Birth of Democracy and the Struggle to Create America* (New York: Penguin Books, 2005).

4. The Confederation period in the Lower South has not received adequate atten-tion, but Charles Singer's 1941 dissertation presents an informative, though limited and outdated, study: *South Carolina in the Confederation* (Philadelphia: n.p., 1941). Jerome Nadelhaft's dissertation, which later became a book, provides the most de-tailed and useful examination of the period, though a unity of planter interest is often assumed: "The Revolutionary Era in South Carolina, 1775–1788" (Ph.D. diss., Univer-sity of Wisconsin, 1965); *The Disorders of War: The Revolution in South Carolina* (Orono: University of Maine at Orono Press, 1981). George Rogers Jr.'s biography of William Loughton Smith provides an interesting glimpse of several of the topics dis-cussed here through the eyes of individuals close to British merchants and lowcountry

planters: *Evolution of a Federalist: William Loughton Smith of Charleston* (Columbia: University of South Carolina Press, 1967), esp. 97–158. Chapters in Robert Weir's book suggest that continuity dominated South Carolina leadership: *"The Last of American Freemen": Studies in the Political Culture of the Colonial and Revolutionary South* (Macon, Ga.: Mercer University Press, 1986), esp. 1–32, 213–30. Robert M. Weir, "'The Violent Spirit,' the Reestablishment of Order, and the Continuity of Leadership in Postrevolutionary South Carolina," in ibid., 213–30.

For the situation in Georgia, I am reliant on George R. Lamplugh's, *Politics on the Periphery: Factions and Parties in Georgia, 1783–1806* (Newark: University of Delaware Press, 1986); Harvey H. Jackson, *Lachlan McIntosh and the Politics of Revolutionary Georgia* (Athens: University of Georgia Press, 1979), 124–43; Kenneth Coleman, *The American Revolution in Georgia, 1763–1789* (Athens: University of Georgia Press, 1958), 179–275.

5. Joyce Chaplin, *An Anxious Pursuit: Agricultural Innovation and Modernity in the Lower South, 1730–1815* (Chapel Hill: University of North Carolina Press, 1993), 208–19; Laurel Ulrich, *The Age of Homespun: Objects and Stories in the Creation of an American Myth* (New York: Alfred A. Knopf, 2001); T. H. Breen, "Baubles of Britain: The American Consumer Revolutions of the Eighteenth Century," in Cary Carson, ed., *Of Consuming Interests: The Style of Life in the Eighteenth Century* (Charlottesville: University of Virginia Press, 1994), 444–82. In the colonial period, only 5% of rice, the region's largest staple produce, was consumed within North America. By the 1790s, the expansion of wheat production in the Mid-Atlantic, Canada, and the Upper South had reduced that quantity to only 0.7%. Indigo had even less domestic demand. See Peter Coclanis, *The Shadow of a Dream: Economic Life and Death in the South Carolina Low Country, 1670–1920* (New York: Oxford University Press, 1989), 134.

6. Jackson Turner Main's division between "cosmopolitans" and "localists," overlooks the fact that all groups during the Confederation were forced to mediate between domestic and international circumstances: *Political Parties before the Constitution* (New York: Norton, 1973), 268.

7. Jonathan Elliot, *The Debates in the Several State Conventions on the Adoption of the Federal Constitution* (Philadelphia: J. B. Lippincott, 1836–1859), 4: 283–84.

8. William W. Abbott, "The Structure of Politics in Georgia, 1782–1789," *William and Mary Quarterly* 14, no. 1 (January 1957): 47–65; John P. Kaminski, "Controversy amid Consensus: The Adoption of the Federal Constitution in Georgia," *Georgia Historical Quarterly* 57, no. 2 (Summer 1974): 244–57; Edward Cashin, "Georgia: Searching for Security," in Michael Allen Gillespie and Michael Lienesch, *Ratifying the Constitution* (Lawrence: University Press of Kansas, 1989); Ernest M. Lander Jr., "The South Carolinians at the Philadelphia Convention, 1787," *South Carolina Historical Magazine* (July 1956): 134–55. Robert M. Weir, "South Carolinians and the Adoption of the United States Constitution," *South Carolina Historical Magazine* 89 (1988): 73–89. My larger conception of the Constitution's significance has been influenced by David C. Hendrickson's *Peace Pact: The Lost World of the American Founding* (Lawrence: University Press of Kansas, 2003); Cathy Matson and Peter Onuf, *A Union of Interests: Political and Economic Thought in Revolutionary America* (Lawrence: University Press of Kansas, 1990); Max Edling, *A Revolution in Favor of Government: Origins of the U.S. Constitution and the Making of the American State* (New York: Oxford University Press, 2003).

9. Max Farrand, ed., *The Records of the Federal Convention of 1787,* 3 vols. (New Haven: Yale University Press, 1911), 1: 596 (Mr. Charles Pinckney), 1: 605 (Pierce Butler), July 11, 1787. The Georgia and South Carolina delegations were the only ones to vote for Butler's proposal that blacks be counted equally with whites: http://elsinore.cis.yale.edu/lawweb/avalon/debates/711.htm (accessed March 19, 2008).

10. Jack Rakove, *Original Meanings: Politics and Ideas in the Making of the Constitution* (New York: Alfred A. Knopf, 1996). For the political and policy effects of the three-fifths compromise, see Garry Wills, *"Negro President": Jefferson and the Slave Power*(Houghton, Mifflin, 2003); Robin Einhorn, *American Taxation, American Slavery* (Chicago: University of Chicago Press, 2006); and Leonard L. Richards, *The Slave Power: The Free North and Southern Domination, 1780–1860* (Baton Rouge: Louisiana State University Press, 2000).

11. Farrand, *Records,* 2: 95.

12. Ibid., 2: 369–70 (Mason); 363–5 (Martin).

13. Ibid., 2: 364.

14. Ibid., 2: 306.

15. Ibid., 2: 372.

16. Ibid., 2: 374. Historians have long disagreed on the extent or necessity of this so-called dirty compromise. For two of the more recent opposing views, see Paul Finkelman, "Slavery and the Constitutional Convention: Making a Covenant with Death," in Richard Beeman et al., eds., *Beyond Confederation: Origins of the Constitution and American National Identity* (Chapel Hill: University of North Carolina Press, 1987), 188–225, and Don Fehrenbacher, *The Slaveholding Republic: An Account of the United States Government's Relations to Slavery* (New York: Oxford University Press, 2001).

17. U.S. Constitution, Article I, Section 10.

18. Farrand *Records,* 2: 449–50.

19. Ibid., 2: 451.

20. Luther Martin, "The Genuine Information, Delivered to the Legislature of the State of Maryland," reprinted in ibid., 3: appendix A, 210–11.

21. Farrand, *Records,* 2: 443, 453–54.

22. Elliot, *Debates,* 4: 285–86.

23. Ramsay to Benjamin Lincoln, January 29, 1788, reprinted in Robert L. Brunhouse, ed., "David Ramsay: Selections from His Writings," *Transactions of the American Philosophical Society,* new series, 55, no. 4 (1965): 118–19.

24. Farrand, *Records,* 2: 452.

25. Pinckney in Elliot, *Debates,* 4: 253.

26. Rebecca Starr, *A School of Politics: Commercial Lobbying and Political Culture in Early South Carolina* (Baltimore: Johns Hopkins University Press, 1998), shows South Carolinians' success in lobbying the British government officials for beneficial commercial arrangements during the colonial period. For the attempt to resurrect commerce after the war, see Singer, *South Carolina in the Confederation,* 88–101. For more on reasons for ratification in the Lower South, see Robert M. Weir, "South Carolina: Slavery and the Structure of the Union," in Gillespie and Lienesch, *Ratifying the Constitution,* 201–34, and Cashin, "Georgia: Searching for Security," in ibid., 93–116 (esp. 97–101); Rogers, *Evolution of a Federalist.*

27. Elliot, *Debates,* 4: 333. After detailing the history of wartime suffering, the long struggle with debtor relief, and the hope of great agricultural exports, Pinckney concluded that the Constitution would "tend to restore your credit with foreigners—to rescue your national character from that contempt which must ever follow the most flagrant violations of public faith and private honesty! No more shall paper money, no more shall tender-laws, drive their commerce from our shores, and darken the American name in every country where it is known. No more shall our citizens conceal in their coffers those treasures which the weakness and dishonesty of our government have long hidden from the public eye . . . Your government shall now, indeed, be a government of laws." Elliot, *Debates,* 4: 335–36. Echoing the nationalist position, John Rutledge, another of South Carolina's delegates, told the state legislature that fortunately treaties were to be paramount to any state or national law and would necessarily have to be enforced, preventing the dislocation that had occurred during the debt crisis. Elliot, *Debates,* 4: 267.

28. Cited in Merril Jensen, *The Documentary History of the Ratification of the Constitution* (Madison: State Historical Society of Wisconsin, 1978), 3: 289. See also Cashin, "Georgia: Searching for Security," 95–96.

29. Clay to James Thomson, April 24, 1790, *Collections of the Georgia Historical Society* (Savannah: The Morning News, 1913), 8: 223–28.

30. Main, *Political Parties,* 268–95.

31. "A Georgian," *Gazette of the State of Georgia,* November 15, 1787, reprinted in Jensen, *Documentary History,* 3: 236–43. Private reservations are expressed in Lachlan McIntosh to John Wereat, December 17, 1787, in ibid., 259–61. For a discussion of McIntosh's opinions, see Jackson, *Lachlan McIntosh,* esp. 144.

32. Lowndes, in Elliot, *Debates,* 4: 271–72, 308. For an explanation of Rawlins Lowndes's anti-Federalist views and his alliance with backcountry interests, see Carl Vipperman, *The Rise of Rawlins Lowndes, 1821–1800* (Columbia: South Carolina Tricentennial Commission by the University of South Carolina Press, 1978), 241–45. Supporters of the new Constitution denied that the South's population would remain smaller than the North's, downplaying the possibility that the North would dominate the House: see "Demosthenes Minor," *Gazette of the State of Georgia,* November 22, 1787.

33. Saul Cornell, *The Other Founders: Anti-Federalism and the Dissenting Tradition in America, 1788–1828* (Chapel Hill: Published for the Omohundro Institute of Early American History and Culture, Williamsburg, Virginia, by the University of North Carolina Press, 1999); Norman K. Risjord, *The Old Republicans: Southern Conservatism in the Age of Jefferson* (New York: Columbia University Press, 1965).

34. Morris & Brailsford to Thomas Jefferson, October 31, 1787, reprinted in "Letters of Morris & Brailsford to Thomas Jefferson," *South Carolina Historical Magazine* 58, no. 3 (July 1957): 138.

35. The perceived economic and geopolitical advantages of union have been spelled out in Matson and Onuf, *A Union of Interests;* Leonard Sadosky, "Revolutionary Negotiations: A History of American Diplomacy with Europe and Native America in the Age of Jefferson" (Ph.D. diss., University of Virginia, 2003); Frederick W. Marks, *Independence on Trial: Foreign Affairs and the Making of the Constitution* (Baton Rouge: Louisiana State University Press, 1974).

36. Tench Coxe, *An enquiry into the principles on which a commercial system for the United States of America should be founded; to which are added some political . . .* ([Philadelphia]: Printed and sold by R. Aitken, 1787), 31–32.

37. Tench Coxe, *An Address to an Assembly of the Friends of American Manufactures* ([Philadelphia]: R. Aitken & Son, 1787), 5 ("August Body"), and 29–30, ("improve our agriculture . . . and the destructive torrent of luxury" and "political salvation").

38. Ibid., 16.

39. Lawrence A. Peskin, *Manufacturing Revolution: The Intellectual Origins of Early American Industry* (Baltimore: Studies in Early American Economy and Society from the Library Company of Philadelphia by the Johns Hopkins University Press, 2003), esp. 84–92, discusses manufacturers' hopes for the new Constitution as well as concern that their minority position might lock them out of favorable legislation that they could better facilitate at the state level.

CHAPTER ONE: The Threads of a Global Loom

1. *State Gazette of South-Carolina*, May 14, 1787.

2. Thomas Ellison, *The Cotton Trade of Great Britain* (1886; London: Frank Cass, 1968), 81–82; Norman Sidney Buck, *The Development of the Organisation of the Anglo-American Trade, 1800–1850* (New York: Greenwood Press, 1925), 33–34.

3. Istvan Hont, *Jealousy of Trade: International Competition and the Nation-State in Historical Perspective* (Cambridge: The Belknap Press of Harvard University Press, 2005).

4. Peter and Nicholas Onuf, *Federal Union, Modern World: The Law of Nations in an Age of Revolutions, 1776–1814* (Madison: Madison House, 1993); R. R. Palmer, *The Age of Democratic Revolution: A Political History of Europe and America, 1760–1800* (Princeton: Princeton University Press, 1959); David Brion Davis, *The Problem of Slavery in the Age of Revolution, 1770–1823* (Ithaca: Cornell University Press, 1975).

5. Henry Laurens to John Lewis Gervais, April 9, 1774, *The Papers of Henry Laurens*, ed. Philip M. Hamer et al. (Columbia: University of South Carolina Press, 1968–1992), 9: 390–91; also 8: n52.

6. The version of Jeffersonian political economy presented here has been informed by the work of John Crowley, *The Privileges of Independence: Neomercantilism and the American Revolution* (Baltimore: Johns Hopkins University Press, 1993); John Nelson, *Liberty and Property: Political Economy and Policymaking in the New Nation, 1789–1812* (Baltimore: Johns Hopkins University Press, 1989); Burton Spivak, *Jefferson's English Crisis: Commerce, Embargo, and the Republican Revolution* (Charlottesville: University of Virginia Press, 1978); Doron Ben-Atar, *The Origins of Jeffersonian Commercial Policy and Diplomacy* (New York: St. Martin's Press, 1993); Drew McCoy, *The Elusive Republic: Political Economy in Jeffersonian America* (Chapel Hill: Institute of Early American History and Culture by the University of North Carolina Press, 1980); Lawrence A. Peskin, *Manufacturing Revolution: The Intellectual Origins of Early American Industry* (Baltimore: Studies in Early American Economy and Society from the Library Company of Philadelphia by the Johns Hopkins University Press, 2003).

7. Norbert Elias, *The History of Manners*, vol. 1, *The Civilizing Process*, trans. Edmund Jephcott (1939; New York, 1978), 151; Richard L. Bushman, *The Refinement of America: Persons, Houses, Cities* (New York: Vintage Books, 1993).

8. On the legislative history of cotton, see George W. Daniels, *The Early English Cotton Industry: With Some Unpublished Letters of Samuel Crompton* (Manchester: The University Press, 1920), 16–24; Michael M. Edwards, *The Growth of the British Cotton Trade, 1780–1815* (New York: Augustus M. Kell[e]y, 1967), 35. For more on the fashion trends of the eighteenth century, see Beverly Lemire, *Fashion Favourite: The Cotton Trade and the Consumer in Britain, 1660–1800* (Oxford: Oxford University Press, 1991); Doreen Yarwood, *English Costume from the 2nd Century to 1952* (London: Batsford, 1952); Sarah Levitt, "Clothing," in Mary B. Rose, ed., *The Lancashire Cotton Industry: A History since 1700* (Oxford: The Alden Press, 1996), 154–86.

9. Economic historians have struggled to explain the causes and timing of the British textile industry's "takeoff." For recent discussions, see Rose, *Lancashire Cotton Industry,* esp. the editor's introduction, "The Rise of the Cotton Industry in Lancashire to 1830," in ibid., 1–28, and Geoffrey Timmins, "Technological Change," in ibid., 29–62. Ralph Davis, *The Industrial Revolution and British Overseas Trade* (Atlantic Highlands, N.J.: Humanities Press, 1979); Douglas A. Farnie and David J. Jeremy, eds., *The Fibre That Changed the World: The Cotton Industry in International Perspective, 1600–1990s* (Oxford: Oxford University Press, 2004). Particularly useful on the gradual diffusion of cotton skills from Britain elsewhere is David J. Jeremy, "The International Diffusion of Cotton Manufacturing Technology, 1750–1990s," in ibid., 85–128.

10. For an excellent discussion of commerce and England's "blue water" policy, see Eliga H. Gould, *The Persistence of Empire: British Political Culture in the Age of the American Revolution* (Chapel Hill: University of North Carolina Press, 2000), 35–71; Linda Colley, *Britons: Forging the Nation, 1707–1837* (New Haven: Yale University Press, 1992); C. A. Bayly, *Imperial Meridian: The British Empire and the World, 1780–1830* (1989; New York: Longman, 1994), esp. 100–132. For cotton's place within that empire, see John Singleton, "The Lancashire Cotton Industry, the Royal Navy, and the British Empire, c.1700–1900," in Farnie and Jeremy, *Fibre That Changed the World,* 57–85.

11. The primary destination for Hove's seeds was the British West Indies, which along with the Mediterranean region provided over 90% of new cotton supplies in the 1780s (see table 3 in chapter 1 this volume). At the request of Manchester manufacturers, led by John Hilton and William Frodsham, the colonial secretary sent a circular to the islands' governors to enlist their support in extending cotton growth. The request met with mixed reaction. Some governors laid small bounties; others distributed the scarce lands of their islands to those willing to produce the white fiber. Initial results were moderately promising, especially in the Bahamas, where the government sponsored the development of a more effective cotton gin. Edwards, *Growth of the British Cotton Trade,* 77.

12. As part of a larger debate over the importance of the Caribbean economy, historians have shown that West Indian sugar continued to remain important well into the nineteenth century as sugar consumption burgeoned within Britain and America. J. R. Ward, "The British West Indies, 1748–1815," in Peter Marshall, ed., *The Oxford History of the British Empire: The Eighteenth Century* (New York: Oxford University Press, 1998), 421–24; P. J. Marshall, "Britain without America: A Second Empire?" in ibid., 576–95.

13. Manufacturer William Frodsham attempted, with only limited success, to grow cotton near British slaving colonies around the Gambia River. A group of

antislavery London merchants encouraged free blacks, resettled in British-controlled Sierra Leone, to grow cotton, but the soil could only muster small amounts of the material. Edwards, *Growth of the British Cotton Trade,* 79, 82.

14. East India briefly became important during the War of 1812 era, when southern supplies were largely unattainable. For more on problems of control within India, see H. V. Bowen, "British India: The Metropolitan Context," in Marshall, *Oxford History of the British Empire: The Eighteenth Century,* 530–51. See also L. S. Sutherland, *The East India Company in Eighteenth-Century Politics* (Oxford: Oxford University Press, 1952); table 3 later in chapter 1.

15. Recent work has shown that Americans, no less then Europeans, shared in the global consumer revolution. Cary Carson, Ronald Hoffman, and Peter J. Albert, *Of Consuming Interests: The Style of Life in the Eighteenth Century* (Charlottesville: Published for the United States Capital Historical Society by the University of Virginia Press, 1994); T. H. Breen, *The Marketplace of Revolution: How Consumer Politics Shaped American Independence* (New York: Oxford University press, 2004); Bushman, *Refinement of America;* Karen Halttunen, *Confidence Men and Painted Women: A Study of Middle-Class Culture in America, 1830–1870* (New Haven: Yale University Press, 1982). On the role of women, cotton, and homespun in America, see Ulrich Thatcher, *The Age of Homespun: Objects and Stories in the Creation of an American Myth* (New York: Alfred A. Knopf, 2001); Joyce Chaplin, *An Anxious Pursuit: Agricultural Innovation and Modernity in the Lower South, 1730–1815* (Chapel Hill: Institute of Early American History and Culture, Williamsburg, Virginia, by the University of North Carolina Press, 1993). On the limits of American raw cotton production immediately after the war, see Edwards, *Growth of the British Cotton Trade,* 72–73 and table B.3.

16. U.S. Constitution, Article 1, Section 8.

17. General studies of the politics of the 1790s include James Roger Sharp, *American Politics in the Early Republic: The New Nation in Crisis* (New Haven: Yale University Press, 1993), and Joanne Freeman, *Affairs of Honor: National Politics in the New Republic* (New Haven: Yale University Press, 2002), which interestingly uncovers the "grammar" that anxious politicians deployed. The analysis presented here is drawn from the invaluable primary source collection, Kenneth Bowling et al., eds., *Documentary History of the First Federal Congress* (hereafter *DHFFC*), 13 vols. (Baltimore: Johns Hopkins University Press, 1972–).

18. See, for example, "Tradesmen and Manufacturers of Boston, May 1789," presented June 5, 1789, *DHFFC,* 8: 351–52; George Cabot to Benjamin Goodlue, March 16, 1790, *DHFFC,* 8: 364–68 (quote from 367); "Petition of Thomas Ruston in Behalf of the Cotton Manufactory of Philadelphia, 30 June 1790," *DHFFC,* 8: 372–73.

19. *Diary of William Maclay,* June 2, 1789, *DHFFC,* 9: 64.

20. These arguments can be traced in the debates during the summer of Congress's first session surrounding the Impost Act (HR-2) and Tonnage Act (HR-5). They continued in the second session with debates over the Trade and Navigation Bill (HR-66) and the Tonnage Act (HR-78), available in *DHFFC.* Also see William W. Bates, *American Marine: The Shipping Question in History and Politics* (Boston and New York: Houghton, Mifflin, 1892), 93–97.

21. William Smith to Edward Rutledge, June 6, 1789, *DHFFC,* 16: 710.

22. Burke, House Debates, *DHFFC*, 13: 1258.

23. Jackson, House Debates, May 13, 1790, *DHFFC*, 13: 1259.

24. Jackson, House Debates, May 11, 1790, *DHFFC*, 13: 1243–47, 1249–50.

25. Pierce Butler to James Iredell, August 11, 1789, *DHFFC*, 16: 1289. A notable exception to this pessimism at the close of the First Congress was William Smith, who told fellow planter Edward Rutledge that "upon the whole, [the Bills] are as favorable to the Southern Interests as we could have expected." William Smith to Edward Rutledge, July 5, 1789, *DHFFC*, 16: 959.

26. James Madison to Tench Coxe, June 24, 1789, *DHFFC*, 16: 852.

27. George Clymer to Tench Coxe, June 28, 1789, *DHFFC*, 16: 873.

28. The duty on raw cotton did rise to 6 cents during the War of 1812 but then dropped back down to 3 cents. See Edward Young, *Special Report on the Customs-Tariff Legislation of the United States* (Washington, D.C.: Government Publishing Office, 1873). Though he misidentifies the duty on raw cotton after 1790, an excellent discussion of these policies is provided by Douglas A. Irwin, "The Aftermath of Hamilton's 'Report on Manufacturing,'" *Journal of Economic History* 64, no. 3 (September 2004): 800–821.

29. Madison's resolutions and his January 4, 1794, speech on discrimination sparked a prolonged congressional debate. See *Annals of Congress* (hereafter *AC*), 3rd Cong., 1st sess., 155–57 and after.

30. Jefferson's "Report on the Privileges and Restrictions on the Commerce of the United States in Foreign Countries," December 16, 1793, reprinted in Merrill D. Peterson, ed., *Writings: Thomas Jefferson* (New York: Literary Classics of the United States, 1984), 435–48.

31. The interpretation presented here and in the following chapters challenges Doron Ben-Atar's assertion that Jeffersonians had little regard for the merchant class. *Origins of Jeffersonian Commercial Policy*. I side instead with the work of Burton Spivak, *Jefferson's English Crisis*, and John Nelson, who asserted that Jeffersonians hoped "to loosen . . . the hegemonic grip of Great Britain on America's market system." Nelson, *Liberty and Property*, 74–75.

32. Pierce Butler to James Madison, February 4, 1794, *Papers of James Madison* (Charlottesville: University of Virginia Press, 1985), 15: 246. Butler had opposed Madison's commercial plan in 1789. See Lewright B. Sikes, *The Public Life of Pierce Butler, South Carolina Statesman* (Washington: University Press of America, 1979), 60.

33. From Thomas P. Carnes, May 2, 1794, reprinted in Noble Cunningham, *Circular Letters of Congressmen to their Constituents, 1789–1829* (Chapel Hill: University of North Carolina Press, 1978), 1: 23–27.

34. Aedanus Burke was a loud supporter of the French cause, rejecting Jefferson's lukewarm attitude toward Genet and actively pursuing a commercial and military alliance with France. See John C. Meleney, *The Public Life of Aedanus Burke: Revolutionary Republican in Post-Revolutionary South Carolina* (Columbia: University of South Carolina Press, 1989), 204, 215–16. James Jackson expressed support for the aims of the French Revolution, though he disliked its excesses and supported the recall of Genet. For uncertain reasons, Jackson did not participate in the vote on a Republican plan to boycott British goods. He did, however, decry the Jay Treaty—making special arrangements to be in New York for the debate—and noted it to be an abuse

of executive power. William Omer Foster Sr., *James Jackson: Duelist and Militant Statesman, 1757–1806* (Athens: University of Georgia Press, 1960), 102, 104, 109, 151.

35. *AC*, 3rd Cong., 1st sess., 178–92 (quote from 188–89). Southern Federalist thoughts are discussed in George C. Rogers Jr., *Evolution of a Federalist: William Loughton Smith of Charleston* (Columbia: University of South Carolina Press, 1962); James H. Broussard, *The Southern Federalists, 1800–1815* (Baton Rouge: Louisiana State University Press, 1978); Lisle A. Rose, *Prologue to Democracy: The Federalists in the South, 1789–1800* (Lexington: University of Kentucky Press, 1968).

36. Crowley, *Privileges of Independence*, 156–68.

37. "Letter to the President of the United States," *Columbian Herald*, August 14, 1795.

38. Quote from minutes and a description from Savannah and Augusta's meet-ings are given in the *Augusta Chronicle and Gazette of the State*, August 15, 1795, and August 22, 1795, respectively. Led by prominent merchant William Jones, this assem-bly appealed directly to Washington to use his veto power, confident that he would not "impair" American rights and liberties for a treaty that would have "the most ruinous consequences to the United States." Savannah, Georgia, Citizens Meeting to George Washington, August 1, 1795, George Washington Papers, Library of Congress, 1741–1799, series 4, General Correspondence, 1697–1799.

39. Read's effigy burning took place on September 12, 1795, and was recorded in the *City Gazette*, October 20, 1795. For incidents in Georgia, see "At a Meeting . . . respecting the impending Treaty with Great Britain," n.p., n.d., Broadside Collec-tion, Georgia Historical Society; *Georgia Gazette*, August 6, 1795, and September 24, 1795. Also *Augusta Chronicle and Gazette of the State*, August 22 and 29, 1795, September 5, 1795. All are cited in George Lamplugh, *Politics on the Periphery: Fac-tions and Parties in Georgia, 1783–1806* (Newark: University of Delaware Press, 1986), 127–28, 141, n34. And for Gunn's hanging, see *Federal Intelligencer*, August 14, 1795, cited in Foster, *James Jackson*, 109. See also John Harold Wolfe, *Jeffersonian Democ-racy in South Carolina* (Chapel Hill: University of North Carolina Press, 1940), 71–81.

40. James Haw, *John and Edward Rutledge of South Carolina* (Athens: University of Georgia Press, 1997), 250–52; Rogers, *Evolution of a Federalist*, 277. Some of the private correspondence opposing the treaty is detailed in Meleney, *Public Life of Ae-danus Burke*, 102–4, 114–16, 122, 134, and esp. 222–36. George C. Rogers Jr., *Charleston in the Age of the Pinckneys* (1969; Columbia: University of South Carolina Press, 1987), 132. For McIntosh, see *Georgia Gazette*, April 10 and April 17, 1795; August 5, 1795, cited in Harvey H. Jackson, *Lachlan McIntosh and the Politics of Revolutionary Geor-gia* (Athens: University of Georgia Press, 2003), 150.

41. William Smith, *An Address from William Smith, of South Carolina to his Con-stituents* (Philadelphia: n.p., 1794), and *A Candid Examination of the Objections to the Treaty of Amity, Commerce, and Navigation, between the United States and Great Britain* (Charleston: W. P. Young, 1795); Robert Goodloe Harper, *An Address from Robert Goodloe Harper of South Carolina, to His Constituents. Containing His Rea-sons for Approving the Treaty of Amity, Commerce, and Navigation, with Great Britain* (Philadelphia: Ormrod and Conrad, 1795). The Rutledge-Pinckney factions, who gen-erally represented that state's ideological middle, continued to oppose the treaty but

tempered more radical voices desiring outright condemnation of the acts of the general government.

42. *South Carolina Journals of the House of Representatives,* 1795, 122, 235, 241–42. Haw, *John and Edward Rutledge,* 254–55; Jerald A. Combs, *The Jay Treaty: Political Battleground of the Founding Fathers* (Berkeley: University of California Press, 1970), 172. Unlike in Georgia, where the Yazoo affair soured most Georgians to the Federalist administration, the majority of South Carolina's political elites managed to separate opposition to the treaty from opposition to the federal government.

43. *Augusta Chronicle and Gazette of the State,* August 15, 1795.

44. The interpretation here opposes Stanley M. Elkins and Eric L. McKitrick's charge that southern opposition to Jay's Treaty primarily reflected a "habitual Anglophobia" and was "in no way a response to the actual terms of the Treaty." *The Age of Federalism: The Early American Republic, 1788–1800* (New York: Oxford University Press, 1993), 415–22, quotes from 415 and 432. A good summary of the South's reception of the Jay Treaty can be found in Rose, *Prologue to Democracy,* 114–25. For more specific examples, see the activities of several town meetings printed in the *Augusta Chronicle and Gazette of the State,* August 15, 1795, August 29, 1795, September 5, 1795, November 14, 1795; also "Meeting of Columbia, SC Militia" and "Toasts" to "The sister republics of France and Holland," in ibid, July 23, 1796; *Georgia Gazette* (Savannah), July 30, 1795, August 6, 1795, August 20, 1795, and August 27, 1795. In South Carolina, see *Columbia Herald or Southern Star,* August 14, 1795, October 21, 1795. See also the voice of "Horatio," who railed against the treaty and its supporters, *Augusta Chronicle and Gazette of the State,* October 2, 1795. There were some less adverse voices, such as "Moderato," in *Augusta Chronicle and Gazette of the State,* September 12, 1795, and the voices of representatives Harper and Smith, who began a counteroffensive in the early winter of 1795.

45. My understanding of diplomacy in the revolutionary era is indebted to Jonathan Dull, *A Diplomatic History of the American Revolution* (New Haven: Yale University Press, 1985); James Hutson, *John Adams and the Diplomacy of the American Revolution* (Lexington: University Press of Kentucky, 1980); and Leonard Sadosky, "Revolutionary Negotiations: A History of American Diplomacy with Europe and Native America in the Age of Jefferson" (Ph.D. diss., University of Virginia, 2003).

46. Cited in Ulrich B. Phillips, *Georgia and States' Rights* (1902; Macon: Mercer University Press, 1984), 42. For more, see Claudio Saunt, *A New Order of Things: Property, Power, and the Transformation of the Creek Indians, 1733–1816* (New York: Cambridge University Press, 1999).

47. Whitemarsh B. Seabrook, *A Memoir on the Origin, Cultivation, and Uses of Cotton* (Charleston: Miller & Browne, 1844), 18.

48. Letter of Thomas Spaulding to W. B. Seabrook, January 20, 1844, in *Southern Agriculturist,* new series, 4, no. 107, reprinted in J. A. Turner, *The Cotton Planter's Manual* (New York: C. M. Saxton & Co., 1857), quote from 282. Decades-old connections with the British Caribbean provided the knowledge southerners needed for early experiments in cotton production, making the West Indies "literally, the seedbed of the later Cotton South." Chaplin, *Anxious Pursuit,* 153–55.

49. E. Merton Coulter, *Thomas Spaulding of Sapelo* (Baton Rouge: Louisiana State University Press, 1940), 63–64.

50. "The Beginning of Cotton Cultivation in Georgia," *Georgia Historical Quarterly* (March 1917), 39–45.

51. Leslie Hall, *Land and Allegiance in Revolutionary Georgia* (Athens: University of Georgia Press, 2001), 170–71.

52. *Georgia Gazette,* December, 4, 1788, cited in Chaplin, *Anxious Pursuit,* 154.

53. George Washington to Thomas Jefferson, February 13, 1789, Dorothy Twohig, ed., *The Papers of George Washington* (Charlottesville: University of Virginia Press), Presidential Series, 1: 299–303.

54. Stuart Bruchey, *Cotton and the Growth of the American Economy, 1790–1860: Sources and Readings* (New York: Harcourt, Brace & World, 1967), table 1.A.

55. Hindley & Gregorie to McConnel & Kennedy, July 13, 1809, McConnel and Kennedy Papers, MSS John Rylands Library, University of Manchester.

56. Entries for April 6, 1788, May 24, 1792, August 15, 1797, Richard Leake Plantation Journal, Georgia Historical Society, and Pierce Butler to Thomas Young, October 28, 1793, Pierce Butler Letterbook, South Carolina Library. Quote from Chaplin, *Anxious Pursuit,* 223. S. G. Stephens, "Origins of Sea Island Cotton," *Agricultural History* 50 (April 1976): 391–99; "The Beginning of Cotton Cultivation in Georgia," *Georgia Historical Quarterly* 1, no. 1 (March 1917): 39–45.

57. Those in the English-speaking Atlantic, as Richard Drayton and Joyce Chaplin have shown, stood at the forefront of such efforts and used science as an instrument for conforming nature to imperial ends: Richard Drayton, *Nature's Government: Science, Imperial Britain and the "Improvement" of the World* (New Haven: Yale University Press, 2000); Chaplin, *Anxious Pursuit;* Asa Briggs, *The Age of Improvement, 1783–1867* (London: Longman, 1959). See Whitemarsh B. Seabrook, *A Report, accompanied with sundry letters, on the causes which contribute to the production of fine Sea-Island cotton* (Charleston: A. E. Miller, 1827), 25–27. For examples of a continued intellectual engagement with the modern world, see correspondences and reprints in the *Southern Agriculturist,* which was published from 1828 to 1846. J. D. Legaré, *The Southern Agriculturist and Register of Rural Affairs: Adapted to the Southern Section of the United States* (Charleston: A. E. Miller, 1828). See also *Southern Review* and *Southern Quarterly Review,* founded by E. H. Britton (Columbia, S.C.: 1842–1857), and the *Southern Literary Messenger,* founded by T. W. White (Richmond: 1834–1864). My analysis supports the study of Mark Smith, which shows that southerners continued to embrace modern advances, like workdays wed to watch time, even as they perpetuated a slave society. Smith, *Mastered by the Clock: Time, Slavery, and Freedom in the American South* (Chapel Hill: University of North Carolina Press, 1997). Also Richard Follett, "Slavery and Plantation Capitalism in Louisiana's Sugar Country," *American Nineteenth Century History* 1 (Autumn 2000): 1–27. Techniques included fertilizing cotton fields with manure (especially after 1825), applying marsh mud rich in minerals, composting, and using early commercial fertilizers like guano. Also in 1826 Thomas Coffin of St. Helena Island sent a questionnaire to other planters inquiring into ways of improvement. See "Letters from Coffin," in Guion Griffis Johnson, *A Social History of the Sea Islands: With Special Reference to St. Helena Island, South Carolina* (1930; New York: Negro Universities Press, 1969), 50–59. On specific innovations, see Chaplin, *Anxious Pursuit,* 299, and Alan L. Olmstead and Paul W. Rhode, "Biological Innovation and Productivity Growth in the Antebellum Cotton Economy" (June 2008), NBER Working Paper no. W14142.

58. Angela Lakwete, *Inventing the Cotton Gin: Machine and Myth in Antebellum America* (Baltimore: John Hopkins University Press, 2003); Bruchey, *Cotton and the Growth of the American Economy*, table 3.A.

59. T. G. Thomas, *Contribution to the History of the Huguenots of South Carolina* (New York: Knickerbocker Press, 1887), 22, in Edwards, *Growth of the British Cotton Trade*, 91.

60. Work Projects Administration, "The Plantation at Royal Vale," *Georgia Historical Quarterly* 27, no. 1 (1943): 88–110.

61. *Columbian Museum and Savannah Advertiser*, October 15, 1799.

62. Malcolm Bell Jr., *Major Butler's Legacy: Five Generations of a Slaveholding Family* (Athens: University of Georgia Press, 1987), 39.

63. Butler to Thomas Young, March 25, 1794, Pierce Butler Letterbook, 1790–1794, South Caroliniana Library, cited in Bell, *Major Butler's Legacy*, 110–11.

64. A 1793 survey reveals that there were a total of 441 slaves (141 males, 160 females, and 140 children) at the Hampton plantation. Bell, *Major Butler's Legacy*, 128. Though it is hard to know how many actually cultivated cotton, it is hard to imagine that it would be fewer than 250 to 300. Average New York prices were 36 cents, and Liverpool prices garnered between 15 and 27 pence. Bruchey, *Cotton and the Growth of the American Economy*, table 3.A.

65. Curtis P. Nettels, *The Emergence of a National Economy: 1775–1815* (New York: Holt, Rinehart and Winston, 1962), 192.

66. David Ramsay, *History of South Carolina from its First Settlement in 1670 to the year 1808* (1809; Spartanburg: Reprint Co., 1968–71), 2: 248–49; Edward Hooker, Journal, November 4, 15, 1805; both cited in Rachel Klein, *The Unification of a Slave State: The Rise of a Planter Class in the South Carolina Backcountry, 1760–1808* (Chapel Hill: University of North Carolina Press, 1992), 248–49.

67. George Sibbald, *Notes and Observations on the Pinelands of Georgia . . .* (Augusta: William J. Bunch, 1801), 6. Also, John Drayton, *A View of South Carolina, as Respects Her Natural and Civil Concerns* (Charleston: W. P. Young, 1802), 130–31; Lewis Du Pre, *Observations on the Culture of Cotton* (Georgetown, S.C., 1799). As Joyce Chaplin poetically noted, it entered "more like William of Orange than William the Conqueror: an *invited* invader that created a kingdom of cotton in an already commercialized region." Joyce Chaplin, "Creating a Cotton South," *Journal of Southern History* 57, no. 2 (May 1991): 193–94. Statistics from Bruchey, *Cotton and the Growth of the American Economy*, table 3.A.

68. Jon Kukla, *A Wilderness So Immense: The Louisiana Purchase and the Destiny of America* (New York: Alfred A. Knopf, 2003), 336.

69. See table 3 in chapter 1.

70. John Nodin, *The British Duties of Customs, Excise, &c* (London: n.p., 1792), 5–6.

71. Edwards, *Growth of the British Cotton Trade*, 75–106.

72. Rogers, *Evolution of a Federalist*, 97–99. Though the exception rather than the rule, Savannah merchant-planters Joseph and Robert Habersham's leadership helped to create a commercial family dynasty that exchanged the family's and other planters' cotton for European goods until the Civil War. See Julia Floyd Smith, *Slavery and Rice Culture in Lowcountry Georgia, 1750–1860* (Knoxville: University of Tennessee Press, 1985), 78.

73. On the influence of local merchants, see two very useful new studies: Jonathan Daniel Wells, *The Origins of the Southern Middle Class, 1800–1861* (Chapel Hill: University of North Carolina Press, 2004), esp. 207–34, and Frank Byrnes, *Merchant Culture in the South, 1820–1865* (Lexington: University of Kentucky Press, 2006). Byrnes has convincingly demonstrated the continued significance of native merchants in the South, revealing that in 1850 78% of those employed in commercial businesses were born in slave states. He does not, however, distinguish between types of commercial occupations, and his evidence is likely skewed somewhat due to overreliance on inland counties. Ibid., 19, table 4. As evidenced in chapter 1, the export-import trade appears to have been increasingly controlled by nonsoutherners.

74. The reintegration of British-American trade after the American Revolution remains an understudied subject, but the cotton trade suggests that new geopolitical circumstances did not prevent a quick reintegration. In his masterful study of an eighteenth-century London merchant community, David Hancock has demonstrated how a diverse group of merchants positioned at the center of the British world integrated a British Atlantic through trade and investment. David Hancock, *Citizens of the World: London Merchants and the Integration of the British Atlantic Community, 1735–1785* (Cambridge: Cambridge University Press, 1995). See also W. O. Henderson, "The American Chamber of Commerce for the Port of Liverpool," *Transactions of the Historical Society of Lancashire and Cheshire* (Liverpool: Historic Society of Lancashire and Cheshire, 1935), 1–62; C. H. Lee, *A Cotton Enterprise, 1795–1840: A History of McConnel & Kennedy Fine Cotton Spinners* (Manchester, UK: Manchester University Press, 1972), 90–91; Rogers, *Evolution of a Federalist*, 100. The important British cotton firm, McConnel & Kennedy used the Tunnos and Gregorie as their factors.

75. From 1790 to 1792 the direct trade between the Lower South and Great Britain seems to have been predominantly carried in British vessels. Shepherd and Walton suggest that 155 of the 199 vessels entering the port were foreign-owned during that period. This would change considerably in the nineteenth century. James F. Shepherd and Gary Walton, "Economic Change after the American Revolution: Pre- and Post-War Comparisons of Maritime Shipping and Trade," *Explorations in Economic History* (November 1976), 417.

76. Nelson Miles Hoffman Jr., "Godfrey Barnsley, 1805–1873: British Cotton Factor in the South" (Ph.D. diss., University of Kansas, 1964).

77. By comparison only 6% of the tonnage departing New York was on foreign vessels. From October 1820 to September 1821, two-thirds of the tonnage of foreign vessels leaving the United States departed from the cotton ports of South Carolina, Georgia, and Louisiana. Timothy Pitkin, *A Statistical View of the Commerce of the United States of America* (New Haven: Durrie & Peck, 1835), table 5: 58–59.

78. *DHFFC*, 8: 355–56.

79. Robert Greenhalgh Albion, *The Rise of New York Port, 1815–1860* (New York: Charles Scribner's Sons, 1939), 100, and *Square-Riggers on Schedule: The New York Sailing Packets to England, France, and the Cotton Ports* (Princeton: Princeton University Press, 1938), passim.

80. Frances W. Gregory, *Nathan Appleton: Merchant and Entrepreneur, 1779–1861* (Charlottesville: University of Virginia Press), 24–26.

81. Albion, *Square-Riggers on Schedule*, 49–76, and *Rise of New York Port*, 95–121.

82. Sibbald, *Notes and Observations,* 51–52. On the cotton triangle, see Albion, *Rise of New York Port,* 95–121.

83. Harold Woodman, *King Cotton and His Retainers: Financing and Marketing the Cotton Crop of the South, 1800–1925* (1968; Columbia: University of South Carolina Press, 1990).

84. Perhaps the best-known firms involved in the cotton trade were the Baring Brothers and the House of Brown. For more on their roles in the financing of cotton in the antebellum period, see Edwin J. Perkins, *Financing Anglo-American Trade: The House of Brown, 1800–1880* (Cambridge: Harvard University Press, 1975), esp. 88–113; Ralph W. Hidy, *The House of Baring in American Trade and Finance: English Merchant Bankers at Work, 1763–1861* (Cambridge: Harvard University Press, 1949); Woodman, *King Cotton,* 98–138, 165–76; Howard Bodenhorn, *A History of Banking in Antebellum America: Financial Markets and Economic Development in an Era of Nation-Building* (Cambridge, UK: Cambridge University Press, 2000), 10.

85. Woodman, *King Cotton,* 19.

86. For example, James Gregorie (Charleston Factor) to McConnel & Kennedy (hereafter MCK), January 16, 1809, February 16, 1809, Papers of MCK, John Rylands Library, MSS letterbook, February 1, 1815; quote from Trapmann, Johncke & Co. to MCK, June 23, 1819, MCK, February 1, 1825; second quote from Longsdon (Charleston) to MCK, December 1, 1825, MCK, February 1, 1831.

87. James Mann, *The Cotton Trade* (London: Simpkin, Marshall, & Co., 1860), table in front.

88. Bruchey, *Cotton and the Growth of the American Economy,* table 3.A.

89. Concern over a cholera epidemic led another Charleston factor to preemptively send his clients "a Box containing medicine with instructions how to use it." Other factors sent gifts to the children and spouses of customers. Woodman, *King Cotton,* esp. 43–48; A. H. Stone, "The Cotton Factorage System of the Southern States," *American Historical Review* 20, no. 3 (April 1915): 557–65. Ralph W. Haskins perpetuates Stone's assumption that the relationship between planters and factors was tenuous. "Planter and Cotton Factor in the Old South: Some Areas of Friction," *Agricultural History* 29 (January 1955): 1–14. Woodman's study provides a useful contrast to Stone's much older and briefer study. With no evidentiary basis, Stone claimed that "the cotton factor was the power behind the throne" of King Cotton. Woodman's broadly researched book reveals that cooperation dictated most factor-planter interactions and shows the strength of planters' position within commercial negotiations related to the cotton trade.

90. Ironically, the commercial and military warfare begun in 1806 may have bolstered southern planters' place within the cotton trade. The desire to ensure the best crop available and find illicit sources of cotton during commercial restrictions from 1807 to 1815 seems to have drawn British cotton spinners increasingly into direct contact with American brokers who had personal relationships with southern planters. Lee, *Cotton Enterprise,* 95.

91. John Killick, "Risk, Specialization and Profit in the Mercantile Sector of the Nineteenth Century Cotton Trade: Alexander Brown & Sons, 1820–1880," *Business History* 16 (January 1974): 1–16; Killick, "The Cotton Operations of Alexander Brown and Sons in the Deep South, 1820–1880," *Journal of Southern History* 43 (May 1977): 169–94.

92. Eugene Genovese, *The Political Economy of the South* (New York: Vintage Books, 1967); Gavin Wright, *The Political Economy of the Cotton South* (New York: Norton, 1978), passim; Woodman, *King Cotton*, 139–53; Joseph Persky, *The Burden of Dependency: Colonial Themes in Southern Economic Thought* (Baltimore: Johns Hopkins University Press, 1992).

93. Sibbald, *Notes and Observations,* 50–51.

94. *Columbian Centinel,* no. 2: reprinted in the *Carolina Gazette* (Charleston), October 14, 1802.

95. *Aurora,* reprinted in *City Gazette and Daily Advertiser* (Charleston), August 13, 1803.

96. *Columbian Centinel,* no. 2, reprinted in the *Carolina Gazette,* October 14, 1802.

97. Drayton, *View of South Carolina,* 36, 128–29; quote from *South Carolina House Journal,* November 25, 1802, cited in Klein, *Unification of a Slave State,* 247.

98. *Columbian Centinel,* no. 2, reprinted in the *Carolina Gazette,* October 14, 1802.

99. "Franklin," *Aurora,* reprinted in *City Gazette and Daily Advertiser,* March 12, 1803.

100. *City Gazette and Daily Advertiser,* May 21, 1803.

101. Ibid., May 7, 1803.

102. *Columbian Centinel,* no. 1, "Our Country is Our Theme," reprinted in *Carolina Gazette,* October 14, 1802.

103. *City Gazette and Daily Advertiser,* July 3, 1797.

104. Drayton, *View of South Carolina,* 146–47.

105. Historians have emphasized the resistance yeomen put up to the market and slavery. Stephen Hahn, *The Roots of Southern Populism: Yeoman Farmers and the Transformation of the Georgia Upcountry, 1850–1890* (New York: Oxford University Press, 1983); Charles Sellers, *The Market Revolution: Jacksonian America, 1815–1846* (New York: Oxford University Press, 1991). For a different perspective, see Lacy K. Ford Jr., *Origins of Southern Radicalism: The South Carolina Upcountry, 1800–1860* (New York: Oxford University Press, 1988), 72–84, 253–56; Klein, *Unification of a Slave State,* passim; Chaplin, "Creating a Cotton South," passim.

106. Ramsay, *History of South Carolina,* 2: 248–49.

107. Klein, *Unification of a Slave State,* 252–53.

108. Cited in Chaplin, *Anxious Pursuit,* 321.

109. Charles Ball, *Slavery in the United States: A Narrative of the Life and Adventures of Charles Ball, a Black Man, Who Lived Forty Years in Maryland, South Carolina and Georgia, as a Slave Under Various Masters, and was One Year in the Navy with Commodore Barney, During the Late War,* electronic edition, 184, http://docsouth.unc.edu/ballslavery/ball.html (accessed November 20, 2005).

110. Michael Tadman, *Speculators and Slaves: Masters, Traders, and Slaves in the Old South* (Madison: University of Wisconsin Press, 1989), 226.

111. Ralph Betts Flanders, *Plantation Slavery in Georgia* (Chapel Hill: University of North Carolina Press, 1933), 63.

112. Tadman, *Speculators and Slaves,* 226.

113. Ball, *Slavery in the United States,* 80.

114. See Tadman, *Speculators and Slaves,* table on 116.

115. Ibid., 226. On the expansion of slavery into the Southwest, see Adam Rothman, *Slave Country: American Expansion and the Origins of the Deep South* (Cambridge: Harvard University Press, 2005).

116. Drayton, *View of South Carolina,* 144, 146–47.

117. Thomas Jefferson to William Burwell, January 28, 1805, Papers of Thomas Jefferson, Library of Congress, http://memory.loc.gov/ammem/collections/jefferson _papers (accessed December 13, 2006).

118. Eric Williams, *Capitalism and Slavery* (1944; Chapel Hill: University of North Carolina Press, 1994), esp. 98–108. Robin Blackburn provides a more recent and perhaps more accurate interpretation in *The Making of New World Slavery: From the Baroque to the Modern, 1492–1800* (New York: Verso Press, 1997).

CHAPTER TWO: Calculating the Cost of Union

1. Rachel Klein, *The Unification of a Slave State: The Rise of the Planter Class in the South Carolina Backcountry, 1760–1808* (Chapel Hill: University of North Carolina Press, 1990), 214 (Butler), 230–37 (Hampton), 259 (backcountry). For the role of Native American policy in this, see Andrew R. L. Cayton, "Separate Interests and the Nation-State: The Washington Administration and the Origins of Regionalism in the Trans-Appalachian West," *Journal of American History* 79, no. 1 (June 1992): 39–67.

2. Joyce Chaplin, "Creating a Cotton South," *Journal of Southern History* 57, no. 2 (May 1991): 171–200, and Klein, *Unification of a Slave State,* passim.

3. Paul Finkelman, "The Problem of Slavery in the Age of Federalism," in Doron Ben-Atar and Barbara Oberg, eds., *Federalists Reconsidered* (Charlottesville: University of Virginia Press, 1998), 135–56; Garry Wills, *"Negro President": Jefferson and the Slave Power* (Boston: Houghton, Mifflin, 2003); Anthony A. Iaccarino, "Virginia and the National Contest over Slavery in the Early Republic, 1776–1833" (Ph.D. diss., University of California, Los Angeles, 1999); Richard S. Newman, "Prelude to the Gag Rule: Southern Reaction to Antislavery Petitions in the First Federal Congress," *Journal of the Early Republic* 16 (Winter 1996): 599.

4. For Tench Coxe's conversion to Republicanism, see Tench Coxe, *A Statement of the Arts and Manufactures of the United States of America in 1810* (Philadelphia: A. Cornman, 1819); Jacob E. Cooke, *Tench Coxe and the Early Republic* (Chapel Hill: University of North Carolina Press), 182–216, 274–92. For similar examples, see Sean Wilentz, *Chants Democratic: New York and the American Working Class* (New York: Oxford University Press, 1984), and Lawrence A. Peskin, *Manufacturing Revolution: The Intellectual Origins of Early American Industry* (Baltimore: Studies in Early American Economy and Society from the Library Company of Philadelphia by the Johns Hopkins University Press, 2003).

5. William Appleman Williams first emphasized the neomercantilist tendencies within Republican thought in "The Age of Mercantilism: An Interpretation of the American Political Economy, 1763 to 1828," *William and Mary Quarterly* 15, no. 4 (October 1958): 419–37. John Crowley discusses Jefferson and Madison's calculations in similar terms in his discussion of their affinity for navigation laws as part of larger neomercantilist policies in *The Privileges of Independence: Neomercantilism and the*

*American Revolution* (Baltimore: Johns Hopkins University Press, 1993), esp. 140, 144–45, 159. For a discussion of the early evolution of Jefferson's personal thoughts, see Merrill Peterson, "Thomas Jefferson and Commercial Policy, 1785–1793," *William and Mary Quarterly* 22, no. 4 (October 1965): 584–610. See also John Nelson, *Liberty and Property: Political Economy and Policymaking in the New Nation, 1789–1812* (Baltimore: Johns Hopkins University Press, 1989), 54, 90–93, 135, 146, 173. For the diverse backgrounds of Republican congressional leaders, see Paul Goodman, "Social Status of Party Leadership: The House of Representatives, 1797–1804," *William and Mary Quarterly* 25, no. 4 (July 1968): 465–74. Republicans decried the terms of the Jay Treaty allowing Britain to match American tonnage duties as a policy that could destroy American shipping interests. Vernon G. Setser, *The Commercial Reciprocity Policy of the United States, 1774–1829* (1937; New York: Da Capo Press, 1969), chap. 4, esp. 104–5, 130.

6. Drew McCoy, *The Elusive Republic: Political Economy in Jeffersonian America* (Chapel Hill: Institute of Early American History and Culture by the University of North Carolina Press, 1980), esp. chap. 3; Peter Onuf and Leonard Sadosky, *Jeffersonian America* (London: Blackwell Publishers, 2001), chap. 3. Also Doron Ben-Atar, *The Origins of Jeffersonian Commercial Policy and Diplomacy* (New York: St. Martin's Press, 1993), passim. John Lauritz Larson has ably described the efforts that Republican leaders like Gallatin made for creating a national economy through equitable funding for internal improvements. Larson, "'Bind the Republic Together'": The National Union and the Struggle for a System of Internal Improvements," *Journal of American History* 74, no. 2 (September 1987): 363–87, and *Internal Improvement: National Public Works and the Promise of Popular Government in the Early United States* (Chapel Hill: University of North Carolina Press, 2001).

7. Jefferson, "First Annual Message," December 8, 1801, in Merrill D. Peterson, ed., *Writings: Thomas Jefferson* (New York: Literary Classics of the United States, 1984), 507.

8. John Stagg emphasizes Madison's favorable view of protection for American commerce in *Mr. Madison's War* (Princeton: Princeton University Press, 1979).

9. Republican fears of national debt are thoroughly explained in Herbert Sloan, *Principle and Interest: Thomas Jefferson and the Problem of Debt* (New York: Oxford University Press, 1995). The administration resisted efforts by Maryland's Samuel Smith to end discriminatory duties against foreign shipping. Jefferson left the decision up to Congress but privately desired a continuation of commercial discrimination. William Bates, *American Navigation: The Political History of Its Rise and Ruin and the Proper Means for Its Encouragement* (New York: Houghton, Mifflin, 1902), 133–46; Burton Spivak, *Jefferson's English Crisis* (Charlottesville: University of Virginia Press, 1979), 32–38; and Nelson, *Liberty and Property*, 144, discuss these policies.

10. *Annals of Congress* (hereafter *AC*), 8th Cong., 1st sess., 1036. See Bates, *American Navigation*, 146–48.

11. McCoy, *Elusive Republic*, esp. 76–104; Onuf and Sadosky, *Jeffersonian America*, chap. 3.

12. Adam Rothman, *Slave Country: American Expansion and the Origins of the Deep South* (Cambridge: Harvard University Press, 2005), 27–35. Also Peter J. Kastor,

*The Nation's Crucible: The Louisiana Purchase and the Creation of America* (New Haven: Yale University Press, 2004). For a very good account of slavery's political influence, see Matthew Mason, *Slavery and Politics in the Early American Republic* (Chapel Hill: University of North Carolina Press, 2006).

13. *AC*, 8th Cong., 1st sess., 1002 (Mitchell), 1014 (Gregg).

14. *AC*, 8th Cong., 1st sess., 993 (Lowndes), 1006 (Huger).

15. Don Fehrenbacher, *The Slaveholding Republic: An Account of the United States Government's Relations to Slavery* (Oxford: Oxford University Press, 2001), 142–43. For votes on postponement which show a breakdown, see *AC*, 8th Cong., 1st sess., 1022 and 1035–36. Of the Georgia and South Carolina delegations, only Joseph Bryan, a Savannah planter, voted against postponing, for reasons that are not apparent.

16. Lewis Grey, *History of Agriculture in the Southern United States to 1860* (1933; Clifton: Augustus M. Kelley, 1973), 2: 765; Timothy Pitkin, *A Statistical View of the Commerce of the United States of America* (New Haven: Durrie & Peck, 1835), chap. 3, table 1, 52–53; and Douglass North, *The Economic Growth of the United States* (New York: Norton, 1961), 17–60.

17. Curtis P. Nettels, *The Emergence of a National Economy: 1775–1815* (New York: Holt, Rinehart and Winston, 1962), table 21, 399.

18. Ibid., table 9, 389.

19. Jefferson, "Second Inaugural Address," March 4, 1805, in Peterson, *Writings: Thomas Jefferson*, 518–23. See also Larson, "'Bind the Republic Together,'" 363–87, for a discussion of Jefferson's view of internal improvements, with explicit reference to this address (371). On the centrality of debt as the Jeffersonian measure for a healthy economy, see Sloan, *Principle and Interest*, passim.

20. On tobacco, see Pitkin, *Statistical View*, table 1, 119, and table 9, 131. See Michael M. Edwards, *The Growth of the British Cotton Trade, 1780–1815* (New York: Augustus M. Kell[e]y, 1967); C. H. Lee, *A Cotton Enterprise, 1795–1840: A History of McConnel & Kennedy Fine Cotton Spinners* (Manchester, UK: Manchester University Press, 1972); Thomas Ellison, *The Cotton Trade of Great Britain* (1886; London: Frank Cass, 1968). France imported a small percentage of American cotton but was a very distant second to Britain as an importer of raw Sea Island and inland raw cotton. Pitkin, *Statistical View*, table 13, 135.

21. Nelson, *Liberty and Property*, graph 12, 184. The broader implications of the carrying trade remain contested by economic historians responding to Douglass C. North's arguments in *Economic Growth of the United States*.

22. Gallatin consistently reminded Jefferson not to abandon or appear to abandon the carrying trade. See "Gallatin's notes on President's Message to Congress," in "Drawbacks File," Papers of Thomas Jefferson, Library of Congress. For the ongoing efforts to convert New England to Republicanism, see Paul Goodman, *The Democratic-Republicans of Massachusetts: Politics in a Young Republic* (Cambridge: Harvard University Press, 1964); Peter S. Onuf, *Jefferson's Empire: The Language of Nationhood* (Charlottesville: University Press of Virginia, 2000), 121–29. Jefferson was fully conscious of the threat presented by the carrying trade, preferring instead to focus navigation on the direct trade, but party goals and his Anglophobia compounded to support the rights of the carrying trade. "What a glorious exchange would it be could we persuade our navigating fellow citizens to embark their capital in the internal

commerce of our country, exclude foreigners from that & let them take the carrying trade in exchange: abolish the diplomatic establishments & never suffer an armed vessel of any nation to enter our ports. [illegible] things can be thought of only in times of wisdom, not of party & Folly." Jefferson to Edmund Pendleton, April 22, 1799, Papers of Thomas Jefferson, series 1, General Correspondence, Library of Congress.

23. Despite the significant amount of controversy that it created in later years, Republicans never challenged the drawback system before 1809, and during Jefferson's administration many sought to extend it. See, for example, the report submitted by Samuel Mitchell, December 20, 1803, *AC*, 8th Cong., 2nd sess., 1477 and 1480.

24. Andrew Gregg (Pa.-R), *AC*, 9th Cong., 1st sess., 543.

25. Jacob Crowninshield (Mass.-R), in ibid., 554; Nathan Williams (N.Y.-R), ibid., 578–79; William Findley, ibid., 619, 628–30. See also *Memorial of the Merchants of the City of New York* (New York: Hopkins & Seymour, 1806); McCoy, *Elusive Republic*, 214–15. The nonimportation agreements of 1774 and Madison's 1793 and 1794 resolutions were offered as precedents, stressing the consistency of their demands with prior Republican theory and practice. See Jefferson, "Report on the Privileges and Restrictions on the Commerce of the United States in Foreign Countries," December 16, 1793, and Madison's resolution in *AC*, 3rd Cong., 1st sess., 155. See also Peterson, "Thomas Jefferson and Commercial Policy," 584–610.

26. Early, *AC*, 9th Cong., 1st sess., 623–24.

27. Ibid.

28. The average value of exports from 1802 to 1804 was $20.2 million, $9.9 million of which was exclusively southern products. Adding the amount of other products such as wheat, the South had a clear majority, especially of the trade to England. Early, ibid., 624–25; D. R. Williams (S.C.-R), ibid., 643–50; Randolph, ibid., 555–74; John Eppes (Va.-R), ibid., 670–71; Nicholson, ibid., 681–83. For a response, see Elliot, ibid., 640–41. The treasury report referred to is available in *American State Papers, Commerce and Navigation*, 1: 640–46.

29. Fiscal conservatives argued that the reexport trade contributed only $850,000 in revenue, compared to approximately $6 million from duties on British imports. See Early, *AC*, 9th Cong., 1st sess., 627; D. R. Williams, ibid., 645; Joseph Clay (Pa.), ibid., 549–52; Wilson Cary Nicholson, ibid., 677–80. Paul Varg discusses the Republican fear of credit and revenue problems in *Foreign Policies of the Founding Fathers* (East Lansing: Michigan State University Press, 1963), chap. 5; Sloan, *Principle and Interest*.

30. Early, *AC*, 9th Cong., 1st sess., 624.

31. Proponents of the bill accepted a "temporary inconvenience from a small reduction in the prices of the produce of our farms" but "in competition with the honor and general interest of our country," they argued, it would be nothing. Gregg, ibid., 538–55.

32. Banned items included some metal goods, high-priced woolens and clothing, glass, and alcohol, but the Nicholas resolutions allowed importation of most critical British goods—cottons, cheap woolens, iron, and steel. Compromise was led by the Mid-Atlantic, supporting Rudolph Bell's claim that in foreign policy "New England and the South/West formed the cores of opposing coalitions which depended for success upon the votes of delegates from the middle states whose attachments were not clearly or primarily sectional." Bell, "Mr. Madison's War and Long-Term Congressional Voting Behavior," *William and Mary Quarterly* 36 (July 1979): 387–88.

33. Randolph, *AC*, 9th Cong., 1st sess., 557; D. R. Williams, in ibid., 645, called it a "partial right." In frustration Randolph removed himself from the House before the vote came to the floor. For more on Randolph's acceptance of British supremacy, see Henry Adams, *John Randolph* (Boston: Houghton, Mifflin, 1899), 173, 178, 180. Most others recognized that not supporting it would be a serious rebuff to merchant Republicans and a blatant rejection of the administration's attempts to protect American neutral rights. Spivak, *Jefferson's English Crisis*, 32–38.

34. Jefferson to Monroe, March 16 and 18, 1806, Monroe Papers, Library of Congress, cited in Norman Risjord, *The Old Republicans* (New York: Columbia University Press, 1965), 60–61. It reflected the ability for centrifugal Jeffersonian policies—avoidance of a costly war, fiscal responsibility, and use of commercial retaliation for diplomatic ends—to maintain party consensus.

35. Early, Randolph, and Williams, *AC*, 9th Cong., 2nd sess., 484, 527–28, 626–27.

36. Fehrenbacher, *Slaveholding Republic*, 144–48; Matthew E. Mason, "Slavery Overshadowed: Congress Debates Prohibiting the Atlantic Slave Trade to the United States, 1806–1807," *Journal of the Early Republic* 20, no. 1 (Spring 2000): 59–81.

37. Donald Hickey, "The Monroe-Pinkney Treaty of 1806: A Reappraisal," *William and Mary Quarterly* (January 1987): 65–88. Upon receiving the terms and consulting with members of the merchant community and cabinet, the administration confirmed its opinion that the treaty terms were too vague, made few guarantees to American merchants and prevented America from employing commercial retaliation against Britain. Because the treaty was not published until 1808 there was little public debate over it.

38. It passed without serious debate by a vote of 82 to 44. The Randolph Quids and three of Georgia's four delegates voted in the opposition, protesting a policy they feared would adversely affect the cotton trade.

39. Bradford Perkins and Burton Spivak have effectively communicated the origins of the embargo as a military preparedness policy, while noting that the policy quickly became an experiment in economic coercion. Spivak, *Jefferson's English Crisis*, 110–11, 114–15; Perkins, *Prologue to War: England and the United States* (Berkeley: University of California Press, 1968), 150–51.

40. Though the embargo did not expressly prevent American consumption of British manufactures, connection between consumption and production within the Atlantic economy was implicit. The weak Nonimportation Act of 1806 went into effect in 1807.

41. "Extract of a Letter from a Member of Congress," *Public Advertiser* (New York), January 14, 1808, and *The Democrat* (Boston), January 20, 1808.

42. From *Life of James Sulliven with Selections from His Writings*, 2: 258, cited in Walter Jennings, *The American Embargo, 1807–1809* (Iowa City: The University Press, n.d.), 72.

43. "Cotton Trade: To Southern Planters," *The Repertory* (Boston), January 8, 1808; "Truth vs. Ruin," from the *Centinel*, reprinted in *Salem Gazette* (Mass.), January 15, 1808; "To the Honest Men of All Parties," *Boston Gazette*, January 11, 1808.

44. From *National Intelligencer*, "To the People of the United States, No. 3," *City Gazette and Daily Advertiser* (Charleston, S.C.), June 2, 1808. Also reprinted in *Miller's Weekly Messenger* (Pendleton, S.C.), June 18, 1808.

45. Crawford, *AC*, 10th Cong., 2nd sess., 63–73.

46. "Aristides," *City Gazette and Daily Advertiser,* October 1, 1808.

47. To this end, some embargo supporters accepted nonimportation only as a complement to nonexportation.

48. See Douglas A. Irwin, "The Welfare Cost of Autarky: Evidence from the Jeffersonian Trade Embargo, 1807–1809," *Review of International Economics* (September 2005): 631–45, available at Social Science Research Network, http://ssrn.com/abstract =806315 (accessed December 15, 2008).

49. After its passage, petitions (often betraying their originators' true concern) flooded into Washington, pledging individual and state support for the president's policy and applauding Congress for passing the "wise" measure. For just one example, see "Petition of House of Representatives of South Carolina," June 28, 1808, Papers of Thomas Jefferson, Library of Congress. For other instances, see Louis Sears, *Jefferson and the Embargo* (1927; New York: Octagon Books, 1966), 95–103.

50. Beginning in January 1808, congressmen Adams, Quincy, and Cook of Massachusetts put forward petitions from fishermen seeking relief. See *AC,* 10th Cong., 1st sess., 375, 1246–47, 1694–95, 2070, 2072. Federalists' accusations that the administration attempted to reduce the country to agrarian pastoralism were rejected as partisan haughtiness, and Federalists were derided as being unpatriotic. See passim in ibid., 1235–1386, esp. Macon, 1249–50.

51. Josiah Quincy to John Adams, December 14, 1808, January 17, 1809, Adams Family Papers, Massachusetts Historical Society, reels 406, 407. Cited in Spivak, *Jefferson's English Crisis,* 137.

52. Williams congressional speech printed in *The City Gazette* (Charleston), July 14, 1808.

53. Williams and Troup from congressional report, February 19, reprinted in *The Carolina Gazette* (Charleston), March 11, 1808.

54. One major exception was the opening of coastal trade under strict restrictions and for the trade of necessary foodstuffs. Spivak, *Jefferson's English Crisis,* 156–63. A March 1808 vote for tougher enforcement passed 97 to 22 with only 4 southern dissenters, 2 each from Kentucky and North Carolina. *AC,* 10th Cong., 1st sess., 1712.

55. Even Randolph, who opposed the embargo, saw it as a test of patriotism and virtue and argued that all should suffer equally. See, for example, *AC,* 10th Cong., 1st sess., 2238–40.

56. Sears, *Jefferson and the Embargo,* 143–227, and "Philadelphia and the Embargo of 1808," *Quarterly Journal of Economics* (February 1921): 354–59. Caroline Ware suggests that New England manufacturers were successful but proved incapable of expanding during the embargo: "The Effect of the American Embargo, 1807–1809, on the New England Cotton Industry," *Quarterly Journal of Economics* (August 1926): 672–88. For quote and a discussion of the heightened sectional rhetoric the policy created in the North, see Mason, *Slavery and Politics,* 47.

57. Senator Crawford, *AC,* 10th Cong., 2nd sess., 63–73. Areas that did have strong commercial interests, such as port cities like Charleston, were generally more sympathetic to northern complaints.

58. Crawford, *AC,* 10th Cong., 2nd sess., 66.

59. Macon, ibid., 1490.

60. Crawford, ibid., 66.

61. Peter Freneau to Jefferson, September 18, 1808, Papers of Thomas Jefferson, Library of Congress.

62. See, for example, the *Carolina Gazette,* September 16, 1808; the *Republican and Savannah Evening Ledger,* March 23, 1809.

63. "From the *Washington Monitor,*" in *City Gazette and Daily Advertiser,* July 13, 1808.

64. *Carolina Gazette,* July 22, 1808.

65. "A Discourse delivered on the 4th of July," *Carolina Gazette,* August 12, 1808.

66. See John Pope, of Kentucky, *AC,* 10th Cong., 2nd sess., 49–50, 206, 659. In reality southern agriculture could more easily endure the embargo as a temporary measure. Wheat and flour had sizable domestic markets and had received special coastal trading privileges. Cotton and tobacco had neither, but their longer shelf life allowed planters more patience to wait for a time when markets did open. Plantation slavery also proved more flexible than in urban areas, expanding and contracting small-scale domestic manufacturing as needed.

67. Randolph, *AC,* 10th Cong., 2nd sess., 1465–66; Russell Kirk, *John Randolph of Roanoke: A Study in American Politics* (1954; Indianapolis: Liberty Press, 1978), 147–50, 528–29.

68. The petition of Liverpool merchants was reprinted in the *City Gazette* (Charleston), April 30, 1808.

69. Import house of Cropper, Benson, and Company price circular. Cited in Spivak, *Jefferson's English Crisis,* 200.

70. Prices in G. W. Daniels, "American Cotton Trade with Liverpool under the Embargo and Non-Intercourse Acts," *American Historical Review* 21, no. 2 (January 1916): 287. Jeffery Frankel has suggested that the amount of smuggling was far below what other historians have assumed and even suggested that the embargo was having a more adverse effect on the British economy than on the United States. "The 1807–1809 Embargo against Great Britain," *Journal of Economic History* 42, no. 2 (June 1982): 291–308.

71. *City Gazette,* August 17, 1808.

72. Most New England Republicans came to see the embargo as an ineffective coercive weapon. Spivak, *Jefferson's English Crisis,* 181–84.

73. Matthew Lyon cited the preservation of the Republican Party from Federalist inroads, which had manifested in the 1808 elections, and the need to preserve the Union as justification for abandoning a policy which thus far had not worked. *AC,* 10th Cong., 2nd sess., 551–54.

74. Doron Ben-Atar summarizes the literature nicely, suggesting it was a "culmination of Jefferson's long-held [Anglophobic] commercial views." Ben-Atar, *Commercial Policy,* 164–168. Louis Sears, *Jefferson and the Embargo* (1927; New York: Octagon Books, 1966), 29; Lawrence S. Kaplan, "Jefferson, the Napoleonic Wars, and the Balance of Power," *William and Mary Quarterly,* 3rd ser., 14 (April 1957): 200. For generally complementary accounts of the debates, see Spivak, *Jefferson's English Crisis,* and Perkins, *Prologue to War.*

75. See furious debates in Congress from February 1 to 22, esp. the vote on Troup's Resolution, *AC,* 10th Cong., 2nd sess., 1332. Spivak, *Jefferson's English Crisis,* 190–95.

76. See February 3rd and 24th votes, *AC,* 10th Cong., 2nd sess.

77. Crawford, *AC,* 11th Cong., 2nd sess., 541–43; William Bibb (Ga.), ibid., 1341–54; Macon, ibid., 541–43.

78. Sears argues that it was "fair to say that the embargo contributed the final blow to the old tide-water prosperity, no substitute for which was ever found in the region." In his analysis southerners accepted Jefferson with "simple trust." Sears, *Jefferson and the Embargo,* 125–26.

79. Ibid., 240.

80. Bacon to Story, January 22, 1809, Joseph Story Papers, MSS, Library of Congress, cited in Perkins, *Prologue to War,* 227–28. Bacon voted against nonintercourse to support Jefferson and because he considered the policy to be unenforceable. Bacon, *AC,* 10th Cong., 2nd sess., 1270–88.

81. Historians have too frequently homogenized agricultural interests. Though generally sharing many common interests—prodebtor policies and favorable land policies—different market orientations can lead to divergent policy choices.

82. Crawford, *AC,* 10th Cong., 2nd sess., 63–65.

83. William Burwell (Va.), ibid., 618. Gallatin made the same point in his analysis of the embargo, as did George Washington Campbell, chairman of the House Foreign Affairs Committee.

84. In the Senate, Crawford stated it bluntly: "Whenever we repeal the embargo we are at war or we abandon our neutral rights. It is impossible to take the middle ground, and say that we do not abandon them by trading with Great Britain alone." Crawford, *AC,* 10th Cong., 2nd sess., 63–65.

85. Crawford to Thomas Carr, February 20, 1809, cited in Richard Brown, *The Republic in Peril* (New York: Norton, 1971), 48.

86. G. W. Campbell summarizing Williams, *AC,* 10th Cong., 2nd sess., 1483.

87. Not to be confused with Virginia's John Taylor of Caroline County. Senate Debate: *AC,* 11th Cong., 1st and 2nd sess., 604–9, 579–82.

88. Randolph, ibid., 1469, 1508–9.

89. Cited in Chase Mooney, *William Crawford* (Lexington: University Press of Kentucky, 1974), 33.

90. Troup, 10th Cong., 2nd sess., 605. D. R. Williams of South Carolina continued to support the embargo but was so irritated with northern merchants that he moved for immediate repeal so as to keep icebound northern ships from capturing a monopoly of the shipping of southern trade. Spivak, *Jefferson's English Crisis,* 190.

91. David Ramsay, *History of South Carolina,* 2 vols. (1858; Spartanburg: Reprint Company, 1960), 2: 136.

92. Cited in Mooney, *William Crawford,* 33.

93. Daniels, "Cotton Trade under the Embargo," 281–82.

94. See South Carolina debates, Jonathan Elliot, *The Debates in the Several State Conventions on the Adoption of the Federal Constitution* (Philadelphia: J. B. Lippincott, 1836–1859), 4: 253–341.

95. Troup to Governor Mitchell, March 17, 1810, letter reprinted in Edward Harden, *The Life of George Troup* (Savannah: E. J. Purse, 1859), 94–96. Troup joined the emerging war party in 1810.

96. *AC,* 11th Cong., 2nd sess., 1161–64.

97. Maryland's representative, Samuel Smith, led the Senate opposition, killing the bill. This generally has been perceived as revenge against the Madison administration.

It is entirely likely, however, that it was economic interest, as the indirect trade had been the safest and most lucrative trade under nonintercourse.

98. Perkins, *Prologue to War,* 226–34; Stagg, *Mr. Madison's War,* 7–14.

99. Cited in Brown, *Republic in Peril,* 47.

100. Cited in Perkins, *Prologue to War,* 244.

101. Liverpool prices from Daniels, "Cotton Trade under the Embargo," 287.

102. Margaret I. Manigault to Alice Izard, February 1809, December 1, 1811, Ralph Izard Papers, 2, 3, Library of Congress, cited in Margaret Kinard Latimer, "South Carolina—A Protagonist of the War of 1812," *American Historical Review,* 61, no. 4 (July 1956): 925.

103. Cited in Latimer, "South Carolina," 923.

104. Speech of December 12, 1811, *AC,* 12th Cong., 1st sess., 477.

105. Speech of January 6, 1812, *AC,* 12th Cong., 1st sess., 686.

106. Robert L. Meriwether et al., eds., *The Papers of John C. Calhoun* (hereafter *PJCC*) (Columbia: University of South Carolina Press, 1959–2003), 1: 83.

107. The treasury report referred to is available in *American State Papers, Commerce and Navigation,* 1: 645, 662.

108. "Speech on the Report of the Foreign Relations Committee," December 12, 1811, *PJCC,* 1: 76–77. Steven Watt's *The Republic Reborn: War and the Making of Liberal America, 1790–1820* (Baltimore: Johns Hopkins University Press, 1987) provides a detailed analysis of this committee, arguing for its aggressively liberal bent.

109. "Report on Relations with Great Britain," November 29, 1811, *PJCC,* 1: 63–69.

110. Cited in Brown, *Republic in Peril,* 49.

111. *AC,* 12th Cong., 1281–1312, 1511, 1539 (June 19, 1812).

112. Calhoun to Patrick Calhoun, January 24, 1812, *PJCC,* 1: 89–90; also Calhoun to Patrick Noble, March 22, 1812, *PJCC,* 1: 95–96 and June 17, 1812, 1: 126; to Virgil Maxcy, May 2, 1812, *PJCC,* 1: 101.

113. In the final vote for war, party mattered more than section, but only three southern Republicans, John Randolph of Virginia, and Richard Stanford and Archibald McBryde, both of North Carolina, opposed war. Brown, *Republic in Peril,* 45, also 73. Ronald Hatzenbuehler affirms the necessity of party unity. "Party Unity and the Decision for War in the House of Representatives, 1812," *William and Mary Quarterly* 29, no. 3 (July 1972): 367–90. Norman Risjord has noted that agrarian groups in the West and South were the earliest to come over to war and provided critical leadership. Risjord, *Old Republicans,* 120–22. For Crawford's turn to war, see Philip J. Green, "William H. Crawford and the War of 1812," *Georgia Historical Quarterly* 26, no. 1 (March 1942): 16–39. See also Latimer, "South Carolina," 914–29.

114. See Risjord, *Old Republicans,* chap. 6.

115. The Monroe-Pinkney Treaty remained a nostalgic beacon for a peaceful resolution that gave some protection of neutral commercial rights without implementing a restrictive system premised on economic coercion. Hickey, "The Monroe-Pinkney Treaty"; Risjord, *Old Republicans,* 92–95. After Virginia's John Taylor of Caroline County read a published copy of the treaty, he believed it "to be a good one upon essential points." John Taylor to Wilson Cary Nicholas, May 10, 1808, Edgehill-Randolph Collection, University of Virginia, Charlottesville.

116. John C. Calhoun to Dr. James MacBride, February 16th, 1812, *PJCC,* 1: 90.

117. Quote from *AC*, 12th Cong., 1st sess., 1537. After first being blocked by the Senate, Madison successfully pursued an embargo in the House over the opposition of Calhoun and Langdon Cheves, who had always opposed the "restrictive" system.

118. Daniels, "Cotton Trade under the Embargo," 278.

119. Stuart Bruchey, *Cotton and the Growth of the American Economy, 1790–1860: Sources and Readings* (New York: Harcourt, Brace & World, 1967), Table 3.A.

120. The majority of southern Republicans supported the measure—in part as a desperate attempt to find a focused policy to bring the war to a close. A few diehard war hawks, including half of Georgia's delegation, continued to support restriction. All of South Carolina's delegation voted against it (with one abstention). Virginia had two people still embracing nonintercourse, with a handful of abstentions. See Stagg, *Mr. Madison's War*, 318–19 and 364–44, and for vote, see Thomas Abernethy, *The South and the Nation*, 420.

121. Rothman, *Slave Country*, 119–216.

122. James Lewis Jr. has adopted the terms *active* and *passive* to distinguish between nationalists who advocated more consolidation within the federal government from those who, though still nationalist, continued to embrace decentralization. *The Problem of Neighborhood: The United States and the Collapse of the Spanish Empire, 1783–1829* (Chapel Hill: University of North Carolina Press, 1998).

123. Coxe, *Statement of the Arts and Manufactures.*

124. Adam Seybert, *AC*, 11th Cong., 2nd sess., 1891–1900.

125. Kentucky hemp and Louisiana raw sugar contributed to vibrant manufacturers in those states. Norris W. Preyer, "Southern Support of the Tariff of 1816: A Reappraisal," *Journal of Southern History* 25, no. 2 (August 1959): 306–22. Most National Republicans were uncertain enough about manufacturers' viability in places where they already existed, much less in those areas in which they had no comparative advantage.

126. Secretary of the treasury William Crawford of Georgia, for example, supported protection only so long as it coincided with revenue needs. When he foresaw protection for its own sake, his support stalled. Mooney, *William Crawford*, 166–67.

127. *AC*, 14th Cong., 1st sess., 1335–36.

128. Ibid., 1336.

129. Ibid., 1330. In rebuttal Taylor of Caroline County later argued that the policies of bounties and protective tariffs for the creation of a stronger army or central government confused the order of things by assuming that war was the natural state of things. John Taylor, *Tyranny Unmasked*, Thornton Miller, ed., (Indianapolis: Liberty Press, 1992).

130. Calhoun, *AC*, 14th Cong., 1st sess., 1334.

131. Telfair's arguments against the tariff can be found in *AC*, 14th Cong., 1st sess., 1316–20, quote from 1319.

132. Ibid.

133. Taylor, *Arator*, ed. M. E. Bradford (Indianapolis: Liberty Fund, 1977). nos. 4–7.

134. The best accounts of postwar reciprocity agreements, including the Convention of 1815 remain, Setser, *Commercial Reciprocity*, and Perkins, *Adams and Castlereagh* (Berkeley: University of California Press, 1964), 167–71 and 259–82, and George Dangerfield, *The Era of Good Feelings* (New York: Harcourt, Brace, 1952).

135. Telfair: "A change from peace to war necessarily injures the immediate interests of commerce and agriculture; a return of peace alike injures those institutions which grow amid the circumstances of war. Is the nation, after all these changes and effects, to hold itself as bound to compensate the losses of those who may have suffered [from peace]?" *AC*, 14th Cong., 1st sess., 1317. Taylor, *Arator;* William Strickland, *Observations on the Agriculture of the United States of America* (London: W. Bulmer & Co., 1801). Taylor wrote his essays in opposition to Strickland's claim that American agricultural prospects were hopeless, but he agreed that serious problems existed, blaming them primarily on redistributive policies and poor land management.

136. *AC*, 14th Cong., 1st sess., 1320.

137. *AC*, 14th Cong., 1st sess., 1319.

138. Calhoun, ibid., 1330–36.

139. Bruchey, *Cotton and the Growth of the American Economy*, Table 3.A.

140. Quoted in Daniels, "Cotton Trade under the Embargo," 284.

141. *AC*, 14th Cong., 2nd sess., 769. House of Representatives Bill no. 32, http://memory.loc.gov/cgi-bin/ampage?collId=llhb&fileName=046/llhb046.db&recNum=599; Lowndes amendments offered January 29, 1817 [bill misdated], http://memory.loc.gov/cgi-bin/ampage?collId=llhb&fileName=046/llhb046.db&recNum=732.

142. "Speech on the Loan Bill," February 25, 1814, *PJCC*, 1: 208–40, quote from 217.

143. Important studies on Calhoun include Merrill Peterson's *The Great Triumvirate: Webster, Clay and Calhoun* (New York: Oxford University Press, 1987); Charles M. Wiltse, *John C. Calhoun: Nationalist, 1782–1828* and *John C. Calhoun: Nullifier, 1829–1839* (Indianapolis: Bobbs-Merrill, 1944, 1949) vols. 1 and 2; John Nevin, *John C. Calhoun and the Price of Union* (Baton Rouge: Louisiana State University Press, 1988).

144. Troup to Governor Mitchell of Georgia, March 17, 1810, reprinted in Harden, *Life of Troup*, 94–96.

145. Historians like William Freehling and others have suggested that southern nationalist thought was qualified from the beginning. While this seems to have been true when slavery came to be endangered, before such a threat seriously existed those in the Lower South willingly embraced Republican nationalism. *Prelude to Civil War: The Nullification Controversy in South Carolina, 1816–1836* (New York: Harper & Row, 1966).

146. Calhoun to Francis Wharton, May 28, 1844, *PJCC*, 18: 648–50, and Senate speech, "Further Remarks on the Case of the Brig," April 15, 1840, *PJCC*, 15: 177–80, quote from 179–80.

147. Mason paints Jefferson's embargo and the experience of the War of 1812 as a pivotal moment in forwarding northern, especially Federalist, antislavery sentiment. See Mason, *Slavery and Politics*, 42–74. If correct, this further suggests how central the commercial and diplomatic developments discussed here were, the dynamics of which are only tangentially related to slavery.

CHAPTER THREE: Protecting Slavery and Free Trade

1. "Slavery and Political Economy," *De Bow's Review* 21, no. 5 (November 1856): 445–46. Authorship attributed in Michael O'Brien, *Conjectures of Order* (Chapel Hill: University of North Carolina Press, 2004), 2: 888.

2. O'Brien, *Conjectures of Order,* 877.

3. Adam Smith, *An Inquiry into the Nature and Causes of the Wealth of Nations* (London: W. Strahan, 1776), reprinted and edited. by R. K. Campbell and A. S. Skinner (Indianapolis: Liberty Fund, 1981), 1: 428.

4. Dating back to Arthur Schlesinger's classic study of the Jacksonian period, studies of this period have frequently focused on alleged transformations wrought by what has more recently been called a market revolution and have generally focused on class and/or the bank war as the defining issue. See, for example, Schlesinger, *The Age of Jackson* (Boston: Little, Brown, 1945); Charles Sellers's *The Market Revolution: Jacksonian America, 1815–1846* (New York: Oxford University Press, 1991); James Roger Sharp, *The Jacksonians versus the Banks: Politics in the States after the Panic of 1837* (New York: Columbia University Press, 1970); and Sean Wilentz, *The Rise of American Democracy: Jefferson to Lincoln* (New York: Norton, 2005). Recent discussion of the tariffs have almost exclusively focused on South Carolina (assuming exceptionalism) and have subsumed that debate under discussions of slavery. William Freehling, *Prelude to Civil War: The Nullification Controversy in South Carolina, 1816–1836* (New York: Oxford University Press, 1992), and *Road to Disunion,* vol. 1, *Secessionists at Bay* (New York: Oxford University Press, 1990); Manisha Sinha, *The Counterrevolution of Slavery: Politics and Ideology in Antebellum South Carolina* (Chapel Hill: University of North Carolina Press, 2000); Robert Pierce Forbes, *The Missouri Compromise and Its Aftermath: Slavery and the Meaning of America* (Chapel Hill: University of North Carolina Press, 2007). For taxation policy more generally seen through the lens of slavery, see Robin Einhorn, *American Taxation, American Slavery* (Chicago: University of Chicago Press, 2006). Two notable exceptions are Richard Ellis's excellent study of the constitutional debates raised during this era, *The Union at Risk: Jacksonian Democracy, States' Rights, and the Nullification Crisis* (New York: Oxford University Press, 1987), and Donald J. Ratcliffe, "The Nullification Crisis, Southern Discontents, and the American Political Process," *American Nineteenth Century History* 1, no. 2 (Summer 2000), 1–30.

5. Slaveholders' commitment to laissez-faire macroeconomic principles did not mean that they were opposed to "big government" at the local level. Indeed, their commitment to slavery forced them to construct quite extensive regulatory states, a point which students of American political development have only begun to grapple with. See Sally E. Hadden, *Slave Patrols: Law and Violence in Virginia and the Carolinas* (Cambridge: Harvard University Press, 2001); William J. Novak, *The People's Welfare: Law and Regulation in Nineteenth-Century America* (Chapel Hill: University of North Carolina Press, 1996).

6. Total figure from Alan Knight, "Britain and Latin America," in Andrew Porter, ed., *The Oxford History of the British Empire: The Nineteenth Century* (New York: Oxford University Press, 1999), 127; cotton figure from Ralph Davis, *The Industrial Revolution and British Overseas Trade* (Atlantic Highlands, N.J.: Humanities Press, 1979), 19.

7. Stuart Bruchey, *Cotton and the Growth of the American Economy, 1790–1860: Sources and Readings* (New York: Harcourt, Brace & World, 1967), tables 3.A (New York and Liverpool), 3.Q (Sea Island), and 3.R (Charleston short staple).

8. Cited in Daniel S. Dupre, *Transforming the Cotton Frontier: Madison County, Alabama, 1800–1840* (Baton Rouge: Louisiana State University Press, 1997), 41.

9. Bruchey, *Cotton and the Growth of the American Economy,* New Orleans, table 3.P.

10. Dupre's description of Madison County, Alabama, provides the best examination of the processes that transformed the Southwest into a vibrant agricultural and commercial region wed to the production of cotton. Dupre, *Transforming the Cotton Frontier.*

11. Bruchey, *Cotton and the Growth of the American Economy,* table 3.A.

12. Robert Greenhalgh Albion, *The Rise of New York Port, 1815–1860* (New York: Charles Scribner's Sons, 1939); Douglass North, *Economic Growth of the United States* (New York: Norton, 1961), 177, 179. Tonnage cited in George Dangerfield, *The Awakening of American Nationalism, 1815–1828* (New York: Harper & Row, 1965), 150.

13. Edwin J. Perkins, *Financing Anglo-American Trade: The House of Brown, 1800–1880* (Cambridge: Harvard University Press, 1975); Murray N. Rothbard, *The Panic of 1819: Reactions and Policies* (New York: Columbia University Press, 1962), 7–8; Larry Schweikart, *Banking in the American South from the Age of Jackson to Reconstruction* (Baton Rouge: Louisiana State University Press, 1987), tables 3, 4, 7, 8, 11; Albion, *Rise of New York Port.*

14. (Prices) North, *Economic Growth,* 137; (Volume) Timothy Pitkin, *A Statistical View of the Commerce of the United States of America* (New Haven: Durrie & Peck, 1835), 96–97.

15. Tobacco prices dropped from between $20 and $40 in 1815 and 1816 to $4 to $5 in June 1819. Charles S. Sydnor, *The Development of Southern Sectionalism, 1819–1948* (Baton Rouge: Louisiana State University Press, 1948), 104.

16. The value of total reexports rose from $7 million in 1816 to $17 million in 1817, but even this jump paled in comparison to the prewar peak of $65 million. Vernon Setser, *The Commercial Reciprocity Policy of the United States, 1774–1829* (1937; New York, Da Capo Press, 1969). Reexports cited in Rothbard, *Panic of 1819,* 6.

17. The ad valorem rate of 30% for cotton textiles set in 1817 had been reduced to 25% for the next two years but leveled off at 20%, close to the normal revenue duty.

18. *Mobile Gazette & Commercial Advertiser,* April 27, 1819. New Orleans prices: Bruchey, *Cotton and the Growth of the American Economy,* table 3.P. Charleston prices plummeted from 23 to 25.5 cents per pound in February 1819 to 14 to 18 cents per pound in April. Ibid., table 3.R. For a general discussion of panic, see Rothbard, *Panic of 1819,* 7–13; Daniel Dupre, "The Panic of 1819 and the Political Economy of Sectionalism," in *The Economy of Early America: Historical Perspectives and New Directions,* ed. Cathy Matson (University Park: Pennsylvania State University Press, 2006), 263–97. For the only comprehensive examination of the Panic of 1819, including its role in accelerating the protectionist movement, see Rothbard, *Panic of 1819,* 159–80. Sellers's *Market Revolution* also gives the panic and its consequences a good deal of coverage. For the depressing consequences of the panic on the Southeast and Southwest, see Sydnor, *Southern Sectionalism,* 104; Thomas P. Abernethy, "Andrew Jackson and the Rise of South-Western Democracy," *American Historical Review* 33, no. 1 (October 1927): 66–70; Daniel Dupre, "Ambivalent Capitalists on the Cotton Frontier: Settlement and Development in the Tennessee Valley of Alabama," *Journal of Southern History* 56, no. 2 (May 1990): 221. The branch of the Alexander Brown commercial house in New Orleans nearly closed due to overadvancement of credit but emerged

strong in the 1820s. See John R. Killick, "The Cotton Operations of Alexander Brown and Sons in the Deep South, 1820–1860," *Journal of Southern History* 43, no. 2 (May 1977): 176. The panic contributed to an industrial depression in manufacturing sectors that had drawn upon banks in order to get started. See Percy W. Bidwell, "The Agricultural Revolution in New England," *American Historical Review* 26, no. 4. (July 1921): 685. Some recent studies have traced the importance of the American System. See excellent works by John Larson, *Internal Improvement: National Public Works and the Promise of Popular Government in the Early United States* (Chapel Hill: University of North Carolina Press, 2001), and Maurice Baxter, *Henry Clay and the American System* (Lexington: University Press of Kentucky, 1995).

19. *Mobile Gazette & Commercial Advertiser,* April 27, 1819.

20. Reprinted in *Niles Register,* December 28, 1816, xi, 283–84; For original, see Hansard, "Parliamentary Debates," 33: 1098–99, *Proceedings in House of Commons,* April 9, 1819. Americans mainly read it in print copied from the *Edinburgh Review* 52 (June 1816): 2263–64.

21. Paul Conklin, *Prophets of Prosperity: America's First Political Economists* (Bloomington: Indiana University Press, 1980), 84.

22. Matthew Carey, *Addresses of the Philadelphia Society for the Promotion of National Industry,* 5th ed. (Philadelphia: James Maxwell, 1820), iv. See also the various petitions in *American State Papers, Class 3: Finance,* 16th Cong., 1st sess., cited in Carl Vipperman, *William Lowndes and the Transition of Southern Politics, 1782–1822* (Chapel Hill: University of North Carolina Press, 1989), 207. Robert Hayne called Carey, the "great father of the American System" in 1830. Herman Belz, ed., *The Webster-Hayne Debate on the Nature of the Union: Selected Documents* (Indianapolis: Liberty Fund, 2000), 47–48.

23. Condy Raguet to Matthew Carey, December 16, December 17, and December 30, 1819, Matthew Carey Papers, in Edward Carey Gardiner Collection, Historical Society of Pennsylvania, MSS F3, box 86. Jonathan Pincus provides an excellent, if somewhat overly deterministic, explanation of the tariffs of 1820 and 1824. *Pressure Groups and Politics in Antebellum Tariffs* (New York: Columbia University Press, 1977), 51–60. Taxes on cotton and woolens were to be raised from 25% to 33%. Edward Stanwood, *American Tariff Controversies in the Nineteenth Century* (Boston and New York: Houghton, Mifflin, 1903), 1: 181.

24. Matthew Mason, *Slavery and Politics in the Early American Republic* (Chapel Hill: University of North Carolina Press, 2006), 145–48, quote from 148.

25. Leonard L. Richards, *The Slave Power: The Free North and Southern Domination, 1780–1860* (Baton Rouge: Louisiana State University Press, 2000), 75.

26. Glover Moore, *The Missouri Controversy, 1819–1821* (Gloucester: P. Smith 1967), 179–257, quote from 218. For the general "lack of fervor over Missouri," see also the very important work by Forbes, *Missouri Compromise,* 50–51. Matthew Mason provides compelling evidence of northeastern and northwestern anger at Missouri's proslavery constitution. Yet his evidence for an immediate public outcry provides barely any southern examples, especially in the Lower South, perhaps indicating that Moore's assertion that Virginia, and not the Lower South, was the hotbed of antirestrictionism. *Slavery and Politics in the Early American Republic* (Chapel Hill: University of North Carolina Press, 2006), 177–212.

27. *Annals of Congress* (hereafter *AC*), 16th Cong., 1st sess., 239.

28. John Quincy Adams, *Memorials of John Quincy Adams*, Charles Francis Adams, ed. (Philadelphia: J. B. Lippincott, 1874–1877), 4: 525.

29. James E. Lewis, *The American Union and the Problem of Neighborhood: The United States and the Collapse of the Spanish Empire, 1783–1829* (Chapel Hill: University of North Carolina Press, 1998), 135.

30. Forbes emphasizes Monroe's role in *Missouri Compromise*, 123–24.

31. Claude H. Van Tyne, ed., *The Letters of Daniel Webster* (New York: McClure, Phillips, 1902), 83, in Moore, *Missouri Controversy*, 105–6. On Baldwin and Moore, see Forbes, *Missouri Compromise*, 81–82, 124.

32. Stanwood, *American Tariff Controversies*, 1: 192–93.

33. Henry Clay, "Speech on Tariff," April 26, 1820, reprinted in James F. Hopkins and Mary W. M. Hargreaves, eds., *The Papers of Henry Clay* (Lexington: University of Kentucky Press, 1959–), 2: 836.

34. Thomas Jefferson to Benjamin Austin, January 9, 1816, in Merrill D. Peterson, ed. *Writings: Thomas Jefferson* (New York: Literary Classics of the United States, 1984), 1369–71.

35. Merrill Peterson, *The Great Triumvirate: Webster, Clay, and Calhoun* (New York: Oxford University Press, 1987), 54, 57, 58, makes this linkage. See also Lewis, *American Union and the Problem of Neighborhood*.

36. Norris W. Preyer, "Southern Support of the Tariff of 1816—A Reappraisal," *Journal of Southern History* 25, no. 3 (August 1959): 306–22. For Lowndes's role in both 1816 and 1819, and perhaps the most detailed account of Baldwin's bill, see Vipperman, *William Lowndes*, 126–34 and 201–32. Also Chase Mooney, *William Crawford* (Lexington: University Press of Kentucky, 1974), 153–55; Charles M. Wiltse, *John C. Calhoun: Nationalist, 1782–1828* (Indianapolis: Bobbs-Merrill, 1944), 291. Southerners in the House voted against the 1820 tariff bill 50 to 3. In the Senate it was 15 to 1. See Pincus, *Pressure Groups and Politics*, 62–63. Glover Moore mistakenly sees the debate surrounding the question as an end to southern liberalism and enlightenment thought. *Missouri Controversy*, 348. See also Sydnor, *Southern Sectionalism*, passim; Don Fehrenbacher, "The Missouri Controversy and the Sources of Southern Sectionalism," in *Sectional Crisis and Southern Constitutionalism* (Baton Rouge: Louisiana State University Press, 1980).

37. Forbes, *Missouri Compromise*, 167.

38. Lowndes, *AC*, 16th Cong., 1st sess., 2115–17, 2125.

39. *AC*, 16th Cong., 1st sess., 2118.

40. It was not a "reasonable theory, but a notorious fact" that "the price of agricultural products must be determined by that part of them which is exported and thus would not be effected by duties or prohibitions." *AC*, 16th Cong., 1st sess., 2116–18.

41. John A. James's examination of the economics of the antebellum tariffs suggests that Lowndes and others were right, if not necessarily for the same reasons. "The Optimal Tariff in the Antebellum United States," *American Economic Review* 71, no. 4 (September 1981): 726–34, esp. 733.

42. Lowndes, *AC*, 16th Cong., 1st sess., 2125–26, 2131–32.

43. Ibid.

44. "Remonstrance against an Increase of Duties on Imports," *American State Papers, Class 3: Finance,* 16th Cong., 2nd sess., no. 600, 3: 563–67 (hereafter "Charleston Remonstrance, 1820").

45. See *City Gazette* (Charleston), September, 1, 1820, for the calling of the meeting and authorship of the petition. Theodore D. Jervey, *Robert Y. Hayne and His Times* (New York: Da Capo Press, 1970), 71, 106–8.

46. Though "political economy" principles were implicit in many of the arguments and Charlestonians were undoubtedly familiar with Adam Smith, the "dismal science's" theories and practitioners were not explicitly referenced in the 1820 petition. John Taylor's *Tyranny Unmasked*—the first major American tract against protection—was not published until 1822. Thomas Cooper, in *On the Proposed Alteration of the Tariff* (Charleston: A. E. Miller, 1823), referred back to the memorial, noting that it contained many of the general arguments similar to what he was writing about. See Dumas Malone, *The Public Life of Thomas Cooper, 1783–1839* (Columbia: University of South Carolina Press, 1961), 291. In 1824 petitions from Charleston and Beaufort recalled the 1820 memorial, reaffirming it entirely. In a public speech given in 1831, shortly after Elliot's death, Hayne referred to Elliot's critical role in composing the petition. See Jervey, *Robert Y. Hayne,* 107. In 1846 an article in the *Southern Quarterly* also harkened back to the *Columbia Telescope* and Elliot's 1820 memorial as the moment when the South awoke to the dangers of protectionism. *Southern Quarterly Review* 9, no. 18: 392–44.

47. "Charleston Remonstrance, 1820," 563, 565.

48. Ibid., 565.

49. "Memorial of the Inhabitants of Darlington," read March 3, 1824, *American State Papers, Class 3: Finance,* 18th Cong., 1st sess., no. 101.

50. "Memorial of Sundry Citizens of Putnam County in the State of Georgia," presented March 11, 1824, *American State Papers, Class 3: Finance,* 18th Cong., 1st sess. no. 114.

51. "Charleston Remonstrance, 1820," 565.

52. "Memorial of the Citizens of Madison, in Morgan County, in the State of Georgia," March 8, 1824, *American State Papers, Class 3: Finance,* 18th Cong., 1st sess., no. 110.

53. "Memorial of the Inhabitants of Darlington."

54. "Memorial of the Inhabitants of the City of Darien, in the State of Georgia," *American State Papers, Class 3: Finance,* 18th Cong., 1st sess., no. 98.

55. Ranklin, *AC,* 18th Cong., 1st sess., 2009–2010 (quote). Hamilton, ibid., 2196. See also James Hamilton, who cited a petition from Sea Island planters in Beaufort, South Carolina, which argued that the reduced British market resulting from a high protective tariff would "annihilate their income" because "the manufacturing establishments of our country furnish no demand whatever" for the fine species of cotton they cultivated. *AC,* 18th Cong., 1st sess., 2: 2194–95. For actual statistics, see Bruchey, *Cotton and the Growth of the American Economy,* 3.A.

56. Thomas Cooper, *Lectures on the Elements of Political Economy* (Columbia: M'Morris & Wilson, 1830, reprinted New York: Augustus M. Kelley, 1971), 127–38. For a very good discussion of Cooper's thoughts on political economy, see O'Brien, *Conjectures of Order,* 2: 895–906, "proponent of modernity" quote from 896.

57. "Memorial of the Inhabitants of the City of Darien, in the State of Georgia."

58. "Against an Increase of the Duties on Imports and a System of Internal Improvements, Report of Legislature of Georgia on the Rights of States under Constitution" communicated to Congress February 6, 1828, *American State Papers, Class 3: Finance*, 20th Cong., 1st sess., no. 849, 5: 855, 852.

59. Barbour, *AC*, 18th Cong., 1st sess., 2: 1923–24.

60. D. P. O'Brien, *The Classical Economists* (Oxford: Clarendon Press, 1975), esp. 30; James Hamilton *AC*, 18th Cong., 1st sess., 2: 2180.

61. Quote from "Charleston Remonstrance, 1820," 563. See also Barbour (Va.), 18th Cong., 1st sess., 1923–24.

62. Whereas a more optimistic Ricardo had deemphasized nature's significance in his critique of Malthus, American free traders simply rejected the terms of the particular debate raging in Europe in the early nineteenth century. Quotes from Jacob Cardozo, *Notes on Political Economy* (Charleston: A. E. Miller, 1826; reprinted New York: Augustus M. Kelley, 1960), 5–6.

63. "Speech of Governor Stephen Miller to the Legislature," reprinted in the *United States Telegraph* (Washington, D.C.), December 4, 1829. Both Clay and Carey supported the idea that the American System would aid slaveholders by creating a southern industrial economy and investing northern manufacturers in slavery. Matthew Carey, *Miscellaneous Essays: Containing, among a variety of other articles, history of the yellow fever which prevailed in Philadelphia in the year . . .* (Philadelphia: Carey & Hart, 1830), 232–34, bound collection at the Library Company of Philadelphia.

64. "Speech of Christopher Rankin," April 1 and 2, 1824, reprinted in *Daily National Intelligencer* (Washington, D.C.), April 23, 1824.

65. "Charleston Remonstrance, 1820."

66. James, "The Optimal Tariff in the Antebellum United States," 726–34.

67. Miller, *United States Telegraph*, December 4, 1829, emphasis added.

68. Historians like William Freehling have seen the Negro Seaman's controversy, quite understandably, in light of future events. Freehling, *Prelude to Civil War*. For one of the most recent and analytically rich discussions of the law which, like its predecessors, partially distorts its meaning by failing to provide proper context for the acts, see Forbes, *Missouri Compromise*. To a considerable extent, however, the South Carolina act—and mostly forgotten subsequent acts passed throughout the Lower South—reflected but one stage in the protracted ambiguity about slavery's place within a federated system of local, state, and national governments. The most thorough examination of the acts remains Alan January's unpublished dissertation, "The First Nullification: The Negro Seamen Acts Controversy in South Carolina, 1822–1860" (Ph.D. diss., University of Iowa, 1976).

69. [Benjamin F. Hunt], *The Argument of Benjamin Faneiul Hunt, in the Case of the Arrest of . . . a British Seaman* (Charleston: A. E. Miller, 1823), 7–9, 12, 16. For the legal issues related to the case and Johnson's ruling, I have leaned heavily on Scott Wallace Stucky, "*Elkison v. Deliesseline*: Race and the Constitution in South Carolina, 1823," *North Carolina Central Law Journal* 14 (1983–84): 361–405; Philip M. Hamer, "Great Britain, the United States, and the Negro Seamen Acts, 1822–1848," *Journal of Southern History* 1, no. 1 (February 1935): 3–28, esp. 6–7; Philip M. Hamer, "British

Consuls and the Negro Seamen's Acts, 1850–1860," *Journal of Southern History* 1, no. 2 (May 1935): 138–68.

70. David Lightner, *Slavery and the Commerce Power: How the Struggle against the Interstate Slave Trade Led to the Civil War* (New Haven: Yale University Press, 2006), 66–69. The Supreme Court affirmed the policing power in the 1837 *New York v. Milne*, giving southern states a stronger legal justification for the acts.

71. Quote from Hamer, "Negro Seamen's Acts," 14–15.

72. Edwin Holland, *A Refutation of the Calumnies Circulated against the Southern & Western States* (1822; New York: Negro Universities Press, 1969), 61, 62, 86.

73. In the case of Savannah, African American berths fell from 15% to 9% in 1830 to only 2% by 1836. In New Orleans they fell from 10.8% in 1840 to only 1% by 1851, after Louisiana's 1844 act had been enforced for a number of years. All of this suggests that, criticism aside, the acts might have served their intended purpose of dissuading white shipowners from sending black sailors to southern ports. Because of the centrality of the cotton trade, it is possible that these acts, especially Louisiana's, might have even had a ripple effect, which helps to explain a larger increase in white majorities on all vessels in the 1840s. Jeffrey Bolster, *Black Jacks: African American Seamen in the Age of Sail* (Cambridge: Harvard University Press, 1997), table 1, 235–39.

74. Cooper, *On the Proposed Alteration of the Tariff.*

75. *AC,* 18th Cong., 1st sess., 2019–20.

76. Nicholas Onuf and Peter Onuf, *Nations, Markets, and War* (Charlottesville: University of Virginia Press, 2006), 247–77.

77. Carter (S.C.), *AC,* 18th Cong. 1st sess., 2158.

78. South Carolina representative James Hamilton, *AC,* 18th Cong., 1st sess., 2: 2178.

79. Cooper, *Lectures on the Elements of Political Economy,* 30.

80. Ibid., 30.

81. Cooper, *On the Proposed Alteration of the Tariff,* 12–13.

82. Ibid., 12–13.

83. Not by chance did Henry Clay title his reprinted 1832 congressional speeches, *In Defence of the American System Against the British Colonial System* (Washington: Gales & Seaton, 1832).

84. For an insightful analysis of the debates demonstrating the geographic distinctions and highlighting the importance of the Corn Laws, see British Ambassador's letter to Canning, T. U. Addington to Canning, Washington May 30, 1824, London Public Record Office, Foreign Office Papers 5/185.

85. To Calhoun's disappointment Tazewell had recently declined a post as minister to England, where Calhoun thought he could advance the free trade cause. Calhoun to L. W. Tazewell, April 14, 1829, in Robert L. Meriwether et al., eds., *The Papers of John C. Calhoun* (hereafter *PJCC*) (Columbia: University of South Carolina Press, 1959–2003), 10: 23. He expressed the same sentiment to recently appointed U.S. minister to France, William Rives, June 21, 1829, *PJCC,* 11: 55.This is not to suggest that those in the Lower South were Anglophiles, though in some instances they did come close. For example, W. W. Boyce, "Direct Taxation and Free Trade," *De Bow's Review* 25, no. 1 (July 1858): 23: "Standing as Great Britain does at the head of the great movement of civilization administered as her government is with such profound wisdom,

her example, in this particular [free trade] commands our attention, and her remarkable success invites our cooperation." The actual policy of Tory governments can be traced in Boyd Hilton's *Corn, Cash, Commerce: The Economic Policies of the Tory Governments, 1815–1830* (New York: Oxford University Press, 1977).

86. Calhoun to Samuel D. Ingham, October 30, 1830, *PJCC*, 11: 252.

87. The cotton-centered assumptions of Lower South political economists forecasted those presented by Douglass North, who argued that "the demands for western foodstuffs and northeastern services and manufactures were basically dependent upon the income received from the cotton trade." See North, *Economic Growth*, 67. Subsequent historians have, with some effectiveness, challenged this claim, showing that interregional trade was more limited and the South more self-sufficient then previously thought, at least in the later antebellum period. See Diane Lindstrom, *Economic Development in the Philadelphia Region, 1810–1850* (New York: Columbia University Press, 1971); and "Southern Dependence upon Interregional Grain Supplies," in William Parker, ed., *The Structure of the Cotton Economy of the Antebellum South* (Washington D.C., 1970); also, Robert Gallman, "Self-Sufficiency in the Cotton Economy of the Antebellum South," in ibid.; Lawerence Herbst, *Interregional Commodity Trade from the North to the South and American Economic Development in the Antebellum Period,* (New York: Arno Press, 1978); Paul J. Uselding, "A Note on the Inter-Regional Trade in Manufactures in 1840," *Journal of Economic History* 36, no. 2 (June 1976): 428–35; Albert Fishlow, "Antebellum Interregional Trade Reconsidered," *American Economic Review* 54, no. 3 (May 1964): 352–64.

88. "Charleston Remonstrance, 1820"; Albion, *Rise of New York Port*, 95–121, and *Square-Riggers on Schedule: The New York Sailing Packets to England, France, and the Cotton Ports* (Princeton: Princeton University Press, 1938). For shipping statistics, see William W. Bates, *American Marine: The Shipping Question in History and Politics* (New York: Houghton, Mifflin, 1892), 34.

89. "Memorial of the Inhabitants of St. Luke's Parish," South Carolina, April 5, 1824, *American State Papers, Class 3: Finance,* 18th Cong., 1st sess., no. 124.

90. McDuffie, *AC,* 18th Cong. 1st sess., 1: 1677–78, and on manufacturing activity, see Lacy K. Ford Jr., *Origins of Southern Radicalism: The South Carolina Upcountry, 1800–1860* (New York: Oxford University Press, 1988), 64.

91. Joseph Persky, *The Burden of Dependency: Colonial Themes in Southern Economic Thought* (Baltimore: Johns Hopkins University Press, 1992), 53.

92. Though in its final analysis, protectionism represented a break from traditional calculations of national wealth, critics believed the rhetoric and remedies its supporters sought harked back to monopolistic and mercantilist policies. This concept is explored in Conklin, *Prophets of Prosperity,* and with greater sophistication in Onuf and Onuf, *Nations, Markets, War,* chaps. 8 and 9.

93. George McDuffie, *AC,* 18th Cong., 1st sess., 1495–97, 1552–57.

94. Bruchey, *Cotton and the Growth of the American Economy,* tables 3.A, 3.P.

95. Such an analysis would be used by southerners as they replayed the tariff debates. See, for example, William Harper and Thomas R. Dew "Communication in Relation to the Memorial of the Committee of the Free Trade Convention against the Tariff," 22nd Cong., 1st sess., annex to doc. no. 82, February 13, 1832.

96. Hamilton, *AC,* 18th Cong., 1st sess., 2177.

97. For example, J. D. B. De Bow, "The Progress of American Commerce," *De Bow's Review* 2, no. 6 (December 1846): 408.

98. The Boston-based *North American Review* continued to oppose protective tariffs until the Woolens Bill of 1827. See, for example, "The Tariff Question," *North American Review* 19, no. 44 (July 1824): 223–53, esp. 246.

99. "One of the People" [George McDuffie], *National and States Rights, Considered by "One of the People," in Reply to the "Trio"* (Charleston, 1821).

100. Daniel Feller, *The Public Lands in Jacksonian Politics* (Madison: University of Wisconsin Press, 1984), 64–66, 89.

101. *AC,* 18th Cong., 1st sess., 2: 2025.

102. North, *Economic Growth,* charts 1–11, 137.

103. John Taylor, *Tyranny Unmasked,* ed. Thornton Miller (Indianapolis: Liberty Press, 1992), 167–68, quotes from "Charleston Remonstrance, 1820," 567.

104. *American State Papers, Class 3: Finance,* 20th Cong., 1st sess., 5: 829.

105. Alabama Legislative Acts, Annual Sessions, November 22, 1826–January 13, 1827, 120–21, resolutions approved January 13, 1827, www.legislature.state.al.us/misc/history/acts_and_journals/1826/acts/Resolutions.html (accessed March 29, 2007).

106. Cited in Feller, *Public Lands,* 104.

107. Call for a Public Meeting, *Charleston Mercury,* reprinted in *United States Telegraph,* June 30, 1827.

108. Thomas Cooper, "Value of the Union" Speech, July 2, 1827, reprinted in William Freehling, *The Nullification Era: A Documentary Record* (New York: Harper Torchbooks, 1967), quotes from 20–21, 24–25. Originally published in *Niles Weekly Register* 33 (September 8, 1827): 28–32, quote from 25.

109. Robert J. Turnbull, "The Crisis," 1827, reprinted in Freehling, *Nullification Era,* 26–47. Originally published in the summer of 1827 in the *Charleston Mercury* under the pen name Brutus.

110. "Memorial of the Inhabitants of the City of Darien."

111. *American State Papers, Class 3: Finance,* 20th Cong., 1st sess., 5: 852–57.

112. Ibid.

113. General Assembly of Alabama's Joint Remonstrance against the Increase of Duties on Imports, communicated February 4, 1828, *American State Papers, Class 3: Finance,* 20th Cong., 1st sess., 5: 848–49.

114. For a general discussion of this, see George Dangerfield, *The Era of Good Feelings* (New York: Harcourt, Brace, 1952), 402–12; also John Niven, *John C. Calhoun and the Price of Union: A Biography* (Baton Rouge: Louisiana State University Press, 1988), 154–99. It has been debated whether Van Buren intended the tariff bill to fail or not. Robert Remini provides solid evidence that he did not while also stressing its importance for Van Buren's party vision. "Martin Van Buren and the Tariff of Abominations," *American Historical Review* 63 (July 1958): 903–17, and *Martin Van Buren and the Making of the Democratic Party* (New York: Columbia University Press, 1959), 129–46. Joel H. Sibley suggests that the tariff was more a thorn than an opportunity, as Van Buren struggled to find a "middle way." *Martin Van Buren and the Emergence of American Popular Politics* (New York: Rowman & Littlefield, 2002), 52–53. Recent histories have challenged the idea that there was a "plot." Donald B. Cole, *Martin Van Buren and the American Political System* (Princeton: Princeton University Press,

1984), 167–68. Suffice it to say, however, that South Carolinians like Calhoun and McDuffie did not see the tariff as legitimate but supported it in hopes of killing the protective system.

115. Calhoun, "Exposition and Protest," December 19, 1828, in Ross M. Lence, ed., *Union and Liberty: The Political Philosophy of John C. Calhoun* (Indianapolis: Liberty Fund, 1992). Calhoun waited until he was forced to come into the open in 1831, though his supporters pushed nullification hard in 1830. Freehling, *Road to Disunion*, 1: 275.

116. Open letter reprinted in *Statesman & Gazette* (Natchez), November 20, 1828.

117. Donald J. Ratcliffe, "The Crisis of Commercialization: National Political Alignments and the Market Revolution, 1819–1844," in Melvyn Stokes and Stephen Conway, *The Market Revolution in America: Social, Political, and Religious Expressions, 1800–1880* (Charlottesville: University of Virginia Press, 1996), 181–83.

118. For a good discussion on the economic and cultural components of this debate, see James David Miller, *South by Southwest: Planter Emigration and Identity in the Slave South* (Charlottesville: University of Virginia Press, 2002), esp. 39–59; Feller, *Public Lands*, esp. chap. 8.

119. *Register of Debates in Congress* (Washington, D.C.: Gales & Seaton, 1825–1837), 21st Cong., 1st sess., 22–27.

120. Adams to Alexander Everett, April 15, 1830, in *American Historical Review* 11 (January 1906): 335–36.

121. One of the earliest works to claim this was Woodrow Wilson, *Division and Reunion, 1829–1889* (New York: Longmans, Green, 1897), 43–44. The most critical speeches during this debate have been reassembled and reprinted in Belz, *Webster-Hayne*.

122. Interestingly, given his appreciation for the doctrine of state interposition, Hayne later softened his criticism of the Hartford Convention, noting that if gentlemen felt they had truly been abused they could have a "right to constitutional redress." Belz, *Webster-Hayne*, 57, 73–80, quote on 67.

123. Feller, *Public Lands*, 119–36.

124. Ibid., 118.

125. Ibid., 111–42.

126. Smith address reprinted in *Niles Register* 39 (December 4, 1830): 245.

127. *United States Telegraph* (Washington, D.C.), April 17, 1830. On praise bestowed, see Charleston "Meeting of the Free Trade and States' Rights Party," *United States Telegraph* (Washington, D.C.), August 10, 1831.

128. "Fort Hill Address," July 26, 1831, in *PJCC*, 2: 430.

129. See, for example, *Dover Gazette & Strafford Advertiser* (Dover, N.H.), August 9, 1831.

130. Condy Raguet, while a state representative of Harrisburg, Pennsylvania, had been employed by Matthew Carey as a congressional lobbyist for protection in 1820. After serving as a diplomat and merchant in South America and returning in 1827, he picked up the banner of free trade and became a loyal advocate of the South, even embracing nullification. A copy of the journal exists at the Library Company of Philadelphia.

131. "Address to the People of the United States," reprinted in *Journal of the Free Trade Convention* (Philadelphia: T. W. Ustick, 1831), 32–33.

132. See vote on October 7, 1831, *Journal of the Free Trade Convention*, 19–20.

133. See examples in Raguet, *Banner of the Constitution* (Philadelphia: Condy Raguet, 1831–32), 1831–1832. Some northerners like Philadelphian Raguet concurred with the southern economic assessment of the detriments of protection. As late as 1853, Israel Andrews proclaimed the "futility of warring against the natural laws governing trade and commerce . . . and the folly and presumption of any nation striving to establish for itself an exclusive and selfish monopoly or control of all things." From U.S. Congress, Senate, *Report of Israel D. Andrews . . . on Trade and Commerce of the British North American Colonies,* Senate Executive doc. no. 112, 32nd Cong., 1st sess., 1853 (Washington: Robert Armstrong Printer, 1853), 818–21, reprinted in Bruchey, *Cotton and the Growth of the American Economy,* 71–73.

134. Quote from *Daily National Intelligencer* (Washington, D.C.), October 10, 1831. *Daily National Journal* (Washington, D.C.), October 11, 1831.

135. John C. Calhoun to Francis Pickens, March 2, 1832, *PJCC,* 11: 558–59.

136. John C. Calhoun to James Edward Colhoun, February 26, 1832, *PJCC,* 11: 557.

137. Ratcliffe, "The Nullification Crisis," 12–13.

138. "Report of Alabama Legislature on the Tariff and Nullification," House Documents no. 141, 22nd Cong., 2nd sess.

139. Freehling, *Road to Disunion,* 1: 276–77.

140. Reprinted from "Western Carolina," in *United States Telegraph* (Washington, D.C.), November 1, 1832.

141. *State Papers on Nullification* (1834; New York: Da Capo Press, 1970), 222.

142. Ellis, *Union at Risk,* 102–22; Merrill D. Peterson, *Olive Branch and Sword: The Compromise of 1833* (Baton Rouge: Louisiana State University Press, 1982).

143. "Charleston Remonstrance, 1820," 565.

144. See the sympathetic resolutions of Alabama and Mississippi, which affirm their opposition to the tariff and suggest politicians in those states thought it violated the spirit of the Constitution, though they rejected nullification as a feasible measure. Alabama "Report" and "Resolves," *State Papers on Nullification,* 119–225; Mississippi "Report" and Resolves," ibid., 229–31.

145. Freehling, *Road to Disunion,* 1: 279; Ellis, *Union at Risk,* 185.

146. Recent historical analysis has given the impression that southern anxiety over antislavery motives, given the relative small number of abolitionists, stemmed from irrational fears. Such analysis fails to appreciate the real agency that potentially insurrectionist slaves had in creating legitimate economic concerns. Additionally, southern planters feared that in the long term, a national political economy, with the South in a peripheral place, could prevent the economic alliances necessary to protect slavery in the future.

CHAPTER FOUR: Building Bridges to the West and the World

1. *Baltimore Patriot,* July 23, 1836, cited in U. B. Phillips, *A History of Transportation in the Eastern Cotton Belt to 1860* (New York: Columbia University Press, 1908), 184.

2. In the 1820s, South Carolina's legislature actively sought to tie the state to the new capital at Columbia through a system of canal and river projects as well as the

creation of a "State Road" linking Charleston to Columbia. Phillips, *History of Transportation*, 88–93. By 1829, Georgia had overcome local jealousies to pass the Market Road Act, intended to coordinate municipal efforts to create a comprehensive state road system tying together the state's population centers. Under the leadership of Wilson Lumpkin, governor from 1831 to 1835, Georgia railroad companies were granted charters and invested. Milton Heath, *Constructive Liberalism: The Role of the State in Economic Development in Georgia* (Cambridge: Harvard University Press, 1954), 239–53.

3. For coverage of this event, see "Extract of a Letter from Liverpool, to a Gentleman in Savannah," *Mobile Gazette & Commercial Advertiser,* September 22, 1819.

4. The skill of English engineer, Horatio Allen, helped the South Carolina Canal & Railroad Company succeed in tying Charleston to the Savannah River by a 138-mile line. John F. Stover, *Iron Road to the West: American Railroads in the 1850s* (New York: Columbia University Press, 1978), 10. In 1833 the Eatonton project merged with efforts from Athens, Georgia, to create the "Union Railroad," a line that would join Augusta to the heaviest cotton-growing regions in the state. Reacting to these developments and fearing a direct line from the center of the state to Charleston, previously hesitant Savannah merchants sprang into action and mobilized to achieve a direct connection with the center of the state in Macon. Heath, *Constructive Liberalism,* 256–58.

5. The committee included archnullifers like James Hamilton and Hayne as well as moderates like Mitchell King, and unionists like Alexander Black and Jacob Cardozo. Stephen Elliot, who had drafted the 1820 Charleston memorial, is believed to have been the first South Carolinian to advocate linking Charleston to the West through internal improvements. *Southern Review* 2 (August–November 1828): 485. Elias Horry, *An Address respecting the Charleston and Hamburg Railroad and on the Railroad System as regards a large portion of the Southern and Western States of the American Union, Delivered at Charleston, at the Medical College . . .* October 2, 1833, Charleston, 1833, cited in Phillips, *History of Transportation,* 169. Quote from *Charleston Courier,* October 8, 1835, in Theodore D. Jervey, *Robert Y. Hayne and His Times* (New York: Macmillan; New York: Da Capo Press, 1970), 385. The Charleston-Cincinnati plan had first gained the public's attention in October of 1835, when former senator and governor Robert Hayne presented a letter from a public meeting in Cincinnati, Ohio, appealing to the "energies of feeling and action" of "the oldest Southern member of the original thirteen." The Cincinnati meeting, though likely organized by South Carolina boosters, was led by former senator General William Henry Harrison. A Whig presidential aspirant, it is possible that Harrison hoped to broaden his appeal by reaching out to the South. One way to do this was by encouraging South Carolina to take the lead in connecting the Ohio River to the South Atlantic seaboard at Charleston via Lexington, Kentucky, eastern Tennessee, and western North Carolina. For Harrison's presidential aspirations during this time, see Michael Holt, *The Rise and Fall of the American Whig Party* (New York: Oxford University Press, 1999), 41.

6. *Charleston Courier,* November 9, 1835, in Jervey, *Hayne,* 389.

7. Report reprinted in *Charleston Courier,* November 5, 1835. *Memorial in Relation to the Charleston & Cincinnati Railroad,* 1835 (no location given), cited in Charles Roy Schultz, "Hayne's Magnificent Dream: Factors which Influenced the Efforts to Join Cincinnati and Charleston by Railroad" (Ph.D. diss., Ohio State University, 1966), 24.

See also Alexander Blanding, *Address of Col. A. Blanding to the Citizens of Charleston: Convened in Town Meeting on the Louisville, Cincinnati, and Charleston Railroad* (Columbia, S.C.: A. S. Johnson, 1836), 1–3.

8. Report reprinted in *Charleston Courier*, November 5, 1835.

9. Blanding, *Address of Col. Blanding.*

10. In his excellent book, John Larson describes the great Founding hope that national public works would extend the republican vision and promise of popular sovereignty. John Larson, *Internal Improvement: National Public Works and the Promise of Popular Government in the Early United States* (Chapel Hill: University of North Carolina Press, 2001). In addition to spoils and internal division, which Larson argues ruined this vision, we might also note that internal improvements were seen as a way of cementing nonslaveholders to slavery. See, for example, Kenneth Noe, *Southwest Virginia's Railroad: Modernization and the Sectional Crisis* (Urbana: University of Illinois Press, 1994).

11. Act approved December 18, 1835, in Thomas Cooper and David McCord, eds., *The Statutes at Large of South Carolina* (Columbia: A. S. Johnston, 1836–1898), 8: 406.

12. Phillips, *History of Transportation*, 195–97; "Louisville, Cincinnati, and Charleston Railroad Company," *Niles Register*, (September 15, 1838), 40. For more on Hamilton, see J. B. O'Neall, *Biographical Sketches of the Bench and Bar of South Carolina* (Charleston, S.C.: S. G. Courtenay, 1859), 2: 236.

13. *American Railroad Journal* 4 (December 6, 1835): 753, in Schultz, "Hayne's Magnificent Dream," 18.

14. Clay to Francis T. Brooke, August 28, 1838, and to Harrison G. Otis, September 1, 1838, James F. Hopkins and Mary W. M. Hargreaves, eds., *The Papers of Henry Clay* (Lexington: University of Kentucky Press, 1959–), 9: 224, 225–26.

15. Citizens of other states, with a multiplicity of projects to invest in, failed to muster any significant funds. Aided by a state grant, Tennesseans subscribed to $355,400, Kentuckians only $187,100, North Carolinians $102,600, and Ohio citizens a mere $12,200. Jervey, *Hayne*, 407. See also, *Charleston Courier*, November 25, 1836.

16. Calhoun declared that the "humburg" had finally ended "with a debt of several millions on the state, great loss to those concerned, and the loss of credit and mortification to the projectors." Calhoun to Andrew P. Calhoun, September 25, 1840, Robert L. Meriwether et al., eds., *The Papers of John C. Calhoun* (hereafter *PJCC*) (Columbia: University of South Carolina Press, 1959–2003), 15: 359–60. Long-term, Calhoun's assessment was perhaps a bit too harsh. When higher cotton prices returned in the late 1840s, the company, reconstituted as the South Carolina Railroad Company, became profitable.

17. "Minutes and Resolutions," reprinted in *American Railroad Journal*, December 10, 1836. Also, Heath, *Constructive Liberalism*, 267–68. For discussions in Savannah, see Walter J. Fraser Jr., *Savannah in the Old South* (Athens: University of Georgia Press, 2003), 241–46.

18. The act passed on December 21, 1838. See Heath, *Constructive Liberalism*, 269.

19. For more on Georgia's railroad efforts, see Phillips, *History of Transportation*, 303–34.

20. Heath, *Constructive Liberalism,* 369–70.

21. John C. Calhoun to A[ugustin] S. Clayton, August 5, 1836, *PJCC,* 13: 264. The communiqué was published in several local and national papers: *States Rights' Sentinel* (Augusta, Ga.), August 19, 1836; *Chronicle* (Augusta, Ga.), August 20, 1836; *Mercury* (Charleston), September 5, 1836; *Whig* (Richmond, Va.), August 26, 1836; *Globe* (Washington, D.C.), August 31, 1836, and September 2 & 3, 1836.

22. Calhoun to Robert Hayne, October 28, 1838, *PJCC,* 14: 450–51.

23. Calhoun to David Hubbard, June 15, 1838, *PJCC,* 14: 344–45.

24. McDuffie to Hon. Richard H. Welde, May 10, 1835, George McDuffie Papers, South Caroliniana Library.

25. Heath, *Constructive Liberalism;* Michael J. Gagnon, "Transition to an Industrial South: Athens, Georgia, 1830–1870" (Ph.D. diss., Emory University, 2000).

26. For useful but outdated discussions of these early conventions, see Thomas Wender, *Southern Commercial Conventions, 1837–1859* (Baltimore: Johns Hopkins Press, 1930), 11–48; John G. Van Deusen, *The Ante-Bellum Southern Commercial Conventions* (Durham: Duke University Press, 1926); Robert Royal Russell, *Economic Aspects of Southern Sectionalism* (New York: Russell & Russell, 1960), 15–32. For a newer examination, especially of late antebellum conventions, see Vicki Vaughn Johnson, *The Men and the Vision of the Southern Commercial Conventions, 1845–1871* (Columbia: University of Missouri Press, 1992).

27. Quote from Wender, *Southern Commercial Conventions,* 11. The driving force behind the Athens proposal seems to have been William Dearing, an Athens entrepreneur and president of the Georgia Railroad Company, who had been a key proponent of the Western and Atlantic project. What would later become known as the impetus for southern commercial conventions began as part of a desire to extend Georgia's internal improvements out of state. Biographical information on Dearing can be found in Ernest C. Hynds, *Antebellum Athens and Clarke County, Georgia* (Athens: University of Georgia Press, 1974), 22, 27–30.

28. *Georgia Messenger,* April 12, 1838.

29. McDuffie's report, along with other reports of the early commercial conventions, was reprinted in *De Bow's Review* in the 1840s. See "Direct Trade of Southern States with Europe," *De Bow's Review* 3, no. 6 (June 1847): 557–59, and 4, no. 2 (October 1847): 208–26.

30. *Georgia Messenger,* October 26, 1837.

31. Russell, *Economic Aspects,* 26; Heath, *Constructive Liberalism,* 312. An example of an editorial favorable to this measure and stressing its assistance in raising capital investment can be found in *Georgia Messenger,* November 23, 1837.

32. William H. Brantley, *Banking in Alabama, 1816–1860* (Birmingham: Oxmoor Press, 1961), 1: 320.

33. Anglo-American partnerships have received some attention. See Ralph Hidy, *The House of Baring in American Trade and Finance* (Cambridge: Harvard University Press, 1949); Edwin J. Perkins, *Financing Anglo-American Trade: The House of Brown, 1800–1880* (Cambridge: Harvard University Press, 1975).

34. James Baker (confidential) to John Backhouse, January 13, 1838, and March 8, 1838. London, British National Archives, Foreign Office Papers, 5/236. Consular reports from Mobile.

35. James Baker (private) to John Backhouse, March 26, 1838, ibid.

36. See reprinted message from Liverpool paper dated October 24, 1837, in *Georgia Messenger,* December 21, 1837.

37. Quoted in Mira Wilkins, *The History of Foreign Investment in the United States to 1914* (Cambridge: Harvard University Press, 1989), 255.

38. See Hidy, *House of Baring,* 254–59. The Barings' chief rival, the Baltimore-Liverpool firm of Alexander Brown & Sons also increased its consignments in a highly competitive market year in 1838. Perkins, *Financing Anglo-American Trade,* 101.

39. McDuffie to J. H. Hammond, March 31, 1839, reprinted in Thomas P. Martin, "The Advent of William Gregg and the Graniteville Company," *Journal of Southern History* (August 1945): 405. Amongst the concerns that McDuffie felt hindered the success was likely the banking crisis, which he observed while in England. McDuffie (London) to Richard H. Wilde, Esq., May 1, 1839, George McDuffie Papers, South Caroliniana Library.

40. Thomas Downey, *Planting a Capitalist South: Masters, Merchants, and Manufacturers in the Southern Interior, 1790–1860* (Baton Rouge: Louisiana State University Press, 2006); Gagnon, "Transition to an Industrial South"; William Scarborough, *Masters of the Big House: Elite Slaveholders of the Mid-Nineteenth Century South* (Baton Rouge: Louisiana State University Press, 2003), 217–37.

41. See, for example, McDuffie's 1838 report, *De Bow's Review* 3, no. 6 (June 1847): 557–59, and 4, no. 2 (October 1847): 208–26. McDuffie to John Banskett, Esq., February 3, 1838, George McDuffie Papers, South Caroliniana Library; Brian Schoen, "Alternatives to Dependence: The Lower South's Antebellum Pursuit of Sectional Development through Global Interdependence," in Susanna Delfino and Michele Gillespie, *Global Perspectives on Industrial Transformation in the American South* (Columbia: University of Missouri Press, 2005).

42. Gavin Wright, *The Political Economy of the Cotton South* (New York: Norton, 1978), and John Majewski, *A House Dividing: Economic Development in Pennsylvania and Virginia before the Civil War* (Cambridge: Cambridge University Press, 2000).

43. The interpretation provided here challenges the interpretations offered by scholars like Eugene Genovese, John McCardell and Fred Bateman and Thomas Weiss, who believe that the desire to promote southern distinctiveness prevented success. McCardell, *The Idea of a Southern Nation: Southern Nationalists and Southern Nationalism, 1830–1860* (New York: Norton, 1979), 92, 118.

44. Quitman's most recent biographer has suggested that these might have been the reasons, along with the advice of Mississippi senator George Poindexter, a supporter of nullification whom Quitman met in Charlottesville, Virginia, in 1831. Quitman's political past could more easily be reconciled in a postnullification period, when opposition to Jackson's heavy-handedness enabled an alliance of southern "True Whigs" and states' righters. Robert E. May, *John A. Quitman: Old South Crusader* (Baton Rouge: Louisiana State University Press, 1985), 46–49.

45. See toasts featuring Quitman and the project in "Railroad Celebration and Dinner," *Mississippi Free Trader and Natchez Gazette,* March 18, 1836.

46. May, *Quitman,* 99–100.

47. William Brune to John A. Quitman, July 12, 1839, in the J. F. H. Claiborne Papers, University of North Carolina, Southern Historical Collection (hereafter

UNC-SHC), no. 151, series 1, box 1, Correspondence; John A. Quitman to Eliza Quitman (wife), May 11, 1839, Quitman Family Papers, UNC-SHC, no. 616; May, *Quitman*, 101–4.

48. Peter Temin's analysis of the Panic of 1837 stresses that international pressures constricted money supplies, noting that "unlike 1837, no recovery followed the Panic of 1839. Prices did not recover, and the signs of prosperity disappeared." *Jacksonian Economy* (New York: Norton, 1969), 154. More recent work by John Wallis admits that international forces might have been involved, especially in 1837, but then highlights the role that debt accumulation for internal improvement projects in southern and western states played in bringing about the Panic of 1839. Wallis, "What Caused the Crisis of 1839?" NBER Historical Paper no. 133, April 2001. For the retraction of British investment, see Wilkins, *History of Foreign Investment*, 66–75. In reality both international pressures and domestic overinvestment could have shaped the location and depth of the economic depression in the Lower South. The analysis here, emphasizing the damaging effects of the panic, conforms to that of James A. Ward, "A New Look at Antebellum Southern Railroad Development," *Journal of Southern History* 39, no. 3 (August 1973): 409–20.

49. Heath, *Constructive Liberalism*, 307, chart 2; J. Mills Thornton III, *Politics and Power in a Slave Society: Alabama, 1800–1860* (Baton Rouge: Louisiana State University Press, 1978), 292, table.

50. For a recent example, see Kathryn Kish Sklar and James Brewer Stewart, *Women's Rights and Transatlantic Antislavery in the Era of Emancipation* (New Haven: Yale University Press, 2007).

51. Hugh Swinton Legaré to Isaac E. Holmes, April 8, 1833, in Hugh Swinton Legaré, *Writings of Hugh Swinton Legaré*, ed. Mary S. Legaré (Charleston: Burges & James, 1846), 2: 215.

52. *United States Telegraph*, June 18, 1833, and *Charleston Mercury*, May 17, 1833, cited in Joe Wilkins, "Window on Freedom: South Carolina's Response to British West Indian Slave Emancipation, 1833–1834," *South Carolina Historical Magazine*, 85 (April 1984), 141–42.

53. Fourth of July Address (1834), *Publications of the Mississippi Historical Society* (1911–1912), cited in "peculiar," *Oxford English Dictionary*, definition 8d, http://dictionary.oed.com.proxy.lib.csus.edu/cgi/entry/50173737/50173737se7?single=1&query_type=word&queryword=peculiar+institution&first=1&max_to_show=10&hilite=50173737se7 (accessed April 1, 2006).

54. Cited in Wilkins, "Window on Freedom," 141–42. See also Edward B. Rugemer, "The Southern Response to British Abolitionism: The Maturation of Proslavery Apologetics," *Journal of Southern History* 70 (May 2004): 221–48.

55. This story is told in depth in William Lee Miller, *Arguing about Slavery: The Great Battle in the United States Congress* (New York: Knopf, 1996).

56. William Harper, "Colonization Society," *Southern Review* 1 (February 1828): 233.

57. Though informed by Judeo-Christian ideas about original sin, stewardship, and proslavery religion, Harper explicitly removed the debate from the arena of religion, suggesting that the Bible sanctions slavery primarily as "a civil institution, with which religion has no concern." Instead, Harper's logic was premised largely on his understanding of civilization as a material and intellectual pursuit, originating with the "accumulation of property," "providence for the future," and "tastes for comfort

or elegancies"—characteristics that historically had only, he asserted, been achieved through the coerced labor of others. Philosophically, Harper's analysis emerged from what he called "the common moral sense of mankind," Scottish Enlightenment phraseology that he merged, with some ambivalence, with a utilitarian outlook concerned with material as well as moral "consequences" for society. William Harper, *Memoir on Slavery,* reprinted in *The Proslavery Argument* (Philadelphia: Lippincott, Grambo, & Co., 1853), 5–6, 8–9, 17–18. See also Drew Gilpin Faust, *A Sacred Circle: The Dilemma of the Intellectual in the Old South, 1840–1860* (Baltimore: Johns Hopkins University Press, 1977), 119–20. The literature on proslavery thought is vast. I have relied largely on the essays in Paul Finkelman, ed., *Proslavery Thought, Ideology, and Politics* (New York: Garland Publishing, 1989); William Sumner Jenkins, *The Pro-Slavery Argument in the Old South* (Chapel Hill: University of North Carolina Press, 1935); and Larry Tise, *Proslavery: A History of the Defense of Slavery in America, 1701–1840* (Athens: University of Georgia Press, 1987). For a pathbreaking new work on the localized roots of proslavery Christianity in Virginia, see Charles F. Irons, *The Origins of Proslavery Christianity: White and Black Evangelicals in Colonial and Antebellum Virginia* (Chapel Hill: University of North Carolina Press, 2008).

58. Wakefield, *England and America,* 339, reprinted in M. F. Lloyd Prichard, ed., *The Collected Works of Edward Gibbon Wakefield* (Glasgow: Collins, 1969), 311–588.

59. Ibid., 470–90, quote from 471.

60. Harper, *Memoir on Slavery,* 25.

61. For more on race and American expansion, see Reginald Horsman, *Race and Manifest Destiny: The Origins of American Racial Anglo-Saxonism* (Cambridge: Harvard University Press, 1981); Frederick Merk, *Slavery and the Annexation of Texas* (New York: Knopf, 1972), 83–100.

62. Perhaps the most sophisticated analysis of this question is Gavin Wright's *Slavery and American Economic Development* (Baton Rouge: Louisiana State University Press, 2006), 48–82, which demonstrates that property rights in slaves increased slaveholders' ability to mobilize labor in new areas. Wright also shows that high slave prices slowed economic diversification efforts. Yet southern industrialists shifted the logic to argue that slavery could concentrate labor toward manufacturing. See, for example, Charles Dew's book, *Bond of Iron: Master and Slave at Buffalo Forge* (New York: Norton, 1994); Robert S. Starborn, *Industrial Slavery in the Old South* (New York: Oxford University Press, 1970); and Mariana Dantas, *Black Townsmen: Urban Slavery and Freedom in the Eighteenth-Century Americas* (New York: Palgrave Macmillan, 2008). For a contemporary account highlighting the higher wages slavery brought to free white laborers, see James De Bow, "The Interest in Slavery of the Southern Non-Slaveholder" (Charleston, 1860), in Eric L. McKitrick, ed., *Slavery Defended: The Views of the Old South* (Englewood Cliffs, N.J.: Prentice-Hall, 1963), 171.

63. Jeffrey Robert Young's interesting work and use of the term *corporate individualism* helps provide the cultural and political framework around which Harper's argument developed and perhaps offers a paradigm for moving beyond the debates over whether slavery was patriarchal or capitalistic. *Domesticating Slavery: The Master Class in Georgia and South Carolina, 1670–1837* (Chapel Hill: University of North Carolina Press, 1999), 9 and passim.

64. Harper, *Memoir on Slavery,* 19.

65. Ibid., 27. He failed to mention, of course, the economizing that took place on the plantation that likely drastically worsened the slave's quality of life.

66. James Huston, "The Panic of 1857, Southern Economic Thought, and the Patriarchal Defense of Slavery," *Historian* 46 (1984): 163–86. His analysis is framed by the older historiography of patriarchy versus capitalism, which was perhaps not as stark a dichotomy as contemporaries would have recognized. Recent work, examining labor and property law, have suggested that these arguments may have influenced southern law. See Jennifer Wahl, *The Bondsman's Burden: An Economic Analysis of the Common Law of Southern Slavery* (New York: Cambridge University Press, 2002), 49–100; Wright, *Slavery and American Economic Development,* 73–74.

67. Harper, *Memoir on Slavery,* 6. Useful studies of racial thought in America during this time include William Stanton, *The Leopard's Spots: Scientific Attitudes towards Race in America, 1815–59* (Chicago: University of Chicago Press, 1960); Robert F. Durden, *The Self-Inflicted Wound: Southern Politics in the Nineteenth Century* (Lexington: University Press of Kentucky, 1985); George Fredrickson, *The Black Image in the White Mind: The Debate on Afro-American Character and Destiny, 1817–1914* (New York: Harper & Row, 1971).

68. Harper, *Memoir on Slavery,* 20.

69. Duff Green, *United States Telegraph,* August 21, 1833, quoted in Wilkins, "Window on Freedom," 139.

70. "East Indian Cotton," *Southern Quarterly Review* 1, no. 2 (April 1842): 449. Duff Green, who was in England, perpetuated that idea among his southern friends. After observing the Peel government in London during the forties, Green concluded that British pressure for emancipation resulted from a desperate effort to allow the stagnating West Indian islands to compete globally again by removing the source of their competitors' vitality. See William Freehling, *Road to Disunion,* vol. 1, *Secessionists at Bay* (New York: Oxford University Press, 1990), 385–87.

71. *De Bow's Review* 14, no. 3 (March 1853): 289–90. Ultimately the author believed the people of England would learn the error of their nation's calculation and remove opposition to the reopening of the slave trade: "Britain's citizens will largely and fully participate in it, in all its ramifications." After all, many southerners knew, they had been complicit in it for a very long time. As outrageous as this contention might now seem, historians as far back as Eric Williams have sought to minimize the influence of religion or culture and embraced a similar assumption—that abolition succeeded primarily because of a shift in British imperial policy that gave primacy to the East. See Eric Williams's influential and controversial 1944 classic, *Capitalism and Slavery* (1944; Chapel Hill: University of North Carolina Press, 1994).

72. Jan Rogozinski, *A Brief History of the Caribbean: From the Arawak and the Carib to the Present* (New York: Meridian, 1992), 185; also Gad Heuman, "The British West Indies," in Andrew Porter, ed., *The Oxford History of the British Empire: The Nineteenth Century* (New York: Oxford University Press, 1999), 481–82. For an illuminating analysis of the role of the British West Indies in America's debate, see Edward B. Rugemer, "The Southern Response to British Abolitionism: The Maturation of Proslavery Apologetics," *Journal of Southern History* 70 (May 2004): 221–48.

73. "British and American Slavery," *Southern Quarterly Review* 8, no. 16 (October 1853): 402–3. Obviously, this story must be skeptically received. No attempt has been

made to locate the original article or locate a Jamaican account that the person was real or these events ever took place.

74. Many questioned whether such laborers could even be called free, proposing that anyone who believed that either East Indian or free blacks were truly "free-laborers" or had been positively affected by emancipation had been seriously "hum-bugged." *De Bow's Magazine* 14, no. 5 (May 1853): 438.

75. Reprinted from *New Orleans Bee* in *Mississippi Free Trader and Natchez Gazette,* May 8, 1844. In 1844 the British government committed itself to the coolie trade by sponsoring transportation and attempting to regulate previous private action. Edgar L. Erickson, "The Introduction of East Indian Coolies into the British West Indies," *Journal of Modern History* 6, no. 2 (June 1934): 127–46.

76. "England and Slavery," *Mississippi Free Trader and Natchez Gazette,* February 27, 1845.

77. India Board to J. Backhouse, Esq., March 19, 1839, and to Thomas Bayles, undated, Public Record Office, Foreign Office, Domestic Papers, 5/328A, both marked "Secret and Immediate."

78. "East Indian Cotton," *Southern Quarterly Review* 1, no. 2 (April 1842): 458.

79. D. A. Washbrook, "India, 1818–1890: The Two Faces of Colonialism," in Porter, *Oxford History of the British Empire: The Nineteenth Century,* 408–12; C. A. Bayly, *Rulers, Townsmen and Bazaars: North Indian Society in the Age of British Expansion, 1770–1870* (Cambridge, 1983), chaps. 2–5, 7. For Niger River expedition, see Howard Temperley, *White Dreams: Black Africa: The Antislavery Expedition to the River Niger, 1841–1842* (New Haven: Yale University Press, 1991).

80. "East Indian Cotton," 449.

81. Ibid.

82. James H. Hammond, "Two Letters on Slavery in the United States," in *Proslavery Argument,* 135–39, quote from 137.

83. Ibid., 139. Conveniently ignored, of course, was the fact that abolitionists were also among the most concerned about these very issues. For a historical analysis of these debates, see Douglas A. Lorimer, *Colour, Class, and the Victorians: English Attitudes to the Negro in the Mid-Nineteenth Century* (Bristol: Leicester University Press, 1978), esp. 131–77.

84. For the broader significance of this court case, though without connecting it to the Negro Seaman's Acts, see William J. Novak, *The People's Welfare: Law and Regulation in Nineteenth-Century America* (Chapel Hill: University of North Carolina Press, 1996), 210.

85. Eugene Genovese, *The Slaveholders' Dilemma: Freedom and Progress in Southern Conservative Thought, 1820–1860* (Columbia: University of South Carolina Press, 1992); James Oakes, *Slavery and Freedom: An Interpretation of the Old South* (New York: Knopf, 1990); and *The Ruling Race: A History of American Slaveholders* (New York: Knopf, 1982).

86. Michael Holt, "The Election of 1840, Voter Mobilization, and the Emergence of the Second American Party System: A Reappraisal of Jacksonian Voting Behavior" and "Winding Roads to Recovery: The Whig Party from 1844 to 1848," in *Political Parties and American Political Developments from the Age of Jackson to the Age of Lincoln* (Baton Rouge: Louisiana State University Press, 1992). For the politics of slavery,

see William J. Cooper Jr., *The South and the Politics of Slavery, 1828–1856* (Baton Rouge: Louisiana State University Press, 1978).

87. The Whig Party in the Lower South remains woefully understudied, but general accounts of the Whig Party include Charles G. Sellers, "Who Were the Southern Whigs?" *American Historical Review* 59 (January 1954): 335–46; Arthur C. Cole, *The Whig Party in the South* (1912; Gloucester: Peter Smith, 1962). I am also indebted to Holt, *Whig Party*.

88. Demonstrating its dissatisfaction with the two emerging parties altogether, South Carolina's legislature cast its electoral votes for North Carolina states' righter Willie Mangum.

89. Thornton, *Politics and Power*, 37–38. Holt demonstrates that in Alabama Whigs benefited from the additional turnout in the 1840 elections more than Democrats did (+6,959W to +4,894D), though Van Buren still won a comfortable majority in 1840. "Election of 1840," Voter Mobilization, table 5, 182; and also *Whig Party*, 75, table 6 and chap. 5.

90. As several historians have suggested, these issues more than any other defined partisan division in the early 1840s. Michael Holt, *The Political Crisis of the 1850s* (New York: Norton, 1978), 17–38; Holt, *Whig Party*, 76–82; William Gerald Shade, *Banks or No Banks: The Money Issue in Western Politics* (Detroit: Wayne State University Press, 1972), 40–59; and Richard L. McCormick, *The Party Period and Public Policy: American Politics from the Age of Jackson to the Progressive Era* (New York: Oxford University Press, 1986), 162–66. The best discussion of the origins of the Independent Treasury may be James Roger Sharp, *The Jacksonians versus the Banks: Politics in the States after the Panic of 1837* (New York: Columbia University Press, 1970), esp. 8–14. See also Bray Hammond, *Banks and Politics in America from the Revolution to the Civil War* (Princeton: Princeton University Press, 1957), 226–450; Larry Schweikart, *Banking in the American South from the Age of Jackson to Reconstruction* (Baton Rouge: Louisiana State University Press, 1987).

91. Calhoun to Nathaniel Beverley Tucker, January 2, 1838, *PJCC*, 14: 45. In 1840 Van Buren won the support of the South Carolina legislature, which had scorned him four years earlier.

92. See Temin, *Jacksonian Economy*, 150–51.

93. Quote in Anthony Gene Carey, *Parties, Slavery, and the Union in Antebellum Georgia* (Athens: University of Georgia Press, 1997), 42.

94. Thornton, *Politics and Power*, 281–85; Edwin A. Miles, *Jacksonian Democracy in Mississippi* (New York: Da Capo Press, 1970), 1960.

95. In 1840, Alabama and Mississippi Whigs succeeded in downplaying their close affiliation with commercial banking and pinned the devastating results of the panic on a Democratically controlled legislature's poor handling of state banks. After making gains in that election year, however, the tables were turned, as in 1841 and 1842 Democrats attacked Whigs' inability to make good on their pledges for reform. Sharp, *Jacksonians versus the Banks*.

96. Carey, *Georgia Parties*, 57–58.

97. Ibid., 59.

98. Clay's support for this policy is traced in Maurice Baxter, *Henry Clay and the American System* (Lexington: University Press of Kentucky, 1995).

99. Mark Anthony Cooper, *Congressional Globe,* 27th Cong., 2nd sess., appendix, 844–46.

100. Rhett: May 1844, *Congressional Globe,* 28th Cong., 1st sess., appendix, 658.

101. Russell, *Economic Aspects,* 156–57; Jones: *Congressional Globe* 29th Cong., 1st sess., 991.

102. Bagby, *Congressional Globe,* 27th Cong., 2nd sess., appendix, 663, 664.

103. Gwin, ibid., appendix, 637.

104. Gwin, ibid., 636.

105. Gwin, ibid., 638; Bagby, ibid., 663. Indeed, Clay's long-held policy of distributing land revenues back to the states was itself suspected of being a nefarious strategy designed to buy off the states, bankrupt the federal government, and thus make a higher tariff necessary to fund the government. The charge was absurd, but in actuality Clay had tried to logroll the tariff, internal improvements, and land distribution as part of a legislative package, first in 1831 and again in 1841. His objectives, however, were arguably less to raise protection for manufactures than to salvage the internal improvement policies that had been thwarted, in the first instance by Jackson's Maysville veto and in the second by the economic downturn. Baxter, *Henry Clay and the American System,* 116, 168.

106. Nine of Virginia's twenty-one congressmen and eight of North Carolina's thirteen were Whigs, many of whom were believed by one Georgia Democrat to be representing newly emerging manufacturing interests in their regions. The degree to which participants in these debates assembled detailed statistics of each states' interests is astounding and revealing. M. A. Cooper's speech and notes, *Congressional Globe,* 27th Cong., 2nd sess., appendix, 834–59.

107. *Congressional Globe,* 27th Cong., 2nd sess., appendix, 634.

108. Harper, *Memoir on Slavery,* 19n.

109. One possible exception might be Massachusetts Cotton Whigs (joined by Webster in 1850), who, in extreme circumstances like in 1850, remained somewhat willing to accommodate slaveholders in order to preserve the Union.

110. Gwin, *Congressional Globe,* 27th Cong., 2nd sess., appendix, 637.

111. Ibid.

112. Baxter, *Henry Clay and the American System,* 177–78.

113. Georgia Democrat Edward Black unabashedly played to his Georgia constituency by bashing his Whig counterpart Roger Gamble, who though he voted against the measure, had supported the idea that revenue tariffs had protective qualities. Black, *Congressional Globe,* 27th Cong., 2nd sess., 678–88. In Congress, during the initial vote, not a single representative—Whig or Democrat—from South Carolina, Georgia, Alabama, Mississippi, or Arkansas voted in favor of the bill. Louisiana continued its legacy of protection, with two of three representatives favoring it. July 16, 1842, vote. These and subsequent voting results are taken from the *Voteview for Windows* software project coded and maintained by Boris Shor at Princeton University. *Congressional Globe,* 27th Cong., 2nd sess., 1841–42, 111–23, 531, 758 (Warren). Carey also suggests that Georgia Whigs did not support the protective tariff. Carey, *Georgia Parties,* 59–62.

114. Berrien, *Congressional Globe,* 28th Cong., 1st sess.; Toombs, *Congressional Globe,* 28th Cong., 1st sess., appendix, 1034–35.

115. William Gregg, *Essays on Domestic Industry: Or an Inquiry into the Expediency of Establishing Cotton Manufactures in South Carolina*, (Charleston: Burges & James, 1845); Broadus Mitchell, *William Gregg: Factory Master of the Old South* (Chapel Hill: University of North Carolina Press, 1928), 15–32. Even Gregg, though, refused to believe that a protective tariff was necessary for southern efforts at manufacturing, or that it would even provide considerable assistance. He also ultimately supported the cause of direct imports. Gregg, "Southern Patronage to Southern Imports and Domestic Industry," *De Bow's Review* 29, no. 1 (July 1860): 77–83; 29, no. 2 (August 1860): 226–32; 29, no. 4 (October 1860): 494–500; 29, no. 5 (November 1860): 623–31; 29, no. 6 (December 1860): 771–78; 30, no. 1 (January 1861): 102–4; 30, no. 2 (February 1861): 216–23.

116. John Berrien, *Congressional Globe*, 28th Cong., 1st sess., 324–26.

117. Berrien, ibid., 326.

118. Stuart Bruchey, *Cotton and the Growth of the American Economy, 1790–1860: Sources and Readings* (New York: Harcourt, Brace & World, 1967), table 3.A.

119. On Toombs's later opposition to tariffs, see William Y. Thompson, *Robert Toombs of Georgia* (Baton Rouge: Louisiana State University Press, 1966), 129, and speech, *Congressional Globe*, 35th Cong., 2nd sess., 1452.

120. A closer examination of the Zollverein Treaty's defeat at the hands of northern Whigs exists in W. Stull Holt, *Treaties Defeated by the Senate* (Baltimore: Johns Hopkins Press, 1933), 79–82; Joel H. Silbey, *The Shrine of Party: Congressional Voting Behavior, 1841–1852* (Pittsburgh: University of Pittsburgh Press, 1972).

121. Merk, *Slavery and Annexation*; Freehling, *Road to Disunion*, 1: 353–452; Thomas Hietala, *Manifest Design: American Exceptionalism and Empire* (1985; Ithaca: Cornell University Press, 2003), 65–71.

122. Duff Green to John C. Calhoun, January 24, 1842, in John Franklin Jameson, ed., *Correspondence of Calhoun* (Washington D.C.: Government Printing Office: 1900), 2: 842–43. On 1844 legislation, see Robert Stewart, "The Ten Hours and Sugar Crises of 1844: Government and the House of Commons in the Age of Reform," *Historical Journal* 12, no. 1 (1969): 39–42.

123. Green to Calhoun, January 24, 1842, in Jameson, *Correspondence of Calhoun*, 2: 842–43.

124. Green to Abel Upshur, July 3rd, 1843, reprinted in Merk, *Slavery and Annexation*, 221–24.

125. This letter is discussed at great length in Freehling *Road to Disunion*, 1: 408–10; Merk, *Slavery and Annexation*, esp. 44–83. John Niven, *John C. Calhoun and the Price of Union: A Biography* (Baton Rouge: Louisiana State University Press, 1988), 275–77.

126. Calhoun to Francis Wharton, May 28, 1844, *PJCC*, 18: 648–50.

127. Calhoun to William King, August 12, 1844, *PJCC*, 19: 568–78; James McQueen, *Blackwood's Edinburgh Magazine* (William Blackwood & Sons), 55, no. 344 (June 1844), 731–48. Available online at www.bodley.ox.ac.uk/cgi-bin/ilej/pbrowse.pl?item= jnl (accessed December 19, 2008).

128. "Letter of Mr. Walker Relative to Texas Annexation," reprinted in Frederick Merk in collaboration with Louis Bannister Merk, *Fruits of Propaganda in the Tyler Administration* (Cambridge: Harvard University press, 1971), 221–52. On Robert J.

Walker, see William Edward Dodd, *Robert J. Walker: Imperialist* (Gloucester: Peter Smith, 1967), 18–27.

129. "Letter of Mr. Walker," 229. On the letter's proliferation and effect, see Hietala, *Manifest Design*, 18–25.

130. Hietala, *Manifest Design*, 31–35; David Roediger, *Wages of Whiteness: Race and the Making of an American Working Class* (London: Verso, 1991).

131. James C. N. Paul, *Rift in the Democracy* (New York: A. S. Barnes, 1961), 114–83.

132. Roy M. Robbins, *Our Landed Heritage: The Public Domain, 1776–1970,* 2nd rev. ed. (Lincoln: University of Nebraska Press, 1976), 94–96.

133. See Charles Kershaw Rowley, Robert D. Tollison, and Gordon Tullock, *The Political Economy of Rent Seeking* (Boston: Kluwer Academic Publishing, 1988), 207–8.

134. George McDuffie to George Wilson, March 11, 1845, MSS, Papers of George Wilson, Manchester Central Library, M20/vol. 8. For the initial correspondence presenting McDuffie with a copy of the league, see George Wilson to McDuffie, December 5, 1844, George McDuffie Papers, South Caroliniana Library. This myth of peace-loving southerners, no doubt, obscured their treatment of Native Americans and Mexico, reflecting their Eurocentric understanding of these developments.

135. Wilson Lumpkin to John C. Calhoun, May 20, 1846, *PJCC,* 23: 128.

136. F. C. Mathiesson to Edward Tootal, n.d., forwarded to Robert Peel by Tootal, MSS, Peel Papers, British Library, 40588 ff 70–71. No date given, but the letter references the recent repeal of the Corn Laws.

137. One should not conflate free trade with an antimanufacturing stance. By the late 1840s even South Carolina's James H. Hammond, a leader of the radically anti-tariff Bluffton Movement, believed southern industrialization politically and economically desirable, wanting "to reconcile industry with free trade, slave labour, agricultural advancement & Southern tone." Quoted in Drew Faust, *James Henry Hammond and the Old South: A Design for Mastery* (Baton Rouge: Louisiana State University Press, 1982), 275–76; Hammond, *An Address Delivered before the South. Carolina Institute* (Charleston: Walker and James, 1849); also address to State Agricultural Society, cited in Russell, *Economic Aspects,* 35–36. Calhoun, too, repeated his earlier position that he was not opposed to manufacturing. Calhoun to Abbott Lawrence, May 13, 1845, *PJCC,* 21: 549–51. In 1843 South Carolina exempted "the products of this State, and the unmanufactured products" of other states from state taxes, a policy Alabama embraced the following year. Russell, *Economic Aspects,* 156. South Carolina's efforts at manufacturing are explored in Alfred Glaze Smith Jr., *Economic Readjustment of an Old Cotton State* (Columbia: University of South Carolina Press, 1958), 112–34. Such policies, it was thought, could provide the incentives and materials necessary to encourage industry's natural development within the South. These ideas are explored more fully in Schoen, "Alternatives to Dependence."

138. For more on the dire straits that Deep South Whigs faced and their inability to resurrect themselves, see Holt, *Whig Party,* 220–21, 795–99, quotes from 221 (Toombs). Alexander Barrow of Louisiana also seems to have opposed the bill.

139. Quoted in Holt, *Whig Party,* 223.

140. Holt, *Political Parties,* table 2, 204–5.

141. Calhoun to Thomas G. Clemson, July 11, 1846, and September 20, 1846, *PJCC*, 23: 300–301, 451–52.

142. In 1845 Calhoun traveled to Memphis and presided over a commercial convention on internal improvements. Afterward he attempted, unsuccessfully, to navigate a series of resolutions that would allow some limited and indirect federal support for internal improvements.

143. For the most thorough examination of these debates, see Michael Morrison, *Slavery and the American West* (Chapel Hill: University of North Carolina, 1997).

144. Calhoun to A. P. Calhoun, May 14, 1846, *PJCC*, 23: 106.

145. *Congressional Globe*, 29 Cong., 1 sess., 296 (February 1846).

146. On cotton's early diplomatic power, see Hietala, *Manifest Design*, 74–79, 120–21, 178–80.

147. Thomas Clemson to John C. Calhoun, June 12, 1846, *PJCC*, 23: 173–75.

148. George Bancroft to Polk, January 19, 1847, M. S. DeWolfe Howe, ed., *The Life and Letters of George Bancroft*, 2: 7–8, cited in David M. Pletcher, *Diplomacy of Annexation: Texas, Oregon, and the Mexican War* (Columbia: University of Missouri Press, 1973), 502–3.

149. Pletcher, *Diplomacy of Annexation*, 502–4.

150. John Tyler to the *Richmond Enquirer*, September 1, 1847, reprinted in the *National Intelligencer* (Washington, D.C.), September 9, 1847.

151. For the terms of these treaties, most of which liberalized trade, see U.S. Government, *Treaties and Conventions Concluded between the United States of America and Other Powers*, rev. ed. (Washington, D.C: Government Printing Office, 1873), 58, 450, 535, 641, 856.

152. William Henry Trescot, *A Few Thoughts on the Foreign Policy of the United States* (Charleston: John Russell, 1849), 11.

CHAPTER FIVE: An Unnatural Union

1. William Trescot, "The Position and Course of the South," reprinted in Jon L. Wakelyn, *Southern Pamphlets on Secession, November 1860–April 1861* (Chapel Hill: University of North Carolina Press, 1996), 15, 17.

2. Ibid., 20–23.

3. Ibid.; article from the *London Times*, September 7, 1850.

4. [W. P. Miles] to James Chesnut, July 1, 1851, "Plantation & Political Papers, 1851," folder 12/36/31, Chesnut Family Papers, South Carolina Historical Society.

5. Trescot, "Position and Course," 23, 24, 29.

6. Laura A. White, *Robert Barnwell Rhett: Father of Secession* (Gloucester: Peter Smith, 1965), 120–21.

7. Eric H. Walther, *The Fire-Eaters* (Baton Rouge: Louisiana State University Press, 1992), 99.

8. Trescot, "Position and Course," 14–15.

9. Charles and Mary Beard, *The Rise of American Civilization* (New York: Macmillan, 1927), 2: 3–10; Algie H. Simons, *Class Struggles in America* (Chicago: C. Kerr, 1906), 32–36; Louis Hacker, *Triumph of American Capitalism* (New York: Simon & Schuster, 1940); and more recently Eugene Genovese, *The Political Economy of Slavery:*

*Studies in the Economy and Society of the Slave South* (New York: Pantheon Books, 1966), and John Ashworth, *Slavery, Capitalism, and Politics in the Antebellum Republic,* 2 vols. (New York: Cambridge University Press, 1995, 2008).

10. Trescot, "Position and Course," 24.

11. Walther, *The Fire-Eaters,* 100.

12. Trescot, "Position and Course," 29. This interpretation parallels that offered by Michael O'Brien in *Conjectures of Order: Intellectual Life and the American South, 1810–1860* (Chapel Hill: University of North Carolina Press, 2004), 1176–86.

13. Brown quote from Avery O. Craven, *The Growth of Southern Nationalism* (Baton Rouge: Louisiana State University Press, 1953), 129. On the role of Cotton Whigs in acquiescing to southern aspirations, see Kinley J. Brauer, *Cotton versus Conscience: Massachusetts Whig Politics and Southwestern Expansion, 1843–1848* (Lexington: University of Kentucky Press, 1967).

14. Gavin Wright, *The Political Economy of the Cotton South: Households, Markets, and Wealth in the Nineteenth-Century* (New York: Norton, 1978); William Barney, *The Secessionist Impulse: Alabama and Mississippi in 1860* (Princeton: Princeton University Press, 1974), 296; Ralph A. Wooster, *The Secession Conventions of the South* (Princeton: Princeton University Press, 1962); Peyton McCrary, Clark Miller, and Dale Baum, "Class and Party in the Secession Crisis: Voting Behavior in the Deep South," *Journal of Interdisciplinary History* 8 (Winter 1978): 452–54.

15. Michael Holt, *The Political Crisis of the 1850s* (New York: Norton, 1978), 67–99, quote from 236. Christopher Olsen, *Political Culture and Secession in Mississippi: Masculinity, Honor and the Antiparty Tradition, 1830–1860* (New York: Oxford University Press, 2000), provides a sociocultural explanation of this phenomenon. See also J. Mills Thornton III, *Politics and Power in a Slave Society, Alabama, 1800–1860* (Baton Rouge: Louisiana State University Press, 1978), 364–65; James L. Huston, "Southerners against Secession: The Arguments of the Constitutional Unionists in 1850–1851," *Civil War History* 46, no. 4 (2000): 281–99.

16. Prices from Stuart Bruchey, *Cotton and the Growth of the American Economy, 1790–1860: Sources and Readings* (New York: Harcourt, Brace & World, 1967), table 3.A; Demand chart from Robert William Fogel and Stanley L. Engerman, *Time on the Cross: The Economics of American Negro Slavery* (New York: Norton, 1974), 92, fig. 28.

17. David Christy, *Cotton is King: Or, the Culture of Cotton . . .* (Cincinnati: Moore & Co., 1855), 186–87.

18. Vicki Vaughn Johnson, *The Men and the Vision of the Southern Commercial Conventions, 1845–1871* (Columbia: University of Missouri Press, 1992), 87–168.

19. Richard Austin Springs to John Springs, December 18, 1846, cited in Lacy K. Ford Jr., *Origins of Southern Radicalism: The South Carolina Upcountry, 1800–1860* (New York: Oxford University Press, 1988), 220.

20. Ford, *Origins of Southern Radicalism,* 239–40.

21. Milton Heath, *Constructive Liberalism: The Role of the State in Economic Development in Georgia* (Cambridge: Harvard University Press, 1954), 272–77, table 21, 306.

22. Thornton, *Politics and Power,* 268–73.

23. Bradley G. Bond, *Political Culture in the Nineteenth-Century South: Mississippi, 1830–1860* (Baton Rouge: Louisiana State University Press, 1995), 110–12, quote from 111.

24. On elite planters' investments, see William Scarborough, *Masters of the Big House: Elite Slaveholders of the Mid-Nineteenth-Century South* (Baton Rouge: Louisiana State University Press, 2003), 228–30; Ford, *Origins of Southern Radicalism*, 239–40; Thomas Downey, *Planting a Capitalist South: Masters, Merchants, and Manufacturers in the Southern Interior, 1790–1860* (Baton Rouge: Louisiana State University Press, 2006); Edward M. Steel Jr., *T. Butler King of Georgia* (Athens: University of Georgia Press, 1964).

25. Downey, *Planting a Capitalist South,* 226.

26. For public expenditures in each state prior to 1861, see Milton S. Heath, "North American Railroads: Public Railroad Construction and the Development of Private Enterprise in the South before 1861," *Journal of Economic History* 10, Supplement: The Tasks of Economic History (1950): 40–52.

27. The presence of European trade houses in the Lower South gave supporters of direct trade some hope. Even prior to the 1850s cotton boom, 43% of British mercantile houses in the United States (58 of 134, including all 14 shipping merchants) operated in the cotton ports of Charleston, Savannah, Mobile, and New Orleans. See Mira Wilkins, *The History of Foreign Investment in the United States to 1914* (Cambridge: Harvard University Press, 1989), 74. For the disproportionately high amount of foreign investment in bank capital and state bonds, see table 3, "Report of the Secretary of Treasury in Answer to a Resolution of the Senate Calling for the Amount of American Securities held in Europe and other Foreign Countries, on the 30th June 1853," U.S. Senate, Executive Document no. 42, 33rd Cong., 1st sess., Washington D.C., 1854, reprinted in Mira Wilkins, ed., *Foreign Investments in the United States* (New York: Arno Press, 1977). On railroad investment, see Cleona Lewis, *America's Stake in International Investments* (Washington, D.C.: Brookings Institution, 1938), 29–30; P. L. Cottrell, *British Overseas Investment in the Nineteenth Century* (London: Macmillan, 1975), 19–29. For one example involving a London loan to the Mobile-Ohio Railroad, see Harriet Amos, *Cotton City: Urban Development in Antebellum Mobile* (University: University of Alabama Press, 1985).

28. *Proceedings of the Cotton Planters Convention held in Macon, Georgia on the 27th, 28th, 30th and 31st October, 1851* (Macon: Georgia Telegraph Print, 1851). "Direct Trade" speech of C. G. Baylor, Esq., U.S. Consul, Amsterdam, Delivered at the Invitation of a Committee of the Legislature of the State of Georgia in the Hall of the House of Representatives, December 1851 (Washington: Jno. T. Towers, 1852), quote from 28.

29. James Hemphill to Robert W. Hemphill, March 18, 1853, Hemphill Family Papers, Duke University, cited in Ford, *Origins of Southern Radicalism*, 265.

30. Nil Desperandum, *Remarks on the Practicability of the Establishment and Profitable Prosecution of the Manufacture of Cotton in the Immediate Vicinity of New Orleans* (New Orleans: William H. Toy, 1849), 5. Pamphlet in Historical Collection of New Orleans.

31. See James Hammond, *An Address Delivered before the South Carolina Institute* (Charleston: Walker & James, 1849); William Gregg, "Southern Patronage to Southern Imports and Domestic Industry," *De Bow's Review* 29, no. 1 (July 1860): 77–83; 29, no. 2 (August 1860): 226–32; 29, no. 4 (October 1860): 495–500; 29, no. 5 (November 1860): 623–31; 29, no. 6 (December 1860): 771–78; 30, no. 1 (January 1861): 102–4; 30, no. 2 (February 1861): 216–23. It may not be coincidence that William Harper's *Memoir on*

*Slavery* was reprinted in *De Bow's Review* beginning in March 1850. *De Bow's Review* 8, no. 3 (March 1850): 232–43; 8, no. 4 (April 1850): 339–47. Battles over slavery in California heightened Jefferson Davis and the *Charleston Mercury*'s awareness that "the mines of Mexico were the original cause of African slavery" and urged "that the pursuit of gold-washing and mining is better adapted to slave labor than to any other species of labor recognized amongst us." "The Territorial Right of the South 'Barren Abstractions'—No Territory," *Charleston Mercury*, February 28, 1860; Davis, *Congressional Globe*, 31st Cong., 1st sess., 202. In the 1850s, several textile mills that had used free white labor, including the Tuscaloosa and Woodville Manufacturing Companies in Mississippi, converted to slave labor. Robert S. Starobin, *Industrial Slavery in the Old South* (New York: Oxford University Press, 1970), 120.

32. Ford, *Origins of Southern Radicalism*, 311: table 9.2.

33. Downey, *Planting a Capitalist South*, 226.

34. Heath, *Constructive Liberalism*, table 17, 298 and table 21, 308; and table 22, 305–8.

35. Calculated from Thornton, *Politics and Power*, table on 282.

36. On specific industrial endeavors and contemporary responses, see Starobin, *Industrial Slavery*, appendix, table 1, 291. For a historian's assessment of Alabama development, see Thornton, *Politics and Power*, 273–81, quotes from 273 and 281, respectively.

37. John Hebron Moore, *The Emergence of the Cotton Kingdom in the Old Southwest: Mississippi, 1770–1860* (Baton Rouge: Louisiana State University Press, 1988), 205.

38. John Forsyth, "The North and South," *De Bow's Review*, 17, no. 4 (October 1854): 375.

39. These arguments are catalogued by Robert Royal Russell, *Economic Aspects of Southern Sectionalism* (New York: Russell & Russell, 1960), 156–61, quote from 157.

40. See Paul F. Paskoff, *Troubled Waters: Steamboat Disasters, River Improvements, and American Public Policy, 1821–1860* (Baton Rouge: Louisiana State University Press, 2007), 96–101. There may have been some reason to support this claim. Of total expenditures for river and harbor bills between 1790 and 1860, the cotton-growing states of Georgia, South Carolina, Mississippi, Florida, Alabama, Louisiana, Arkansas, and Texas received only around 9%, despite possessing a significantly higher percentage of the nation's rivers and coastline. Calculated from ibid., table D.7.

41. Calhoun, "Address on Taking the Chair of the Southwestern Convention," November 13, 1845, Robert L. Meriwether et al., eds., *The Papers of John C. Calhoun* (hereafter *PJCC*) (Columbia: University of South Carolina Press, 1959–2003), 22: 276–85, quotes from 284, 276, 281. *Journal of the Proceedings of the Southwestern Convention at Memphis on the 12th November, 1845* (Memphis: n.p., 1845): 9, 29–41. *De Bow's Review* 1, no. 1 (January 1846), 7–22. No policy measure captured regional aspirations more than the drive to "do what Christopher Columbus was attempting when he discovered a new world—find a direct passage to the East Indies by going west." Mississippi Pacific Railroad, Committee of Correspondence, *Circular to the Citizens of the United States* (Memphis), 1849. Also J. D. B. De Bow, "The Progress of American Commerce," *De Bow's Review* 2, no. 6 (December 1846): 422. The following account of the transcontinental railroad debates comes from Robert R. Russel's *Improvement*

*of Communication with the Pacific Coast as an Issue in American Politics* (Cedar Rapids, Iowa: The Torch Press, 1948).

42. *Proceedings of the Southern and Western Commercial Convention, Memphis, Tennessee, in June, 1853* (Memphis, 1854), 18–19, 61, cited in Johnson, *Men and the Vision of the Southern Commercial Conventions*, 107–9.

43. Pike to Trezevant of Memphis, reprinted in *Arkansas State Gazette and Democrat*, February 25, 1853, quoted in Russel, *Improvement of Communication*, 122.

44. Butler, *Congressional Globe*, 32 Cong., 2nd sess., 709; Russel, *Improvement of Communication*, 103–7, Borland cited on 104.

45. Pike's resolutions reprinted in "Pacific Railroad-Plan of the Southern Convention," *De Bow's Review* 17, no. 6 (December 1854), 593–99.

46. Stephen A. Douglas, *Letter of Stephen Douglas, Vindicating His Character and His Position . . .* (Washington, D.C., 1854), 14, cited in Michael Morrison, *Slavery and the American West: The Eclipse of Manifest Destiny and the Coming of the Civil War* (Chapel Hill: University of North Carolina Press, 1997), 146.

47. *Charleston Mercury,* October 5, 1854.

48. Trescot, "Position and Course," 14–15.

49. Cited in Robert E. May, *The Southern Dream of a Caribbean Empire, 1854–1861,* 2nd ed. (Gainesville: University Press of Florida, 2002), 51.

50. It continues: "Cotton is shipped from Charleston, Savannah, Mobile and New-Orleans, mainly to Liverpool. There the ships take in a return cargo—in a great measure previously transported from the continent—for New-York, Philadelphia and Boston; and to these cities our Southern merchants repair to lay in their stocks, to be reshipped by them to the South, at a cost almost equal to that of the original transport from Liverpool or the continent. Thus we pay double tribute for the great bulk of foreign goods consumed at the South—first to Liverpool, and then to New-York, Philadelphia and Boston. Surely it must be the finest country of the world, not only to live, but to flourish, under such unnatural and enormous drafts upon our industry." *De Bow's Review* 17, no. 3 (September 1854): 253.

51. Thomas D. Morris, *Free Men All: The Personal Liberty Laws of the North, 1780–1861* (Baltimore: Johns Hopkins University Press, 1974), 166–85. On northern political realignment, see James L. Huston, *Calculating the Value of Union* (Chapel Hill: University of North Carolina Press, 2003), 190–232; Ashworth, *Slavery, Capitalism, and Politics*, vol. 2, esp. 471–579; Jonathan H. Earle, *Jacksonian Antislavery and the Politics of Free Soil, 1824–1854* (Chapel Hill: University of North Carolina Press, 2004), 181–98; Michael Holt, *The Fate of Their Country: Politicians, Slavery Extension, and the Coming of the Civil War* (New York: Hill & Wang, 2004).

52. Viscount Palmerston to Sir Henry Bulwer, no. 105, October 11, 1850, *Correspondence Relative to the Prohibition Against the Admission of Free Persons of Colour,* F.O. 5/579, British National Archives, 140–42.

53. Philip M. Hamer, "British Consuls and the Negro Seamen's Acts, 1850–1860," *Journal of Southern History* 1, no. 2 (May 1935): 156; Alan Frank January, "The First Nullification: The Free Negro Seamen Acts Controversy in South Carolina, 1822–1860" (Ph.D. diss., University of Iowa, 1976).

54. On other states, see Hamer, "British Consuls and the Negro Seamen's Acts," 143. Bunch seems to have followed advice that senators Andrew Butler and William

Aiken had given to Crampton. See Crampton to Clarendon, April 4, 1853, reprinted in James J. Barnes and Patience P. Barnes, *Private and Confidential: Letters from British Ministers in Washington to the Foreign Secretaries in London, 1844–67* (Selinsgrove: Susquehanna University Press, 1993), 71–72.

55. Hamer, "British Consuls and the Negro Seamen's Acts," 164.

56. Bunch to Adams, September 1, 1855, FO 5: 626, in Hamer, "British Consuls and the Negro Seamen's Acts," 165.

57. Follow in Hamer, "British Consuls and the Negro Seamen's Acts," 161–66; January, "The First Nullification," 386. Bunch to Clarendon, January 1, 1858, *Foreign Office*, 5/698, consular dispatches from Charleston. (matter resolved).

58. Alfred Huger to William Porcher Miles, November 28, 1859, William Porcher Miles Papers, University of North Carolina, Southern Historical Collection (hereafter UNC-SHC), microfilm no. 1-4485, folder 17.

59. Scott Wallace Stucky, "*Elkison v. Deliesseline:* Race and the Constitution in South Carolina, 1823," *North Carolina Central Law Journal* 14 (1983–84): 399.

60. Robert E. May, *Manifest Destiny's Underworld: Filibustering in Antebellum America* (Chapel Hill: University of North Carolina Press, 2002), 241–42.

61. Cited in May, *Southern Dream*, 51.

62. Mr. Soulé to Mr. Marcy, October 20, 1854, reprinted in *Daily Chronicle & Sentinel* (Augusta, Ga.), March 28, 1855.

63. J. Preston Moore, "Pierre Soulé: Southern Expansionist and Promoter," *Journal of Southern History* 21, no. 2 (May 1955): 203–23. In June 1855, *De Bow's Review* reprinted Mr. Muscoe R. H. Garnett's 1850 pamphlet, "The South and the Union," which in Trescot-like fashion argued that "in the event of a dissolution of the Union it would be," in Britain's "interest to strengthen us [in the Gulf region], and she would be bound to the southern alliance by natural ties, and would have natural causes of hostility to the north. The dependence of four millions of her people on the south for cotton, and of many more for food, would give the slave States a powerful hold upon the good will of her government—a hold that would strengthen with every year." Mr. Garnett, "The South and the Union, Part V," *De Bow's Review* 18, no. 6 (June 1855): 683–84.

64. British response to the Ostend Manifesto had been muted, partly because of the Pierce administration's quick dismissal of it, but also because of Britain's deepening military commitments against Russia. British chargés d'affaires in Belgium and Spain informed their American counterparts that aggressive action would not be viewed favorably. Seaford to Lord Clarendon, November 1, 1854, reprinted in Gavin B. Henderson, "Southern Designs on Cuba and Some European Opinions," *Journal of Southern History* (August 1939): 377–78. A summary of British chargé d'affaires to Spain, Horatio J. Perry's, remarks to Soulé is included in Howden to Clarendon, October 23, 1854, ibid., 376–77; Clarendon to Lord Howard de Walden (British ambassador in Belgium), November 11, 1854, in ibid., 379, however, disavowed hostile action.

65. Clarendon to Palmerston, December 23, 1855, cited in Kenneth Bourne, *Britain and the Balance of Power in North America, 1815–1908* (Berkeley: University of California Press, 1967), 191.

66. In the words of one diplomatic historian, the attempt to intimidate and "create an anti-American balance of power had been challenged and publicly defeated." Bourne, *Balance of Power,* 200.

67. Clarendon to Palmerston, December 30, 1857; Palmerston to Clarendon, Private, December 31, 1857; Earl of Malmesbury to Queen Victoria, July 8, 1858, all reprinted in Kenneth Bourne, "The Clayton-Bulwer Treaty and the Decline of British Opposition to the Territorial Expansion of the United States, 1857–60," *Journal of Modern History* 33, no. 3 (September 1961): 287–91.

68. Palmerston to Clarendon, July 4, 1857, in Henderson, "Southern Designs on Cuba," 385.

69. Lord Napier to Clarendon, May 26, 1857, in ibid., 383–84.

70. Sumner's comments to British officials are quoted in Richard W. Van Alstyne, "Anglo-American Relations, 1853–1857: British Statesmen on the Clayton-Bulwer Treaty and American Expansion," *American Historical Review* 42, no. 3 (April 1937): 492, n3. On the French accusations and Napier's response, see Barnes and Barnes, *Private and Confidential,* 174–75. When Napier unwisely tipped off U.S. officials to Britain's willingness to revisit the Clayton-Bulwer Treaty and offered a conciliatory public speech, even Napoleon III inquired whether Britain had changed its official policy of opposing America's "annexing propensities." The British, of course, denied it, blaming France for its own timidity in the region. Bourne, *Balance of Power,* 202.

71. Edward B. Bryan, *Letters to the Southern People Concerning the Acts of Congress and Treaties with Great Britain, in relation to the African Slave Trade* (Charleston: Press of Walker, Evans & Co., 1858), esp. 20.

72. Catherine Hall, *Civilising Subjects: Colony and Metropole in the English Imagination, 1830–1867* (Chicago: University of Chicago Press, 2002), 338–79.

73. Edgar L. Erickson, "The Introduction of East Indian Coolies into the British West Indies," *Journal of Modern History* 6, no. 2 (June 1934): 143–45.

74. "The African Slave Trade to Be Revived by Great Britain and France," *Charleston Mercury,* June 17, 1857.

75. "Message of the President of the United States . . . with accompanying papers, in relation to the African slave trade," April 21, 1858, 35th Cong., 1st sess., 929, Senate Executive Document no. 49, 56. Excerpts from Mason's correspondence were reprinted in, among other southern papers, the *Charleston Mercury,* April 28, 1858.

76. Napier to Clarendon, March 8, 1858, reprinted in Barnes and Barnes, *Private and Confidential,* 195.

77. *Houma Ceres,* cited in William Freehling, *Road to Disunion,* vol. 2, *Secessionists Triumphant, 1854–1861* (New York: Oxford University Press, 2007), 182.

78. Quote from Jackson, *Semi-Weekly Mississippian,* April 26, 1859, cited in Ronald T. Takaki, *A Pro-Slavery Crusade: The Agitation to Reopen the African Slave Trade* (New York: Free Press, 1971), 41. "Why," asked a contributor to the *Edgefield Advertiser,* "contend for the abstract right to extend the area of slavery in Kansas, California and other localities without furnishing the Africans necessary to accomplish it?" quoted in ibid., 26. Leonidas Spratt blamed Kansas's rejection of the proslavery Lecompton government on the lack of slaves: "Ten thousand masters have failed to take Kansas, but so would not have failed ten thousand slaves. Ten thousand of the rudest Africans . . . would have swept the free soil party from the land." Spratt, speech in the *Liberator* (Boston), August 12, 1859.

79. "Mark of Cain," *Report to Montgomery Commercial Convention,* 1858, cited in Eric H. Walther, *William Lowndes Yancey and the Coming of the Civil War* (Chapel Hill: University of North Carolina Press, 2006), 217. See also *De Bow's Review* 27

(September 1859): 364. The subject of reopening the slave trade has been hotly contested by historians, some seeing support of it as evidence of the reactionary views of the South and others seeing the region's rejection of it as evidence that the South desired to develop internal manufacturing. For the first, see Manisha Sinha, *The Counterrevolution of Slavery: Politics and Ideology in Antebellum South Carolina* (Chapel Hill: University of North Carolina Press, 2000), versus Gavin Wright, *Political Economy of the Cotton South*. The most comprehensive examination that demonstrates the diverse motives is Takaki, *Pro-Slavery Crusade*. I am indebted to Walter Johnson for sharing some of the ideas informing his new work: *River of Dark Dreams: Slavery, Capitalism, and Imperialism in the Mississippi Valley's Cotton Kingdom* (Cambridge: Harvard University Press, forthcoming).

80. See Freehling, *Road to Disunion*, 2: 168–84.

81. Walther, *William Lowndes Yancey*, 216–28, cite from 216–17.

82. *De Bow's Review* 26, no. 6 (June 1859): 713; 27, no. 1 (July 1859): 94–99, 205–14.

83. Freehling, *Road to Disunion*, 2: 180.

84. Yancey's letter reprinted in *Milwaukee Daily Sentinel*, July 2, 1858.

85. Cited in Don E. Fehrenbacher, *The Slaveholding Republic: An Account of the United States Government's Relations to Slavery* (New York: Oxford University Press, 2001), 185.

86. *London Times*, November 24, 1857, cited in Harral E. Landry, "Slavery and the Slave Trade in Atlantic Diplomacy, 1850–1861," *Journal of Southern History* 27, no. 2 (May 1961): 184–207, quote from 202.

87. On Napier's urging of caution, see letter to Malmesbury, April 5, 1858, in *Private and Confidential*, 198–99. For a contemporary explanation of the legal issues at work, read Richard Core, "The African Slave Fleet and Right of Search," *De Bow's Review* 25, no. 5 (November 1858): 512–45. This subject is briefly discussed in Fehrenbacher, *Slaveholding Republic*, 185–86, but a more detailed account is provided in Hugh Soulsby, *The Right of Search and the Slave Trade in Anglo-American Relations, 1814–1862* (Baltimore: Johns Hopkins Press, 1933), 118–76; see also Landry, "Slavery and the Slave Trade." Landry's article supports the argument presented here, that the 1858–1859 backing down of Britain on matters of slavery and the slave trade empowered southern slaveholders. See esp. 206–7.

88. Quote from General William Walker, *The War in Nicaragua* (1860; Tuscon: University of Arizona Press, 1985), 270.

89. Takaki, *Pro-Slavery Crusade*, 231–34.

90. "Remarks on an Appropriation for Warships," June 7, 1858, *The Papers of Jefferson Davis*, ed. Lynda Crist et al. (Baton Rouge: Louisiana State University Press, 1971–), 6: 183–87.

91. *Daily Morning News* (Savannah, Ga.), June 3, 1858.

92. "Settlement of the Difficulty between the United States and Great Britain," *Mississippian and State Gazette* (Jackson, Miss.), July 7, 1858.

93. The interpretation presented here challenges the belief that southerners simply merged Britain and the North into a common antislave enemy. Kenneth S. Greenberg, *Masters and Statesmen: The Political Culture of American Slavery* (Baltimore: Johns Hopkins University Press, 1985).

94. John C. Claiborne, *Report of the Secretary of the Interior* (hereafter Claiborne Report), 35th Cong., 1st sess., Executive Document no. 35, read and ordered tabled

March 22, 1858, 93. The Senate deemed Claiborne's report significant enough to have 10,000 copies printed and disseminated. 35th Cong., *Senate Journal,* March 30, 1858, 297.

95. Claiborne Report, 1858, 93. According to the statistic compiled by Claiborne, 3,424,502,072 lbs of the total 4,361,526,047 lbs., or 78.5%, of raw cotton imported came from the U.S.

96. Claiborne Report, 6–18.

97. Robert Greenhalgh Albion, *The Rise of New York Port, 1815–1860* (New York: Charles Scribner's Sons, 1939), 399, appendix 8, demonstrates a larger number of shipments directly to France and Germany. By 1860, fifty-three ships left Mobile for France, twenty-one from Charleston and six from Savannah.

98. Claiborne Report, 9.

99. "Consumption of Cotton in Europe," *De Bow's Review* 25, no. 1 (July 1858): 75–76. Also "Cotton Crop of the United States," *De Bow's Review* 28, no. 4 (October 1860): 528–29; "Cotton Is King," 28, no. 5 (November 1860): 588–90; 28, no. 6 (December 1860): 721–23.

100. Quoted in David L. Cohn, *The Life and Times of King Cotton* (New York: Oxford University Press, 1956), 122.

101. "King Cotton," *Semi-Weekly Mississippian* (Jackson), September 23, 1859.

102. *Hunt's Merchants' Magazine* 39: 459; 42: 157; 43: 455, cited in Russell, *Economic Aspects,* 205. The effects of the Panic of 1857 are brilliantly analyzed in James Huston's *The Panic of 1857 and the Coming of the Civil War* (Baton Rouge: Louisiana State University Press, 1987).

103. Boyce's report reprinted in the *Charleston Mercury,* May 31, 1858.

104. C. C. Clay to Wm. Burwell, May 7, 1858, *William M. Burwell Letters,* Library of Congress, cited in Russell, *Economic Aspects,* 164.

105. *Charleston Mercury,* May 24, 1858.

106. Clay's speech, May 4, 1858, *Congressional Globe,* 35th Cong., 1st sess., 1930–1936; vote on passage of repeal, ibid., 35th Cong., 1st sess., 2239.

107. Jefferson Davis, May 11, 1858, *Congressional Globe,* 35th Cong, 1st sess., 2052–54.

108. Senate Vote, May 19, 1858, *Voteview for Windows* software project coded and maintained by Boris Shor at Princeton University; House Vote, February 29, 1859, ibid.

109. In addition to the most common objective, repealing the Navigation Acts, some also included the federal government's ban on the international slave trade in their attack. C. C. Clay to Wm. Burwell, May 7, 1858, *Wm. M. Burwell Letters,* in Russell, *Economic Aspects,* 164.

110. Yancey to Thomas J. Orme, May 22, 1858, in John Witherspoon Du Bose, *The Life and Times of William Lowndes Yancey: A History of Political Parties in the United States from 1824–1864* (Birmingham: Roberts & Son, 1892), 368.

111. "Steam Between New Orleans and Europe," *De Bow's Review* 28, no. 4 (April 1860): 462–64.

112. "Editor's Miscellany," *De Bow's Review* 28, no. 4 (April 1860): 492.

113. Clay's speech, May 4, 1858, *Congressional Globe,* 35th Cong., 1st sess., 1930–1936; vote on passage of repeal, ibid., 35th Cong., 1st sess., 2239.

114. *PJCC,* 1: 217.

115. *New York Weekly Tribune,* July 18, 1846, quoted in Roy M. Robbins, *Our Landed Heritage: The Public Domain, 1776–1936* (Princeton: Princeton University Press, 1942), 96.

116. Huston, *Panic of 1857,* 191; Helene Sona Zahler, *Eastern Workingmen and National Land Policy, 1829–1862* (New York: Columbia University Press, 1941); David M. Potter, *The Impending Crisis, 1848–1861* (New York: HarperCollins, 1976), 391–92, 418–20, 423, 430.

117. May 12, 1852, tabulated from *Voteview for Windows.*

118. Robert W. Johnson of Alabama, quoted in Robbins, *Our Landed Heritage,* 177.

119. The uncertainty created by popular or "squatter" sovereignty precluded slaveholders from risking their extensive capital and fortunes in a place where not even their short-term protection could be guaranteed. The issue became particularly relevant after 1858, when Stephen Douglas, in answer to Lincoln's critique of the Dred Scott decision at Freeport, noted "that slavery cannot exist a day or an hour anywhere, unless it is supported by local police regulations." Allen Johnson, *Stephen A. Douglas* (New York: Chelsea House, 1983), 373.

120. *Voteview for Windows,* Roll Call Statistics, February 1, 1859, Roll Call no. 424, Homestead Bill, House no. 35, 1857–1858; *Voteview for Windows,* Roll Call Statistics, March 12, 1860, Roll Call no. 92, Secure Homesteads to Actual Settlers, House no. 36, 1859–1860. Interestingly, future unionist candidates John Bell of Tennessee and Andrew Johnson viewed the homestead policy more sympathetically, perhaps indicating another difference in the rigidity of Upper and Lower South views on this issue.

121. *Congressional Globe,* 35th Cong., 2nd sess., 242–44, quoted in Russel, *Improvement of Communication,* 229.

122. Cited in Allan Nevins, *The Emergence of Lincoln: Douglas, Buchanan, and Party Chaos, 1857–1859* (New York: Charles Scribner's Sons, 1950), 448.

123. Boyce's speech reprinted in *Daily National Intelligencer* (Washington D.C.), February 19, 1859.

124. Davis to a meeting of the Mississippi Democratic state convention, Jackson, MS, July 6, 1859, cited in May, *Southern Dream,* 188.

125. On the importance of the Cuban debate, see May, *Southern Dream,* 163–89; on continued aspirations, see 235–39.

126. Speech discussed here and and in the subsequent paragraphs is reprinted in *Charleston Mercury,* July 7, 1859.

127. Yancey's Columbia speech, delivered July 8, 1859, is reprinted in *Charleston Mercury,* July 14, 1859.

128. Thomas M. Hanckel, *Government and the Right of Revolution: An Oration Delivered before the '76 Association and the Cincinnati Society* on Monday July 4, 1859 (Charleston: A. J. Burke, 1859), 1–3.

129. *Charleston Mercury,* July 14, 1859.

130. George Holt, "Journal of a Journey to North America," April 12–July 16, 1857, Liverpool Public Record Office, 920DUR2/32/entry from May 1, 1857.

131. W. A. Gregory to William Porcher Miles, February 17, 1860, Miles Papers, UNC-SHC.

132. For Douglass, see John Blassinghame, ed., *The Frederick Douglass Papers* (New Haven: Yale University Press, 1979–), 3: 335–36; Gregory to W. P. Miles, February

17, 1860, Miles Papers, UNC-SHC; Thomas Carlyle, "Occasional Discourse on the Nigger Question," in Carlyle, *Latter Day Pamphlets* (London: Chapman & Hall, 1858). See also Thomas Holt, *The Problem of Freedom: Race, Labor, and Politics in Jamaica and Britain, 1832–1938* (Baltimore: John Hopkins University Press, 1992), 179–82, and Richard Blackett, *Divided Hearts: Britain and the American Civil War* (Baton Rouge: Louisiana State University Press, 2001), 36–38.

133. Evelyn Ashley (10 Downing Street) to William Porcher Miles, August 18, 1859, Miles Papers, UNC-SHC, folder 15.

134. W. H. Gregory to W. P. Miles, May 22, 1860, Miles Papers, UNC-SHC, file 20.

135. Ian Radforth, *Royal Spectacle: The 1860 Visit of the Prince of Wales to Canada and the United States* (Toronto: University of Toronto Press, 2005). The effort and "snub" received some national attention, see "Slavery Agitation Invitation for the Prince of Wales to Visit the South," *New York Times,* September 21, 1860.

136. Longstreet's public letter was picked up in southern newspapers. *Charleston Courier, Tri-Weekly,* August 9, 1860. Several papers reported the incident as a southerner standing up for the insulted Pennsylvanian minister George M. Dallas. See, for example, "Lord Brougham's Insult to Mr. Dallas Resented by a Southerner," *Weekly Mississippian* (Jackson), August 29, 1860; *Charleston Courier, Tri-Weekly,* August 25, 1860.

137. G. Barnsley to Wm. Duncan, Esq., February 25, 1860, Godfrey Barnsley Papers, MSS 1737, Hargrett Rare Book and Manuscript Library, University of Georgia (typescript, 1860).

138. *Congressional Globe,* 37th Cong., 1st sess., 658. The proposal stood in stark contrast to the Mississippi legislator's 1854 state intention "to counteract and prohibit all attempts by Congress to impose slavery restriction on any territory of the United States; and that any territory has the indisputable right to seek admission; as a State of the Union, with or without slavery, as the people thereof may determine." Series 1701, box 6818, folder "Resolutions," Mississippi State Archives (Jackson, Miss.).

139. Morrison, *Slavery and the American West,* 211–15.

140. Barney, *Secessionist Impulse,* 151.

141. J. H. Hammond to M. C. M. Hammond, April 22, 1860, cited in Harold S. Schultz, *Nationalism and Sectionalism in South Carolina, 1852–1860: A Study of the Movement for Southern Independence* (Durham: Duke University Press, 1950), 205.

142. Morrison, *Slavery and the American West,* 213.

143. "The Secession of the South," *De Bow's Review* 28, no. 4 (April 1860): 382.

144. Alfred Huger to W. P. Miles, April 4, 1860, Miles Papers, UNC-SHC.

145. Roy Franklin Nichols, *The Disruption of American Democracy* (New York: Macmillan, 1948); *Official Proceedings of the Democratic National Convention Held in 1860 at Charleston and Baltimore, Proceedings at Charleston,* April 23–May 3, Prepared and Published under the Direction of John G. Parkhurst, Recording Secretary (Cleveland: Nevins' Print, 1860).

146. Anthony Gene Carey, *Parties, Slavery, and the Union in Antebellum Georgia* (Athens: University of Georgia Press, 1997), 216–17; Thornton, *Politics and Power,* 418.

147. "Aid and Comfort to the Enemy—The Cloven Foot Visible," *Semi-weekly Mississippian* August 7, 1860.

148. William Windom, "The Homestead Bill—Its Friends and its Foes: Speech of Hon. William Windom of Minn.," delivered March 14, 1860 (Washington, D.C., 1860), 6, 2.

149. Horace Greeley to Mrs. R. M. Whipple, April 1860, quoted in Potter, *Impending Crisis*, 420.

150. My understanding of Republican ideology and the party draws from both Holt's *Political Crisis*, esp. 183–218, and Eric Foner, *Free Soil, Free Labor, Free Men: The Ideology of the Republican Party before the Civil War* (New York: Oxford University Press, 1970); Hutson, *The Panic of 1857*, esp. 264–69; John R. Commons, "Horace Greeley and the Working Class Origins of the Republican Party," *Political Science Quarterly* 24 (1909): 468–88. On the convention, see Potter, *Impending Crisis*, 430–31.

151. This theme is discussed in Thomas P. Martin, "Conflicting Cotton Interests at Home and Abroad, 1848–1857," *Journal of Southern History* 7, no. 2 (May 1941): 173–94. Yancey, in an October Cooper Institute address, noted that "Mr. Seward sneers at" the forty millions of dollars in interregional trade, most of it in cotton and textiles and said, "Lincoln, I presume, would never think of making it a material subject of consideration in the way of legislation." "The Impending Crisis," *New York Herald*, October 11, 1860.

152. The connection was occasionally explicit. Campaigning in the years leading up to 1860 drew heavily on competing portraits of the meaning of early "Republicanism." Lincoln supporters elevated themselves as the true heirs to a party which had, among other things, passed the Northwest Ordinance precluding slavery in the Northwest Territories, sought to end economic dependence on Great Britain, and rallied the military forces to preserve a diverse nation. Politicians in the South, in turn, elevated their own understanding of the roots of what they were now forced to call the "Democratic" Party.

153. *Charleston Mercury,* April 30 and August 28, 1860.

154. John Townsend, *The South Alone Should Govern the South and African Slavery Should be Controlled by those only who are Friendly to it* (Charleston, 1860), 8. At least one historian, inclined to see secession as a conspiracy led by the secretive South Carolina Association, overlooks the fact that perhaps the most prominent secessionist tract emerged out of resolutions passed during a community meeting. Freehling, *Road to Disunion,* 2: 391.

155. Townsend, *The South Alone,* mistake quote (18), abolition (19), British views (20); *Charleston Courier, Tri-Weekly,* September 13, 1860.

156. *Charleston Courier, Tri-Weekly,* September 13, 1860; Townsend, *The South Alone,* 20.

157. Townsend, *The South Alone,* 54.

158. Thomas Prentice Kettell believed southern manufacturing had advanced out of its infant stage. *Southern Wealth and Northern Profits* (1860; Tuscaloosa: University of Alabama Press, 1965), 61.

159. Holt, "Journey to North America," Liverpool Public Record Office, May 1 and 3; To John Frazer & Co., September 22, 1829, McConnel and Kennedy (hereafter MCK), February 2, 1818, letterbook of MCK, December 1828–April 1830, Papers of McConnel & Kennedy and McConnel & Co., 1715–1888, John Rylands Library. J. J. Pringle Smith and Gourdin applied to Miles for a passport in late June 1858. J. J. Pringle Smith to W. P. Miles, June 3, 1858, Miles Papers, UNC-SHC.

160. Numbers from Freehling, *Road to Disunion*, 2: 393–94. John Townsend, *The Doom of Slavery in the Union: Its Safety Out of It*, 2nd ed. (Charleston: Evans & Cogswell), 13.

161. Steven Channing, *Crisis of Fear: Secession in South Carolina* (New York: Simon & Schuster, 1970), 245.

162. "The Impending Crisis," *New York Herald*, October 11, 1860. For an insightful account of this tour, see Walther, *William Lowndes Yancey*, 251–73, quotes from 262, 259.

163. Du Bose, *Life and Times of William Lowndes Yancey*, 532–34.

164. *New Orleans Daily Crescent*, November 15, 1860, reprinted in Dwight L. Dumond, *Southern Editorials on Secession* (1931; Gloucester: Peter Smith, 1964), 241.

165. For a brief discussion of New York City politics in the buildup to secession, see Sven Beckert's *The Monied Metropolis: New York City and the Consolidation of the American Bourgeoisie, 1850–1896* (New York: Oxford University Press, 2001), 78–97.

166. *New Orleans Bee*, December 5, 14, 1860, quoted in Donald E. Reynolds, *Editors Make War: Southern Newspapers in the Secession Crisis* (Nashville: Vanderbilt University Press, 1970), 156–57.

167. Dumond, *Southern Editorials*, 243.

168. S. D. Moore, "The Irrepressible Conflict and Impending Crisis," *De Bow's Review* 28, no. 5 (November 1860): 531–51, quotes from 532–33.

169. Howell Cobb, "Letter . . . to the People of Georgia," in Wakelyn, *Southern Pamphlets*, 88–89.

170. Trescot, "Position and Course," 15.

171. These themes, and especially the centrality of property rights for southern arguments, are superbly explored in three recent works: Huston, *Calculating the Value of Union;* David L. Lightner, *Slavery and the Commerce Power: How the Struggle against the Interstate Slave Trade Led to the Civil War* (New Haven: Yale University Press, 2006), esp., 140–64; and Gavin Wright, *Slavery and American Economic Development* (Baton Rouge: Louisiana State University Press, 2006). Each of these studies, along with my own, suggest the limits of approaches centered on honor or rhetoric. See, for example, Elizabeth R. Varon, *Disunion!: The Coming of the American Civil War, 1789–1859* (Chapel Hill: University of North Carolina Press, 2008).

172. Jabez Lamar Monroe Curry, "The Perils and Duty of the South," speech delivered in Talladega, Alabama, November 26, 1860, reprinted in Wakelyn, *Southern Pamphlets*, 51.

173. W. H. C., "A Southern View of Affairs," reprinted from *New York Express*, in *Charleston Courier*, November 1, 1860.

174. Morris, a poet for *Harper's Weekly*, unintentionally aided the effort, having composed a poem, "King Cotton," that in the summer of 1860 was set to music on Broadway, dedicated to Savannah's port collector John Boston, and sold in local music stores. See, for example, *Charleston Courier, Tri-Weekly*, September 1, 1860.

175. In early November the French-speaking *New York Courrier des États Unis* reported rumors that South Carolina disunionists had already made "preparatory overtures" to French officials in hopes of placing Charleston's port under French protection. The following week, eager New York journalists reported news of an "informal meeting" of "distinguished Southern statesmen from the cotton and Gulf States" of Alabama, South Carolina, Georgia, Florida, and Mississippi. That meeting

purportedly drafted a "Southern Manifesto" and a "Declaration of Independence" and instructed "a distinguished Southerner now in Paris" to extract "promise of friendly recognition from Louis Napoleon." "South Carolina and the Emperor Napoleon," reprinted from *New York Courrier des États Unis,* in *Fayetteville Observer* (N.C.), November 8, 1860. Reports of the "diabolical" secessionist meeting circulated widely through papers outside the south, which printed the "Manifesto," "Declaration," and "Instructions." *New York Herald,* November 14, 1860; *Daily Evening Bulletin* (San Francisco), November 17, 1860; *Bangor Daily Whig & Courier,* November 17, 1860.

176. Even Miles's close friend, Trescot, however, informed him of the difficulty of continuing to assert secession as a constitutional rather than a natural right. "Narrative of William Henry Trescot, concerning the Negotiations between South Carolina and President Buchanan," in December 1860, *American Historical Review* 13, no. 3 (April 1908): 528–56.

177. Lyons forwarded the message on to Lord Russell because he had "heard it represented as an overture from South Carolina," though he did not "bear that construction" of it and would not make an answer. Lyons to Russell, December 4, 1860, dispatch 303, in James J. Barnes and Patience P. Barnes, *The American Civil War through British Eyes: Dispatches from British Diplomats* (Kent: Kent State University Press, 2003), 1: 4. Wm. D. Porter, *State Sovereignty and the Doctrine of Coercion together with a Letter from J. K. Paulding, Former Sec. of Navy,* 1860 Association, tract 2, (n.p., n.d.).

178. "Despatch from the British Consul at Charleston to Lord John Russell, 1860," *American Historical Review* 18, no. 4 (July 1913): 783–87.

179. Ibid., 785–86.

180. Ibid.

181. William Mure to Russell, December 13, 1860, Fo5/744, cited in Walther, *William Lowndes Yancey,* 303.

182. "Stephens's Unionist Speech," November 14, 1860, in William W. Freehling and Craig M. Simpson, eds., *Secession Debated: Georgia's Showdown in 1860* (New York: Oxford University Press, 1992), esp. 60–66. For Stephens's own journey from disillusionment with the election of 1860, to hope for compromise, to supporter of secession, see Thomas E. Scott, *Alexander H. Stephens of Georgia: A Biography* (Baton Rouge: Louisiana State University Press, 1988), 301–28.

183. Both Freehling and Michael Johnson have stressed that unionist sentiment was more pervasive in the Lower South than previously thought. Freehling and Simpson, *Secession Debated,* introduction; Johnson, *Toward a Patriarchal Republic: The Secession of Georgia* (Baton Rouge: Louisiana State University Press, 1977). This may be true, but both authors have interpreted votes for "cooperation" as "unionist." It is important to remember that "cooperation" still often pointed toward disunion as an end. An examination of the secession conventions throughout the South can be found in Wooster, *Secession Conventions.* Examinations of secessionist leaders include David S. Heidler, *Pulling the Temple Down: The Fire-Eaters and the Destruction of the Union* (Mechanicsburg, Pa.: Stackpole Books, 1994); Walther, *The Fire-Eaters.*

184. *Charleston Courier,* December 8, 1860.

185. Joseph Jones, M.D., *Agricultural Resources of Georgia: Address before the Cotton Planters' Convention of Georgia at Macon,* December 13, 1860 (Augusta: Steam Press of Chronicle & Sentinel, 1861), 10, 11; Jones, *First Report to the Cotton Planters'*

*Convention of Georgia* (Augusta: Steam Press of Chronicle & Sentinel, 1860), *Memorial of the Cotton Planters' Convention to the Honorable Senate and House of Representatives of the State of Georgia in General Assembly Met* (Augusta: Steam Press of Chronicle & Sentinel, 1860), Georgia State Archives.

186. Jones, *Agricultural Resources of Georgia*, 11–12.

187. Laurent de Give to the Belgian minister of foreign affairs, January 20, 1861, in Paul Evans and Thomas P. Govan, eds., "A Belgian Consul on Conditions in the South in 1860 and 1862," *Journal of Southern History* 3, no. 4 (November 1938): 481. Governor Joseph Brown had met with a special envoy from Belgium in May Brown to His Excellency Blondell Van Culebreck, May 8, 1860, Georgia, Executive Department Collection, Governor's letterbooks, 1860, Georgia State Archives.

188. De Give to the Belgian Minister, January 20, 1861, in Evans and Govan, "Belgian Consul," 481. This law was the first passed during the legislative session, December 18, 1860, *Acts of the General Assembly of Georgia*, 1: 7, accessible through Galileo: http://dlg.galileo.usg.edu/zlgl.

189. *De Bow's Review* 29, no. 6 (December 1860): 800.

190. Molyneaux to Russell, November 28 and December 13, 1860, F05/744, cited in Walther, *William Lowndes Yancey*, 303.

191. For Brown's requests for the service of Lt. Col. Hardee to travel to Europe for arms, see Brown to Howell Cobb, November 22, 1860, Georgia Executive Department, Governor's letterbooks, Georgia State Archives; *New York Herald*, January 10, 1860. For King's appointment and instructions, see *The Confederate Records of the State of Georgia* (Atlanta: Chas. P. Byrd, 1909), 2: 18–24.

192. On the importance of political dynamics, see Holt, *Political Crisis of the 1850s;* Daniel W. Crofts, *Reluctant Confederates: Upper South Unionists in the Secession Crisis* (Chapel Hill: University of North Carolina Press, 1989), chaps. 2 and 3; William G. Shade, *Democratizing the Old Dominion: Virginia and the Second Party System, 1824–1861* (Charlottesville: University of Virginia Press, 1996). For an explanation of the divisions in the Lower South premised partly on the different "cultural hearths" of Virginia versus Georgia and South Carolina, see Marc Egnal, "Rethinking the Secession of the Lower South: The Clash of Two Groups," *Civil War History* 50, no. 3 (September 2004): 261–90.

193. For analysis stressing this, see esp. Channing, *Crisis of Fear;* William Freehling, *Road to Disunion*, vol. 2; Charles Dew, *Apostles of Disunion: Southern Secession Commissioners and the Causes of the Civil War* (Charlottesville: University of Virginia Press, 2002).

194. Huston, *Calculating the Value of Union;* Wright, *Political Economy of the Cotton South* and *Slavery and American Economic Development;* Lightner, *Slavery and the Commerce Power.*

195. As Georgia secessionist Thomas R. R. Cobb later emphasized, the "protective tariffs and homestead bills—acquisition of territory—peace or war with foreign powers" were, unlike slavery, more "*temporary in their nature.*" Cobb, "Secessionist Speech, Monday Evening, November 12," in Freehling and Simpson, *Secession Debated,* 15.

196. McCrary, Miller, and Baum, "Class and Party in the Secession Crisis," 452–54; see also, Wright, *Political Economy of the Cotton South;* Barney, *Secessionist Impulse,* 296; Wooster, *Secession Conventions.*

197. Toombs rejoinder to Stephens's speech, in Freehling and Simpson, *Secession Debated*, 63.

198. No complete text of Stephens's "Cornerstone Address" exists, but a newspaper edition was reprinted in Frank Moore, ed., *The Republican Record: A Diary of American Events*, 12 vols. (New York: G. P. Putman, 1862–1867), 1: 44–49, and has been reprinted in Wakelyn, *Southern Pamphlets*, 402–12.

199. Trescot to Governor of State of So. Ca. (Confidential), December 14, 1860, reprinted in "Narrative of William Henry Trescot," 556.

200. Remarks written in February 1861, reprinted in "Narrative of William Henry Trescot," 552.

201. Gavin Wright's important work provides convincing evidence of the general economic optimism of the 1850s and of the fear that Republican control would lead to a drop in cotton prices. See Wright, *Political Economy of the Cotton South*, 128–57. At least some people overseas shared their expectation and funneled illicit support to the Confederate cause, most notoriously in a guns-for-cotton trade through the Mexican port of Matamoros. There were many British authors emphasizing the desirability of an independent Southern Confederacy. For one written by a Member of Parliament, see George McHenry, *The Cotton Trade: Its Bearing upon the Prosperity of Great Britain and Commerce of the American Republics* (London: Saunders, Otley, & Co., 1863).

202. Jonathan Elliot, *The Debates in the Several State Conventions on the Adoption of the Federal Constitution* (Philadelphia: J. B. Lippincott, 1836–1859), 4: 244–45.

## Epilogue, 1861

1. William C. Davis, *A Government of Our Own: The Making of the Confederacy* (New York: Free Press, 1994), 31–42 (Montgomery and background), 23 (flag).

2. Constitution of the Confederate States of America, Article 1, Section 9.4.

3. Reprinted in Henry Cleveland, *Alexander H. Stephens, in Public and Private: With Letters and Speeches, before, during, and since the War* (Philadelphia: National Pub. Co., 1886), 717–29.

4. Constitution of the Confederate States of America, Article 1, Section 8.3 and Section 10.3.

5. Robert Barnwell Rhett, *A Fire-Eater Remembers: The Confederate Memoir of Robert Barnwell Rhett*, ed. William C. Davis (Columbia: University of South Carolina Press, 2000), 28. See also the reprint of a letter reminiscing on these events (along with Davis's helpful editorial notes), in ibid., 118–23.

6. Jabez Curry to Anderson, February 20, 1861, Petrie Scrapbook, cited in Davis, *A Government of Our Own*, 202.

7. Rhett, *A Fire-Eater Remembers*, 28.

8. James W. Daddysman, *The Matamoros Trade: Confederate Commerce, Diplomacy and Intrigue* (Newark: University of Delaware Press, 1983).

9. T. R. R. Cobb to wife, February 19, 1861, in *The Correspondence of Thomas Reade Rootes Cobb, 1860–1862*, Southern History Association Publications, 11 (May and June 1907), 185, 257–60.

10. Bunch to Russell, no. 9, June 1861, FO 780, part 1, cited in Frank Lawrence Owsley, *King Cotton Diplomacy: Foreign Regions of the Confederate States of America* (1931; Chicago: University of Chicago Press, 1959), 22.

11. Journal entry, May 21, 1861, in Beth G. Patton and James W. Patton, eds., *Journal of a Secesh Lady: The Diary of Catherine Ann Devereux Edmondston, 1860–1866* (Raleigh: North Carolina Division of Archives and History, 1979), 63, electronic version at Alexander Street: www.alexanderstreet4.com/cgi-bin/asp/philomain/con textualize_?p.14380./projects/artfla/databases/asp/nawld/fulltext/IMAGE/.12480 (accessed January 3, 2009).

12. William Howard Russell, *Civil War: Private Diary and Letters, 1861–1862* (Athens: University of Georgia Press, 1992), passim. Bunch cited in Henry Blumenthal, "Confederate Diplomacy: Popular Notions and International Realities," *Journal of Southern History* (May 1966): 153.

13. On Mercier and Slidell, see Blumenthal, "Confederate Diplomacy," 154. The meeting between Lyons and Mercier is described in Lyons to Russell, March 30, 1861, reprinted in James J. Barnes and Patience P. Barnes, eds., *The American Civil War through British Eyes: Dispatches from British Diplomats* (Kent: Kent State University Press, 2003), 1: 42–45. Lyons did acknowledge that though he agreed with the arguments he did not wish the power of recognition to be placed in the hands of U.S. ministers, as Mercier contended should happen. Mercier's activities and the economic rationale behind them are detailed in Daniel B. Carroll, *Henry Mercier and the American Civil War* (Princeton: Princeton University Press, 1971).

14. Quoted in Michael Fellman, Lesley Gordon, and Daniel Sutherland, *This Terrible War: The Civil War and Its Aftermath* (New York: Longman Press, 2003), 98.

15. Yancey and Rost to Toombs, May 10, 1861, in *A Compilation of the Messages and Papers of the Confederacy, including the Diplomatic Correspondence, 1861–1865* (Nashville: United States Publishing Company, 1905), 2: 18.

16. I thank Scott Marler for letting me preview his insightful article, "'An Abiding Faith in Cotton': The Merchant Capitalist Community of New Orleans, 1860–1862," *Civil War History* 54, no. 3 (August 2008): 247–76.

17. Ibid. Bunch to Russell, no. 93, August 3, 1861, FO, 781: 2, cited in Owsley, *King Cotton Diplomacy*, 27.

18. The bonds were printed using New York connections through former Savannah resident and president of New York's Bank of the Republic, Gazaway B. Lamar. See Edwin B. Coddington, "The Activities and Attitudes of a Confederate Business Man: Gazaway B. Lamar," *Journal of Southern History* 9, no. 1 (February 1943): 3–36; Davis, *A Government of Our Own*, 347.

19. Howell and T. R. R. Cobb, "To the Planters of Georgia," 1861, *Confederate Imprints, 1861–1865* (New Haven, Conn.: Research Publications, [1974]), reel 94, no. 2904–2.

20. Richard Cecil Todd, *Confederate Finance* (Athens: University of Georgia Press, 1954), 25–64, fig. 63.

21. Sven Beckert, "Emancipation and Empire: Reconstructing the Worldwide Web of Cotton Production in the Age of the American Civil War," *American Historical Review* 109, no. 5 (December 2004): 1405–38.

22. Robert Toombs, Secretary of State, to William Yancey, Pierre A. Rost, A. Dudley Mann, March 16, 1861, in *Compilation of the Messages and Papers of the Confederacy*, 2: 7. Relying on Rhett's self-serving account, most historians have entirely mischaracterized Davis's position, arguing that he (and not public opinion) had pressed the cotton embargo and, secondly, that he had not empowered the European

commissioners to negotiate treaties, which their instructions clearly did provide for. Blumenthal, "Confederate Diplomacy," and Charles Hubbard, *The Burden of Confederate Diplomacy* (Knoxville: University of Tennessee Press, 1998), 15; Davis, *A Government of Our Own*, 204.

23. *Journal of the Congress of the Confederate States of America* (Washington, D.C.: Government Printing Office, 1904), 1: 253. Both William Davis and Hubbard mistakenly identify Rhett's last maneuver as taking place in mid-May and argue that it had not been discussed after it was put on the calendar on May 15. It was on May 20, when Cobb moved to have the time reduced to five (not six, as Rhett suggested) years. The subjects of duties also briefly reemerged the following February, until a bill by John Perkins and an amendment by Kenner postponed all discussion of duty collection indefinitely, this being the final attempt Rhett refers to in his memorial. Rhett, *A Fire-Eater Remembers*, 124, n12; Hubbard, *Burden of Confederate Diplomacy*, 24–25. For the last-ditch effort, see *Journal of the Confederate Congress* 1: 757, and Perkins/Kenner amendment, 828. On Varina Davis's own self-serving defense of Davis's actions, see *Jefferson Davis, Ex-President of the Confederate States of America: A Memoir by His Wife* (New York: Belford Co., 1890), 159–61.

24. For one of the many fine studies on the memory of the war, see David W. Blight, *Race and Reunion: The Civil War in American Memory* (Cambridge: Belknap Press, 2002).

# Essay on Sources

PRIMARY SOURCES

This book is largely about how elites, responding to constituents' interests, defined and articulated political and economic positions to local, national, and international audiences. Accordingly, it relies heavily on materials intended for the broader public, including printed speeches, national and regional periodicals, pamphlets, and newspapers. Records of the debates in the U.S. Congress—some of which were subsequently reprinted in pamphlet form—have proven particularly invaluable for every stage of this project. In them, politicians and policymakers calculated, prepared, and presented key articles meant to win over not just their colleagues but also, in many cases, voters at home. Though often speeches were prepared in advance, responses were more often than not unscripted. As a result these records bring together an extensive, though certainly not exhaustive, discussion of interests, ideas, and pure politics to help explain much about American society, politics, and thought during that period. They remain, I believe, one of the least-tapped resources for current historians of any genre and are easily accessible. For the years covering 1789 to 1824, see the *Annals of Congress* (Washington, D.C.: Gales & Seaton, 1834–56); for 1824 to 1837; *Register of Debates* (Washington, D.C.: Gales & Seaton, 1835–37); and for the remainder of the antebellum period, the *Congressional Globe* (Washington, D.C.: Office of the Congressional Globe, 1833–1860). I have also used petitions and reports available as part of the *American State Papers,* especially those series labeled "Commerce" and "Finance."

The interpretation of the 1787 federal convention and South Carolinian and Georgian delegates' roles in it relies on Max Farrand, ed., *The Records of the Federal Convention,* 3 vols. (New Haven: Yale University Press, 1911). Jonathan Elliot's, *Debates in the Several State Conventions on the Adoption of the Federal Constitution* (Philadelphia: J. B. Lippincott, 1836–1859), and Merrill Jenson et al., eds., *The Documentary History of the Ratification of the Constitution* (Madison: State Historical Society of Wisconsin, 1976–), were especially useful for identifying how they and other leaders perceived the document within their respective states. The analysis of commercial policy offered in chapter 1 relies on the immensely valuable debates and private correspondence collected in Kenneth Bowling et al., eds., *Documentary History of the First Federal Congress* 13 vols. (Baltimore: Johns Hopkins University Press, 1972–).

Not all public discourse, of course, happens within clearly delineated political institutions. Consequently, this book draws heavily upon national, regional, and local print culture. Early state and national debates, including those over amnesty to

Loyalists and the Jay Treaty were followed through the *South Carolina Gazette and General Advertiser* (Charleston: J. Miller, 1783–1784), the *Columbian Herald* (Charleston: Harrison, Bowen & Markland, 1785–1792); the *Augusta Chronicle and Gazette of the State* (Augusta, Ga.: John E. Smith, 1789–1806); the *Georgia Gazette* (Savannah: James & Nicholas Johnston, 1788–1802). On the debates over Jefferson's embargo and the buildup to the War of 1812, I consulted the *Carolina Gazette* (Freneau & Paine, 1798–1840) and the *Republican and Savannah Evening Ledger* (Savannah, Ga.: John Everitt, 1807–1816) as well as the full-text newspaper database offered by Readex, *Early American Newspapers,* series 1.

The debates over the nullification period and the American System were traced through the numerous public petitions sent to Congress found in the *American State Papers, Class 3: Finance,* and in the appendixes to the *Annals of Congress,* 18th Cong., as well as the *Register of Debates.* In addition, I used the documents in William Freehling's useful (but unfortunately abridged) *The Nullification Era: A Documentary Record* (New York: Harper Torchbooks, 1967); Herman Belz, ed., *The Webster-Hayne Debate on the Nature of the Union: Selected Documents* (Indianapolis: Liberty Fund, 2000); and *State Papers on Nullification* (1834; New York: Da Capo Press, 1970). The nationally prominent *Niles Weekly Register*'s (Baltimore: 1811–1849) support for protectionism and critiques of free trade provided context for the political economic debates of the period. The *Southern Review* (Charleston, S.C.: 1828–1832) and Thomson-Gale's *Nineteenth-Century U.S. Newspapers* provided snapshots into how powerful editors and contributors shaped and responded to local public opinion over these and other controversial subjects. The Rare Americana Collection at the Library Company of Philadelphia remains one of the most extensive collections of books, tracts, and pamphlets from the early to mid-nineteenth century, resources that were particularly useful in tracking the debates over political economy and slavery. Included at that repository are full runs of Condy Raguet's *Banner of the Constitution* (Philadelphia, 1831–1832), which proved invaluable for shedding light on previously unstudied aspects to the crisis, including the 1832 Free Trade Convention.

Efforts to promote a southern regional identity and articulate interests in a regional manner accelerated during the late antebellum period and can be traced through journals such as the *Southern Quarterly Review* (Columbia, S.C.: 1842–1857), *Southern Literary Messenger* (Richmond, Va.: 1835–1861), and most significantly for this study, *De Bow's Review* (New Orleans: 1846–1861), which reprinted records of many of the various commercial conventions. On secession the edited collections by Dwight L. Dumond, ed., *Southern Editorials on Secession* (1931; Gloucester, Mass.: Peter Smith, 1964), and Jon L. Wakelyn, *Southern Pamphlets on Secession, November 1860–April 1861* (Chapel Hill: University of North Carolina Press, 1996), provided useful glimpses into those debates, as did the Thomson and Gale *Nineteenth-Century Newspaper* collection and Readex's *Early American Newspapers,* series 2, 3, and 4. Records for individual states' legislatures and conventions tasked with discussing secession have been digitized at the University of North Carolina as part of its Historical Southern Collection.

Sources intended for public consumption have been strategically supplemented with reprinted and archived personal papers that allow for a clearer understanding of individuals' thoughts and actions. In addition to the dozens of biographies or early historical journals that reprint entire or excerpted letters and are cited in the notes, I have leaned heavily on paper projects tasked with bringing together a comprehensive record of men in key policy-making positions. The most frequently used for this project were the Jefferson Papers, which have found their way to print in Julian Boyd et al., *The Papers of Thomas Jefferson* (Princeton: Princeton University Press, 1950–), and those that have not yet but are available through the digital archive at the Library of Congress: http://memory.loc.gov/ammem/collections/jefferson_papers. The recently completed *Papers of John C. Calhoun,* ed. Robert Lee Meriwether et al. (Columbia: University of South Carolina Press, 1959–2003), 28 vols., provide invaluable insights into the private thoughts and public actions of an individual often at the center of these debates or corresponding with people who were. The same can be said about the first six volumes of *The Papers of Jefferson Davis,* ed. Lynda L. Crist et al. (Baton Rouge: Louisiana State University Press, 1971–).

Various manuscript collections, papers, and correspondences at the University of North Carolina Southern Historical Collection (hereafter UNC-SHC) were instrumental in identifying private strategies of key players in the sectional and subsequently secessionist movement. By far the most revealing was the "William Porcher Miles Papers," microfilm no. 1-4485. Miles's close proximity to events in Washington, D.C., in the years prior to war and his close correspondence with secessionists provide fascinating glimpses as events unfolded. Also consulted were the Christopher G. Memminger Papers, UNC-SHC, no. 502, and the Robert Barnwell Rhett Papers, UNC-SHC, no. 3204. The Quitman Family Papers, UNC-SHC, no. 616, and J. F. H. Claiborne Papers, UNC-SHC, no. 151, proved especially important for understanding Mississippi's efforts at economic diversification in the 1830s. So, too, were the John Quitman Papers available at the Mississippi State Archives, z66.

In addition to holding copies of some of the early direct trade conventions, the Hargrett Rare Book and Manuscript Library at the University of Georgia possesses the Godfrey Barnsley Papers, MSS 1737. Barnsley was a cotton factor and planter whose vast networks throughout the world made him an invaluable and largely untapped source for information about the cotton trade and southern commerce. The Georgia State Archives has copies of the memorial of the 1860 cotton planter and direct convention. The "Governor's letterbooks" available under the Executive Department Collection provide an interesting glimpse into the official (and at times unofficial) correspondence of the state leader, Joseph Brown, tasked with readying the state for secession. "The Letters of Joseph Clay," published as part of *The Collections of the Georgia Historical Society* (Savannah: The Morning News, 1913), illuminated aspects of the early cotton business.

Paper collections at the University of South Carolina's South Caroliniana Library offer a treasure trove of prominent South Carolinians important for this work. Collections that were used include the George McDuffie Papers, Christopher Gustavus Memminger Papers, 1803–1888, Robert Young Hayne Papers, Rutledge Family Papers, William Campbell Preston Papers, and the Williams-Miller-Chesnut-Manning Family Papers. Also used were papers at the South Carolina Historical Society, namely from the Bacot-Huger Collection: R. Dewar Bacot Business Papers, Chesnut Plantation & Political Papers, and the Robert Barnwell Rhett Papers.

In addition to its vast collection of images and pamphlets, the Williams Research Center at the Historical New Orleans Collection contains a number of collections affording access to the commercial life of the South's chief port city. Those consulted for this work include Commercial Files, MSS 405; Allen Holland Financial Papers, MSS 461; Charles Monnot Family Papers, MSS 466; John J. Moore Papers, 1847–1865, MSS 12; Enoch Silsby Letters, MSS 413; and Thomas Murdoch Letters, MSS 439. The Matthew Carey Papers are part of the Edward Carey Gardiner Collection (MSS F3) at the Historical Society of Pennsylvania and helped with the tariff debates.

Published collections of correspondence between British officials provide a revealing look into their public and private assessment of the power of cotton as it related to specific policies, including the Negro Seaman's Acts and expansion: James J. Barnes and Patience P. Barnes, *Private and Confidential: Letters from British Ministers in Washington to the Foreign Secretaries in London, 1844–67* (Selinsgrove: Susquehanna University Press, 1993). James J. Barnes and Patience P. Barnes, *The American Civil War through British Eyes: Dispatches from British Diplomats* (Kent: Kent State University Press, 2003); Kenneth Bourne, "The Clayton-Bulwer Treaty and the Decline of British Opposition to the Territorial Expansion of the United States, 1857–60," *Journal of Modern History* 33, no. 3 (September 1961): 287–91; Richard W. Van Alstyne, "Anglo-American Relations, 1853–1857: British Statesmen on the Clayton-Bulwer Treaty and American Expansion," *American Historical Review* 42, no. 3 (April 1937), 491–500; Gavin B. Henderson, "Southern Designs on Cuba and Some European Opinions," *Journal of Southern History* 5, no. 3 (August 1939), 371–85; and "Despatch from the British Consul at Charleston to Lord John Russell, 1860," *American Historical Review* 18, no. 4 (July 1915): 783–87. For a Belgian perspective, see Thomas P. Govan, ed., "A Belgian Consul on Conditions in the South in 1860 and 1862," *Journal of Southern History* 3, no. 4 (November 1938): 478–91.

These printed materials were supplemented with materials from a variety of archives in Britain. The Consulate and Foreign Office Papers at the British National Archives in Kew include many revealing facets of American policy and of diplomatic relations between the two countries. Foreign Office Papers in series 4 and 5, especially reports from consuls dispatched to Charleston, Savannah, Mobile, and New Orleans, were examined. Particularly helpful was the *Correspondence Relative to the Prohibition Against the Admission of Free Persons of Colour*, F.O. 5/579. The Aberdeen Papers (4.2131), Huskisson Papers (no. 38756), and Peel Papers (no. 40588) in the British Library all provided revealing nuggets related to the political and economic situation of the period. A window into the early transatlantic cotton trade was offered by an examination of two firms available in the *Papers of McConnel & Kennedy* and the *Papers of the Fielden Brothers, 1811–1906* at the John Rylands Library in Manchester. Smaller collections at the British Library, Manchester Central Library, and Liverpool Public Record Office provided interesting morsels of information about the Atlantic context for these developments. Too little is known about William Henry Trescot, but the Miles Papers (cited above) and the "Narrative of William Henry Trescot, concerning the Negotiations between South Carolina and President Buchanan," *American Historical Review* 13, no. 3 (April 1908): 528–56, provide interesting firsthand accounts during a critical moment.

SECONDARY SOURCES
## Context and Cotton

This book is largely about economic and political ideas, and several recent works provide the context for that discussion. Istvan Hont, *Jealousy of Trade: International Competition and the Nation-State in Historical Perspective* (Cambridge: The Belknap Press of Harvard University Press, 2005); and Douglas A. Irwin, *Against the Tide: An Intellectual History of Free Trade* (Princeton: Princeton University Press, 1997); and Bernard Semmel, *The Rise of Free Trade Imperialism: Classical Political Economy and the Empire of Free Trade and Imperialism, 1750–1850* (Cambridge: Cambridge University Press, 1970), offer very different accounts of how and why Atlantic political and economic thought began to be reconceived in the eighteenth century. The role of the American Revolution in American economic thinking is explored in Lawrence A. Peskin, *Manufacturing Revolution: The Intellectual Origins of Early American Industry* (Baltimore: Johns Hopkins University Press, 2003). The influence of Peter Onuf and Nicholas Onuf, *Federal Union, Modern World: The Law of Nations in an Age of Revolutions, 1776–1814* (Madison: Madison House, 1993), and *Nations, Markets, and War: Modern History and the American Civil War* (Charlottesville: University of Virginia Press, 2006); John McCardell, *The Idea of a Southern Nation: Southern Nationalists and Southern Nationalism, 1830–1860* (New York: Norton,1979); and Michael O'Brien's *Conjectures of Order: Intellectual Life and the American South, 1810–1860* (Chapel Hill: University of North Carolina Press, 2004), will be apparent to anyone who has digested these thoughtful works. David Brion Davis, *The Problem of Slavery in the Age of Revolution, 1770–1823* (Ithaca: Cornell University Press, 1975), must frame any discussion of slavery during this important period, while a useful introduction to slavery's broader Atlantic context is offered in Robin Blackburn, *The Making of New World Slavery: From the Baroque to the Modern, 1492–1800* (New York: Verso Press, 1997).

Cultural shifts often drive economic forces, and this seems to have been the case with the cotton business. For more on cotton's consumer culture and fashion trends during the eighteenth and nineteenth century, see Beverly Lemire, *Fashion Favourite: The Cotton Trade and the Consumer in Britain, 1660–1800* (Oxford: Oxford University Press, 1991); Cary Carson, Ronald Hoffman, and Peter J. Albert, *Of Consuming Interests: The Style of Life in the Eighteenth Century* (Charlottesville: Published for the United States Capital Historical Society by the University of Virginia Press, 1994); Karen Halttunen, *Confidence Men and Painted Women: A Study of Middle-Class Culture in America, 1830–1870* (New Haven: Yale University Press, 1982). On the role of women, cotton, and homespun in America, see Ulrich Thatcher, *The Age of Homespun: Objects and Stories in the Creation of an American Myth* (New York: Knopf, 2001).

We know quite a bit about the transatlantic cotton trade and its financing from business and industry histories generally focused on Britain. Thomas Ellison, *The Cotton Trade of Great Britain* (1886; London: Frank Cass & Co., 1968), still remains a much-relied-upon statistical work, though it must be viewed in light of Ralph Davis, *The Industrial Revolution and British Overseas Trade* (Atlantic Highlands, N.J.: Humanities Press, 1979), and more focused examinations like Michael M. Edwards, *The Growth of the British Cotton Trade, 1780–1815* (New York: Augustus M. Kell[e]y, 1967). The diverse essays included in Douglas A. Farnie and David J. Jeremy, eds., *The Fibre*

*That Changed the World: The Cotton Industry in International Perspective, 1600–1990s* (Oxford: Oxford University Press, 2004), will provide an invaluable source for future work, though the South receives little attention. Sven Beckert's two recent articles, "Emancipation and Empire: Reconstructing the Worldwide Web of Cotton Production in the Age of the American Civil War," *American Historical Review* 109, no. 5 (December 2004): 1405–38, and "From Tuskegee to Togo: The Problem of Freedom in the Empire of Cotton," *Journal of American History* 92, no. 2 (September 2005): 498–526, heighten anticipation of his forthcoming global history of cotton.

Useful case studies of how the trade was financed are offered in Edwin J. Perkins, *Financing Anglo-American Trade: The House of Brown, 1800–1880* (Cambridge: Harvard University Press, 1975), and Ralph W. Hidy, *The House of Baring in American Trade and Finance: English Merchant Bankers at Work, 1763–1861* (Cambridge: Harvard University Press, 1949). For more general discussions, see Howard Bodenhorn, *A History of Banking in Antebellum America: Financial Markets and Economic Development in an Era of Nation-Building* (Cambridge, UK: Cambridge University Press, 2000), and Mira Wilkins, *The History of Foreign Investment in the United States to 1914* (Cambridge: Harvard University Press, 1989). On the shipping industry's connection to the trade, Robert Greenhalgh Albion's two works on New York remain essential: *The Rise of New York Port, 1815–1860* (New York: Charles Scribner's Sons, 1939) and *Square-Riggers on Schedule: The New York Sailing Packets to England, France, and the Cotton Ports* (Princeton: Princeton University Press, 1938). So is Beckert's first work, *The Monied Metropolis: New York City and the Consolidation of the American Bourgeoisie, 1850–1896* (New York: Cambridge University Press, 2003). Statistical evidence on cotton's impact on the national economy is also thoroughly explored in Douglass North, *Economic Growth of the United States* (New York: Norton, 1961), Curtis P. Nettels, *The Emergence of a National Economy: 1775–1815* (New York: Holt, Rinehart and Winston, 1962), and most invaluably, Stuart Bruchey, *Cotton and the Growth of the American Economy, 1790–1860: Sources and Readings* (New York: Harcourt, Brace & World, 1967).

We know appallingly little about southern commerce during the antebellum period. The only major study of the cotton trade in the region remains Harold Woodman's *King Cotton and His Retainers: Financing and Marketing the Cotton Crop of the South, 1800–1925* (1968; Columbia: University of South Carolina Press, 1990), and one continues to hope that his half-century appeal for more systematic commercial histories may yet be realized. Though my interpretation differs from theirs on particulars, Frank J. Byrne's *Becoming Bourgeois: Merchant Culture in the South, 1820–1865* (Lexington: University of Kentucky Press, 2006), and Scott P. Marler's recent dissertation, "Merchants and the Political Economy of Nineteenth-Century Louisiana: New Orleans and Its Hinterlands" (Ph.D. diss., Rice University, 2007), provide some reason for optimism. For a fascinating look into the business history and fiction related to the cotton gin, see Angela Lakwete, *Inventing the Cotton Gin: Machine and Myth in Antebellum America* (Baltimore: Johns Hopkins University Press, 2003).

## Politics, Policy, and Political Economy

Politics, especially at the national level, is driven by the complex interaction of ideas, institutions, identities, personal jealousies, and interests defined in any number of individual, local, regional, national, and even international ways. The political history presented here joins others in an attempt to move us past purely ideological, anecdotal, or biographical histories while at the same time not forgetting that people, ideas, and historical contingencies matter, often a great deal.

My understanding of the context and specific debates centered around the constitution draws from David C. Hendrickson, *Peace Pact: The Lost World of the American Founding* (Lawrence: University Press of Kansas, 2003); Max M. Edling, *A Revolution in Favor of Government: The Origins of the U.S. Constitution and the Making of the American State* (New York: Oxford, 2003); Cathy D. Matson and Peter S. Onuf, *A Union of Interests: Politics and Economics in Revolutionary America* (Lawrence: University Press of Kansas, 1990); Jack N. Rakove, *Original Meanings: Politics and Ideas in the Making of the Constitution* (New York: Knopf, 1996); and for slavery, Paul Finkelman, *Slavery and the Founders*, 2nd ed. (New York: M. E. Sharpe, 2001).

That slavery critically informed American politics from the outset is becoming clearer with each passing day. Mason's *Slavery and Politics in the Early American Republic* (Chapel Hill: University of North Carolina Press, 2006) nicely situates slavery's political importance within other debates of that period. Other important new works include Robert Pierce Forbes's important work, *The Missouri Compromise and Its Aftermath* (Chapel Hill: University of North Carolina Press, 2007), and Robin Einhorn's *American Taxation, American Slavery* (Chicago: University of Chicago Press, 2006).

When possible, national politicians preferred to push slavery outside of regular political discourse. They sometimes succeeded because of the pressing need to deal with economic or foreign policy crises. Overviews that show the regional component of these include James Roger Sharp, *American Politics in the Early Republic: The New Nation in Crisis* (New Haven: Yale University Press, 1993), and Peter Onuf and Leonard Sadosky, *Jeffersonian America* (London: Blackwell Publishers, 2001). A number of important works have examined the intersection of ideas, political economy, and diplomacy in the Jeffersonian period, many searching for an underlying ideological coherence. See James Lewis Jr., *The Problem of Neighborhood: The United States and the Collapse of the Spanish Empire, 1783–1829* (Chapel Hill: University of North Carolina Press, 1998). Drew McCoy shows a Republican-minded obsession with social decay in *The Elusive Republic: Political Economy in Jeffersonian America* (Chapel Hill: Institute of Early American History and Culture by the University of North Carolina Press, 1980). Others have seen Jeffersonianism as rooted in a burgeoning faith in individual liberalism, a case stated forcefully in Joyce Appleby, *Liberalism and Republicanism in the Historical Imagination* (Cambridge: Harvard University Press, 1992), and *Thomas Jefferson* (New York: Times Books, 2003). For the Federalists' own participation in these ideological turf wars, see James H. Broussard, *The Southern Federalists, 1800–1815* (Baton Rouge: Louisiana State University Press, 1978), and Lisle A. Rose, *Prologue to Democracy: The Federalists in the South, 1789–1800* (Lexington: University of Kentucky Press, 1968). The picture of early national politics presented in chapters 1 and 2 accepts that so-called republican and liberal ideas informed politicians (likely coexisting in their heads) but also that tangible economic interests limited rigid adherence to either. When interests and ideas butted heads (as they did when American cotton planters warred against British cotton manufacturers), new political dynamics and tensions emerged.

This can especially be seen as the earliest generation of politicians struggled to define the nation's place in the world. On the diplomatic front, the effect of the Jay Treaty and diplomacy of the Federalist period are nicely discussed in Jerald A. Combs, *The Jay Treaty: Political Battleground of the Founding Fathers* (Berkeley: University of California Press, 1970). The Jeffersonians' less successful efforts in keeping the peace have been well documented. Bradford Perkins, *Prologue to War: England and the United States* (Berkeley: University of California Press, 1968), remains an invaluable narrative of the events culminating in war with Britain. Burton Spivak's *Jefferson's English Crisis* (Charlottesville: University of Virginia Press, 1979) provides a more detailed and satisfactory explanation of Jefferson's embargo, joining Louis Sears, *Jefferson and the Embargo* (1927; New York: Octagon Books, 1966), to illuminate that often overlooked policy decision. Richard Brown, *The Republic in Peril* (New York: Norton, 1971), artfully shows how Jeffersonians' anxiety about party and principle drove them to a war with Britain, while Steven Watt's *The Republic Reborn: War and the Making of Liberal America, 1790–1820* (Baltimore: Johns Hopkins University Press, 1987), sees that conflict as a more confident turn toward liberal values. Very useful accounts of how the earliest Republican presidents viewed the broader geopolitical challenges of their day are offered in Robert W. Tucker and David C. Hendrickson, *Empire of Liberty: The Statecraft of Thomas Jefferson* (New York: Oxford University Press, 1992), and John Stagg's *Mr. Madison's War* (Princeton: Princeton University Press, 1979). Norman Risjord provides one of the few examinations of the political divisions which Republicans experienced as a result of the war and its aftermath in *The Old Republicans: Southern Conservatism in the Age of Jefferson* (New York: Columbia University Press, 1965).

A particularly rich and closely related literature exists on Jeffersonian commercial and economic policy, one that the issues raised in chapter 2 speak directly to: John Nelson, *Liberty and Property: Political Economy and Policymaking in the New Nation, 1789–1812* (Baltimore: Johns Hopkins University Press, 1989); Doron Ben-Atar, *The Origins of Jeffersonian Commercial Policy and Diplomacy* (New York: St. Martin's Press, 1993); John Crowley, *The Privileges of Independence: Neomercantilism and the American Revolution* (Baltimore: Johns Hopkins University Press, 1993). Vernon G. Setser, *The Commercial Reciprocity Policy of the United States, 1774–1829* (1937; New York: Da Capo Press, 1969), remains indispensable. Herbert Sloan, *Principle and Interest: Thomas Jefferson and the Problem of Debt* (New York: Oxford University Press, 1995), provides a useful examination of national financing.

Banking and finance, culminating in the "bank war," has dominated political and policy histories of what we now somewhat awkwardly refer to as the "Market Revolution." See James Roger Sharp, *The Jacksonians versus the Banks: Politics in the States after the Panic of 1837* (New York: Columbia University Press, 1970); Bray Hammond, *Banks and Politics in America from the Revolution to the Civil War* (Princeton: Princeton University Press, 1957); Larry Schweikart, *Banking in the American South from the Age of Jackson to Reconstruction* (Baton Rouge: Louisiana State University Press, 1987); Peter Temin, *Jacksonian Economy* (New York: Norton, 1969). Jackson's war against the bank remains at the heart of two of the most popular surveys of that time: Arthur Schlesinger Jr., *The Age of Jackson* (1945; n.p., Back Bay Books, 1988), and Charles Sellers's deceptively complicated *The Market Revolution: Jacksonian America,*

*1815–1846* (New York: Oxford University Press, 1994). Two very different accounts of politics during this period promise to revitalize and hopefully nuance our understanding of economics and politics: Sean Wilentz, *The Rise of American Democracy: Jefferson to Lincoln* (New York: Norton, 2005), and Daniel Walker Howe's much-needed *What God Hath Wrought: The Transformation of America, 1814–1848* (New York: Oxford University Press, 2007).

Some recent histories of Jacksonian politics invaluable to this work have highlighted the need to understand institutions and other specific policies: Daniel Feller, *The Public Lands in Jacksonian Politics* (Madison: University of Wisconsin Press, 1984); John Larson, *Internal Improvement: National Public Works and the Promise of Popular Government in the Early United States* (Chapel Hill: University of North Carolina Press, 2001); Robert Angevine, *The Railroad and the State: War, Politics, and Technology in Nineteenth-Century America* (Stanford: Stanford University Press, 2004); Laurence Malone, *Opening the West: Federal Internal Improvements before 1860* (Westport: Greenwood Press, 1998); Paul F. Paskoff, *Troubled Waters: Steamboat Disasters, River Improvements, and American Public Policy, 1821–1860* (Baton Rouge: Louisiana State University Press, 2007); Robert R. Russel's *Improvement of Communication with the Pacific Coast as an Issue in American Politics* (Cedar Rapids, Iowa: The Torch Press, 1948); as well as the several articles and local studies listed below or in the notes. William J. Novak, *The People's Welfare: Law and Regulation in Nineteenth-Century America* (Chapel Hill: University of North Carolina Press, 1996); Richard R. John, *Spreading the News: The American Postal System from Franklin to Morse* (Cambridge: Harvard University Press, 1995), and Richard R. John, ed., *Ruling Passions: Political Economy in Nineteenth Century America* (University Park: Pennsylvania State University Press, 2006).

Despite this resurgence of policy history, it is baffling that no systematic histories of commercial or tariff policies during the Jacksonian period have been recently attempted. This is all the more troubling given the endurance and ferocity of the debates that ensued over such matters. Despite some interesting work on maritime history, for a systematic examination of American navigation policy one must reach back to William Bates's *American Navigation: The Political History of Its Rise and Ruin and the Proper Means for Its Encouragement* (Boston and New York: Houghton, Mifflin, 1902). To find a book-length study of the debates over the tariff, one has only Jonathan Pincus's interesting but largely tangential study of lobbying groups during the 1820s debates presented in *Pressure Groups and Politics in Antebellum Tariffs* (New York: Columbia University Press, 1977) before having to travel back over a hundred years to the works of Frank W. Taussig, *The Tariff History of the United States* (New York: Putnam, 1888), and Edward Stanwood, *American Tariff Controversies in the Nineteenth Century*, 2 vols. (Boston: Houghton, Mifflin, 1904). It is hoped that the original research offered here (albeit channeled for more narrow ends) might join the broader studies of U.S. trade history by Dartmouth economist Douglas A. Irwin and Einhorn's above-cited and spirited work on domestic tax policy to peak further interest on such matters.

The global focus of this work has left me reliant on more local and state studies than can appropriately be cited here. Some, however, are especially noteworthy given their sensitivity to cotton's role within the region or engagement with themes of special significance in this book. For South Carolina, see Rachel Klein, *The Unification of a Slave State: The Rise of a Planter Class in the South Carolina Backcountry, 1760–1808* (Chapel Hill: University of North Carolina Press, 1992); John Harold Wolfe, *Jeffersonian Democracy in South Carolina* (Chapel Hill: University of North Carolina Press, 1940); Joyce Chaplin, *An Anxious Pursuit: Agricultural Innovation and Modernity in the Lower South, 1730–1815* (Chapel Hill: University of North Carolina Press, 1993); Lacy K. Ford Jr., *Origins of Southern Radicalism: The South Carolina Upcountry, 1800–1860* (New York: Oxford University Press, 1988).

For Georgia politics, see George Lamplugh, *Politics on the Periphery: Factions and Parties in Georgia, 1783–1806* (Newark: University of Delaware Press, 1986); Leslie Hall, *Land and Allegiance in Revolutionary Georgia* (Athens: University of Georgia Press, 2001); and E. Merton Coulter, *Thomas Spaulding of Sapelo* (Baton Rouge: Louisiana State University Press, 1940), which provides a good examination into cotton's introduction into the region and Loyalist roots. The best examination of antebellum politics in the states is Anthony Gene Carey, *Parties, Slavery, and the Union in Antebellum Georgia* (Athens: University of Georgia Press, 1997).

Politics in the Old Southwest has received somewhat more attention of late, complementing some useful older works. See Adam Rothman, *Slave Country: American Expansion and the Origins of the Deep South* (Cambridge: Harvard University Press, 2005); Edwin A. Miles, *Jacksonian Democracy in Mississippi* (New York: Da Capo Press, 1970); Bradley G. Bond, *Political Culture in the Nineteenth-Century South: Mississippi, 1830–1860* (Baton Rouge: Louisiana State University Press, 1995); Christopher Morris, *Becoming Southern: The Evolution of a Way of Life, Warren County and Vicksburg, Mississippi, 1770–1860* (New York: Oxford University Press, 1995); J. Mills Thornton III, *Politics and Power in a Slave Society: Alabama, 1800–1860* (Baton Rouge: Louisiana State University Press, 1978); Daniel S. Dupre, *Transforming the Cotton Frontier: Madison County, Alabama, 1800–1840* (Baton Rouge: Louisiana State University Press, 1997).

Southern Economic Thought and Development

Any study of the South's political economy cannot help but be influenced by the long-running debate over whether the South and slavery were capitalist or not. The works that have drawn the most attention are, of course, Eugene Genovese's *The Political Economy of Slavery: Studies in the Economy and Society of the Slave South* (New York: Random House, 1967), and with Elizabeth Fox-Genovese, *Fruits of Merchant Capital: Slavery and Bourgeois Property in the Rise and Expansion of Capitalism* (New York: Oxford University Press, 1983); Robert William Fogel, *Without Consent or Contract: The Rise and Fall of American Slavery* (New York: W. W. Norton & Co., 1994), and with Stanley L. Engerman, *Time on the Cross: The Economics of American Negro Slavery* (New York: Norton, 1974); and James Oakes, *The Ruling Race: A History of American Slaveholders* (New York: Knopf, 1982). The subtle influence of all three of these interpretations can be seen in various places in this work, though its overall tone probably comports most closely to Oakes's. A good summary of these debates can be found in Mark Smith, *Debating Slavery: Economy and Society in the Antebellum American South* (Cambridge: Cambridge University Press, 1998). Jeffrey Young's concept of "corporate individualism" offers an attractive linguistic compromise in *Domesticating Slavery: The Master Class in Georgia and South Carolina, 1670–1837* (Chapel Hill: University of North Carolina Press, 1999). The idea of dependence has dominated studies of southern economics and thought and is most forcefully expressed in Joseph Persky, *The Burden of Dependency: Colonial Themes in Southern Economic Thought* (Baltimore: Johns Hopkins University Press, 1992). Though conceptually enriching, the modernization theories of development underlying these studies often fail to capture the more complicated thoughts and actions of contemporaries.

Though it occasionally engages these often ideologically driven works, this project's primary focus is less on "labeling" and more on exploring economic reality and its intersection with the ideas and political actions contemporary to the time. Consequently, it has drawn heavily from more narrow studies that root people and policies in specific places and time. On the commercial convention movement, see Thomas Wender, *Southern Commercial Conventions, 1837–1859* (Baltimore: Johns Hopkins Press, 1930); John G. Van Deusen, *The Ante-Bellum Southern Commercial Conventions* (Durham: Duke University Press, 1926); Vicki Vaughn Johnson, *The Men and the Vision of the Southern Commercial Conventions, 1845–1871* (Columbia: University of Missouri Press, 1992). On the regional and national debates over railroads, see Kenneth Noe, *Southwest Virginia's Railroad: Modernization and the Sectional Crisis* (Urbana: University of Illinois Press, 1994); U. B. Phillips, *A History of Transportation in the Eastern Cotton Belt to 1860* (New York: Columbia University Press, 1908); and John F. Stover, *Iron Road to the West: American Railroads in the 1850s* (New York: Columbia University Press, 1978). The pathbreaking work of William Thomas on Civil War–era railroads promises to move this discussion onto an entirely new plane: *Jupiter's Bow: Railroads, the Civil War, and the Roots of Modern America* (New Haven: Yale University Press, forthcoming).

Of the local studies that informed the interpretation presented in chapters 4 and 5, several stand out: Milton Heath, *Constructive Liberalism: The Role of the State in Economic Development in Georgia* (Cambridge: Harvard University Press, 1954); Thomas Downey, *Planting a Capitalist South: Masters, Merchants, and Manufacturers in the Southern Interior, 1790–1860* (Baton Rouge: Louisiana State University Press, 2006); John Hebron Moore, *The Emergence of the Cotton Kingdom in the Old Southwest: Mississippi, 1770–1860* (Baton Rouge: Louisiana State University Press, 1988). William Scarborough, *Masters of the Big House: Elite Slaveholders of the Mid-Nineteenth Century South* (Baton Rouge: Louisiana State University Press, 2003), provides a multiple biography of the region's wealthiest elites with an eye toward their economic actions and views. I have benefited greatly from John Majewski's comparative study, which suggests that some, but not all, of the same dynamics were at work in the Upper South: *A House Dividing: Economic Development in Pennsylvania and Virginia before the Civil War* (Cambridge: Cambridge University Press, 2000). For still-useful examinations of industrial efforts, see Alfred Glaze Smith Jr., *Economic Readjustment of an Old Cotton State* (Columbia: University of South Carolina Press, 1958); Robert S. Starobin, *Industrial Slavery in the Old South* (New York: Oxford University Press, 1970); and Michael Gagnon's excellent dissertation, "Transition to an Industrial South: Athens, Georgia, 1830–1870" (Ph.D. diss., Emory University, 1999).

Most of these case studies indicate that the move toward industrialization was well under way by the late 1850s. One study which presents a more pessimistic portrait is Fred Bateman and Thomas Weiss, *A Deplorable Scarcity: The Failure of Industrialization in the Slave Economy* (Chapel Hill: University of North Carolina Press, 1981).

Some of the most illuminative recent work stressing the dynamism of slavery and the southern economy has focused on the domestic slave trade explored statistically by Michael Tadman, *Speculators and Slaves: Masters, Traders, and Slaves in the Old South* (Madison: University of Wisconsin Press, 1989), culturally by Walter Johnson, *Soul by Soul: Life inside the Antebellum Market* (Cambridge: Harvard University Press, 1999), and perhaps most comprehensively by Steven Deyle, *Carry Me Back: The Domestic Slave Trade in American Life* (New York: Oxford University Press, 2006).

More general studies have conceptually enriched this project. By far the most important and influential of these for me has been Gavin Wright's work, *The Political Economy of the Cotton South* (New York: Norton, 1978), and *Slavery and American Economic Development* (Baton Rouge: Louisiana State University Press, 2006). I have few quibbles with Wright's interpretation but believe its detachment from historical events, processes, and, somewhat ironically at times, global circumstance limits its ability to explain human action. In this sense the approach (if not always the analysis) of essays in David Carlton and Peter Coclanis, *The South, the Nation, and the World: Perspectives on Southern Economic Development* (Charlottesville: University of Virginia Press, 2003), and Susanna Delfino and Michele Gillespie, *Global Perspectives on Industrial Transformation* (Columbia: University of Missouri Press, 2005), are more in line with my own. See also Jennifer Wahl, *The Bondsman's Burden: An Economic Analysis of the Common Law of Southern Slavery* (New York: Cambridge University Press, 2002), and the still-very-useful Robert Royal Russell, *Economic Aspects of Southern Sectionalism* (New York: Russell & Russell, 1960). I have also benefited from exchanges with Walter Johnson and eagerly anticipate his forthcoming work, *River of Dark Dreams: Slavery, Capitalism, and Imperialism in the Mississippi Valley's Cotton Kingdom* (Cambridge: Harvard University Press).

## Race and Proslavery Thought

There remains considerable work to be done to demonstrate how economic realities shaped racial and proslavery thinking in the postrevolutionary period. One fruitful attempt has been offered by James Huston in "The Panic of 1857, Southern Economic Thought, and the Patriarchal Defense of Slavery," *Historian* 46 (1984): 163–86. On racial theories prevalent during the time, see William Stanton, *The Leopard's Spots: Scientific Attitudes towards Race in America, 1815–59* (Chicago: University of Chicago Press, 1960); Robert F. Durden, *The Self-Inflicted Wound: Southern Politics in the Nineteenth Century* (Lexington: University Press of Kentucky, 1985); George Fredrickson, *The Black Image in the White Mind: The Debate on Afro-American Character and Destiny, 1817–1914* (New York: Harper & Row, 1971); Ronald T. Takaki, *Iron Cages: Race and Culture in Nineteenth-Century America* (New York: Knopf, 1979).

For relevant studies that approach these matters in an Atlantic-centered perspective, see Douglas A. Lorimer, *Colour, Class, and the Victorians: English Attitudes to the Negro in the Mid-Nineteenth Century* (Bristol: Leicester University Press, 1978);

Catherine Hall, *Civilising Subjects: Colony and Metropole in the English Imagination, 1830–1867* (Chicago: University of Chicago Press, 2002); and Edward B. Rugemer, "The Southern Response to British Abolitionism: The Maturation of Proslavery Apologetics," *Journal of Southern History* 70 (May 2004): 221–48. Rugemer's *The Problem of Emancipation: The Caribbean Roots of the American Civil War* (Baton Rouge: Louisiana State University Press, 2008) independently has traced many of the developments this book does but was published too late to inform my analysis.

Proslavery thought has received a good deal of attention. In addition to O'Brien's own insightful remarks, see Drew Gilpin Faust, *A Sacred Circle: The Dilemma of the Intellectual in the Old South, 1840–1860* (Baltimore: Johns Hopkins University Press, 1977); Paul Finkelman, ed., *Proslavery Thought, Ideology, and Politics* (New York: Garland Publishing, 1989); William Sumner Jenkins, *The Pro-Slavery Argument in the Old South* (Chapel Hill: University of North Carolina Press, 1935); Ronald T. Takaki, *A Pro-Slavery Crusade: The Agitation to Reopen the African Slave Trade* (New York: Free Press, 1971); Larry Tise, *Proslavery: A History of the Defense of Slavery in America, 1701–1840* (Athens: University of Georgia Press, 1987); and most recently, Charles F. Irons, *The Origins of Proslavery Christianity: White and Black Evangelicals in Colonial and Antebellum Virginia* (Chapel Hill: University of North Carolina Press, 2008).

## Party Politics and the Sectional Crisis

The decision to go to war in 1860 was, first and foremost, a political decision. State-level and national politicians, informed by their own judgment and the demands of constituents with tangible concerns and aspirations, faced very difficult challenges. The choices they made in addressing them (choices generally supported by majorities at home who backed them) brought the nation to and over the abyss into a bloody conflict few had the foresight to envision.

Though this book suggests that certain choices made decades in advance and for quite different reasons would contribute to this decision, the specific events of the period from 1846 to 1860 were obviously the most critical. In particular the political realignment that began in the late 1840s and culminated in the destruction of the second party system proved significant for explaining why many Americans stopped worshipping at the shrine of interregional parties in favor of more sectionalized ones. For the depth of partisan loyalty, see Joel Silbey, *The Shrine of Party: Congressional Voting Behavior, 1841–1852* (Pittsburgh: University of Pittsburgh Press, 1967), and the encyclopedic study of the Whig Party offered by Michael Holt, *The Rise and Fall of the American Whig Party* (New York: Oxford University Press, 1999). It must be remembered, however, that sectional commitments, and even identities, could form within nationalism and national parties, a point made clear in David Waldstreicher, *In the Midst of Perpetual Fetes: The Making of American Nationalism, 1776–1820* (Chapel Hill: University of North Carolina Press, 1997), and William J. Cooper Jr., *The South and the Politics of Slavery, 1828–1856* (Baton Rouge: Louisiana State University Press, 1978).

Despite their lack of attention to cotton or international events, a number of important studies of realignment were useful for this book: Michael Holt, *The Political*

*Crisis of the 1850s* (New York: Norton, 1978), and *The Fate of Their Country: Politicians, Slavery Extension, and the Coming of the Civil War* (New York: Hill & Wang, 2005); Michael Morrison, *Slavery and the American West: The Eclipse of Manifest Destiny and the Coming of the Civil War* (Chapel Hill: University of North Carolina Press, 1997). James L. Huston's emphasis on wealth, property rights, and slaveholders' aggression in *Calculating the Value of Union* (Chapel Hill: University of North Carolina Press, 2003), fits nicely with this work, as does his exceedingly useful earlier work emphasizing the economic situation framing the lead-up to war, *The Panic of 1857 and the Coming of the Civil War* (Baton Rouge: Louisiana State University Press, 1987). See also John Ashworth, *Slavery, Capitalism, and Politics in the Antebellum Republic*, 2 vols. (New York: Cambridge University Press, 1995, 2008); Roger L. Ransom, *Conflict and Compromise: The Political Economy of Slavery, Emancipation, and the American Civil War* (New York: Cambridge University Press, 1989); Richard Franklin Bensel, *Yankee Leviathan: The Origins of Central State Authority in America, 1859–1877* (New York: Cambridge University Press, 1990). For two accounts that include cotton's political place in these calculations, see: Thomas P. Martin, "Conflicting Cotton Interests at Home and Abroad, 1848–1857," *Journal of Southern History* 7, no. 2 (May 1941): 173–94; and Kinley J. Brauer, *Cotton versus Conscience: Massachusetts Whig Politics and Southwestern Expansion, 1843–1848* (Lexington: University of Kentucky Press, 1967). Though related because of the issue of slavery, the fall of the second party system and rise of the third did not necessarily make secession and war inevitable.

The actions of southerners with disunionist desires and northerners determined to stop them made that happen. Explaining the former of these actions has left generations of historians puzzled. One approach, with its roots tracing back to the Progressive-era histories of Charles and Mary Beard, *The Rise of American Civilization* (New York: Macmillan, 1927), has seen the war as the natural outgrowth of a battle between two incompatible societies. They and their heirs, foremost amongst them the Genoveses, have seen secession as a logical outgrowth of the incompatibility of free and slave labor systems: Eugene D. Genovese, *The World the Slaveholders Made: Two Essays in Interpretation* (New York: Pantheon Books, 1969); *The Political Economy of Slavery;* and with Elizabeth Fox-Genovese, *Fruits of Merchant Capital.* My own account agrees that many secessionists had come to believe that, but it rejects the notion that such belief reflected a structural reality. The degree to which nonagrarians embraced the secessionist movement should also caution against assuming secession was an antimodern action intended to defend some traditional and outdated labor system.

Where some historians have seen divergent economic structures as the foremost reasons for secession, others have focused on divergent ways of thought or ideas about government. Older and newer works starting with W. J. Cash, *The Mind of the Old South* (1941; New York: Vintage Books, 1991); Clement Eaton, *The Mind of the Old South*, rev. ed. (1964; Baton Rouge: Louisiana State University Press, 1967); and more recently Bertram Wyatt-Brown, *Southern Honor: Ethics and Behavior in the Old South* (New York: Oxford University Press, 1982), assumed that some sort of "savage ideal," "noblesse oblige," or "primal honor" are necessary to explain the secession crisis. This book rejects such views, which at times border on ideological or cultural determinism. Ideas about honor, and certainly savagery, factored into how southerners responded to crisis; it does not seem likely, however, that they were in any way determinative. More satisfactory examinations of culture's influence in shaping southern nationalism are presented in John McCardell's classic work, *The Idea of a Southern Nation;* Elizabeth R. Varon, *Disunion!: The Coming of the American Civil War, 1789–1859* (Chapel Hill: University of North Carolina Press, 2008); and Robert E. Bonner, "Americans Apart: Nationality in the Slaveholding South" (Ph.D. diss., Yale University, 1997). Marc Egnal interestingly attempts to merge the best of the progressive argument with the best of cultural approaches in "Rethinking the Secession of the Lower South: The Clash of Two Groups," *Civil War History* 50, no. 3 (September 2004): 261–90. It and a number of other articles by him lay the groundwork for a forthcoming neo-Progressive account of the Civil War.

Many of the most recent works on secession have traced it back to the less democratic (some say antidemocratic) political system that slavery created, suggesting that secessionists simply couldn't handle the idea of majority rules: William Freehling, *The Road to Disunion,* vol. 1, *Secessionists at Bay, 1776–1854* (New York: Oxford University Press, 1990); and Manisha Sinha, *The Counterrevolution of Slavery: Politics and Ideology in Antebellum South Carolina* (Chapel Hill: University of North Carolina Press, 2000). That may, I emphasize may, help explain South Carolina's response to Lincoln's election. But it can't explain the reaction of those in the Southwest, something that Freehling tacitly admits in his second volume of that very impressive work. Freehling's work, especially vol. 2., *Secessionists Triumphant, 1854–1861* (New York: Oxford University Press, 2007), offers the most comprehensive examination of the march to secession yet written. Though riveting, its search for contingency occasionally stretches beyond what historical reality suggests. The work's deemphasis of economic factors also limits its explanatory reach.

Racially driven fears of slave insurrections have recently, and with a great deal of accuracy, been identified as a key motive in secession, as Charles Dew, *Apostles of Disunion* (Charlottesville: University of Virginia Press, 2001), and Steven Channing, *Crisis of Fear: Secession in South Carolina* (New York: Simon & Schuster, 1970), have recently shown. The demands of protecting slavery as a social system from potential attack were absolutely critical, but at least as important are the economic demands explained most convincingly in the works of Gavin Wright and Huston cited above and the perceptions discussed in this work. See also Frank Tower's *The Urban Crisis and the Coming of the Civil War* (Charlottesville: University of Virginia Press, 2004).

Several recent works suggest the possible move toward a neorevisionist account of the origins of the Civil War by highlighting the reluctance of many Upper South groups. See especially Daniel W. Crofts, *Reluctant Confederates: Upper South Unionists in the Secession Crisis* (Chapel Hill: University of North Carolina Press, 1989), and Edward Ayers, *In the Presence of Mine Enemies: The Civil War in the Heart of America* (New York: Norton, 2003). See also Peter B. Knupfer, *The Union as It Is: Constitutional Unionism and Sectional Compromise, 1787–1861* (Chapel Hill: University of North Carolina Press, 1991).

This work has also been informed by older state studies of the secession movement, several of which intimate the popularity of secession in the newest cotton lands of the Southwest: William L. Barney, *The Secessionist Impulse: Alabama and Mississippi in 1860* (Princeton: Princeton University Press, 1974); Ralph A. Wooster, *The*

*Secession Conventions of the South* (Princeton: Princeton University Press, 1962); Peyton McCrary, Clark Miller, and Dale Baum, "Class and Party in the Secession Crisis: Voting Behavior in the Deep South," *Journal of Interdisciplinary History* 8 (Winter 1978): 452–54, as well as Thornton's work on Alabama, cited earlier. Also very helpful for this book were examinations of specific secessionist leaders, including Laura A. White, *Robert Barnwell Rhett: Father of Secession* (Gloucester, Mass.: Peter Smith, 1965); David S. Heidler, *Pulling the Temple Down: The Fire-Eaters and the Destruction of the Union* (Mechanicsburg, Pa.: Stackpole Books, 1994); Eric H. Walther, *The Fire-Eaters* (Baton Rouge: Louisiana State University Press, 1992); and especially *William Lowndes Yancey and the Coming of the Civil War* (Chapel Hill: University of North Carolina Press, 2006).

## King Cotton Diplomacy and Confederacy

Several useful diplomatic histories of the late antebellum period helped frame the discussion of American foreign policy during the 1840s and 1850s. The most recent and useful, because of its cognizance of cotton, is Thomas Hietala, *Manifest Design: American Exceptionalism and Empire* (1985; Ithaca: Cornell University Press, 2003). Also informing my discussion of American expansionism was Reginald Horsman, *Race and Manifest Destiny: The Origins of American Racial Anglo-Saxonism* (Cambridge: Harvard University Press, 1981); Frederick Merk, *Slavery and the Annexation of Texas* (New York: Knopf, 1972); David M. Pletcher, *Diplomacy of Annexation: Texas, Oregon, and the Mexican War* (Columbia: University of Missouri Press, 1973); Robert E. May, *The Southern Dream of a Caribbean Empire, 1854–1861*, 2nd ed. (Gainesville: University Press of Florida, 2002), and *Manifest Destiny's Underworld: Filibustering in Antebellum America* (Chapel Hill: University of North Carolina Press, 2002). In many ways, however, Kenneth Bourne's *Britain and the Balance of Power in North America, 1815–1908* (Berkeley: University of California Press, 1967) remains unsurpassed in its appreciation for the diverse factors that informed foreign policy on both sides of the Atlantic.

On the long-neglected Free Black Port Acts, see Philip M. Hamer's two still-useful articles: "Great Britain, the United States, and the Negro Seamen Acts, 1822–1848," *Journal of Southern History* 1, no. 1 (February 1935): 3–28, and "British Consuls and the Negro Seamen's Acts, 1850–1860," *Journal of Southern History* 1, no. 2 (May 1935): 138–68; and Alan Frank January, "The First Nullification: The Free Negro Seamen Acts Controversy in South Carolina, 1822–1860" (Ph.D. diss., University of Iowa, 1976).

Useful accounts of the formation of the Confederate government are provided in William C. Davis's *A Government of Our Own: The Making of the Confederacy* (New York: Free Press, 1994), and George Rable, *The Confederate Republic: A Revolution against Politics* (Chapel Hill: University of North Carolina Press, 1994). Confederate diplomacy has been the focus of a number of thorough studies, including Frank Lawrence Owsley, *King Cotton Diplomacy: Foreign Regions of the Confederate States of America* (1931; Chicago: University of Chicago Press, 1959); Henry Blumenthal, "Confederate Diplomacy: Popular Notions and International Realities," *Journal of Southern History* (May 1966): 151–71; and Charles Hubbard's, *The Burden of Confederate Diplomacy* (Knoxville: University of Tennessee Press, 1998). On the broader global context for these negotiations, see D. P. Crook's classic, *The North, the South, and the Powers, 1861–1865* (New York: Wiley, 1974), and newer work by Howard Jones, *The Union in Peril: The Crisis over British Intervention in the Civil War* (Chapel Hill: University of North Carolina Press, 1992), and Robert E. May, ed., *The Union, the Confederacy, and the Atlantic Rim* (West Lafayette: Purdue University Press, 1995). Lynn M. Case and Warren F. Spencer's *The United States and France: Civil War Diplomacy* (Philadelphia: University of Pennsylvania Press, 1970) provides an all-too-rare window into Confederate efforts on the continent, as does Daniel B. Carroll, *Henri Mercier and the American Civil War* (Princeton: Princeton University Press, 1971).

Appeals to the European public and the variety of responses they evoked are covered in R. J. M. Blackett's superb *Divided Hearts: Britain and the American Civil War* (Baton Rouge: Louisiana State University Press, 2000); Charles P. Cullup, *Confederate Propaganda in Europe, 1861–1865* (Coral Gables: University of Miami Press, 1969); George M. Blackburn, *French Newspaper Opinion on the American Civil War* (Westport: Greenwood Press, 1997); and Martin Crawford, *The Anglo-American Crisis of the Mid-Nineteenth Century: The Times and America, 1850–1862* (Athens: University of Georgia Press, 1987). Cotton features prominently in James W. Daddysman, *The Matamoros Trade: Confederate Commerce, Diplomacy and Intrigue* (Newark: University of Delaware Press, 1983). On Confederate economic policy, Richard Cecil Todd's *Confederate Finance* (Athens: University of Georgia Press, 1954) remains useful, as does Richard Bensel's invaluable *Yankee Leviathan: The Origins of Central State Authority, 1859–1877* (Cambridge: Cambridge University Press, 1990).

# Index

Page numbers in *italics* indicate figures and tables.